The River Is in Us

Fighting Toxics in a Mohawk Community

ELIZABETH HOOVER

University of Minnesota Press

Minneapolis

London

The University of Minnesota Press gratefully acknowledges the generous assistance provided for the publication of this book by the Office of the Dean of the Faculty, Brown University.

Portions of chapter 3 were published as "'We're Not Going to Be Guinea Pigs': Citizen Science and Environmental Health in a Native American Community," *Journal of Science Communication* 15:01 (A05) 2016. Published online January 21, 2016, and reproduced under a Creative Commons 4.0 by-nc-nd license.

Published by the University of Minnesota Press
111 Third Avenue South, Suite 290
Minneapolis, MN 55401-2520
http://www.upress.umn.edu

ISBN 978-1-5179-0303-9 (pb)
ISBN 978-1-5179-0302-2 (hc)
A Cataloging-in-Publication record for this book is available from the Library of Congress.

Printed in the United States of America on acid-free paper

The University of Minnesota is an equal-opportunity educator and employer.

22   10 9 8 7 6

The River Is in Us

Contents

Cultural Touchstones

The Mohawk, or Kanien'kéha:ka (People of the Flint), are part of the Haudenosaunee (People of the Longhouse) Confederacy of Six Nations, known to the French as the Iroquois.[1] While traditional Mohawk territory stretches north to south across what is now eastern New York State, the contemporary reserves that many Mohawk people call home lie mostly north of there, including Kahnawà:ke and Kanesatake in Quebec; Wahta, Tyendinaga, and Six Nations of the Grand River (which is home to all six nations of Haudenosaunee peoples) in Ontario; and Akwesasne, which stretches across Ontario, Quebec, and northern New York. There are also two independent Mohawk communities in New York State, Kanienkeh and Kanatsiohareke.

As the "eastern door" nation of the Haudenosaunee Confederacy, Mohawks were the first to experience the impact of settlers moving inland from the Atlantic coast. Regardless, members of this nation have worked creatively against, within, and around the influx of settler influence, maintaining distinctly Indigenous cultures and communities. While Akwesasne has come to embrace a range of religious traditions (in addition to longhouse adherents, a majority of residents belong to Catholic or other Christian churches), elements of what is thought of as traditional Mohawk culture are laid out in well-known stories and prayers that have structured how Akwesasro:non (people of Akwesasne) have approached environmental health research, environmental cleanup, and the preservation of food culture. Among the stories and prayers that have been particularly influential are the Haudenosaunee creation story, the Ohen:ton Karihwatehkwen (Thanksgiving Address), the "one dish, one spoon" story, and the history of the formation of the Haudenosaunee Confederacy—including the establishment of the Kaianerekowa (Great Law of Peace).[2]

Creation Story

The Haudenosaunee creation story, the Tsi Kiontonhwentsison, demonstrates the importance of women's bodies not only as the basis of all human life but also as the source of original foods. Prior to the coming of Sky Woman, this earthly plane was dark, and covered with water. Humans lived in the Sky World above, illuminated by a celestial tree. The Tsi Kiontonhwentsison tells of a pregnant woman, Sky Woman, Otsitsisohn (Mature Flowers), who fell through a hole in the Sky World, bringing with her the seeds of strawberries and tobacco. As she plummeted toward the watery world below, birds caught her in their wings and laid her on the back of a large turtle. A number of water creatures attempted to bring up sediment from far below the water's surface to support Sky Woman; the muskrat finally succeeded, but perished in the process. Sky Woman spread this sediment over the turtle and danced in counterclockwise circles to enlarge the land surface. She gave birth to a daughter, Iakotsisionite (She Has a Flower on Her), who matured and was impregnated by Rawenhontsiowaikon (Turtle Man). Iakotsisionite in turn gave birth to twin sons, the good-minded right-handed son, Sonkwaiathison (He Made All of Our Bodies, or Creator), who was born naturally, and his contrary left-handed brother, Sahwiskeh:ra (Flint), who insisted on making his own entrance through her armpit, killing her. Sky Woman covered her daughter's body with a mound of soil, and from it sprouted tobacco and strawberries, from seeds that she had grabbed from the celestial tree before her plummet. In addition, her body produced corn, beans, and squash, the "three sisters" crops that would sustain the Haudenosaunee and other nations of the Northeast. The two brothers fought constantly, Sonkwaiathison forming plants, animals, and humans in his image and his brother corrupting them. Sonkwaiathison gave ceremonies to the people to celebrate all that they were thankful for, and so they would remain triumphant over his brother, Sahwiskeh:ra. These ceremonies are still practiced in Haudenosaunee longhouses, and many are based on the horticultural cycle, celebrating events around maple sugaring, seed planting, strawberries, string beans, green corn, and the fall harvest. Some aspects of the ceremonies reflect qualities of the plants being celebrated: as Mohawk midwife Katsi Cook described to me, when the women dance during ceremonies, they "weave like bean runners." This horticultural tradition that began in the body of Sky Woman's daughter continues to shape Haudenosaunee culture today.

Akwesasne residents still relate the importance of taking part in the growing cycle to the creation story. One woman, Gina, described to me how her father would instruct her in growing, based on this story:

> He'd tell me plant three seeds, one for the birds, one for the Creator, and one to grow up. And then he'd make me dance around it and—I guess that was his way of giving thanks or praying, saying "Please grow" . . . and then as I got older and I read the creation story and that's what it says in there that she danced around and Mother Earth became bigger and bigger.

As a man who plants extensive gardens in Akwesasne explained to me, "We relate everything to the creation story. Our answers are in the creation story. So that's how we plant."

Imagery from the creation story has been utilized in promoting both horticultural traditions and the value of women's bodies. Wakerakatsiteh (Louise McDonald), a Bear Clan mother at Akwesasne, has begun to host rites of passage ceremonies for the young men and women, called Ohero:kon.[3] These ceremonies bring adolescents together as a cohort for fasting and participating in sweat lodge and other ceremonies, as well as for teachings from respected community members about coming into adulthood, learning necessary skills, and respecting their bodies. Wakerakatsiteh decided to develop a Mother Earth garden based on the creation story, so that the girls can understand the importance of planting at the same time they are coming into an understanding of their own fertility. Each spring, she has the boys create a mound of dirt in the shape of a woman, gently moving the dirt while discussing the importance of respecting women's bodies. Just as the crops sprang forth from the body of Sky Woman's daughter, the young women tuck seeds in around the figure. They

Akwesasne Bear Clan mother Wakerakatsiteh (Louise McDonald).
Photograph by Elizabeth Hoover, 2016.

"Uncles" help with an Ohero:kon rites of passage ceremony, shaping the soil that will become one of the Mother Earth gardens. Photograph by Jessica Sargent, 2016.

plant tobacco at her head, because burning tobacco brings a good mind. A strawberry plant, whose crushed berries resemble blood, is planted at her heart. Corn, whose kernels turn milky as they ripen, is planted at her breasts. Squash, with a curly vine like an umbilical cord, grows from her belly button. String beans are planted at her hands, reflecting the fingerlike qualities of the long beans that come to dangle from the plants later in the season. At her feet, they plant potatoes, which grow to look like the bottoms of human feet that have been walking in fresh dirt.

When they finish, Wakerakatsiteh explains to the girls that they will have to come back to take care of this garden—seeds are like babies and need to be nurtured and cared for properly. At the same time, the girls are meant to identify with this fertile woman-garden—in Mohawk culture, understandings of the garden and the body are woven together—women and plants share certain qualities and sustain each other. Qualities of the human body are passed along to plants, which then nourish Mohawk bodies. The creation story is also used as a metaphor to explain other female biological processes. Bev Cook, the former director of the Saint Regis Mohawk Health Services clinic (and currently an elected chief), gives a presentation each year for the adolescents in which she describes the process of ovulation in the context of this story—the egg falls from the follicle, down the fallopian tube, and lands on the soft lining of the uterus, in a manner similar to Sky Woman's journey. In light of the importance of women's bodies in Mohawk culture, it is not surprising that it was a midwife concerned about breast milk who initiated interest in health studies after the discovery of environmental contamination.

Ohen:ton Karihwatehkwen, the Thanksgiving Address

Ceremonies and important events at Akwesasne, and in other Haudenosaunee communities, are opened with the Ohen:ton Karihwatehkwen—the "Words That Come before All Else," or Thanksgiving Address—which addresses different aspects of the environment as family and expresses gratitude to and for them. This includes sections for the People, the Waters, the Fish, the Plants, the Food Plants, the Medicinal Herbs, the Animals, the Trees, the Birds, the Four Winds, the Grandfather Thunderers, Elder Brother the Sun, Grandmother Moon, the Stars, the Enlightened Teachers, and the Creator, each section concluding with "Now our minds are one," addressing the importance of peace, balance, and consensus. In addition to elders, who have commonly been the ones asked to recite the Ohen:ton Karihwatehkwen at events, a number of younger people are now invited to offer the address, thanks to the Akwesasne Freedom School (a Mohawk-language immersion school), a language immersion program at the Akwesasne Mohawk Board of Education, and the promotion of the Mohawk language through Ohero:kon and other cultural programs. Segments of the address are featured in materials produced by the Saint Regis Mohawk Tribe (such as the newest fish advisory issued by the Environment Division) as a way of highlighting the importance of, and the community's relationship to, natural elements.

Kaianerekowa, Great Law of Peace

Kaianerekowa is cited as the source of traditional laws and principles that provide the political and spiritual structure of the Haudenosaunee Confederacy. The Great Law also reaffirms sacred ceremonies, songs, dances, and the clan system.[4] The telling of the entire story of the Great Law can take days, according to former Wolf Clan subchief Jake Swamp, whom I heard narrate what he called a "*Reader's Digest* version" of the story that lasted an hour and a half, during which he was only able to scratch the surface.

The story generally begins in a time when the separate nations who would eventually come to form the Confederacy were at war. A man known as the Peacemaker was born on the shores of Lake Ontario to a Huron woman. When he grew older, he carved a canoe from stone, paddled it across Lake Ontario, and then traveled throughout territories of the warring nations, spreading a message of peace and strength in unity. He recruited Jigonsaseh, a female Seneca leader, to join in his cause and promote peace, initially by withholding food from passing warriors.[5] For her cooperation, she was made the head clan mother, and the roles of other clan mothers were revived and strengthened. The Peacemaker also recruited Hiawatha (or Aiionwatha), a Mohawk man who created the condolence prayer after the death of his daughters, and who became the spokesman for the movement. Together, they worked to recruit each of the five Haudenosaunee nations to come together to form a confederacy that would bring peace among member nations and strengthen them to act as a unified body in peace and war with other nations. They demonstrated to the people how one arrow could be easily broken, but when brought together, a bundle of arrows was almost impossible to break. The last nation to agree was the Onondaga, led by an evil-minded chief named Tadodaho (or Adodaroh), who had a nest of snakes for hair. The Peacemaker (or, in some versions, Hiawatha) combed the snakes from Tadodaho's hair and straightened his twisted and misshapen body, and thereby his mind. The Onondaga Nation was then offered the position of fire keepers. A great white pine tree was uprooted, and the weapons of war from all of the five nations were buried under it. An eagle was placed atop the tree to stand guard and sound a warning should anyone try to disturb the peace. The tree is said to have four white roots, which nations can follow back to the tree to achieve peace.[6]

The Confederacy is symbolized as a great longhouse, with the Mohawk as the keepers of the eastern door, the Seneca the keepers of the western door, and the Oneida, Onondaga, and Cayuga in between. Within each nation, clan mothers, who are select older women of each clan, choose and depose chiefs. Each clan mother appoints a roiane (chief), as well as a subchief, a male faithkeeper, and a female faithkeeper, and these four people, along with the clan mother, work together under one hereditary title.[7] For the Mohawk Nation, there are nine hereditary titles, three in each of the Turtle Clan, Wolf Clan, and Bear Clan.[8] Decisions are made through consensus rather than through democratic vote. As an entire council, the chiefs of the Five (later Six) Nations meet at Onondaga, the most centrally located nation and the seat of the fire.[9] Before any action can be taken by the Confederacy, all of the fifty chiefs who constitute the council have to agree, have to be of "one heart, one mind, one law."[10] When an issue is raised in the Confederacy council, it can be brought forward three times. After the third time, if it is not approved, it can never be raised again, in order to prevent divisiveness in the Confederacy.

The Kaianerekowa is not just an origin story for the Confederacy; it represents a complex combination of spiritual and political rules and regulations for spiritual ceremonies, political leadership, warfare against enemies, justice, international relations, funerals, adoptions and the resolution of internal disputes.[11] Three concepts have come to be synonymous with the Great Law of Peace: skennen (peace), kasatstenhse:ra (power), and kanikonri:io or kariwiio (righteousness).[12]

The Peacemaker brought skennen in order to end the bloodshed between nations. The white pine tree under which the weapons of the warring nations were buried has come to stand for peace.[13] Skennen, as applied to the body politic, denotes peace and tranquility. As applied to the individual human mind/body, it denotes health or soundness, the normal functioning condition. Its antithesis is war, strife, and contention, or disease, illness, and obsession.

The Peacemaker demonstrated the second concept, kasatstenhse:ra, when he held up the bundle of arrows to show that unification means strength. Kasatstenhse:ra denotes the force of a strong community, its potential power in war, but also an individual's power, the authority of the orenda, or, as Kanetohare terms it, the life energy force.[14] A strong, healthy society has the power to enact peace.

The third concept, kanikonri:io (good mind) or kariwiio (good word, or good message), is not as easy to translate into English but has generally come to be called righteousness.[15] This concept entails ethical teachings, values, justice, and righteousness as formulated in customs, later developed in institutional form through the teachings of Handsome Lake, a Seneca prophet who revitalized the longhouse religion at the beginning of the nineteenth century.[16] On the level of the individual, kanikonri:io or kariwiio denotes the healthy mind of a person who follows and promotes these teachings and values.

Together, these concepts create the Great Law of Peace. Inherent in the notion that each concept has an individual denotation and a body politic denotation is the idea that for a society to be healthy, each of its individual members must be healthy, and vice versa. This sentiment was reflected in the conversations I had with Akwesasro:non that focused on the importance of community cooperation in improving health for Mohawk people. In addition, Mohawk scholar Taiaiake Alfred has used these concepts as the basis of his "Indigenous manifesto," to inspire tradition-based leadership, and the Akwesasne Task Force on the Environment Research Advisory Committee (ATFE RAC) has used them as base principles in developing its Good Mind Research Protocol.[17]

One Dish, One Spoon

Lessons around consensus and cooperation, and the importance of sharing food, are also built into the stories documenting the formation of the Haudenosaunee Confederacy, in particular the "one dish, one spoon" philosophy. When the Peacemaker gathered a circle of fifty chiefs representing the member nations of the Confederacy together for the first time, he worked to establish what it would mean to work together. The Peacemaker passed around a bowl of beaver tail, a delicacy, of which the assembled leaders were expected to take only as much as they needed, so that there would be enough for all in the circle.[18] This dish demonstrated the collective responsibility of the people to share equally, with a spoon rather than a knife offered to prevent possible bloodshed and disruption of peace. In a community that is often fractured along political and religious lines, the "one dish, one spoon" philosophy is frequently evoked as a reminder of the necessity of working together.

Akwesasro:non draw on cultural elements like the touchstones described above to frame understandings of health and the environment, and the ways in which community action to address issues should be carried out. In this book, these stories and philosophies are cited in the ways in which many Mohawks shaping environmental policy and environmental health research think and speak about health, women's roles, food culture, and environmental governance.

Abbreviations

Alcoa: Aluminum Company of America

ARAR: applicable or relevant and appropriate requirement

ATFE: Akwesasne Task Force on the Environment

ATFE RAC: Akwesasne Task Force on the Environment Research Advisory Committee

ATSDR: Agency for Toxic Substances and Disease Registry

BMI: body mass index

CBPR: community-based participatory research

CBSA: Canada Border Services Agency

CDC: Centers for Disease Control and Prevention

CERCLA: Comprehensive Environmental Response, Compensation, and Liability Act of 1980

DEP: dominant epidemiological paradigm

EJ: environmental justice

EPA: U.S. Environmental Protection Agency

FERP: First Environment Research Project

GM: General Motors

IHS: Indian Health Service

IRB: institutional review board

MASH: Mohawks Agree on Safe Health

MAWBS: Mohawk Adolescent Well-Being Study

MCA: Mohawk Council of Akwesasne

NIEHS: National Institute of Environmental Health Sciences

NRDA: Natural Resource Damages Assessment

NYSDEC: New York State Department of Environmental Conservation

NYSDOH: New York State Department of Health

OU: operable unit

PCBs: polychlorinated biphenyls

ppb: parts per billion

ppm: parts per million

ROD: Record of Decision

SBRP: Superfund Basic Research Program

SRMHS: Saint Regis Mohawk Health Services

SRMT: Saint Regis Mohawk Tribe

SUNY Albany: State University of New York at Albany

USDA: U.S. Department of Agriculture

WARN: Women of All Red Nations

Environmental Justice, Political Ecology, and the Three Bodies of a Mohawk Community

"This is God's country here," an Akwesasne Mohawk woman explained to me as we sat at her kitchen table over cups of coffee. She stared past me out her kitchen window, which overlooks the Saint Lawrence River and the General Motors Central Foundry. She had just been describing how she stood in her front yard and watched men in "moon suits" work to clean up the industrial site a few years prior. "They'd come in here in their space suits and take your water, a sample of it. If that's not alarming, then I don't know what is." She described how "we used to play in that dump. We used to go play in it. We would just scavenge in the junk and go sort through it, pick aluminum and stuff like that, play with paint." She reduced the family's fish consumption after the government of the Saint Regis Mohawk Tribe (SRMT) issued advisories against eating locally caught fish, and after her husband started noticing changes in the fish. But she was not sure these changes had come in time to protect their health. She had always wanted a big family, but several miscarriages (which she connected to exposure to the contamination) made that impossible. Even so, when I asked her if she ever considered moving, she said no. As a resident of the Raquette Point region of the Saint Regis Mohawk Reservation, she had the dubious honor of both living on a beautiful waterfront property and having a front-row seat to observe a Superfund cleanup.

Another resident, Mark, lived a little farther downriver. He described his battle with cancer and told me that the residents of

Raquette Point were constantly barraged with pollution from three local industrial sites: General Motors (GM), Reynolds Metals, and the Aluminum Company of America (Alcoa).[1] We talked about whether contamination from these industrial plants had affected the number of gardens that had been planted in Akwesasne, a community where gardens are materially and symbolically important. He told me: "I decided to keep eating. . . . No, I never did stop planting." He went on to emphasize:

> I never did stop planting, you know. Hoping that . . . the stuff I produced was healthier than what I bought from an unknown source, you know, at least I knew the pollutants I was getting from the yard, so I could say yeah, mine is polluted but it's my own pollution. I don't know, that doesn't make sense but somewhere in my head it did.

As far as Mark was concerned, it seemed that all food had the chance of being somewhat tainted, so by continuing to produce food in his own gardens he at least had some modicum of control over the source of the contamination. When I asked him if he had ever considered moving, even to another area of the reservation, he replied, "Are you kidding me? I live in heaven!"

These conversations are emblematic of the complicated feelings that many Akwesasro:non express about their homeland, a place that has sustained Indigenous people for eons but has been impinged on by environmental contamination as well as state and federal governments. These two examples are drawn from dozens, all collectively emphasizing the strange tension between the beauty, history, and productivity of the land and the devastating environmental impact of industry. As people reputed to be fighters and activists, Mohawks have battled to preserve who they are, confronting state and federal governments and the scientific–industrial complex to maintain their homeland. This book is about those fights and those confrontations.

Akwesasne is a Mohawk community that straddles the borders of New York State and the Canadian provinces of Ontario, and Quebec.[2] The portion of the community below the U.S.–Canadian border is known as the Saint Regis Mohawk Reservation. The portion north of the border is known as the Akwesasne Mohawk Reserve. The entire community, currently about 13,000 people living across 25,712 acres, is called Akwesasne, which means "land where the partridge drums."[3] Sitting at the confluence of the Saint Lawrence, Saint Regis, Raquette, Grasse, and Salmon Rivers, the community has relied for generations on the region's abundance of fish and wildlife and rich alluvial soils.

Akwesasne is downwind, downriver, and down gradient from one federal and two state Superfund sites, one of which, the General Motors plant, has been determined to be a serious hazardous waste site. The Comprehensive Environmental Response, Compensation, and Liability Act (CERCLA), commonly known as Superfund, was enacted by Congress in 1980 and amended in 1986 by the Superfund Amendments and Reauthorization Act. This law gave the U.S. federal government broad authority to respond directly to releases of hazardous substances that might endanger public health or the environment, established prohibitions and requirements concerning closed and abandoned hazardous waste sites, and provided for the liability of persons responsible for releases of hazardous waste. The trust fund part of Superfund, which was established to pay for cleanup when no responsible party could be identified, was funded initially through a tax on chemical and petroleum industries. Starting in the mid-1990s, however, due to industry lobbying and efforts by a Republican Congress to weaken the law, input to the Superfund trust diminished, and cleanup rates for contaminated sites slowed. Since 2001, most of the funding for cleanups of hazardous waste sites has come from taxpayers and from "potentially responsible parties," when they can be identified and held accountable.[4]

Once a site is identified as releasing hazardous substances, the U.S. Environmental Protection Agency (EPA) conducts a site inspection and gives the site a score based on the EPA's hazard ranking system. This score determines whether the site should be placed on the National Priorities List of more serious sites. A Remedial Investigation/Feasibility Study is then conducted to determine the degree of site contamination, and this leads to a Record of Decision (ROD), which explains the methods that will be used to clean up the site. Remedial action then begins. In 1983, New York State discovered that the GM industrial plant directly adjacent to the Raquette Point portion of Akwesasne had been leaching polychlorinated biphenyls (PCBs) into the Saint Lawrence River. This discovery, fueled by community outrage, triggered an official reaction.

The Superfund cleanup was staged on a complicated landscape. Akwesasne is one of eight Mohawk communities spread across Quebec, Ontario, and New York, although it is the only one to straddle the geopolitical territorial lines of so many nations, states, and provinces. Because of the myriad borders that crisscross Akwesasne, residents must contend with two federal, three state/provincial, and three tribal governments, along with all of their accompanying agencies. If they step off either end of the reservation, they are also dealing with two different New York counties, Franklin County and Saint Lawrence County. Children in Akwesasne have the option of attending public schools on either side of the international border (or the community-based Akwesasne Freedom School), and many have dual U.S. and Canadian citizenship in addition to their tribal citizenship. The southern portion of the community is governed by the SRMT, the elected tribal government recognized by the U.S. federal government. The Mohawk Council of Akwesasne (MCA), the elected tribal government recognized by the Canadian government, governs the northern half of the community. A third governing body, the traditional clan-based government empowered by the Haudenosaunee Confederacy, the Mohawk Nation Council of Chiefs, considers the entire territory of Akwesasne as its jurisdiction, although it is not recognized by either the U.S. or the Canadian federal government. Most Native American communities are jurisdictionally challenging, but Akwesasne is exceptionally so.

After the discovery of leaching PCBs and other contaminants in the 1980s, the community rallied across social, cultural, and political divides to fight for environmental justice. A midwife, Mohawk scientists, and other community members, concerned about the potential health impacts of this contamination, worked to revolutionize how environmental health research is done in Indigenous communities and pushed to influence how the cleanup would be conducted. Drawing on interviews with community members and scientists, and framing my discussion within the literatures of Native American studies, critical medical anthropology, environmental anthropology and sociology, and political ecology, I set out here to explore the history of how these projects came together and to reveal how taking part in this research affected the Akwesasne Mohawk community, the scientists who worked with the community, and the ways in which environmental health research would be conducted after this case.

Throughout this book, I try to highlight those moments when Indigenous methods informed the scientific outcomes and when local ways of knowledge production came into dynamic relation with the state, with corporations, and with the existing scientific community outside Akwesasne.

At first glance, the situation of the Akwesasne Mohawk community would appear to be a standard case of environmental racism, but the proliferation of borders and boundaries, the disconnects among overlapping agencies and identities, and the distinctiveness of local cultural history set this particular case apart and demonstrate that it needs to be examined on its own terms. To accomplish this, I include in this book the voices of people on the ground, mobilized for environmental justice, but working through a kaleidoscope of identities, affiliations, and political structures. I highlight the material history and symbolic impact of settler colonialism and dramatize the interplay between political activism and political ecology. Through this book's focus, plotlines, and conclusions, I intend to spotlight how we might learn from community-based research projects that are built, at the very foundation, in partnership with Indigenous communities. I also aim to model how we might actually write about those same sorts of projects. Such partnerships do not merely change how we understand—they also alter *what* and *for whom* we learn.

Katsi Cook: Midwife, Activist, and Grassroots Leader

The story outlined in this book began in large part with the actions of a remarkable woman who has made it her life's work to help Indigenous women reclaim sovereignty over their bodies, their birthing practices, and the health of their communities. Katsi Cook was born at home, delivered by her midwife grandmother, and raised in Akwesasne.[5] As she prepared for the birth of her own first child in 1975, Katsi sought out traditional birthing methods as a means to avoid the sterile "white" institution of the hospital and to assert herself as a Mohawk woman. Throughout the 1970s, as she became more involved in Indian activism and took part in the founding of Women of All Red Nations (WARN), she identified control over reproduction as one of the essential elements of Native sovereignty.[6] She decided to take up midwifery, a profession practiced by women in her family for several generations. In 1978, Katsi completed an apprenticeship in spiritual midwifery at The Farm in Tennessee; a completely self-sufficient "hippie commune," as she describes it, The Farm, run by Plenty International, trained midwives and emergency medical technicians for Akwesasne through its own medical programs. She then received clinical training at the University of New Mexico Women's Health Training Program, which included working with Navajo and Pueblo women, whom Katsi was concerned were also becoming estranged from their cultures' traditional birthing methods. She subsequently completed a clinical placement in the Twin Cities at the Red Schoolhouse Clinic, a WARN project in Minneapolis–St. Paul. There she trained an Anishnaabe birthing crew and created the Women's Dance Health Program through a grant administered by the Youth Project in Minneapolis.

The Women's Dance is a traditional Haudenosaunee dance in which the women's feet never leave the ground; it is performed to remind women of their connection to the earth. In the creation story, Sky Woman made the earth larger through a dance done on the back of a turtle, and women carry on a reminder of this creation through this traditional, shuffling dance. Katsi organized a core group of four women to continue the project, and in 1980 she returned to Akwesasne, where she gave birth at home to her second son.[7] She then became involved in the standoff between New York State and the Tribe over jurisdictional issues on the Raquette Point portion of the reservation.[8]

Katsi joined the standoff in 1980 and helped to develop the Akwesasne Freedom School, an alternative school that taught students in the Mohawk language and served to educate children who lived in the encampment as well as those living elsewhere on the reservation. Katsi also continued her midwifery practice. While the battle over jurisdictional issues raged, outside communities would not provide emergency medical services, so Akwesasne developed its own volunteer group of emergency medical technicians, trained at The Farm, and Katsi delivered babies in mothers' homes. In a 1981 grant application for funding for the Women's Dance Health Program, she described how on average she oversaw a home delivery every six weeks. She also provided complete prenatal care, labor and delivery assistance at home and in the hospital, postpartum care, family planning services, family counseling, and general obstetrical, gynecological, and infant care, which she estimated to be about $1,600 worth of services for each mother. She noted: "While we do not charge for our services, this does not mean that it is free. Our birthing families are primarily motivated by their commitment to traditional understandings of health and community. Along these lines, they are encouraged to offer their volunteer services to other nation projects, such as the Akwesasne Freedom School, community gardens, and Akwesasne Emergency Team."[9] Katsi also worked with her husband, Jose Barreiro, at the offices of the newspaper *Akwesasne Notes*, which, along with the Freedom School, were directly adjacent to the General Motors dump, a source of contamination that continues to shape life at Akwesasne decades after its discovery.

Katsi partnered with her fellow community members to insist that the impacts of this contamination on their health and environment be properly investigated. Their research and persistence, coupled with the willingness of scientists at SUNY Albany to work with community members to reimagine their methods, changed the way such environmental health research is now done in tribal communities. In the literature on research methods, Akwesasne is often referenced as an example of an Indigenous community that took control of its research destiny, and the scholarly data about the site are held up as an example of the results that can come from community-based participatory research (CBPR).[10]

Environmental Justice

Katsi Cook's local struggles intersect with the national history of the concept of environmental justice, which first appeared on the political and academic radar in 1982, at roughly the moment Katsi began actively pressing the state to confront the massive cleanup needed at the GM site. In that year, African American activists in Warren County, North Carolina, stood up to protest the construction in their neighborhood of a dump for PCB-contaminated waste. That people of color were disproportionately affected by environmental contamination, and that race was the most important factor in predicting where toxic waste sites would be located, was confirmed by a study conducted by the U.S. General Accounting Office in 1983 and by a national study conducted by the United Church of Christ's Commission for Racial Justice, reported in the 1987 publication *Toxic Wastes and Race in the United States*.[11] Environmental justice (EJ) studies emerged as an interdisciplinary field with a body of literature documenting the disproportionate impacts of pollution on communities of color. Since then, as Mohai et al. note, "hundreds of studies" have concluded that, in general, "ethnic minorities, indigenous persons, people of color, and low-income communities confront a higher burden of environmental exposure from air, water, and soil pollution from industrialization, militarization, and consumer practices."[12]

Environmental racism, which lies at the root of struggles for environmental justice, has been defined as "any policy, practice, or directive that differentially affects or disadvantages (whether intended or unintended) individuals, groups, or communities based on race or color."[13] This leads to the "systematic exclusion of people of color from environmental decisions affecting their communities."[14] On the flip side, environmental justice is the principle that all people and communities are entitled to equal protection by environmental and public health laws and regulations. The EJ movement has expanded definitions of "the environment" to include where people live, work, play, and pray and has fought to institutionalize the "fair treatment and meaningful involvement of all people regardless of race, color, national origin, or income, with respect to the development, implementation, and enforcement of environmental laws, regulations, and policies" in agencies like the EPA.[15]

While Katsi Cook's activism could be viewed as an outgrowth of the radical social movements of the 1960s and 1970s—and there are obvious connections between Akwesasne and North Carolina at the start of this national movement—Indigenous communities have a unique stake in the history of environmental racism. In the United States, Native communities live in close proximity to approximately six hundred Superfund sites, and environmental mitigation for these communities lags significantly behind that for nontribal communities.[16] Sites ranging from industrial plants to mines to military bases—as well as places affected by the release of pesticides and other agricultural by-products—have negative effects not only on their surrounding environments but also on the health, cultures, and reproductive capabilities of the Indigenous communities they border.[17] When the study of EJ is applied to a tribal context, environmental issues cannot be contemplated apart from a recognition of American Indian tribes' unique historical, political, and legal circumstances.[18] As geographer Ryan Holifield notes, "Environmental justice in Indian country is intimately bound up in the complex matter of tribal sovereignty," which differentiates EJ cases in these communities from those in other racial or ethnic communities.[19]

Katsi Cook highlighted this important difference between American Indians and other EJ groups in a keynote speech she delivered to environmental health researchers in 2015:

> It's important to understand that North American Indigenous are not a racial or ethnic minority, but are one of three sovereignties in the United States. These are the federal, state and tribal levels of government. And so our traditional cultural property is protected by whole body of case law and Supreme Court decisions, treaty rights, and has significance for the work that's being done to recover our community from this historic moment of the post-WWII economic boom and the development of the St Lawrence Seaway.[20]

The political, social, and environmental history of Akwesasne reveals how promoting environmental justice in an Indigenous community can be challenging, necessitating a consideration of these unique factors. More specifically, any consideration of environmental issues in Indian Country needs to take into account the unique colonial history of Native Americans and the relationship that tribes have with the United States. Writing from the perspective of a member of the Muskogee Creek Nation of Oklahoma, Daniel Wildcat refers to the dislocation of Native peoples from the environment as the "fourth removal," following relocation from tribal homelands through forced removal, the compulsory attendance of Indigenous children in boarding schools, and the removal of tribal identity through assimilationist programs.[21] Jace Weaver similarly considers environmental issues across Indian Country with this history in mind, noting, "As Indian lands are assaulted, so are Indian peoples. . . . Environmental destruction is simply one manifestation of the colonialism and racism that have marked Indian/White relations."[22]

Exploring environmental issues in Indian Country through the lens of settler colonialism—and differentiating cases of EJ in Indigenous communities from struggles for justice in other types of communities—also contributes to an understanding of the full impacts of settler colonialism on Indigenous lifeways. Patrick Wolfe defines settler colonialism as an inclusive, land-centered project with a view to eliminate Indigenous societies.[23] As Scott Morgensen notes, the elimination of Indigenous peoples necessary for settler societies is pursued via "amalgamation and replacement"—that is, through the physical removal of Indigenous peoples from the land or through their assimilation into Western society.[24] This assimilation can come in part through a "structure of oppression that wrongfully interferes with Indigenous capacities to maintain an adaptive capacity in their homelands," robbing Indigenous peoples of the ability to carry out relational responsibilities and land-based culture.[25] In describing the legacy of uranium mining on Navajo land, Traci Voyles asserts, "Settler colonialism is so deeply about resources that environmental injustices, whether on Native lands or lands of other others, must always be viewed through the lens of settler colonialism. While the connections between the two forms of power are various, the body is a good place to start—just as race and racial power are organized at the level of the body, so too are the functions of environmental violence."[26] She goes on to state that Native American encounters with settler colonialism are so deeply entangled with environment and resources that "even the phrase 'environmental racism' can seem to lose all meaning in a tribal context, quite simply because 'racism' has *always* meant environmental violence for Native peoples."[27] Voyles calls to move EJ studies, particularly studies of environmental injustices on Native lands, to a more complex understanding of nature and justice in the past, present, and future of settler colonialism. Part of what I am setting out to do here is to examine how settler colonial encroachment on Akwesasne's self-governance and relational responsibilities has affected the health and environment of Akwesasro:non, but without diminishing the ways in which the community has pushed back against these forces and their assimilative impacts in the fight to maintain and re-create identity and lifeways.

Environmental justice activists and scholars have focused their efforts on different avenues of justice: distributive justice, procedural justice, and recognition justice. *Distributive justice* addresses the over-representation of toxic waste sites in communities of color, advocating for the equal distribution of such environmental harms as well as environmental benefits like green space. The early EJ reports, like the one drafted by the United Church of Christ's commission, focused primarily on inequitable siting practices—on who was bearing burdens. *Procedural justice* centers on ensuring that all communities are able to participate in the environmental decision-making process, in the hope that this will both help prevent inequitable siting and better involve affected communities in site cleanups. While this type of inclusion is what many EJ organizations are fighting for, Penobscot anthropologist Darren Ranco has noted that procedural inclusion looks different for tribes than it does for other communities fighting environmental injustice because of EPA policies necessitating that federally recognized tribes be given "treatment as state" in cases that affect their territories. Ranco notes that many EJ groups are fighting to "get a seat at the table," but just being involved in the regulatory process may not be enough. He goes on to describe how the EPA is required to include and consult with Indian nations during regulatory decisions when tribal resources are affected, but, he notes, quoting Eileen Guana, "A place at the table does not ensure a comparable serving of the environmental protection pie."[28] Tribes can set standards, but they might not have the funds to monitor and enforce compliance with those standards.

Some critical EJ scholars have noted that being included in the procedures is irrelevant to community health and safety when the system in which these procedures are embedded is designed to exploit some members of the community for the benefit of others. David Schlosberg, who has studied conceptions of justice in the context of the EJ movement, argues that what is important is not just the fight for equal distribution of goods and bads in society or equal participation in environmental decision-making processes—we also need to examine the processes that construct the maldistribution and unequal participation, which allow for the application of justice only to certain human communities.[29] As critical EJ scholars argue, the system that allows for environmental degradation in some communities is not broken, it is designed to work that way. They argue that environmental problems and inequities are produced—they are not accidents. These inequities are evidence of the normal routine functioning of modern market economies.[30] For these reasons, Anishnaabe activist and author Winona LaDuke has stated, "We don't just want a piece of the pie. We want a different pie."[31]

Wary of the dangers posed by entanglements with the federal government, tribal leaders have still worked incredibly hard to ensure Native inclusion in environmental processes. As this book will describe, community and tribal government leaders in Akwesasne fought for a seat at the regulatory table, to develop their own policies and regulations, and to have a voice in the research and cleanup processes. But what some are calling for is a step beyond achieving equal inclusion in the political process. They are calling for *recognition justice*—the affirmation of group identity and acknowledgment that as a distinct and sensitive group they do not want to receive the same treatment as, for example, white middle-class suburbanites. Because of subsistence lifestyles, spiritual practices, and other cultural behaviors, Indigenous people often suffer multiple exposures from resource use that result in environmental health impacts disproportionate to those seen in the general population.[32] "Exposure scenarios designed for suburban activities and lifestyles are not suitable for tribal communities," note Stuart Harris and Barbara Harper, who have conducted extensive work around developing Native American exposure scenarios and risk assessment tools. For this reason, they argue, risk needs to be calculated differently in Indigenous communities.[33] Potawatomi environmental philosopher Kyle Whyte asserts that the maintenance of "relational responsibilities," which are necessary for tribal "collective continuance," includes the maintenance of relationships not only between family and community members and across human communities but also across species and with features of the land (like rivers or mountains) and ecosystems.[34] Members of the Akwesasne Task Force on the Environment (ATFE) have published multiple articles demanding that their community be recognized as a distinct tribal community and culture, with a relationship to the natural world and a culturally based lifestyle that are different from those of other Americans.

In a way, then, this story about industrial environmental contamination, histories of settler colonialism, and heroic community struggles for justice is also, in the end, about food. There is increasing convergence in many communities between environmental justice and food justice, as people work to have their environments cleaned up and to make safe food more available. In contrast with many urban communities, rural and Indigenous communities often rely on the immediate environment as their main source of food. Both the environmental justice and food justice movements have a place-based focus and are health related. Further, both focus on addressing corporate dominance and system-related issues, the empowerment of community members, and the development of sustainable and livable communities.[35] Advocates of both environmental justice and food justice seek to alter the power relations at the root of social and ecological problems. As Whyte notes, in Indigenous communities, the structure of environmental injustice is "often tied to notions of wrongful disruption of Indigenous food systems."[36] He goes on to explain that "Indigenous food systems refer to specific *collective capacities* of particular Indigenous peoples to cultivate and tend, produce, distribute, and consume their own foods, recirculate refuse, and acquire trusted foods and ingredients from other populations."[37] Protective measures like fish advisories, made necessary by environmental contamination, disrupt these systems and capacities.

Much of the organizing around EJ issues in Indigenous communities involves the protection of traditional food sources. The notion that Indigenous peoples have a sovereign "right to food" has been affirmed in an array of instruments created by international governmental and nongovernmental alliances, including the United Nations Declaration on the Rights of Indigenous Peoples, which specifies the range of rights required for the full exercise of food sovereignty, paying particular attention to the connections between the right to cultural self-determination and the right to maintain and protect seeds and land.[38] But, as Whyte notes, "many of the more visible theories of environmental justice have not explicitly referenced the relationship between food and environmental justice."[39] In chronicling the story of Akwesasne, I have been struck by the power of this relationship, by the connection between a change in diet and activity, and by the ensuing health issues on the ground.

David Pellow and Paul Brulle call for a move toward critical environmental justice studies, which does not just document cases and successes but also provides a more critical examination of the movement's tactics, strategies, discursive frames, organizational structure, and resource base.[40] They note that it is imperative for EJ scholars to make more significant links between EJ research and literatures on social movements, environmental sociology, history, and ethnic studies. EJ scholars need to engage in conversations across disciplines that redefine the ways those disciplines approach questions concerning not only the environment but also race and ethnicity, class, gender, and nation; as well as the application of participatory methods being used in collaboration with communities fighting environmental injustice.[41]

Political Ecology

In this book, I demonstrate how aspects of the Akwesasne community—whether through grassroots organizations like the Akwesasne Task Force on the Environment and the First Environment Research Collaborative, or through tribal departments like the Saint Regis Mohawk Tribe's Environment Division—sought to challenge the durable, dangerous political power imbalances that made contamination possible. But although Akwesasro:non demanded and earned the opportunities to create environmental policies and shape environmental health research for their communities by establishing governance models and developing new research protocols, it is also important to note that Akwesasne (and tribal communities more generally) is not one monolithic political entity. It encompasses a number of different political factions and subcommunities, as well as divisions of class, gender, and religion. Examining the uneven interactions and negotiations between and among these socially and politically constructed categories is what Native American and Indigenous studies is meant to do, but here, in this book, it also contributes to an understanding of political ecology.

The premise of political ecology is that environmental changes and ecological conditions are the products of political processes. This includes the fundamental assumption that the costs (often hidden) and benefits associated with environmental change are distributed among actors unequally, usually reproducing or reinforcing social and economic inequities. Research in political ecology explores the root causes of environmental issues, who benefits and who loses when environmental changes take place, the political actors who contribute to environmental transitions, and the political movements that grow from these transitions. The goal of political ecological research is to identify root causes rather than just symptoms.[42]

As Beth Rose Middleton notes, the political ecology approach has increased our understanding of the relationships between resource control and governance, but it has not yet deeply engaged with

Native and Indigenous studies and other related disciplines. Middleton argues that one cannot understand human–environment interactions within formerly colonized (or, some would argue, continually colonized) communities without both an explicit examination of coloniality through critical ethnic studies and analyses from third and fourth world scholars of their experiences of coloniality at multiple scales.[43] Similarly, in his book about environmental governance in the Cherokee Nation, Clint Carroll describes how political ecology as a field stands to benefit from Native American and Indigenous studies through an analysis of the unique political histories of American Indian nations and their relationships to the U.S. settler state.[44]

Political ecologists have increasingly argued that "the terrain of human health must be acknowledged as an 'environment' in its own right, thus necessitating that we examine (un)healthy bodies within the wider ecological context of (un)healthy landscapes."[45] In documenting the activist and environmental history of Akwesasne, and then moving through decades of remediation to present-day food-related health concerns that Mohawks see as still connected to this damaged landscape, I seek to contribute in this book to a developing political ecology of health and a political ecology of the body.[46] While the full range of concerns ordinarily associated with the political ecological perspective—such as conflicts over resources, challenges inherent in environmental governance, and human–environment relationships—are all present at Akwesasne, we can also present "the body" as a site in which these concerns intersect.[47]

Methods

Much of this book is about method—and about what happens when Indigenous methods are brought together with conventional academic practice in pursuit of environmental justice. It is not surprising, then, that my own method was shaped by the history shared in this book.

In many Indigenous communities, research has been perceived as an activity to benefit academics rather than community members.[48] Many communities feel "researched to death" and have no desire to allow or take part in any further projects that they do not feel will directly benefit them. Tribal institutional review boards (IRBs) like the Akwesasne Task Force on the Environment Research

Advisory Committee have been established to prevent further re-search exploitation by approving or rejecting projects based on how the board members perceive these projects will affect their commu-nities. Community-based participatory research, described as much as a process as a method, is one type of approach that researchers in the health sciences and social sciences have used as a means for achieving broader community input and greater community accep-tance of research projects. Indigenous researchers have taken this a step further, advocating for "decolonizing methodologies," which fur-ther deepen CBPR's ethical commitments to communities. As Dakota scholar Kim TallBear describes, "Rather than integrating community priorities with academic priorities, changing and expanding both in the process, decolonizing methods begin and end with the standpoint of indigenous lives, needs, and desires, engaging with academic lives, approaches, and priorities along the way."[49] An important aspect of this is what Cree scholar Shawn Wilson refers to as "shared aspects of relationality and relational accountability" that can be put into practice "through choice of research topic, methods of data collec-tion, form of analysis and presentation of information."[50] This rela-tional accountability, he notes, "requires me to form reciprocal and respectful relationships within the communities where I am con-ducting research."[51]

As I conducted the research for this book, it was important to me that the project meant something to the people with whom—and for whom—I was working. The selection of the different themes and topics presented here was an iterative process, developed through conversations and work parties with Akwesasro:non, in addition to an interest in the literature of environmental health research. As a person of Indigenous ancestry who is not from Akwesasne, I knew that I needed to develop the right relationships with, and responsibil-ities to, the people, seeds, and soil of this community before, during, and after the drafting of the manuscript.[52]

The idea that this book should explore the impact of environ-mental health research on Akwesasro:non was first developed in Katsi Cook's living room, during a casual visit with her son, who was a friend of mine. As we sipped tea, Katsi described to me her work helping nursing mothers in the community determine the safety of their breast milk. Over the years, Katsi has striven to combine her knowledge of midwifery, women's health issues, traditional Mohawk culture, and scientific health studies, and she is almost perpetually traveling—giving talks, working with Indigenous communities developing birthing centers, and collecting information for new health-based projects. As someone who helped to initiate the health studies at Akwesasne, but who has since taken on several other projects, she was interested in having me dedicate my fieldwork to a better understanding of people's opinions of, and reactions to, these health studies—work that she felt could contribute to future health research.

At the same time, I could not explore issues of health and the environment in a community like Akwesasne without taking into account the connections between these issues and food production. This became apparent one day while my friend Gina and I were standing in her front yard on Cornwall Island. Gina described to me how she grew up around extensive gardens and had always tended a garden of her own until she was advised not to because of concerns about the contamination that might be coming from the neighboring industrial plants. From Gina's yard, there was a clear view of the GM Central Foundry Division, directly across the river on the New York shore of the Saint Lawrence River. She pointed farther upstream, to the smokestacks of the Reynolds Metals foundry. Concerns about the possible effects on gardens of fluoride contamination from Reynolds and PCB contamination from General Motors led to the warning that Gina should not plant food.

Literature published by members of the grassroots Akwesasne Task Force on the Environment illustrates a trajectory of health and social ills linked to environmental contamination. These publications describe how Mohawks were robbed of the ability to grow or harvest free, healthy, culturally relevant food and were left with the only option of purchasing cheap, processed foods, with the end result being an increasingly unhealthy population.[53] Shortly after the founding of Kanenhi:io Ionkwaienthon:hakie (We Are Planting Good Seeds), a grassroots organization with a focus on supporting families interested in starting farming or gardening projects, I began volunteering with the organization to help with planting activities and to learn more about gardening efforts in the community. I sought to integrate community members' thoughts on the changing food system, and efforts to reclaim it, with their concerns about the environment and their experiences with environmental health research. In this work

I spent a lot of time planting seeds, pulling weeds, butchering chickens, harvesting vegetables, canning pickles and tomatoes, shelling beans, and braiding corn, in the process engaging in conversation about the past, present, and future of the food system in Akwesasne, and Indian Country more broadly. This work carried into taking part in the Ohero:kon rites of passage programs and ceremonies. With the encouragement of Wakerakatsiteh (Louise McDonald), the clan mother at the forefront of reviving these ceremonies, I have since 2008 helped the girls prepare for their fast, assisted with event setup, cut cedar, and tended gardens. The privilege of being able to take part in this work helped me to contextualize the multigenerational battle against environmental contamination and social ills that many people in the community have been waging.

A majority of the interviews that I conducted with community members took place in 2008, although I also conducted some targeted interviews to fill in knowledge gaps in 2009 and 2014.[54] The interview protocol was structured similarly from one interviewee to the next, although I focused most on what each individual could bring to the discussion. The questions pertained to health studies, participants' perceptions of change in the health and environment of the community, and their suggestions for how to improve the health of the community. We also discussed changes in diets related to a decrease in farming and fishing, and the possibility of community members returning to either of those activities with the proper support. Visiting is a valued form of social interaction in this community, and my interviews were often treated as "visits" over coffee. Some interviewees joked that they were envious I had managed to obtain a grant that allowed me to spend several months visiting with people, even if it meant I always had to be jotting down notes. As noted in chapter 3, some suggested that more visiting should be done in the context of sharing the results of studies and environmental information. Many of these visits led to "kitchen table stories," as Gwen Ottinger labels them. Such stories offered deeper critiques of environmental injustices by highlighting an assortment of structural issues that have led to health conditions in Akwesasne, as opposed to "strategic stories," which drew direct and uncritical lines of causation between environmental contamination and every health and social ill in the community.[55] In exploring these honest stories, my intention is not to lessen any of the responsibility of polluting industries for the environmental and health disasters they have created but to explore additional factors that have contributed to social and health problems, as well as actions beyond environmental cleanup that can be supported to address these problems.

All interviewees were presented with informed consent forms that gave them the opportunity to choose whether they wanted their identities to remain confidential (I would remove their names and identifying information from the transcripts) or if they were comfortable leaving their identities on the transcripts. In the following pages in which I share and discuss their words, I give direct credit by using the first names of those who chose to allow me to do so. In quoting from public presentations, I generally provide the speakers' full names.

I transcribed each of the sixty-three community interviews and then uploaded both the interviews and my field notes into the qualitative data analysis software NVivo 7 to code for relevant themes. Some of these themes arose from the interview questions, such as references to health studies and fish consumption, and others arose independently, such as references to distrust of the state and federal governments and concerns about health and habits of youth. I continue to have conversations and e-mail exchanges with some interviewees about the progress of the Superfund cleanup, environmental governance, and health programming, as well as farming and gardening programs. Publications that have come from this work have all been vetted through the Akwesasne Task Force on the Environment, and one of ATFE's members, Brenda LaFrance, served as the community editor for this book. This gave members of the community featured in the book the opportunity to ensure that this publication meets ATFE's goals for all research about the community to provide respect, equity, and empowerment.

I also worked to establish a level of accountability to members of the scientific community who shared their time, words, and articles with me. As described in greater detail in chapter 3, I interviewed seven scientists at SUNY Albany who had collaborated with Akwesasro:non on environmental health research, in response to Laura Nader's call for "studying up"—turning the ethnographic lens on those in society who are not often seen as a cultural group because of their institutionalized positions of power.[56] I spoke with each of them about their experiences in organizing the studies and working directly with Akwesasne community members, and I asked for their ideas about what they might do differently if they were to conduct the studies again. I also attended community meetings in Akwesasne in 2012 and 2014, during which the SUNY scientists presented years' worth of results of environmental health research to the community. My purpose was to observe the ways in which the scientists worked to articulate dense scientific information for a lay audience, as well as the community's responses. Dr. Lawrence Schell and Dr. David Carpenter were kind enough to provide comments on drafts of the chapters about their work in this book, to ensure that I had summarized their science correctly and represented the efforts of their research teams fairly.

Structure

Understanding the political, cultural, and environmental history of Akwesasne is key to understanding how it became the locus of the first large-scale CBPR study in an Indigenous community. In chapter 1, I lay out the history of this community in the context of a driving tour to provide a sense of the physicality of the location. To illustrate salient issues in the community's social and political history, the tour includes landmarks such as border markers, the casino, the longhouses, the tribal offices, the Kateri Tekakwitha Catholic Center, the Saint Lawrence Seaway, industrial plants, and the smattering of signs put up by residents warning state police that they are no longer in New York but on Mohawk land. The "ecosocial history" of Akwesasne as an Indigenous community surrounded by two settler colonial nations and myriad other political bodies that impinge on environmental quality and self-governance makes the fight for environmental justice in Akwesasne a unique case.[57] The road-map-structured history presented in chapter 1 demonstrates the historico-political lens through which Akwesasro:non perceive the imposition of environmental contamination, the government agencies that should have done a better job defending them, and the obstacles to their collaboration with state agencies on the first big CBPR project to take place in an Indigenous community.

In chapter 2, I draw from interviews, archival materials, minutes of public meetings, and newspaper clippings to document the multifaceted history of environmental contamination and environmental health research at Akwesasne. Fluoride contamination from the Reynolds Metals aluminum foundry and PCB contamination from the GM plant decimated the dairy and fishing industries, leading to Akwesasne being targeted for conventional environmental health research studies. But community members organized to demand action, forming first Mohawks Agree on Safe Health (MASH) and then the Akwesasne Task Force on the Environment in order to ensure that the community's interests were represented in the "mitigation politics" that would play out.[58] Despite a lack of trust toward the state government based on suspicions that it has never had Mohawks' best interests in mind, Katsi Cook convinced the New York State Department of Environmental Conservation (NYSDEC) and the New York State Department of Health (NYSDOH) to work with the Mohawks to determine the impact of contamination on the community, conducting environmental sampling and a health risk assessment. This work eventually led to nearly two decades of research with SUNY Albany that documented the levels of contaminants in Mohawk breast milk and blood, and, more recently, investigated some of the potential health effects of these burdens. Chapter 2 also traces the history of the cleanup process at this Superfund site, which, after GM declared bankruptcy, was turned over to an environmental trust.

Rooted in interview material as well as the literatures of citizen science, CBPR, and study report-back, chapter 3 addresses the benefits and challenges of this large-scale CBPR project for both the scientists and community members. Through frank discussions with scientists and Mohawk fieldworkers, I have constructed a conversation that was never able to take place in one time or space—a conversation about the successes and difficulties that members of both groups experienced in working together, and their suggestions for future researchers. The nature of the relationship between researchers and community members was in part a result of the fact that science is the "language of power"—that is, the scientists' way of speaking about the impacts of contamination was legitimated as "official" or "formal" by the state, as opposed to the rich oral testimonies given by community members at public meetings hosted by the EPA.[59] I also interviewed people who had served as subjects in the environmental health research, who had a number of suggestions for more effective and culturally appropriate report-back methods, targeted at social bodies rather than just individual bodies. In this chapter I also explore how, in addition to contributing to the capacity development of the scientists and community members who worked together on these health studies, environmental health research at Akwesasne contributed to the development of science more broadly, beginning at a time when CBPR was just beginning to become a standard of community research.

The second half of the book unpacks the impacts of contamination on Akwesasne's local food culture, the health issues that developed as a result, and the community's efforts to remedy them. In chapter 4, I discuss how the diets of Akwesasro:non have changed over the past generation and examine the direct and collateral ways in which people connect this shift to environmental contamination and other factors. Prior to the discovery of contamination in the river, Akwesasro:non relied on fishing and farming to sustain their food needs and the local economy. Fish advisories issued to protect human health (and the EPA's reliance on policies focused on risk aversion rather than risk remediation), as well as concerns about the potential impacts of fluoride and PCBs on locally raised farm foods, have led to a decrease in the consumption of local foods. In this chapter I explore the risk assessment process that some people employ in making decisions about their local food consumption, in which they weigh potential health impacts against concerns about culture loss. At the same time, this diminishment in local food consumption has been compounded by other modern factors, such as the wage economy and young people's preference for digital entertainment over gardening work. These elements have combined to lead to what Claude Fischler refers to as "gastro-anomy," an anxiety over food, suffered by a generation whose relationship to food is different from that of preceding generations.[60]

One of the health impacts of the change in food culture has been an increase in rates of diabetes. Akwesasne is not unique in its high rates of diabetes (the disease affects about 25 percent of the community, according to the local diabetes program coordinator). Indigenous peoples the world over are suddenly finding they have this "disease of modernity" in common, and in the past thirty years, medical anthropologists and health care providers have worked to understand both the medical and local etiologies of the disease. Drawing on Margaret Lock's concept of "local biologies" and Sherine Hamdy's "political etiologies," chapter 5 contributes to this conversation,

exploring the ways in which Akwesasne community members con-
ceptualize the environmental, social, and physiological origins of this
disease.[61] Mohawks do not place the blame only on individual noncompliant bodies; rather, they weave a more complex etiology that
indicates direct connections between PCBs and diabetes or points
to the role of environmental contamination in limiting the procurement and consumption of local foods.

To address some of these concerns, community groups like
Kanenhi:io Ionkwaienthon:hakie and ATFE have developed community gardening projects. Recently the Tribe also reached a Natural Resource Damages Settlement with local industries that resulted
in funds being made available for programs to support traditional
Mohawk cultural practices, including an apprenticeship program to
promote Mohawk language, horticulture, fishing, trapping, and traditional medicine. In addition, the Saint Regis Mohawk Tribe's Environment Division has recently created a new fish advisory, based on
fish testing and community interviews, which seeks to provide more
nuanced information about which fish can be eaten. I explore these
programs in depth in the book's conclusion.

THREE BODIES

One of the threads weaving all these chapters together is a framework
I have assembled from community suggestions for solutions to everything from health study report-back to health interventions, cultural
programming, and the creation of healthier bodies through the growing of traditional foods. I have structured the suggested solutions
around each of these topics into three layers, loosely incorporating
the concept of the three levels of the body (the individual body-self,
the social body, and the body politic) laid out by medical anthropologists Nancy Scheper-Hughes and Margaret Lock in their explication
of the different perspectives from which culturally perceived bodies
can be understood.[62] I utilize this framework a little differently, as I
find that the idea of the three levels of the body is useful for examining what community members see as the sources of some of their
health issues, and how those can be addressed. Akwesasne community members' suggestions for remedies to many of the local issues
fell into three categories: individual, social, and structural (involving
political bodies). While any issue should be tackled from all three

levels, the social level was often the middle ground, where many community members felt that the most feasible solutions would be implemented. In exploring new ways to frame environmental health research report-back, community members pointed to the social body rather than the individual body as a target of information. In discussing better ways of treating and preventing diabetes, interviewees expressed that rather than working with individuals who have already developed the condition to alter their diet and exercise practices, clinics need to work with the family body to modify behaviors.

Scheper-Hughes and Lock describe the first level as the phenomenally experienced individual body-self: "The human body is an imitation of heaven and earth in all its details."[63] The health of individuals depends on a balance in the natural world, while the health of each organ depends on its relationship to all the other organs. Women's bodies are important in Mohawk culture, as is demonstrated in the creation story, where all human life on earth begins in Sky Woman's womb, and the most important foods for Haudenosaunee people come from her daughter's body. As part of the Ohero:kon rites of passage ceremony, lessons around women's bodies are framed through the creation story. This is reflected in lessons around ovulation described in the context of Sky Woman's descent, and in the formation of gardens in the shape of Sky Woman's daughter, where lessons center on seeds and caring for women's bodies. It is not surprising that the environmental health studies in this community were begun by a midwife who was concerned about the impact of contaminants on women's bodies and those of their babies. In discussing the individual body in the context of environmental health research and health issues like diabetes, the Akwesasne community members I interviewed considered the social and political bodies of the community.

Scheper-Hughes and Lock describe the second level, the social body, as a natural symbol with which to think about nature, society and culture. The body in health offers a model of organic wholeness; the body in sickness offers a model of social disharmony, conflict, and disintegration. Reciprocally, society in "sickness" and in "health" offers a model for understanding the body.[64] As Mary Douglas notes, "Just as it is true that everything symbolizes the body, so it is equally true that the body symbolizes everything else."[65] While this book addresses health concerns around people's individual bodies, these concerns are situated in the social body of Akwesasne, or the ways

Ash-splint basket made by Akwesasne Mohawk artist Carrie Hill. The three feathers on the top of the basket represent the type of kastowa (traditional headdress) that Mohawk men wear to indicate which nation they are from. This basket was part of a series sent to the U.S. embassy in Swaziland, Africa, for an Art in Embassies loan. Photograph by Jessica Sargent, 2015.

that the environment and people of Akwesasne are perceived as one body. Many times interviewees would express to me that "the community" or "Akwesasne" was ill and suffering, indicating that the ailments afflict not just individual bodies but also this greater entity. The social body in Haudenosaunee communities is more inclusive than that in many Western communities. Traditional Haudenosaunee culture conceives of elements of the natural world—in addition to humans—as part of this social body. Enrique Salmón uses the term "kincentric ecology" to describe how many Indigenous people view themselves and nature as part of an extended ecological family.[66] For many Indigenous communities, this means that the "social body" is more inclusive than that of the average American community. As the Akwesasne Task Force on the Environment Research Advisory Committee notes:

> For Native people, pollution problems also result in lost relationships with the natural world, something that can only be likened to mourning. The people actually mourn the loss of the natural world. At the same time though, the ecosystem mourns the loss of Mohawk people, communities that have always worked to maintain a balance and restrict human activity to ensure the survival of all species. The loss of place, relationships and balance can be culturally devastating.[67]

Part of this inclusion of "nonhumans" into Mohawk family systems is achieved through the structuring of Mohawk society around a matrilineal clan system. The clans at Akwesasne are mainly Bear, Turtle, and Wolf, as well as Snipe. The clans originated when, during a time of social unrest, the Creator came to the people and instructed them to break into groups led by elder women, who were directed to go to the river to draw water and take note of the first animals they saw. These animals determined clan names and are held in esteem by clan members today.

As described in the preface, the Ohen:ton Karihwatehkwen addresses aspects of the environment as family—Mother Earth, Grandfather Thunderers, Elder Brother the Sun, Grandmother Moon, and so on. The responsibility that some Akwesasro:non feel toward fish and heritage seeds (described in chapter 4) connects back to the Ohen:ton Karihwatehkwen. In addition, specific crops are given family titles, like the three sisters (corn, beans, and squash), which grow symbiotically in the garden and also work together to provide optimal nutrition when prepared as a meal. Because traditional Mohawk people assign great value to elements of the natural environment, organizations like ATFE have taken it upon themselves to push for a cleanup of the contamination that will restore nature in addition to protecting human health. Some members of the community told me that they were convinced that if the environment could be healed, the community's health and social ills would be healed at the same time. They viewed the health of one as intrinsically tied to the health of the other.

This notion of a social body also came out in discussions with Akwesasro:non around their thoughts on how risk assessment, environmental health research, and health care could be conducted differently—considering "social bodies" rather than just individual bodies. As Harris and Harper write in their work on establishing more effective risk assessment models, "Human health effects can also be synergistic with ecological or cultural effects (and vice versa) to affect not only an individual's personal health but also the health of the community as a single social organism. A true systems approach to assessment is needed, since system-level impacts are more than the sum of individual metrics."[68] Articles and press releases by ATFE, which will be explored in greater depth throughout this book, have similarly called for a more culturally relevant consideration of the social community body and its nonhuman relatives.

The stability of the body politic rests on that body's ability to regulate populations and to discipline social bodies. The regulation, surveillance, and control of bodies (individual and collective) in reproduction and sexuality, in work and leisure, and in health are all goals of the body politic.[69] The body politic can also exert its control over individual bodies in more mundane ways—Scheper-Hughes and Lock note that Foucauldian analyses of the roles of medicine, criminal justice, psychiatry, and the various social sciences in producing new forms of power/knowledge over bodies are illustrative in this regard. Native studies scholars have examined political bodies such as tribal governments, which determine which individual bodies are recognized and included, and which, in turn, are frequently reshaped and remade by their constituents.[70] Some Native political scholars have called on the leadership of their tribal communities to reform—to decolonize and reshape themselves based on traditional Indigenous principles.[71] Similar discussions have arisen in Akwesasne around the myriad political bodies governing the community.

Politics can be complicated in any Native American community, but in Akwesasne they are especially contentious. As noted earlier, exerting some level of control over Akwesasro:non are two federal governments, two federally recognized tribal governments, and a traditional Haudenosaunee Confederacy–backed government.

Three state/provincial governments are also involved. There are two separate longhouses, in addition to a number of other religious establishments (including Catholic, Methodist, Baptist, and Jehovah's Witness churches). There are two separate health clinics—the Saint Regis Mohawk Health Services clinic, funded by the U.S. federal government, and Kanonhkwat'sheri:io, which receives funds from the Canadian government. Similarly, there are two separate federal environmental authorities. Each of these various bodies seeks to control some aspect of the fate of Akwesasro:non, and most elicit some level of distrust from community members. The contentious relationship that Akwesasne has had with outside political bodies (described in chapter 1) has colored community members' perceptions of whether these bodies can be trusted. Indeed, when I asked people what could be done to improve the health of the community, many pointed straight to the tribal governments and their agencies and wondered what they could do to support families and individuals.

The struggle to achieve environmental justice in Akwesasne, which involves the restoration of the natural environment, traditional foods, and good health for human and nonhuman communities, includes roles for each of these three bodies and the social layers they entail. In this book's conclusion, I highlight the ways in which Akwesasro:non are drawing on Indigenous regeneration and survivance to promote the rebuilding of their relationships with the environment and with fellow community members.

CHAPTER 1

Driving Tour through the Political and Environmental History of Akwesasne

While most Native American and First Nations communities are jurisdictionally complex, Akwesasne, which straddles the borders of New York, Ontario, and Quebec, is exceptionally so. Akwesasro:non are constantly working with, around, and against these boundaries and divisions within their community. The contentious relationship between Akwesasne and the surrounding state and federal governments has taken multiple forms over the past three hundred years, as these outside entities have whittled away at Akwesasne's land base and imposed different forms of tribal governance. The expropriation of Mohawk land to create the Saint Lawrence Seaway, a feat of engineering that would irrevocably alter the culture and environment of Akwesasne, is emblematic of this relationship. But for the past two centuries, Mohawks at Akwesasne have fought against state and federal governments to resist the imposition of outside governance and the expropriation of their land.

In addition to lines on maps, other boundaries—those between differing religions, between differing economic beliefs, and between "experts" and "cultural knowledge bearers"—have affected how Akwesasro:non carry out their everyday lives and how they have responded to situations like living downstream from one federal and two New York State Superfund sites.[1] In order to properly introduce some of these boundaries and their origins, this chapter will take you on a driving tour of the landscape and history of Akwesasne, traversing State Route 37 from east to west across the southern half of the

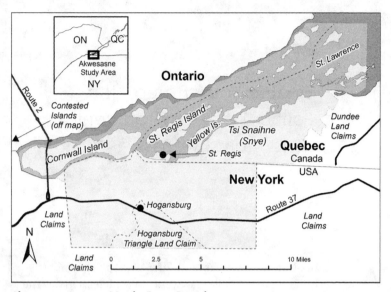

Akwesasne territory. Map by Bruce Boucek.

community. Although not included on the tour, a number of small businesses and artists' studios are found in Akwesasne that showcase the amazing traditional and contemporary artistry for which Mohawks are known. Numerous eateries are also seen along the route, offering everything from steaks to corn soup to burgers and fries to Asian fusion foods. The tour offered in this chapter is not comprehensive, but it will help you to place the history of Akwesasne within the contemporary landscape.

Driving toward Akwesasne from the east, the first indication that you are approaching sovereign Mohawk territory comes before the official welcome sign at the reservation's border. Twin Leaf Express, a tax-free gas station, convenience store, and diner, sits at the edge of the town of Fort Covington. The business, which is owned by the Terrance family of Akwesasne, is on land whose ownership the Saint Regis Mohawk Tribe and New York State have been disputing for decades. The store, which opened in 2009, is stocked with food, soda, beer, and tribal cigarettes, which are cheaper than brand-name cigarettes because they are not subject to the New York State tax. The same is true for the gasoline sold from full-service pumps out front,

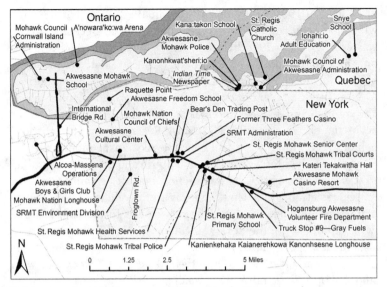

Driving tour through Akwesasne territory. Map by Bruce Boucek.

which is a few cents cheaper per gallon than the gas at other stations in town. The SRMT, not the town of Fort Covington—which attempted to bring suit against the company in 2011 for building code violations—licenses the gas station and convenience store.[2]

Another three and a half miles down the road, past flat, windswept farmland and a few scattered homes, you will come to a sign:

WELCOME TO AKWESASNE

"SEKON"

PLEASE COMPLY WITH OUR VEHICLE AND TRAFFIC LAWS.

IT PROTECTS OUR MOHAWK CHILDREN

WE WISH YOU A SAFE AND ENJOYABLE VISIT

"NIAWEN"

(THANK YOU)

Those who do not comply with the vehicle and traffic laws will likely be stopped by SRMT police officers, who patrol the southern half of the community and enforce all federal, New York State, and Tribal laws. The Tribal Police Department was first established in 1972, disbanded in 1980, and reconstituted in 1990.[3] The Tribal Court, which has been adjudicating traffic offenses since December 2000, was established in 1994.[4] Until recently, Tribal police officers had only limited civil police authority, and only as it related to members of the Tribe. After May 2007, Tribal police officers became authorized by New York State, and they are now able to provide a full range of law enforcement services and make arrests for all criminal offenses occurring on the Saint Regis Mohawk Reservation.[5] The northern half of the community is patrolled by the Akwesasne Mohawk Police Service, which enforces the laws of Ontario and Quebec. According to the service's website, its jurisdiction includes criminal code offenses, violations of by-laws, highway traffic offenses, and Quebec highway safety code offenses. The service was formed in 1970 and worked jointly with the Royal Canadian Mounted Police; it became a stand-alone police force in 1991.[6]

Like many Native communities, Akwesasne is peppered with smoke shops. These range from small businesses like Jenn's, housed in a white shack on your left as you enter the reservation, to larger operations like the Bear's Den, a gas station/restaurant/gift shop/tobacco retailer located five and a half miles up the road. The business of selling tax-free tobacco is emblematic of some of the tensions between tribes in New York and the state and local governments. For decades, non-Native smokers crossed the border from the land of cigarettes with price tags burdened by state taxes (currently $4.35 per pack in New York) to reservation communities where they benefited from the Native insistence that the constitutional clause "Indians not taxed" extended to the ability to sell tobacco products. Not everyone was happy with this arrangement: the non-Native owners of the convenience stores these shoppers were driving past on their way to the reservations argued that the state's selective collection of cigarette taxes was a violation of their constitutional equal protection rights. In 1994, the U.S. Supreme Court decided, in the case *Department of Taxation & Finance of New York et al. v. Milhelm Attea & Bros et al.*, that "enrolled tribal members purchasing cigarettes on Indian reservations are exempt from a New York Cigarette Tax, but non-Indians making such purchases are not." The problem, however, came when the state tried to enter the reservations and collect those taxes. Haudenosaunee communities across the state refused to comply with the ruling, and attempts to seize untaxed cigarettes headed for reservations led to unrest, including the Seneca Nation's closure of the New York State Thruway with a pile of burning tires. Signs across Akwesasne taunted Governor "George Custer" Pataki and reminded those passing through, "This is not New York State. You are on Mohawk Land." A series of court cases and new tax laws followed, culminating in a new collection scheme in which all cigarette packs sold in New York State would bear tax stamps, and all wholesale distributors would prepay taxes by purchasing the stamps. Native American nations would obtain tax-free cigarettes for use only by their tribal members by participating in either a coupon system or a prior approval system.[7]

In June 2011, New York State began enforcing the collection of state excise taxes on Marlboro cigarettes and other "premium" brands sold on reservations to non-Native Americans. This led to an increase in the popularity of locally produced cigarettes, crafted in large square buildings on Frogtown Road at the western end of Akwesasne. These cigarettes are sold under local brand names such as Native, Signal, Nation's Best, and Discount. Billboards advertising these brands are seen along Route 37, and the companies that produce them sponsor local sports teams as well as concerts and other events, including the annual Nation's Best fashion show and calendar. Two of these companies have even become legitimate in the eyes of the U.S. federal government. Ohserase Manufacturing, owned by the Tarbell family, is one of these; the company received a U.S. Treasury Department permit to manufacture cigarettes in 2010. As part of the deal, it paid $1.75 million in fines for prior cigarette trafficking and tax law violations.[8] The Tarbell family's convenience stores, which include the Bear's Den, the Eastern Door, and the Western Door, stopped taking shipments of Marlboro and other major brands, and they now sell mostly Native American cigarettes, some of which are priced as low as $2.00 a pack. However, the major tobacco company Philip Morris USA is now lobbying states to collect more taxes and fees from tribal companies.[9] Truckloads of these locally produced cigarettes have been shipped out to reservations in other parts of the country, but recently they have been seized on the orders of the Saint Lawrence County District Attorney's Office, despite a New York State Tax Department directive to allow the transport of Native-made cigarettes from one reservation to another. The seized cigarettes are tied up in litigation, and the factories are going quiet.[10] The reservation boundaries at one time signaled a separate and foreign economy to cigarette shoppers and retailers, differentiated from the rest of New York and the nation by lower prices for buyers and greater profits for retailers. With the passage of new tax codes and politicians' increasing determination to balance the state budget, the tobacco trade at Akwesasne and at other New York reservations has been affected in a way that reservation communities in other states have yet to face.

Other economic draws to the reservation are tribal gaming ventures like the Akwesasne Mohawk Casino and the Mohawk Bingo Palace ("where the winning never stops!" according to its catchy jingle, which airs frequently on the tribal radio station). The driveway to the casino, which is on the right-hand side about three and a half miles past the welcome sign, is lined with large metal sculptures in the shape of traditional hair combs featuring different clan animals, like the wolf, the snipe, the turtle, and the bear. The casino itself is a single-story brick building featuring four restaurants, twenty-six gaming tables, and hundreds of slot machines. A recent expansion has added a new 150-room hotel with spa, fitness area, conference area, and banquet facility.[11] Although it has arguably been a financial boon to the community, the casino was not unanimously welcomed when it was constructed in 1999. Bitter divisions over the issue of gambling contributed to a civil war in Akwesasne, which led to gun battles between "Antis"—traditionalists and others who wanted to keep gambling out of Akwesasne—and Warrior Society members and a pro-gambling faction who wanted to utilize Akwesasne's sovereign status to generate income. In May 1990, ten months of tension spilled over into violence, leaving two Mohawks dead, two homes burned, and a cultural building firebombed.[12] After the killings, Governor Mario Cuomo dispatched several hundred police officers to the reservation to keep the peace and to escort members of the Quebec police force and the Royal Canadian Mounted Police through the New York portion of the reservation to investigate the shootings, which took place on the New York/Quebec line.[13] Ships from the Canadian armed forces also patrolled the Saint Lawrence River. These events resulted in painful divisions within the community that persist to this day. As Doug George-Kanentiio describes, "Our dreams for a united Mohawk Nation died in the spring of 1990, when we were in a state of civil war from which the wounds have yet to heal."[14] For some, the Akwesasne Mohawk Casino is a reminder

The Akwesasne Mohawk Casino. Photograph by Elizabeth Hoover, 2016.

of those conflicts. Others point to the jobs the casino has created and the revenue it has brought in, some of which has been used to improve the local health clinic and contribute to programs like the Akwesasne Boys & Girls Club, the Hogansburg Akwesasne Volunteer Fire Department, the Tsi Tetewatatkens Saint Regis Mohawk Senior Center, and the Akwesasne Mohawk Ambulance Unit. In addition, the proceeds from the casino provide direct support to community members through funding for the Home Heating Fuel Assistance Program, various sports teams, and the Home Repair Program.[15]

The Akwesasne Mohawk Casino was developed through a compact between the Saint Regis Mohawk Tribe and the state of New York under regulations created through the Indian Gaming and Regulatory Act of 1988. But not all would-be entrepreneurs in the community believe in conceding any authority to the state. In July 2011, members of the Kanienkehaka Kaianerehkowa Kanonhsesne longhouse, who are affiliated with the Warrior Society and do not acknowledge the authority of the Saint Regis Mohawk Tribe, decided to open their own casino. The Three Feathers Casino was located in a sprawling brick building formerly used for manufacturing cigarettes, about two miles west of the SRMT's casino. Despite orders to cease and desist from the Saint Regis Tribal Gaming Commission, the group operated about four hundred gaming terminals. After the casino had operated with minimal profit for about a year and a half, five men were indicted in December 2012 on federal charges of operating an illegal gambling business, unlawfully possessing gambling devices, and stealing electricity through an unauthorized power connection at the site.[16] While the SRMT chiefs pointed out that the revenues from their casino provide funding for government programs and services, representatives of the group that operated the Three Feathers Casino claimed their intention was to support unenrolled Mohawks who do not receive the Tribe's services. Some followers of this longhouse have disenrolled themselves from, or chosen not to become listed on SRMT rolls because they do not recognize the SRMT's authority.[17] While the Warrior Society and the Kanienkehaka Kaianerehkowa Kanonhsesne longhouse have attempted private gambling ventures in the past, the SRMT, with the authority of the U.S. government and the state of New York, has ensured that it has a legally enforced monopoly on this enterprise. The Three Feathers Casino building currently sits abandoned.

As you leave the Akwesasne Mohawk Casino, on your left about half a mile up the road, across from Truck Stop #9 and the Three Feathers Café, is a "For Sale by Owner" sign that non-Native landowner Horst Wuersching had the lack of foresight to post without first approaching the Mohawks. Ordinarily, posting a for-sale sign on private property would not elicit a negative reaction from one's neighbors. But Wuersching's 240 acres of wooded property are on disputed land, the "Hogansburg triangle," part of an ongoing battle between the Akwesasne Mohawk and the state of New York. Akwesasne has irregular borders, like a rhombus someone has chiseled pieces out of. These missing pieces indicate land taken illegally from the Mohawk—by squatters, by the state of New York, and by the Canadian government.

After the American Revolution, the Treaty of Paris (1783) drew the boundary between British North America and the United States at the forty-fifth parallel. In 1791, land speculator Alexander Macomb bought more than three million acres of land in northern New York, setting aside six square miles and two islands for the use of the Mohawks.[18] A series of Mohawk delegations met with representatives of New York State to assert their claims to land that had been taken by the state. The dispute was considered resolved in 1796 when a treaty was signed with the Seven Nations of Canada ceding all of the Saint Regis lands on the American side, except for six square miles near Saint Regis Village, two areas of one square mile situated around mills the Mohawks had constructed (currently in the middle of the town of Massena and in Fort Covington, where Twin Leaf Express is located), and meadows on the Grasse River. The signatories to that treaty were not representatives of the Seven Nations and did not have the authority to cede Akwesasne land, but Washington still considered the agreement legitimate.[19] A series of additional treaties between 1816 and 1845 sold off most of the land that the Mohawks had claim to, except for about 14,000 acres in New York, 7,384 acres in Quebec, and 2,050 acres on Cornwall Island in Ontario, which make up the current community.[20] In recent decades, Akwesasne Mohawks have begun to pursue land claims against the state of New York for acquiring these lands from the Mohawk without the intervention of the U.S. federal government, contrary to the 1790 Trade and Intercourse Act, which prohibits such exchanges.

Another portion of the land claim involves three islands: Barnhart, Baxter (or Croil), and Long Sault. These islands were part of the land granted to Mohawks in the 1796 treaty. The border established by the Treaty of Paris placed Baxter and Barnhart Islands in British territory, though they continued to be part of Mohawk territory. The Treaty of Ghent (1814), which ended the War of 1812, provided a survey of the boundary established by the Treaty of Paris. In 1822, following the Treaty of Ghent Boundary Commission Report, the international boundary was redrawn and lands were exchanged between Britain and the United States, shifting several islands owned and used by the Mohawks from British to American jurisdiction.[21] The British gave Baxter and Barnhart Islands to the United States in exchange for Wolfe Island near Kingston, Ontario. After acquiring the islands, New York sold them to private developers and in 1856 moved to compensate the Mohawks for lost rent from the property, but not for complete loss of the islands.[22] The state did not consider this an outright purchase of land, which would have been in violation of the Trade and Intercourse Act, but rather an "adjustment of a claim that had arisen as the result of the ambiguous language of the 1796 treaty."[23] The Moses–Saunders Power Dam is anchored on Barnhart Island, and federal law provides tribal nations with the right to share in power revenues when their reservations are used for power production.[24]

The Mohawks have been fighting in court for the return of these lands. In 1996, land claims negotiations derailed when New York State insisted that as part of the settlement, Mohawks also had to agree to collect all state taxes on cigarette sales to non-Indians on their reservation and turn them over to state (part of the cigarette saga described above). The Mohawks wanted this issue handled separately from the land claim, since it involved other Native nations living in New York as well. The federal judge overseeing the Mohawk case in Syracuse agreed with the Mohawks and urged the state to handle tax issues separately from land settlement, but the state refused and broke off negotiations.[25]

In 2005, the Mohawks made a second effort to reclaim the contested land, and an agreement was reached between the state and all three governments in Akwesasne that would end land claim litigation involving 12,000 acres of land. All parties had signed the agreement, but in 2006, the local counties withdrew support after a series of federal court decisions against other tribes' land claims, as well as the state legislature's failure to enact the settlement.[26] The Cayuga and Oneida Nations in western New York lost their land claims in 2005 and 2006 because of the length of time that had passed since the land was unlawfully taken and the extent to which the land had become populated by non-Native people. Saint Lawrence and Franklin Counties were emboldened by this news, hoping for a similar outcome in their case.[27]

This is the context in which Wuersching's hand-painted "For Sale by Owner" sign went up in 2009, on land that should have belonged to the Mohawk community were it not for a stalled legal system. When the Men's Council of the Kanienkehaka Kaianerehkowa Kanonhsesne longhouse saw the sign, they promptly painted "NOT" on it in red letters, covered it over with a yellow sign reading "Reclamation Site," raised the red warrior flag on the site, bulldozed a clearing in the woods, and erected a smoke shop. The Saint Regis Mohawk Tribe did not support this unconventional land reclamation; in December 2011, the Saint Regis Mohawk Tribal Police assisted in the arrest of Roger Kaneretiio Jock, one of the men representing the Men's Council (and one of the men arrested for the Three Feathers Casino operation), and turned him over to the Franklin County

District Attorney's Office. The charge was second-degree grand larceny for depriving the deeded owner of his land, a charge recently dropped due to technicalities.[28] While the methods of the Kanienkehaka Kaianerehkowa Kanonhsesne were unconventional, they drew attention once more to the lands under question surrounding the Mohawk community.

In June 2014, the SRMT chiefs signed an agreement with New York State and Saint Lawrence County that would allow the Tribe to buy almost 5,000 acres of land from willing sellers in the towns of Massena and Brasher and add it to the reservation. In return, a share of Akwesasne Mohawk Casino revenues would be paid to the state and the county. Talks are ongoing with Franklin County, which contains contested land east of the reservation. The settlement is controversial—many community members feel as though their tribe should not have to buy back land that was stolen from them.[29]

The Mohawk Council of Akwesasne is fighting similar battles along the northern front of the community. It was recently successful in acquiring funds from the Canadian government as part of the settlement of the Kawenoke-Easterbrook claim, which compensated the tribe for lands illegally leased on Cornwall Island (Kawenoke) between 1820 and 1934.[30] Currently under negotiation are the Dundee land claims in Quebec, on the south shore of the Saint Lawrence River roughly opposite Cornwall, Ontario. These lands were part of Mohawk territory but were leased out to non-Mohawk settlers in the early 1800s and then allegedly surrendered by the Mohawk in 1887, although the nation claimed all along that it intended to reclaim the leased lands. Since 2004, Canada and the MCA have been discussing a "lands selection area"—land that will be added back to the reserve after it is purchased with the proceeds of a settlement.[31] In addition, the MCA submitted claims to Canada in June 2012 for lands on the north shore of the Saint Lawrence River that were historically farmed and hunted by Mohawks and were part of the lands reserved for the Mohawks of Akwesasne through treaty obligations expressed in 1760 and the Royal Proclamation in 1763. A French deed granted in the early 1700s by Father Gordon of Quebec assured Mohawk ownership of the land. After the War of 1812, soldiers began squatting on the land and were also granted lands for their service by the Crown. Since the lands on the north shore were never surrendered, a claim has been filed for them. Current landowners would not be displaced if this claim were to be successful; rather, First Nations may purchase lands from willing sellers as replacement lands for their communities.[32] These claims also have the potential to expand the landscape as well as the legal and cultural purview of Akwesasne.

As you drive west past the reclaimed land site, if you take a right onto Cook Road and follow a series of winding back roads north, you will find yourself in the district of Tsi Snaihne—or Snye, as it is more commonly known—a low-lying riverside community that contains homes, a few small businesses, and the Iohahi:io Akwesasne Adult Education and Training Centre. Probably without realizing it, since there is no Canada Border Services Agency (CBSA) reporting site, you have crossed into land that the province of Quebec considers within its boundaries. Residents of Snye are known as avid fishermen, skilled basket makers, and devoted Mohawk-language speakers. Heading back out onto the main road, and continuing west on Route 37, you will come upon the first traffic light in town. If you take a right onto Saint Regis Road at this intersection and drive north, you will again cross over an invisible line into territory over which Quebec claims jurisdiction. There is no CBSA reporting station here either, but on the side of the road there once stood a stone obelisk marking the U.S.–Canadian border. In October 2009, members of the Kanienkehaka Kaianerehkowa Kanonhsesne used a backhoe to dislodge and cart away the obelisk to remove the border demarcation in the middle of their community. Now as you drive north on Saint Regis Road, the only markers that indicate you have crossed into Canada are the speed limit signs specifying the maximum kilometers per hour rather than miles per hour. This road will take you into the village of Saint Regis, or Kana:takon, which houses some of the government buildings for the Mohawk Council of Akwesasne, the elected government for the northern half of the community. The Kanonhkwat'sheri:io clinic, the health facility for the constituents of the MCA, is located here, in a cluster of buildings that also houses the offices of the community newspaper, *Indian Time*, as well as the community radio station, 97.3 CKON, which plays a mixture of country music, hip-hop, and Mohawk language instruction, as well as the music of local celebrities, like the "Nammy" Award–winning Teresa "Bear" Fox.[33] CKON is considered a pirate radio station; it is licensed by the Mohawk Nation Council of Chiefs, but not by Canadian or

American licensing agencies, even though the building and its sound waves fall under the purview of both entities. It is the only radio station in North America operating under the exclusive jurisdiction of an aboriginal government.[34]

The village of Saint Regis is also home to the large stone Saint Regis Catholic Church, which looks out over the confluence of the Saint Regis and Saint Lawrence Rivers. Completed in 1795, the impressive structure has survived fires, crushing ice from the nearby river, and earthquakes, and has been part of generations of Mohawk history. As Mohawk historian Darren Bonaparte writes,

> This old church, assembled by Mohawk hands 7 generations ago, has been a silent witness to the major events of our ancestors' lives—the baptisms, the confirmations, the weddings, and the funerals. From cradle to grave, this church has been a consistent presence in the lives of Akwesasro:non.[35]

Growing from a log house to a massive stone structure within the first half century of the community's establishment, the church speaks to the complicated times that produced it and stands as a testament to the impact of the Catholic Church on Akwesasne's history.

At the beginning of the seventeenth century, prior to significant settler influence on Haudenosaunee life, Mohawk people lived mainly in three fortified villages in the Mohawk Valley, in what is now part of Montgomery County in central New York State. These villages typically moved every twenty-five years, after the palisades had begun to decay and the local resources had become taxed.[36] Mohawk hunting territories extended north into the Adirondack Mountains and south down to the east bank of the Susquehanna River, nearly to the area where present-day Oneonta is located. As the easternmost of the nations that make up the Haudenosaunee Confederacy, the Mohawk were the first to feel the impact of European activities along the Eastern Seaboard.[37] The seventeenth and eighteenth centuries in North America were characterized by plagues, wars between Europeans and Indigenous peoples, wars among Native nations, and the work of missionaries to convert Indigenous people to Christian religions. Kahnawà:ke (originally spelled Caughnawaga) is a community initially founded by French Catholics in the Mohawk Valley near the

The sanctuary of the Saint Regis Catholic Church in Akwesasne. Photograph by Elizabeth Hoover, 2016.

site of present-day Fonda, New York; it relocated to the banks of the Saint Lawrence River near Montreal in 1669.

By the mid-eighteenth century, contention was developing in Kahnawà:ke. Some scholars cite factional disputes, overcrowding, and soil exhaustion. Ray Fadden attributes the departure of some Mohawks from Kahnawà:ke to the influence of "fire water."[38] The leaving party was led by Zechariah and John Tarbell, English brothers who had been captured as children from Groton, Massachusetts, and taken to Kahnawà:ke, where they were adopted and raised as Mohawks. In the fall of 1754, the Tarbells left Kahnawà:ke with their wives and their wives' families and paddled up the Saint Lawrence River.[39] They spent the winter in what is now known as the district of Tsi Snaihne, and then in the spring crossed the Saint Regis River to establish a new village on the peninsula formed by the Saint Regis and Saint Lawrence Rivers. In describing the site selected for the new community, nineteenth-century historian Franklin Hough effuses:

> Its founders in selecting this site, evinced the possession
> of a taste at once judicious and correct, for it may well be

The Saint Regis Catholic Church has stood for more than two centuries in the village of Saint Regis (Kana:takon) in Akwesasne. Photograph by Elizabeth Hoover, 2016.

questioned whether the shores of the Saint Lawrence, abounding as they do in charming and lovely localities, affords anywhere a spot that will surpass this in beauty of scenery, or pleasantness of location. The village stands on a plain, moderately elevated above the river, which having for more than forty miles been broken by cascades and dangerous rapids, here becomes tranquil.[40]

In 1760 the first group to settle Akwesasne was joined by another group of Mohawks from Kahnawà:ke, led by Father Anthony Gordon. Father Gordon named the place Saint Regis, for Jean-François Régis, a French Jesuit who was canonized by Pope Clement XII in 1737.[41] Mohawks named the area Akwesasne, meaning "land where the partridge drums." Some have said this was due to the great number of partridges that once inhabited the area, and others have described how the local falls, before being reshaped by the seaway, once made sounds like the mating dance of the male partridge.[42] After several wooden iterations, the stone church was constructed on

43

the peninsula that juts into the confluence of the Saint Lawrence and Saint Regis Rivers, on the site that once held a large Native village.[43]

As you head away from the river, back to the traffic light, and turn once again west onto Route 37, on your right is another Catholic community institution, the Saint Kateri Tekakwitha Hall. The small, single-level white building, constructed in the 1960s, serves as a meeting place for the Kateri Tekakwitha Prayer Circle and other Catholic community events. A statue of an Indian maiden in a blue shawl, the Mohawk saint for whom the hall is named, sits under a lean-to on the lawn. Káteri Tekahkwí:tha was born in the 1650s to a Mohawk father and an Algonquian mother who died in a smallpox epidemic.[44] Against the wishes of her father's family, she converted to Catholicism and moved north with the Catholic settlement. After living an austere and pious life, she died at the age of twenty-four and became an example of Catholic devotion held up as an example for other Indigenous people the church was hoping to convert. She was recommended for canonization in 1844 and beatified in 1980.[45] In 2006, a Lummi boy in Washington was miraculously cured of lethal flesh-eating bacteria after his family prayed to Káteri on his behalf.[46] This miracle led to her promotion to sainthood in October 2012, an event celebrated by Native American Catholics around the country, and attended by an entourage from Akwesasne. Catholicism has the largest following of any religion in this community, and the local paper, *Indian Time,* followed the event closely.[47] Native Catholics see the canonization of Káteri as recognition of their contribution to the Catholic faith. Other people in the community have shunned or left the Catholic Church, and some see the canonization of a Mohawk saint as another tool of colonization. Still others take a more complex view, recognizing Káteri as a Mohawk woman symbolic of discipline, fortitude, and perseverance—a complicated relative.[48]

Another mile down the road past the Kateri Hall, on your left in a low-lying, long white building, are the offices of the Saint Regis Mohawk Tribe's elected chiefs and Tribal clerk. A large purple sign out front reads "Saint Regis Mohawk Tribe Administration," and an electronic message board displays the Mohawk word of the day. The Tribal building shares a parking lot with the Saint Regis Mohawk Health Services (SRMHS). Occupying a single-level brick-and-wood building, the SRMHS provides health care services to the constituents of the SRMT. Even though this clinic is only a few miles from the

Kanonhkwat'sheri:io clinic, the two facilities serve mostly different populations and cannot collaborate because of their different federal funding and support streams. Residents enrolled with the MCA can use this SRMT clinic, but they cannot get a referral out for other services that are paid for by the SRMHS. The possibility that residents might use the Canadian-side Kanonhkwat'sheri:io clinic one day and the SRMHS clinic on the American side another day, and may additionally visit doctors or hospitals in other towns in New York or Canada, makes keeping track of medical records very challenging for health staff in any of these facilities. Next door to the SRMHS clinic is a small white house that serves as an office for the Mohawk Nation Council of Chiefs.

The evolution of these elected tribal governments is complex. During the seventeenth century, Akwesasne Mohawks belonged to the Seven Nations of Canada, a union modeled on the Haudenosaunee Confederacy, with twelve chiefs chosen for life by clan mothers.[49] After the Treaty of Paris drew the boundary between British North America and the United States that effectively split Akwesasne, New York State and Canada became more involved in the governance of Akwesasne, replacing the traditional government with two federally imposed tribal governments. In 1802 the New York State Legislature appointed three trustees for the tribe (signers of the 1796 treaty mentioned earlier) and stipulated that from then on, Mohawk males twenty-one years of age and older would elect a clerk and trustees to make rules and regulations to govern Mohawks on the American side of the community. This new government directly contradicted the previous form of government, in which clan mothers chose chiefs who served for life terms, or as long as they were deemed qualified.

In April 1888, a general council of the Six Nations Confederacy was held at the Allegany Seneca Reservation. The council passed a resolution adopting the Saint Regis Mohawks as the successors to the Mohawk position in the Confederacy, essentially making Akwesasne the capital of the Mohawk Nation.[50] The nine original Mohawk titles were given over to Akwesasne, and nine chiefs were selected. However, the U.S. and Canadian federal governments, which recognized only the tribal governments they had installed, did not recognize these chiefs.

Fearful that this Mohawk Nation government would govern

Akwesasne as a singular territory, New York State officials moved to make their three trustees into a governing entity called the Saint Regis Tribal Council. Through an act of the New York State Legislature in 1892, the Tribal Council was given sufficient authority "to counter the move toward nationalizing the reservation," as George-Kanentiio describes.[51] Mohawk people who support the current elective form of government, the Saint Regis Mohawk Tribe, contend that the 1802 statute was enacted at the request of the Mohawks at Akwesasne, and it incorporated elements of the traditional system, including naming some of the life chiefs as trustees.[52] Mohawks who support the traditional government, the Mohawk Nation Council of Chiefs, describe this new government as forced on the people.

The twelve life chiefs affiliated with the Seven Nations continued to serve as the governing body on the northern half of Akwesasne until the Canadian Indian Act of 1876 provided for elected tribal leaders, as well as the registration of Indians according to patrilineal descent. This led to a loss of status among Indian women who married non-Indian men or even Mohawk men from the half of the reservation that fell below the American border. The elected band council government was not peacefully adopted. A supporter of the life chiefs, Jake Ice (Saiowisaké:ron), was shot and killed by Canadian police on May 1, 1899, as they arrested the life chiefs for preventing elections from being held the previous summer. The chiefs were released from jail when they agreed not to oppose future elections and thereupon became the founders of something of an "underground" movement with no formal recognition by outside authorities.[53] A large wooden statue of Jake Ice once stood at the Canadian customs office on Cornwall Island, but was moved to the lawn in front of the MCA Justice Building when the customs office was torn down. During the summer of 2009, when Mohawks were protesting the decision by the Canadian government to arm the country's border guards, Jake Ice was held up as an example of past aggression by armed Canadian authorities. The current elected government of the northern half of Akwesasne is the Mohawk Council of Akwesasne (known until 1984 as the Saint Regis Band Council), which consists of twelve elected district chiefs and a grand chief.

In 1934, the U.S. Congress passed the Indian Reorganization Act, which proposed the reorganization of Indian tribes as constitutionally based governments. Indian people were permitted to vote on whether they wished to organize their governments according to the provisions of the act. A referendum was held at Saint Regis on June 8, 1935, during which Mohawk people voted overwhelmingly to reject the Indian Reorganization Act.[54] Supporters of the traditional government protested the 1935 referendum and the subsequent 1938 election, which was held under the guard of state troopers. In 1948, in an attempt to eliminate the state-supported elected tribal government, Mohawks supported a slate of tribal chiefs who agreed to dissolve the state-sanctioned council upon taking office, in an attempt to turn power over to the traditional chiefs. The state refused to recognize these traditional chiefs, but when the "tribal attorney," accompanied by two state troopers, arrived at the Council House to conduct a new election, he found the doors padlocked and guarded by clan mothers who refused to permit the election to be held.[55] The state then staged an election off reservation, under state police guard; only a small number of Mohawk voted in the election.[56] As historian Thomas Stone notes, "Opposition to the elected system and the attempt to restore the traditional government by life chiefs was motivated at least in part by the desire to assert autonomy from external, white control."[57] But New York State was not willing to relinquish this control.

On July 1, 1948, Congress passed a criminal jurisdictional transfer bill, and then in 1950 a civil jurisdiction bill, which together transferred to the state of New York jurisdiction over all Native nations in the state.[58] The transfer bill was "opposed by 99 percent of all Indians in the state of New York," but it passed nonetheless.[59] This bill declared that tribes within New York were "freed from Federal supervision and control" and were now in the hands of the state. The bill was part of a broader effort to free the federal government of responsibility to Indian tribes by, in this case, transferring tribes from Bureau of Indian Affairs guardianship to state jurisdiction. Similar efforts were implemented for other states. In 1953, Public Law 280 gave the states of California, Minnesota, Nebraska, Oregon, and Wisconsin jurisdiction over the tribes residing within their borders.[60] This legislation continues to shape the relationships among tribes, the federal government, and these states.

Because of this convoluted history, there are currently three tribal governments in Akwesasne. The Saint Regis Mohawk Tribal Council, in the southern half of the community, consists of seven

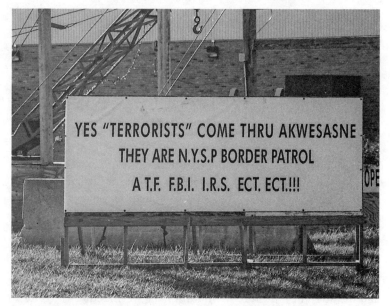

Sign speaking out against New York State and U.S. federal entities that have disrupted the self-governance of Akwesasne. Photograph by Elizabeth Hoover, 2008.

elected officials who serve staggered three-year terms: three chiefs, three subchiefs, and a tribal clerk. The elected government of the northern half of Akwesasne, the Mohawk Council of Akwesasne, also consists of officials elected every three years. In addition to a grand chief elected by the entire community, twelve district chiefs are elected, four from each of the three districts of the northern portion of Akwesasne: Kawehno:ke (Cornwall Island), Kana:takon (Saint Regis), and Tsi Snaihne (Snye). MCA offices are located in all three districts. The Mohawk Nation Council of Chiefs represents the traditional government; it comprises nine chiefs selected by clan mothers representing the three main clans of the Mohawk: Bear, Turtle, and Wolf. The council's office is in the plaza on Route 37, across the parking lot from the state-sanctioned SRMT government offices, but the chiefs conduct most of their business from the Confederacy-authorized longhouse farther down the road, tucked back in the woods at the end of a long driveway. Some traditionalist Mohawks have chosen to identify only as citizens of this traditional government and carry Haudenosaunee Confederacy "red cards" rather than tribal identification cards from either federally sanctioned tribal government. However, New York State and the United States deal exclusively with the SRMT, and the provinces of Quebec and Ontario and the Canadian government deal exclusively with the MCA.[61] While many who are members of the longhouse do not vote in elections on principle, recently individuals associated with the traditional longhouse have successfully run for elected tribal office in an effort to position themselves to bring positive change to the community.

Not all traditionalist Mohawks identify with the Haudenosaunee Confederacy–sanctioned Mohawk Nation Council of Chiefs. The traditionalist community was once united under one longhouse, but after the bitter civil war in Akwesasne in 1990, the longhouse community split over ideological differences. The Kaianerekowa, or Great Law, is a message of peace and unity that was brought to the set of warring nations who would become the Haudenosaunee (Iroquois) Confederacy. The Kariwiio, or Good Word, is a message that was brought by Seneca prophet Handsome Lake in 1799. This code is a blueprint for a reworked traditional culture that embraces the thanksgiving traditions, eschews alcohol and gambling, and promotes male-headed farming households.[62] Opponents of casino gambling in Akwesasne pointed to the Kariwiio, as well as to their concerns about undesirable elements coming into the community. The Warrior Society rejects the Kariwiio as a Christian-influenced creation and follows only the Kaianerekowa. The two parties now celebrate their ceremonies at two separate longhouses, one of which, the Kanienkehaka Kaianerehkowa Kanonhsesne, is across from the Tribal police headquarters; the Confederacy-sanctioned longhouse is two miles farther west down Route 37.

Leaving the tribal buildings complex and driving another mile down Route 37, on the right you will find the Akwesasne Library and Museum. On the upper level of this small brick building is the library and computer center, where residents can access the Internet; check out books, movies, and CDs; or sit and read the local papers and clip coupons. During the public comment period for the remediation of the local Superfund site, the Akwesasne Library served as a repository for public documents. The lower level of the building houses the museum and a gift shop that sells local handcrafts and books. The

The traditional wedding of Kakwiroton and Wabigonikwe at the Mohawk Nation longhouse at Akwesasne, the seat of the Mohawk Nation Council of Chiefs. Photograph by Jessica Sargent, 2016.

museum boasts a fine collection of ash-splint and sweetgrass baskets, an art for which this community is especially renowned. Classes are offered at the museum for community members who want to learn how to make fancy as well as utilitarian baskets, raised beadwork, cornhusk dolls, feather fans, moccasins, and cradleboards.

Leaving the museum, as you continue to head west, past the winding gravel driveway leading to the Confederacy longhouse, you will arrive at the second stoplight in town. If you take a left here onto Frogtown Road, you will find the office of the Saint Regis Mohawk Tribe Environment Division, located immediately on your right in a small business park. The Environment Division grew out of a single position sponsored by the federal Indian Health Service (IHS), through which an environmental health technician was hired in 1977. Today, the division (described in detail in chapter 2) has departments devoted to air quality, brownfields, solid waste management, water resources management, wetlands protection, Natural Resource Damage Assessment, hazardous materials, and Superfund oversight.

Travel another mile down Route 37, and you will arrive at the western boundary of the reservation. To reach the Cornwall Island (Kawehno:ke) portion of the community, you need to first drive over the border into New York State. Upon leaving the reservation, you will take the first right-hand turn at the sign reading "Industrial Plants/Bridge to Canada." The General Motors plant used to be visible from here, bordered by the Saint Lawrence River on one side and the Raquette Point region of the reservation on the other. For neighbors in the upstream town of Massena, this industrial plant represented employment in a postindustrial region that has come to be considered part of the "rust belt" of the Northeast/Great Lakes region. For downstream Akwesasro:non, the PCBs that leached from this site for decades had irreversible negative impacts on the local environment, culture, and community health, and the General Motors Company continues to be a source of contention. The contamination from this site, which includes a twelve-acre landfill that directly abuts Akwesasne, underlies the focus of much of the rest of this book.

As you turn past the site of the former GM plant, the bridge will take you over the Saint Lawrence River, which bisects Akwesasne. The river begins at the northeast end of Lake Ontario and flows eastward to the Gulf of Saint Lawrence on the Atlantic coast. While Mohawk people call the river Kaniatarowanenneh, or the "big waterway," the river was renamed for the feast day of Saint Lawrence by French explorer Jacques Cartier during his travels in the region in 1535.[63] In addition to Mohawk communities, settler towns sprung up along both shores of the Saint Lawrence throughout the nineteenth century; they utilized the river for fishing as well as for transportation of both people (in small boats) and timber.

But, as was first noted by Cartier in the sixteenth century, the Long Sault rapids and Soulanges rapids limited the use of the Saint Lawrence River for transportation, preventing the passage of ships farther inland to Lake Ontario. For nearly five decades, members of the Canadian Parliament and the U.S. Congress debated the expense and merits of creating a seaway out of the river. During the 1950s, Canada's Saint Lawrence Seaway Authority, the United States' Saint Lawrence Seaway Development Corporation, the Hydro-Electric Power Commission of Ontario, and the Power Authority of the State of New York came together for the purpose of developing the river as a shipping passage to the Great Lakes and constructing a hydro-electric dam to provide electricity and spur industry.

Despite staunch efforts on the part of Mohawk people from Akwesasne and Kahnawà:ke to resist relocation during the construction process, 1,260 acres of Indian-owned land were expropriated along the seaway's route, including 130 acres on Cornwall Island for the toll gates, customs house garages, offices, roads, and a bridge that was built there after the seaway was developed.[64] On the southern side, Mohawk land claims to Barnhart Island dating back to 1822 were swept aside by Robert Moses and the New York State Power Authority with the building of two major powerhouses, high-voltage power lines, tow ship locks, and a major beach camp recreation area constructed on the island.[65] Also appropriated were 88 acres from the Raquette Point region of Akwesasne. Mohawks sued for compensation in the 1950s, but the courts denied the claim.[66] Construction on the seaway began in the summer of 1954, and over the next five years, a channel 27 feet deep was opened, stretching 2,350 miles from the Atlantic Ocean to Duluth, Minnesota. The seaway contains fifteen locks and is capable of lifting ships about 600 feet above sea level as they sail inland. During the construction, which cost approximately one billion dollars, more than nine thousand individuals were relocated and nearly one hundred square miles of property were condemned.[67]

This development brought unprecedented change to the region. Prior to the construction of the seaway, Mohawk people had adapted to a series of dramatic economic changes, from their participation in the fur trade of the seventeenth and eighteenth centuries to their work in the nineteenth century as canoe men, timber rafters, fishermen, trappers, farmers, and dairy men. Mohawks have taken part in the bridge construction trades since the 1870s and have become internationally famous as ironworkers. This skill in high steel has led Mohawks to seek employment in cities, where they have adjusted to

A cargo ship approaches a lock on the Saint Lawrence River. The Saint Lawrence Seaway project widened and deepened the river, adding fifteen locks through which ships are lifted 600 feet above sea level as they sail inland from the Atlantic Ocean to the Great Lakes. This feat of engineering displaced residents, destroyed fish habitat, and changed the economy of the region. Photograph by Elizabeth Hoover, 2016.

urban life and formed new communities even as they have commuted home every weekend. Despite these shifts in economy and lifestyle, according to historian Laurence Hauptman, "the Mohawks of Saint Regis and Caughnawaga had faced their first major modern-day crisis to their homeland with the coming of the Saint Lawrence Seaway," a crisis that continues today as the community contends with the legacy of industrial development and contamination.[68] On April 25, 1959, the first ships entered the waterway. Thousands would follow, bringing invasive species from around the world to the Saint Lawrence River.

Elders in Akwesasne who witnessed the building of the seaway noted the social and environmental changes that it brought, including changes in family structure, food culture, and wildlife. Howard David lived most of his life on Cornwall Island, and during the 1950s he worked on the seaway construction. During the time when I was conducting my fieldwork, he was running a small farm on the island, growing raspberries and strawberries as well as vegetables. During our visit, he described how in earlier times many families owned and worked on farms, but the seaway brought jobs that drew the men from the farms and into wage labor, and thus changed the economy. Howard noted that the influx of workers with the coming of the seaway (22,000 men worked on the seaway from 1954 through 1959)[69] also drove up the cost of living in the neighboring town of Massena. When the seaway was completed, prices remained high even after the workers left. According to Howard, the money earned by the seaway workers and the decrease in farming ruined the local bartering economy:

> After the seaway left, after they finished, nobody wanted to farm. The money was good, uh? It wasn't good after though. They got the taste of the good living I guess you'd call it. They didn't realizing that the good living was the way we worked. Growing our own food, even little gardens. Everybody had gardens. Enough for themselves, and if anybody grew more than that, they would trade. They used to trade, trade for flour or something.

Reflecting back on his own employment in the construction, Howard told me:

> I even worked on the seaway, I worked on that dam up there. The both of them; the power dam and then Long Sault Dam. I didn't realized this was going to happen, but there's nothing I could do about it. A lot of people worked there. It ruined them. Big money. They ruined Massena too. Well when they left here the prices stayed up, uh? They raised the prices while they were here, the cost of living. And it stayed. On account of the seaway.

Towns up and down the seaway felt the same economic shift. A great industrial boom was predicted along the river as a result of the Moses–Saunders Power Dam that fed the Saint Lawrence–FDR Power Project on the American side and the Canadian Robert H. Saunders Generating Station. In addition, enhanced activity associated with tourism and shipping fueled optimistic population projections that were never to be realized. Some employment opportunities diminished after the construction was completed, such as the closing of a milk processing plant after the loss of farmland appropriated for the seaway.[70]

In addition to a decrease in farms and a shifted economy, Akwesasro:non noted social changes after the coming of the seaway. As Salli Benedict, who lived on Cornwall Island, described: "It used to be easier. People were more connected before. Before the seaway people went fishing together and you pass on that stuff. . . . Before the seaway people were more dependent on the land and the environment than grocery stores." (This impact on the food culture is discussed further in chapter 4.) Mohawk scholars Mary Arquette and Maxine Cole similarly describe social changes precipitated by the coming of the seaway that fundamentally altered Mohawk families:

> The Project created a dramatic transformation in the community. From a traditional society rooted in the culture and values of the Rotinoshonni, we were forced into the mainstream economy and found ourselves pressured by the values of that competitive, materialistic culture. Our traditional economy was disrupted as a result of not being able to rely upon farming, fishing, trapping, hunting and gathering as a means of living. Lost to our people were the opportunities to engage in important traditional cultural practices. A large number of our men worked on the Project as construction specialists for the short term. When it altered the land and the river, these men were not able to return to their traditional land- and water-based practices. Consequently, they maintained non-traditional jobs, which eventually led them to leave the community. Family life suffered. Aside from the deep social disruption this caused, our community began to suffer culturally from the effects of having the core of our traditional political and social system, the family, ripped apart, as well as having English supplant Kahniakeha, the Mohawk language. We view the building of the Project as a major disruption of our social and cultural continuity.[71]

Mohawk midwife Katsi Cook also notes the extensive impact the seaway had on social life, including, ultimately, birthing practices:

55

The Seaway has changed the whole course of family life there [at Akwesasne]. Although traditional Mohawk family life had already changed greatly under the effects of colonialism, many strengths and values had remained constant. The people at Akwesasne helped one another in work bees and the sharing of property, food and knowledge. The self-subsisting economy of agriculture, fishing and trading was undermined by the Seaway and subsequent industrial development. With industrial development and economic growth soon came "social" development—hospitals, schools, social services—a whole centralization of life based on corporate society and exploitation of local resources. Birthing practices are a microcosm of this process because it is a passage which most intimately affects Indian women, the traditional heart of the Native family.[72]

Katsi's aunt, grandmother, and great-grandmother were all midwives, and Katsi has spent her life trying to help Indigenous women reclaim this birthing process.

The creation of the seaway also had a dramatic effect on wildlife. Akwesasne elder Ernie Benedict, a resident of Cornwall Island, described to me how efforts to deepen the river destroyed the fish habitat:

[The blasting of rocks] affected the spawning grounds of fish, not only by the blasting but also because of when the blasting was done, they had to clean out all the broken bottom soil and then deposit it somewhere. And of course the easiest place to do it were the inlets and the bays, where there were spawning areas, and so for a long time fish couldn't make a living out there and so a lot of their work was not done. The fish, as you know, have sort of a cleaning action there in swimming—absorbing the water and taking in contaminants, depositing it down in the bottom of the river, so getting it out of the way. And so now we had to do without the fish for years.

His description of fish unable to "make a living out there" in the same way they always had, similar to Mohawk people, highlights the connections among the multiple communities affected by this development. Ernie also described how islands in the river were covered over "with diggings from the river. And all of these operations, the river was getting pretty messy." Formerly good farmland along the shore continues to be covered with heavy clay material periodically dredged from the bottom of the river. With the installation of the power dam, Ernie also began noticing cut-up eels festering on the shores of the river, creating a stench and attracting birds and insects. The power dam also brought industry to the region, the waste from which would have further negative impacts on the lives of Mohawk people, as will be discussed in the following chapters.

The lack of attention paid to Mohawk concerns regarding the appropriation of their lands for the seaway contributed to the rise of activism at the time. Hauptman argues that by expropriating Indian lands during the construction of the Saint Lawrence Seaway, "these agencies contributed to a powerful Indian backlash which led directly to the rise of Red Power militancy."[73] In August 1957, approximately two hundred Mohawks from Akwesasne and Kahnawà:ke, led by Akwesasne ironworker Francis "Standing Arrow" Johnson, took over land off Route 5S on the Schoharie Creek near Fort Hunter, New York. Citing the Treaty of Fort Stanwix of 1784, the group claimed fifteen square miles of territory, insisting that the New York State treaty of 1789 that ceded the land was invalid because the state had no legal right to enter into negotiations with the Mohawks after the formal adoption of the U.S. Constitution in 1788. They were also protesting being "blasted from their homes" by the seaway project. They were evicted from the land they had claimed in March 1958, but this event was emblematic of future standoffs between Mohawks and the state and federal governments, including the takeover of land in the Adirondacks in 1974 that would eventually lead to the founding of the community of Ganienkeh in Altona, New York. After a series of armed standoffs and a great deal of negotiation with New York State, Ganienkeh was established, and currently it is home to a few dozen Mohawk families, who plant gardens in the summer and run a few tax-free businesses.

Halfway across the Saint Lawrence River, the South Channel Bridge touches down on Cornwall Island, the Kawehno:ke district of Akwesasne. The North Channel Bridge connects the island to the city of Cornwall, Ontario, on the Canadian mainland. Together, they are known as the Seaway International Bridge. Once you cross over the bridge onto Cornwall Island, you will encounter the intersection of Internation Road with Island Road, the main road that runs east–west the length of the island. If you were headed to the Mohawk Council of Akwesasne Department of Environment, you would take a left. If instead you turn right at the intersection, a little less than a kilometer down the road is the turnoff for the A'nowara'ko:wa (Big Turtle) Arena. Built in 1995, the arena serves as an ice rink in the winter for local hockey teams and a sport court in spring and summer for lacrosse associations.

Lacrosse is a wildly popular sport in Akwesasne, and has been for generations. Initially utilized by Haudenosaunee nations as a means of settling disputes or as a medicine game, lacrosse caught on as a sport across Canada and the United States in the nineteenth century.[74] Now kids in Akwesasne start playing as soon as they can walk, and a number of players from the community have been included on the Iroquois Nationals lacrosse team, touring the world to compete in international competitions. Cornwall Island has also been home to the commercial production of lacrosse sticks for generations—located down the road from the arena, Mohawk International Lacrosse is considered to be the largest supplier of wooden lacrosse sticks still operating; the company produces them in addition to the plastic sticks now more commonly used in the sport.[75] At one time, Akwesasne produced 97 percent of the world's lacrosse sticks.[76] The importance of this production became apparent in 1968, when the Chisholm Lacrosse stick factory in Akwesasne burned down, and there was something of a panic across the United States and Canada over how the demand for lacrosse sticks would be met.[77] Today lacrosse is celebrated in Akwesasne as a modern sport as well as for its historic roots.

Traveling to the Cornwall Island portion of Akwesasne means crossing from the United States into Canada at a point on the border that is policed much more heavily than the previously mentioned points between the United States and Quebec in Saint Regis and Snye. As a result of this imaginary line on the water, the Saint Lawrence River, which brushes against both U.S. and Canadian shores, has supported an alternative economy for centuries, fueled in recent years by out-of-work fishermen and others looking to make a quick dollar. Although it is only in recent decades that intensive media attention has been given to the issue, the smuggling of goods (or the

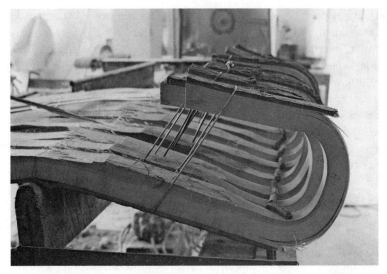

Bending hickory to make wooden lacrosse sticks. Mohawk International Lacrosse is one of the few places that still makes the traditional wooden sticks. Photograph by Elizabeth Hoover, 2016.

"interterritorial import/export business," as one resident described it) across the international border has been a practice ever since the border was created and enforced. During the War of 1812, rations sent to the reservation by the American government were taken by boat to Cornwall, Ontario, where they were sold to emissaries of the British army.[78] During the 1890s, non-Natives in Canada smuggled nails from a factory in Fort Covington, New York, in order to avoid paying customs duties and storekeeper markups.[79] The sweetgrass basket trade was even forced underground, as basket makers from the Canadian side of the community worked to get their wares to American markets while trying to avoid the enforcement of duties on imported goods.[80] Throughout the period of Prohibition in the United States in the 1920s, liquor smuggling was also a profitable business, both for Mohawks and for organized crime operations.[81]

Cigarettes have been traversing the river for decades, owing to the high taxes on this commodity in Canada. Canadian cigarettes are shipped to American wholesalers, who are not required to pay taxes levied by the Canadian federal and provincial governments. People then buy the cigarettes from the wholesalers and smuggle them back into Canada, where they are sold for half the official price for a carton. Cigarettes made on the reservation are also smuggled into Canada, where they are sold tax-free. This business diminished in the 1990s when Canadian cigarette taxes were reduced (in part in an effort to curtail the black market), but the volume of smuggled cigarettes spiked again after Canadian officials boosted cigarette taxes in 2001 to combat smoking.[82] In the past couple of years, the Canadian government has redoubled its efforts to seize cigarettes not bearing tax stamps, and this has slowed some of the illicit tobacco trade.

During the 1990s, human smuggling was also a lucrative business. Immigrants would often get visas into Canada, which is an easier process than legal entry into the United States, and then pay for transport across the Saint Lawrence River.[83] Because smuggling people is more difficult and dangerous than smuggling inanimate products—especially since the terrorist attacks of September 11, 2001 increased the U.S. focus on border security—rates of human trafficking over the river have diminished in recent years. Currently the most lucrative trade is in drugs, which also constitute the contraband seized in greatest quantity, particularly marijuana and ecstasy. According to a 2011 report by the U.S. Department of Justice, about 20 percent of all the high-potency marijuana produced in Canada—multiple tons each week—is smuggled through a patch of border less than ten miles wide on the reservation.[84] Traffickers sell the marijuana and ecstasy in major northern cities and then buy cocaine in Los Angeles from sellers linked to Mexican cartels. The cocaine is then sent back to Canada, where it is sold for a profit.[85] Since 2008, U.S. prosecutors say they have broken up four major smuggling rings operating on the Mohawk territory.[86]

There are conflicting opinions around smuggling in Akwesasne. While the trade has existed in one form or another since the creation of the international border through the center of the community, some residents point to the destruction of the once-prosperous fishing economy by environmental contamination as a catalyst for an increase in rates of smuggling. With their main occupation destroyed, some fishermen found other uses for their boats in order to maintain a livelihood. Proponents of smuggling argue that it is within the sovereign rights of Mohawks to move goods from one area of their territory to another. Their detractors in the community point to the unequal distribution of wealth: successful smugglers are easy to spot because of their conspicuous consumption—large houses surrounded by high walls, shiny new trucks and SUVs with dark tinted windows and spinning rims. While the rhetoric of sovereignty is used to defend the trade, the profits are not given back to the community from which this sovereignty stems. There is also a range of opinions on the matter of smuggling depending on the items being trafficked. Many community members I spoke with are neutral on the matter of cigarette smuggling. Cigarettes are legal items made illegal only by different nations' tax laws. But drugs and weapons are seen as another issue: these are items that can be harmful to the youth of the community, and Akwesasne territory should not be used as a conduit for them. There are also concerns about youth who take up smuggling as a means to earn quick money, as they are not focusing their time on gaining an education or learning a trade, and if they acquire arrest records, they will have even more difficulty finding legitimate work in the future. But while smuggling dominates the news coverage, community members are quick to point out that a vast majority of Akwesasro:non do not take part in these activities and do not appreciate the bad publicity.

This international boundary, and the Seaway International Bridge that traverses it, has also been at the center of decades of activism and protest. Akwesasne is a community known for its activist spirit, and much of the direct action associated with this activism has taken place on this bridge. When boundary commissioners came to Saint Regis in 1814 to survey, they told Mohawks that the international boundary would only be an imaginary line that would go "eight feet over the head of the tallest Indian" and would not affect them.[87] This has proven false, as the myriad complications at border crossings on this bridge have proven.

In 1959, Mohawks on Cornwall Island threatened to cut off all traffic across the bridge that connected New York State to Ontario unless the Saint Lawrence Seaway Authority paid $45,000 to guarantee three years' rental for the new 1.5-mile road that bisected the island. After Mohawks threatened to collect fifty cents per driver from everyone trying to travel over the bridge, authorities acceded to their demands.[88] The bridge served as a site of protest again a decade later, when in December 1968 Mohawks blocked traffic to bring attention to the fact that the 1794 Jay Treaty was being violated.

Following the American Revolution, the United States and Great Britain signed the Treaty of Amity, Commerce, and Navigation, known as the Jay Treaty (for the chief American negotiator, John Jay). Article III of the treaty guaranteed free border-crossing rights for "the Indians dwelling on either side of the boundary line" and also stated that Indians were not to pay duty or taxes on their "own proper goods" when crossing the border. This "free passage" provision has endured differently over time in U.S. and Canadian law. In the United States, Jay Treaty provisions were incorporated into Section 289 of the Immigration and Naturalization Act, and courts and the Board of Immigration Appeals have generally interpreted this section of the act in a way that is beneficial to Native people. The Canadian government, in contrast, never incorporated provisions of the Jay Treaty into permanent statutory law. Rather, the treaty's provisions have been sustained under the "aboriginal rights" doctrine, and Canadian courts have been restrictive in identifying these "aboriginal rights."[89] In the 1950s, Mohawks complained that they were being charged duties for bringing groceries and household goods over the border. They sued in court and lost. They tried bringing their complaints to the elected band council, as well as to the capital in Ottawa, and nothing happened. So on December 18, 1968, one hundred Mohawks blocked the bridge in protest.

One of the protesters, Mike Mitchell, phoned George Stoney, then the executive producer of the Challenge for Change program at the National Film Board of Canada. Stoney was able to assemble a film crew in less than twenty-four hours to be on site during the protest, and the resulting documentary, *You Are on Indian Land,* was released in 1969. The film shows Mohawks gathering on the bridge, explaining to the Ontario provincial police and Cornwall city police that they are blocking traffic in order to draw attention to the imposition of the customhouse on Indian land and the violation of the Jay Treaty by customs officers. A Mohawk woman, wearing a thick coat and a scarf on her head against the cold, describes to reporters how the group tried taking their concerns to the band council, and tried going to Ottawa, but to no avail. One of these band council chiefs, an elderly man, pulls up to the protest in his car and threatens to break up the event (as well as the film crew's cameras) himself with a gun and a billy club. Police usher him back into his vehicle, and he drives off angrily. As police begin to arrest protesters (forty-one in total), children clamor behind them shouting, "Give us back our rights!" and an elderly woman shouts, "The world is watching!" The film begins and ends at a meeting between Mohawks and a government spokesperson, who gives a vague promise to try to find a solution. In the end, the film actually enabled the protesters to get the hearing they had petitioned for in Ottawa.[90] Film scholar Faye Ginsburg argues, "The legacy of *You Are on Indian Land* was not only in the impact of the documentary process at the time. It catalyzed people— then and now—to think about their history and about their need to represent their claims and to take up cameras themselves in order to tell stories that can make a difference."[91] The bridge blockade was followed by takeovers of Stanley Island and Loon Island in 1970, in protest against the leasing of Mohawk land to non-Natives. The band council had been working to take legal action to break the leases, but the protesters felt the process was taking too long and the band council did not have their best interests in mind.[92]

After the bridge blockade in 1968, a group of Mohawks gathered at the home of Ernie Benedict, an Akwesasne Mohawk who had graduated from Saint Lawrence University in Canton and who had edited two reservation newspapers in the 1940s and 1950s. This meeting led to the birth of the newspaper *Akwesasne Notes*, which originally began as a means to get the word out about the bridge blockade and then quickly expanded to include reports about Indigenous events across North America and later the world. The paper was published until 1998; at its peak, it had a circulation of 150,000.[93]

Akwesasne Notes was initially distributed with the help of the White Roots of Peace, a mobile teaching group composed of musicians, dancers, speakers, artists, and writers from dozens of Native nations across North America, operating under the wing of the Mohawk Nation.[94] The White Roots of Peace had its origins in the Akwesasne Counselor Organization, begun in the 1940s by Ray Fadden, who had moved to Akwesasne after marrying a Mohawk woman.[95] Fadden drove carloads of Mohawks "to every Indian reservation north of the Carolinas and east of the Mississippi to visit historical sites and interview Native leaders" and to take part in demonstrations and marches around Native issues.[96] Jerry Gambill, first editor of *Akwesasne Notes*, worked with Ernest Benedict and others to build the White Roots of Peace into a traveling troupe that visited Native peoples, urban and rural, in both the United States and Canada, sharing Iroquois culture and the Great Law.[97] Mike Jock, who traveled with the White Roots of Peace for more than two decades (starting in 1968), recalled loading a tipi on top of a Winnebago and traveling to colleges all over the country, as well as to the White House, to deliver the message of the Great Law and to encourage "our Native children to be proud of who they are, stand up for your rights." In addition to carrying copies of *Akwesasne Notes,* the members of the White Roots of Peace collected material for articles for the paper as they took part in events like the occupation of Alcatraz in 1969, the attempted takeover of Ellis Island in 1970, the takeover of the offices of the Bureau of Indian Affairs in Washington, D.C., in 1972, and the occupation of Wounded Knee in 1973, gaining inside perspectives on events that other reporters did not have access to.

Richard Oakes was an ironworker who left Akwesasne after being displaced by the seaway; he moved west, married a Pomo woman, and enrolled in San Francisco State University. He was moved by presentations of the White Roots of Peace to get involved in Native politics, including the takeover of Alcatraz in 1969, in which he was one of the key players. His murder in September 1972 was one of the catalysts for the Trail of Broken Treaties, a caravan of hundreds of Native people who traveled across the country to Washington, where they took over the Bureau of Indian Affairs building in October 1972.[98] Akwesasne Mohawks were at the heart of most of the pan-tribal Red Power activism of the twentieth century.[99]

This activism also continued at home. Back in Akwesasne, members of the White Roots of Peace and the writers of *Akwesasne Notes* joined the traditional longhouse government in a standoff against New York State and the SRMT government from May 1979 to August 1980. That May, during the occupation of the Tribal government building in protest of the Tribal police force that had been created with U.S. federal funds, traditionalists discovered a secret land claims agreement that had been brokered between the SRMT and New York State (without consultation with the Mohawk Nation Council of Chiefs).[100] In the context of these tensions, that same month, a traditional chief found a work group cutting down trees on his property on Raquette Point. This work was being done as part of a Tribe- and state-supported "boundary delineation project" for a proposed fence around the reservation. Feeling that this delimitation of the reservation symbolically weakened Mohawk claims to traditional territories, the chief and a friend confiscated the group's chainsaws. This, and the confrontation that followed with the Tribal council and state police, led to twenty-three indictments of traditional people. To avoid arrest, the group of traditionalists and their supporters created a defensive encampment in Raquette Point, which is on a peninsula bordered by the Saint Lawrence and Raquette Rivers. There they harvested wildlife for food, including rabbits and fish, because the state police and the Saint Regis Mohawk Tribe's deputized officials had established roadblocks to cut off their supplies. Supporters circumvented the roadblocks by sending supplies to the group across the Saint Lawrence River. Mohawk parents behind the barricade started the Akwesasne Freedom School, a Mohawk-language immersion school dedicated to teaching the cultural material that their children were not getting in public schools.[101] The standoff ended in August 1980, but the repercussions of the event carried into the fall, when a bomb exploded outside the house of Solomon Cook, the only SRMT chief who had lobbied for unity, and a week later the house of Tom Porter, a traditional chief, was burned to the ground. The charges against the traditionalists were dropped in 1981.[102] As a result of the conflict, the land claims agreement between the SRMT and New York State was rejected, a united Mohawk team was formed to negotiate land claims, and the Tribal police force was disbanded.[103]

This tradition of activism continues today. In May 2009, when it was announced that agents of the Canada Border Services Agency would begin carrying guns, Mohawks again blocked the bridge. Unlike most border-crossing checkpoints, the Cornwall Island port of entry was in the middle of a residential community, and it stood beneath a statue of Saiowisaké:ron (Jake Ice), the Mohawk shot by Canadian police in 1899 when he tried to prevent the arrest of life chiefs who were protesting the imposition of an elected government.[104] Several reports had been filed with the MCA about border security officers harassing Mohawks at this checkpoint. In addition, in a violation of Canada's constitution, Mohawk leaders had not been consulted before the Canadian government decided to arm the border guards who would be stationed in this community. Akwesasro:non found all of this unacceptable and held a unity rally at the checkpoint. CBSA officers claimed they felt threatened and walked off the job. The CBSA closed the border crossing, shutting down the Seaway International Bridge between Cornwall and Massena for six weeks, which forced island residents to drive up to two hours out of their way to other bridges and border-crossing stations just to access the southern part of Akwesasne by car. In support of Akwesasne residents, other Mohawk communities in Ontario, including Tyendinaga and Six Nations, also closed down bridges to draw attention to the need for fair negotiations.[105] In July 2009, a temporary port of entry was set up in a traffic circle in Cornwall on the other side of the river, and the bridge was reopened. While this seemed like a victory at the time, it has proven to be a major inconvenience for Mohawk travelers. Now if people who live in the southern half of the community want to visit friends and relatives on Cornwall Island, they first have to drive completely over the river, past the island, to the temporary checkpoint in Cornwall and then drive back over the northern span of the bridge to Cornwall Island. This trip can take up to two hours during periods of heavy traffic. Travelers' license plate numbers are captured by cameras mounted on the U.S. customs building located at the base of the southern bridge on the New York side. Vehicles that do not continue on over the northern bridge to check in with customs during every trip to Cornwall Island are impounded on their next trip to mainland Canada, and the owners are fined a thousand dollars.[106] The CBSA is currently discussing plans to set up a customs agency alongside the American customs office in Massena.[107] While this will be more convenient than having to travel to mainland Canada to check in for visits to Cornwall Island, Akwesasne residents will still have to engage in the invasive process of asking permission from Canadian and American border officers to pass from one portion of their community to the other.

The most recent closure of the Seaway International Bridge occurred on January 5, 2013, in support of the Idle No More movement. This movement, which began in Canada and has been sweeping the globe, arose as a response to an assault on Indigenous rights in Canada: Bill C-45, which passed on December 14, 2012. The bill made changes to the Indian Act, eroded treaties, and removed environmental protections. The Canadian government is required by Section 35 of the Constitution Act to consult with Native people before enacting laws that affect them, but when First Nations leaders came to the House of Commons to share their concerns about the proposed bill, they were blocked from entering. This led Attawapiskat chief Theresa Spence to embark on a hunger strike, and a series of protests took place across Canada, and then the United States, involving flash mobs in shopping malls, highway and railway blockades, and organized rallies. With Twitter and Facebook as major organizing tools, the Idle No More movement spread across North America as well as into Europe, New Zealand, and the Middle East.[108] On January 5, 2013, about a thousand supporters of the movement closed down the Seaway International Bridge and led a huge round dance in the traffic circle in Cornwall. Local response was emblematic of Akwesasne's relationship with its neighbors in general: on newspaper comment pages, some non-Native supporters called on others to recognize that the issues raised by Idle No More affect all residents of Canada and the United States, noting, for example, that clean drinking water is necessary for good health, and pollution does not stop at borders.[109] Detractors, including the town supervisor and mayor of Massena, expressed annoyance that travelers had once again been inconvenienced by Mohawk protests and called the movement's closing of the bridge pointless, foolish, and something that should not be tolerated in the future. The town supervisor issued an apology after Mohawks threatened to boycott Massena businesses, an acknowledgment of the interconnectedness of the economies of these two communities.[110]

This chapter has offered a brief and superficial tour through the community of Akwesasne. While I recognize that I have not been able to include everything that makes up the history and character of this complex place, it is my hope that this overview provides a good sense of the grounding from which community members approached the industrial contamination that was threatening their health and livelihoods, and the scene into which the state and university scientists entered. Environmental sociologists and psychologists inform us that when dealing with environmental issues, individuals look to prior experiences for how to respond.[111] In reflecting on scholarship around contaminated communities, Altman et al. note that collective experiences of community relations, contamination episodes, and media or movement discourse "coalesce into a popularly available set of assumptions, social cues, and social referents that individuals draw upon to guide new encounters with chemical pollutants. These popular assumptions, in turn, inform how participants understand risks, anticipate government and societal responses, and respond to the situation."[112] In this chapter, I have presented an abbreviated account of three centuries of history to demonstrate some of the extended collective experiences that Akwesasro:non are drawing on when they seek to make sense of the environmental contamination affecting them and what they have come to expect from regulators and other government entities.

In applying work on contaminated communities to the context of a tribal nation, one must also consider the additional layer of impact to a land-based culture and tradition. As Potawatomi scholar Kyle Whyte notes, each tribal community is anchored in a specific socioecological context, which he defines as "any arrangement of humans, nonhumans and ecosystems that involves particular cultural, economic and political practices."[113] The ecosocial history of Akwesasne has been shaped by the interruption and alteration of Mohawk socioecological contexts by settler institutions—including state, provincial, municipal, and federal governments, as well as individual settlers and entrepreneurs.

The road-map-structured history laid out above demonstrates the historico-political lens through which Akwesasro:non perceive the imposition of environmental contamination, the government agencies that should have done a better job defending them, and the obstacles to their collaboration with state agencies on the first large community-based participatory research project to take place in an Indigenous community. In addition, as the remainder of this book will show, the tradition of activism against entities interfering with Mohawk self-governance has contributed to and shaped the Mohawks' insistence that that research be conducted on the impacts of environmental contamination and that their voices drive the research process.

CHAPTER 2

Environmental Contamination, Health Studies, and Mitigation Politics

S wiftly moving water has been a draw to industry for centuries. In North America, mechanical hydropower has been used extensively since the 1700s and helped to usher in the Industrial Revolution. The Saint Lawrence River—which for eons has served as a source of food and transportation for the Indigenous people of the region, and for whose rapids places like Akwesasne (land where the partridge drums, referring to the drumming sound of the rapids) and Kahnawà:ke (place by the rapids) were named—became the source of energy for many industrial plants. A number of these plants were upstream and upwind of Akwesasne, and the health, culture, and livelihoods of the area's residents would suffer negative impacts from the ensuing contamination. State and federal regulations are supposed to prevent harmful waste products from entering the environment and damaging human health, but as this case study and thousands of other demonstrate, often those regulations are not strict enough, or they are not rigorously enforced. In the case of Akwesasne, neighboring industries were discovered to have been careless with their waste.

Determined to learn more about the impacts of this contamination on their health and environment, Mohawks turned to scientists and medical researchers for assistance. Considering the historic tensions between their community and state and federal governments—which have not only interfered with Akwesasne's self-governance over the past two centuries but also in many cases failed to enforce the environmental protections necessary to keep industrial waste out of the environment—the partnerships they developed with New York State employees and university researchers took considerable negotiation. As will be described below, after experiencing years of conventional "helicopter research" from which the community did not benefit, Akwesasro:non went on to help develop the first comprehensive community-based participatory research project on environmental health in the nation. This chapter details the history of the discovery of environmental contamination in Akwesasne and the process of establishing these major research projects. Akwesasro:non took part in two decades of environmental health research in the hopes of learning more about how the local industrial contamination affected community health, but also in order to be able to use these data to fight for the most stringent cleanup of the industrial sites possible. Akwesasne Mohawks developed both grassroots organizations and a Tribal government division devoted to environmental issues to ensure that their perceptions of risks and desired outcomes would be properly represented and considered.

The Coming of Industry

Since the late nineteenth century, industry has been gathering on the shores of the Saint Lawrence River. Across the river from Akwesasne in Cornwall, Ontario, a paper mill was built by the Toronto Manufacturing Company in 1881; in 1965, this became the Domtar paper mill.[1] In 1896, the New York State Legislature formed the Saint Lawrence Power Company, with the goal of developing the Saint Lawrence River as an energy source.[2] This led the Aluminum Company of America to locate a plant on the Grasse River in 1903, just south of where the Grasse River meets the Saint Lawrence River, a few miles upstream from Akwesasne. Less than thirty years later a biological survey noted serious local pollution problems, a portent of problems to come.[3] The Moses–Saunders Power Dam (named for Robert Moses and Robert H. Saunders, the chairmen, respectively, of the Power Authority of the State of New York and Ontario Hydro) increased the attraction of this area for industry. After decades of negotiation, construction on the dam began in 1954; upon its completion in 1958, it was placed in service to provide hydroelectricity and to regulate the Saint Lawrence Seaway.

The Alcoa East plant, formerly known as Reynolds Metals. Photograph by Elizabeth Hoover, 2016.

In the 1950s, Reynolds Metals was the second-biggest producer of aluminum in the world. The process of manufacturing aluminum is energy-intensive, so Reynolds sought to set up an operation near the power dam, where electricity was being offered at inexpensive rates. The company convinced the Chevrolet Division of General Motors to set up a plant nearby to cast auto parts from the molten aluminum produced by Reynolds. Between the two plants, 57 percent of the American share of the power generated by the dam was allocated, in what was a clear violation of New York State law, which required that preference be given to domestic and rural customers.[4] The New York State Power Authority was happy to bring employment to the region and welcomed the plants. State and federal organizations—Canada's Saint Lawrence Seaway Authority, the United States' Saint Lawrence Seaway Development Corporation, the Hydro-Electric Power Commission of Ontario, and the Power Authority of the State of New York—worked together to industrialize the region. In doing so they did more than just condemn Mohawk lands, they also weakened tribal self-sufficiency by virtually destroying the fishing and trapping economies and the dairy cattle industries.

Fluoride

The first large-scale environmental impacts from the industrial plants neighboring Akwesasne became apparent when the trees around the Reynolds and Alcoa factories began to brown, and cattle downwind from the factories became crippled and died. According to farmers on Cornwall Island, the first signs of abnormal ill health in their cattle became apparent in the early 1960s.[5] The cattle developed swelling in their leg bones and became lame, to the extent that they would have to lie down in the pasture to eat, crawling to new patches of grass to continue grazing. With increasing age, the cows' teeth began to fail and mastication became difficult—cows would grab hay with their mouths but drop it because it was too painful to chew. They were also unable to drink the cold river water that farmers were pumping into their barns. For the younger cows, first pregnancies would be uneventful, but by the time of their third pregnancies, they were unable to drink or chew; this led to the deaths of many cows during delivery and a high calf mortality rate.[6] Farmers like Noah Point described how the life span of cattle decreased from eleven years to five or six years after Reynolds began operating.[7]

In 1969, the Ontario Ministry of the Environment identified fluoride emissions, a by-product of the aluminum smelting process at Reynolds, as the cause of health problems in Cornwall Island's cattle.[8] As historian Laurence Hauptman relates, the crisis was publicized in 1970 before the Assembly Subcommittee on Indian Affairs by Solomon Cook, a Mohawk dairy farmer (and the first Native American to receive a PhD from Cornell University), "who blamed the declining prosperity of his herd and the reservation dairy cattle industry on the fluoride pollution from Reynolds and other factories."[9] In 1973, the Saint Regis Band Council (renamed the Mohawk Council of Akwesasne in 1984) was informed that fluoride was killing the pine trees near the factory. In response to the situation, the Band Council created the Department of Environment to monitor the contamination and to try to find answers. F. Henry Lickers, a Seneca biologist from the Six Nations reserve, was appointed director and began lobbying for scientific studies of the effects of fluoride poisoning on the human and animal populations on Cornwall Island.

Before 1968, Reynolds had been emitting three hundred pounds of fluoride per hour, which was settling directly on the Cornwall Island portion of Akwesasne.[10] A New York State court ordered Reynolds to reduce emissions, and in 1973, the company installed $17.5 million worth of emission control equipment, which lowered the emissions to about seventy-five pounds per hour. After that, the trees in the area no longer died, but urine samples taken from cows in 1975 still showed abnormally high levels of fluoride.[11] Farmers rebuilt their herds, but the cows still suffered.[12]

In response to residents' concerns about sick and dying livestock, in 1977 Lennart Krook and George Maylin from Cornell University came to Akwesasne to conduct a study on fluoride contamination. What they found was a greatly reduced livestock population that was suffering from severe fluorosis as a result of being downwind from Reynolds. Between 1959 and eighteen years later, when they began their study, the cattle population on Cornwall Island had fallen from 364 head (mostly dairy cows) to 177.[13] In their report, they concluded that severe fluorosis was evidenced by the impacts to the cows' bones and teeth. The fluoride exposure caused osteosclerosis, or abnormal hardening of bones, as well as osteonecrosis, in which lost blood supply causes the bone to die. Analysis of the cows' dental health "showed, with statistical certainty, that all cattle are doomed to exhibit severe teeth lesions in due time," with a "fate [of] starvation and death if the cows are not slaughtered at a relatively young age."[14] In addition to the slow, painful death these animals were suffering, the scientists noted, "the economical impact of stunted growth in beef cattle operations is self-evident."[15] Farmers who received no financial benefit from neighboring industries had their livelihoods destroyed by these factories.

Part of the problem was that regulations based on previously conducted lab research were not protective in real-life settings: the emissions coming from Reynolds were in compliance with New York State and U.S. federal standards, and the fluoride contamination of the forage was within the tolerance levels set by the National Academy of Sciences. These numbers were based on studies conducted with cows that were not chronically exposed as were those on Cornwall Island, where "cattle are exposed in utero and then uninterruptedly for life. Cattle have only fluoride-contaminated forage for consumption. Fluoride polluted air is inhaled through the years—the contribution to the total picture of that source is unknown."[16] As a result, Krook and Maylin noted, "the experimental designs have little relevance to the field situation under study."[17]

In the settlement of a federal lawsuit by Mohawk ranchers against Reynolds, farmers were paid a few thousand dollars for the damage to their cows, but the dairy industry on Cornwall Island collapsed by the mid-1980s.[18] Memories of suffering animals, on both their own farms and those of their neighbors, continue to have negative impacts on Akwesasne residents' perceptions regarding the feasibility of farming in the area.

Mount Sinai School of Medicine Health Study

The results of the Krook and Maylin study, and witnessing the slow, painful deaths of cattle, led to concerns in the Akwesasne community about how the fluoride contamination might be affecting the health of the area's human residents. The Saint Regis Band Council reached out to the Canadian Ministry of Health and Welfare (now known as Health Canada) and requested that a study be conducted to examine the health effects of fluoride and other environmental contaminants on Mohawks. In August 1979, an international panel of scientists visited the reservation to begin work on a $1.6 million study, and in 1981, Irving Selikoff of the Mount Sinai School of Medicine in New York City entered into an agreement to lead the study. He led a team of forty physicians, dentists, and environmental specialists who established an on-site clinic to conduct physical exams, take X-rays, conduct pulmonary function studies, and collect blood, urine, and fat samples. They also collected samples of garden vegetables, fish, and water.[19] In the second phase of the study, the researchers tested the human samples for methyl mercury, PCBs, and mirex (an organochloride used as an insecticide).

On January 12, 1982, researchers from Mount Sinai revealed that traces of PCBs had shown up in fat specimens taken from reserve residents. The tests had been conducted before the contamination leaching from the General Motors foundry had surfaced, but in light of the ongoing discoveries, the Mount Sinai researchers emphasized that the presence of PCBs in Mohawks' bodies did not necessarily correlate with tainted GM groundwater.[20] In March 1984, the first results of their broader study were released in a 400-page report. In the first phase of the study, the investigators found that forty Mohawks had elevated blood fluoride levels, but the levels were no higher than those seen in people living in areas with fluoridated water supplies.[21] The researchers found no adverse human health impacts that they attributed to this fluoride exposure, but they recommended that the individuals with elevated levels be monitored, and they did not rule out the possibility of adverse health problems within the next two decades. Stephen Levin of Mount Sinai stated that the study results were "not a clean bill of health," because while the study found "no current gross health affects," there was "basis to be concerned in the future." The results of the second phase of the study were released in a 250-page report in December 1985. Altogether, the study took six years to complete.[22]

One of the goals of the second phase of the Mount Sinai study was to explore the relationship between PCB blood levels and fish consumption in forty-seven adult residents of Akwesasne. What the researchers found was that although fish consumption was positively associated with blood PCB levels, the average levels in these subjects were comparable to those found in individuals without occupational or other identified PCB exposures. Members of the environment divisions of both the Saint Regis Mohawk Tribe and the Saint Regis Band Council attributed the lower-than-expected blood PCB levels to the fish advisories they had issued prior to the study being conducted, which caused a reduction in fish consumption.[23]

In 1976, concerns about PCB, mirex, and mercury led the New York State Department of Health to advise anglers to reduce consumption of fish from Lake Ontario and the Saint Lawrence River, including the Akwesasne waters, and women of childbearing age and children under the age of fifteen to avoid eating any fish from these waters.[24] Also in 1976, the Canadian Ministry of Health and Welfare approached the Saint Regis Band Council to determine if there were elevated levels of mercury in people of Akwesasne, since mercury had been identified as a problem in Native communities across Canada. The presence of paper companies like Domtar, adjacent to and upstream from Akwesasne, led to the concern that mercury could be a threat to this community as well. In 1978 the Band Council took samples of fish, and when PCBs, mercury, and mirex were found in the samples, the Canadian ministry issued an advisory similar to the one issued in 1976 by NYSDOH.[25] This led to a decrease in fish consumption in the years leading up to the Mount Sinai study. The report issued by the Mount Sinai researchers recommended that fish consumption be further reduced by 90 percent, advice that was especially difficult to follow for a Native community that had subsisted for centuries as fishermen.[26]

Given the conclusion of the Mount Sinai report, the SRMT also issued its own warning, recommending that adults restrict local fish consumption to no more than one-half pound per week. It also recommended that women of childbearing age, pregnant and nursing women, and children under fifteen should avoid the consumption of contaminated fish entirely.[27] The SRMT provided lists of the species to be avoided and those that it recommended for consumption in the amount of only half a pound per week.[28]

Akwesasne residents' main criticism of the Mount Sinai study was that at its conclusion, the researchers packed up and left, and community members felt they had not received any useful information. Midwife Katsi Cook expressed frustration at figuring out "How do we badger Mount Sinai to get that data back to the community?" Another health professional in the community, Agnes, recalled when I interviewed her: "I think the community did go and look for the information. I think one of the end results was that it was gone. So nobody ever really knew what they did with all that, and those were like adipose samples, nail clippings, hair clippings." As was standard for health studies conducted at the time, the physical samples collected, as well as the data, returned to the institution with the scientists, and study participants learned about the results only through newspaper stories.

Today, community response to the Mount Sinai study ranges from vague memories to anger. Seven of the community members I interviewed had been subjects in the study, but since it took place more than twenty-five years before my interviews, most had only cloudy memories on the subject. Most remembered giving samples, being not entirely sure what any of it meant, and then at the end being given the impression that everything was pretty much okay. One elder, Ernie, recalled:

> There was a team that came from New York City and they were pretty gung-ho at the start of the project, but when it came

time to get the results, there are meager results in the reports [laughs]. I don't know, also real big language they were using.

Others, who see their health as having been dramatically affected by fluoride exposure, expressed anger at the lack of action that was taken based on the study results. As one woman angrily expressed, "They got results and they had forewarning. People from China came and said, 'In twenty-five years you're going to see health problems in the population.' So what was the plan twenty-five years before?" She faulted the Tribe's environment program for not working to help people to reduce their fluoride exposure, in ways they could control, since they had little control over their environmental exposure to it:

> Well what do you do? Nothing! Nothing. You wait for people to come twenty-five years later and say uht! They were right! Twenty-five years right on the button people got sick. And now everybody knew so they should have done it themselves, figured out what to do. So that's my gripe, is they knew, Mount Sinai said something, so why didn't somebody make a plan? And say "This is how you reduce fluoride." . . . Where was the awareness? Where was the education campaign? Where was anything that made people aware of where fluoride was? Nobody knew fluoride was in tuna fish. Nobody knew fluoride was in shrimp. Nobody knew fluoride occurred naturally. Nobody knew it's in every canned food, in water. Who knew that? Nobody knows fluoride is high in grapes, in grape jelly? Who knew that? Well I know it now. And toothpaste . . . There's alternatives. Nobody knew that, nobody said. So do a study, a big big big study, and then what? No plan. Very disappointing.

This woman is part of a cohort of women who live on Cornwall Island who all have terrible arthritis problems in addition to myriad other health conditions that they attribute to exposure to contamination. As quoted above, Stephen Levin of Mount Sinai said there was "basis to be concerned in the future." This woman (along with many others her age) was away at college when the sampling occurred for the

Mount Sinai study, and even though she was not part of the sample, she feels that the prediction has been borne out.

Community members challenged the usefulness of the Mount Sinai results in other ways as well. As Katsi Cook has noted, by the time the study was completed, the science used was becoming irrelevant:

> Even before we got to see the study in its finished form in our community, the analytical methods they used for the chemistry analysis of the bloods were already obsolete, because by then, we understood that PCB is not just one kind of a chemical. It's over 200 different species of this chemical. And they all have fingerprints, chemically, and they have different impacts on different body tissues. And so, this multimillion-dollar study by a very well-known research organization led to a dead end.[29]

Henry Lickers, a biologist with the Band Council's Department of Environment who worked on the Mount Sinai study, defended aspects of the research, remarking that the scientists involved were working within the norms and strictures of their time. He noted that Selikoff and his colleagues were not allowed to give people their individual results because of medical confidentiality issues, so they did presentations to the community, but not to individuals. He described how when they first started this study in the 1970s and 1980s, doctors

> had to swear oaths to not reveal anything that was going on and this whole concept of medical confidentiality was right up the wazoo. The concept of community participatory research, that wasn't even considered a viable way of doing research. One of the reasons why the health study that we did with Selikoff at least got better data than others, was because the community participated in it.

So while other community members complained about the lack of information they received back from the researchers, Lickers noted that the data they did get were better than they might have received had the community not been involved at all. He also observed that the results were given to doctors, but the doctors did not feel compelled to share this information with their patients because they did not think they would understand it.

Among the positive outcomes of the study were that it gathered data on long-term trends that future environmental health researchers could work with and that it provided some community members with experience in science. As Lickers noted, "For a number of our people here, it meant very good reputations in those fields, and we were able to spring off those into other jobs." However, it was a struggle at first to convince the Mount Sinai scientists to allow even as much community participation as they did. As Lickers described: "When we first started this, oh jeez I'll tell you, I can remember the arrogance of these doctors was just too much. It was like they came up here to help the Natives, you know." But local Native scientists like Henry pushed to ensure that Mohawk people were included in some way in the process of carrying out the study, even if not to the extent that many people would have preferred.

The negative impression created by the Mount Sinai study left a difficult legacy for other researchers seeking to conduct studies in Akwesasne, as the scientists who worked with the community through the State University of New York at Albany in the two decades subsequent to the Mount Sinai study found. Ed Fitzgerald, the principal investigator for the first SUNY study, explained:

> [The Mount Sinai study] went poorly. They just came in their white coats, did their medical thing and left. And there was very little community involvement, very little feedback to the community, and that went quite poorly, I think there was some bad memories of that. So we kind of had to go out of our way to convince people that no, we are different, we are not like Mount Sinai, we want to include you as partners and we are going to keep you, you know, in the loop at every stage of the way.

David Carpenter, who worked on both phases of the SUNY study, also commented that the Mount Sinai study "led the community to believe that they would be given feedback, that they would be given assistance, and it just didn't happen at all. . . . There was just a great amount of hostility to academic institutions." Joan Newman, another SUNY researcher, emphasized that she and her colleague "were trying not to be people who went up there, got our data, and disappeared and then benefited from the data. I mean Larry and I were very explicitly trying not to be like that." As discussed in greater detail below and in the following chapter, the Akwesasne community worked hard to ensure that subsequent research projects did not take place without their consent and participation.

General Motors, PCBs, and Superfund

While the impacts were subtler at first, the GM plant, which was even closer to Akwesasne than Reynolds, was also emitting contaminants. Over the years since the GM foundry had been established directly adjacent to Raquette Point, Mohawk people had attempted to report issues related to the plant to the New York State Department of Environmental Conservation. But rather than holding GM responsible, the state often blamed Mohawks for the problems. In the early 1970s, when the open dumps at the GM site spontaneously combusted, state agencies blamed Akwesasro:non for setting the fires. In 1972, a nurse at Akwesasne's medical clinic reported to regional environmental officers that open dumping and burning were taking place at the GM site, within 450 feet of Mohawk homes. The district health department director's comment was that "Indians did all the burning at the dumpsite."[30] Jim Ransom remembers reading this statement in the newspaper and feeling angry that Mohawks were being blamed for the reactions of chemicals dumped by GM. The slowness of response from state agencies led someone to call the U.S. Environmental Protection Agency, which acknowledged GM's illegal dumping.[31] Even as NYSDEC acknowledged that GM was operating a landfill in violation of New York law, the director of the state's Division of Solid and Hazardous Waste conceded that it was only one of three hundred illegal landfills in New York at the time.[32] The GM landfill remained open, without a permit, for another six years after NYSDEC discovered the problem.

The main contaminant of concern at the site was polychlorinated biphenyls. Marketed under the brand name Aroclor, PCBs were first fabricated in 1929 in the United States in West Anniston, Alabama—a town whose residents would later sue producer Monsanto for poisoning their community.[33] Until 1977 Monsanto produced Aroclor 1248, a substance that was added to the hydraulic fluids at GM and other companies. In 1978, PCBs were designated a hazardous substance by the Clean Water Act, and their manufacture, processing, and distribution were banned by the Toxic Substances Control Act after the potential negative health impacts linked to PCB exposure—including nervous system delays, cancers, decreased thyroid and liver function, and autoimmune disorders—were discovered.[34] PCBs enter the body either through occupational exposure or through food and then are metabolized by the liver. Some are excreted, and some are stored in the body's fat. The compounds known as PCBs encompass 209 different forms, or congeners; all are largely odorless, colorless, and tasteless.

The GM plant produced aluminum cylinder heads, pistons, and transmission casings using a die casting process, in which large machines applied high pressure and high temperatures to mold the aluminum. From 1969 to 1974, GM added Aroclor 1248 to the hydraulic fluids in these machines to make the fluids resistant to fire.[35] After 1974, GM substituted non-PCB fluids, but residual PCB contamination remained until 1980, when the machines' hydraulic fluid reservoirs were twice flushed and refilled.[36]

The PCB-laden hydraulic fluids were disposed of in reclamation lagoons behind the GM plant; these lagoons were periodically drained and excavated, and the sludge was buried on-site in unlined pits. The use of the lagoons was intended to prevent the direct contamination of the rivers, but the waste overflowed at least seven times between January and September 1982 alone, contaminating the beds of the Saint Lawrence River, the Raquette River, and Turtle Creek.[37] GM also had an outfall that discharged into the Saint Lawrence River that led to sediment contamination, especially in Turtle Creek.[38] The twelve-acre area designated as the Industrial Landfill, which contained more than 300,000 cubic yards of material, also leached PCBs into the groundwater, which then ran into the river.[39] Katsi described how the children from the Freedom School had swum in Turtle Cove, where they played "mudmen," covering their bodies with the thick PCB-laced mud. A few years later Turtle Cove was renamed "Contaminant Cove" by the workers who excavated the toxic sediment. For years the landfill was also an open site, and community members I interviewed described how they had dug there for scrap metal or played there as children.

In addition to the lagoons, in December 1981, NYSDEC found

the groundwater on the GM property to be contaminated with PCBs, heavy metals, chromium, mercury, and cadmium. A month later, tests found PCBs in the 220-foot-deep private well of Raquette Point residents Tony and Ella Cole. Rather than hearing directly from regulators, Mohawks found out about these tests through articles in the local newspaper. NYSDEC blamed the breakdown in communication on the fact that although the GM plant is adjacent to Akwesasne, the plant is in Saint Lawrence County, which is in NYSDEC Region 6, while Akwesasne is in Franklin County, in NYSDEC Region 5.

This failure of either industry or regulatory agencies to communicate with the community, coupled with a general distrust of many of the institutions that were tasked with ensuring the environmental health and safety of people in the region, led to the development of the community organization Mohawks Agree on Safe Health, which was founded in an attempt to ensure that health-related information was reaching residents and that their needs were properly represented. As one resident, Mark, described, everyone had a different opinion about their mission, but concluded,

> "Well, you know it seems like we are never going to get any-where if we disagree" and so we said, "well at least the Mo-hawks agree on safe health." So that is how it came Mohawks Agree on Safe Health. There was nothing else we agreed on but it spelled out MASH and we laughed so that is how it started.

As another MASH founding member, Brenda, explained, "So the Tribe was trying to get a handle on what's this contamination, and the community was trying to get a handle on—the fear factor went up as soon as we heard it caused cancer." Standoffs between traditionalists on one side and the SRMT and New York State on the other during the Raquette Point incident just a few years prior had left some residents concerned about whether the Tribe was acting in the best interests of the people. As Brenda described, "So that's why MASH organized and tried to get outside involvement, expert involvement on environmental contamination and what the issues were, and sort of that intermediary between the panicked community and the tribal council that they didn't trust." According to Leona, another founding member, MASH's intention was to get information out to the community that there were problems with the environment that could affect people's health, and also to make the leadership aware that MASH members were looking into these concerns. Members of MASH worked with the Tribe's Environment Division and made phone calls, attended public meetings from which they would bring information back to the community, and held meetings at the Freedom School. They issued press releases, hired scientists to test wells, and staged protests. As Mark stated:

> I don't want to know after the fact that I shouldn't have drank the water, I don't want to know after the fact that when I smell the stuff, maybe I should tell the kids, come on in, don't play out today. Because with knowledge you can do something. Otherwise, you are stuck with what is dished out to you. That is basically what is was, it wasn't the most organized group I have ever been in, but it did provide us with information to act on.

In February 1982, a month after PCBs were found in Tony and Ella's well, MASH hired a private lab from Tennessee to test the water in twelve wells on Raquette Point, half of which were found to show signs of contamination. NYSDOH officials were skeptical of the results, but in 1983, the department officially announced the discovery of PCBs, benzene, and trichloroethylene in the groundwater near the GM Central Foundry.[40] GM began distributing bottled water to Raquette Point residents, but according to Jim Ransom, who was the environmental health technician for the SRMT at the time, the company refused to communicate with the Tribe about the contamination.[41]

> We tried to contact, reach out to General Motors, they wouldn't respond to our phone calls. They ignored our letters, ended up going through the Saint Lawrence Environmental Management Council and they were much more receptive, had a meeting at our request and GM didn't show up, but New York State DEC did and it was shortly after that, that the state decided to nominate it for the Superfund list, because of their refusal to cooperate.

The 270-acre General Motors site was nominated to the National Priorities List as a Superfund site in the fall of 1983 and was placed on the list in early 1984. The company was fined $507,000 for twenty-one counts of illegally dumping and storing PCB-laden waste.[42]

Even after the GM site was placed on the National Priorities List, MASH continued to work to ensure that community members were informed about the ongoing discoveries regarding the extent of contamination at the site, and to push for a thorough cleanup. Barbara and her sister Leona, two of the founding members of MASH, described their concerns regarding the health and safety of the children who attended the Akwesasne Freedom School on Raquette Point, directly adjacent to the GM plant. But their goal was also to educate people that the contamination could carry beyond Raquette Point— through air pollution and fish consumption. As Barbara reflected:

> I think we made the community aware of what was happening. I think we made New York State government aware that we were not dummies, and that we knew what we were doing, and that we were educated. And we weren't going to stand back and just let things, you know, happen to our people. We weren't going to let that happen.

MASH worked to educate the community by distributing flyers, providing information for newspaper and radio news coverage, and hosting demonstrations. Barbara indicated that the group became less active when the Tribe became more active in the remediation process, "and they made GM accountable for what they have done to us." Looking back, Barbara said:

> I think it served its purpose. I think it made the community conscious of the fact that when there's an environmental issue, it's all of Akwesasne that's affected. And I think the other thing it did was it made the Environmental Division or Department, whatever it was at that time, realize there was a lot of work ahead, and that the people in there had to be dedicated. And they were. And so, they carried on.

In 1987 MASH merged with a new group, the Akwesasne Task Force on the Environment.

The purpose of ATFE, which is still active today and has become well known as an Indigenous grassroots environmental organization, is to bring together representatives from all three tribal governments in the community of Akwesasne, as well as any community members who want to attend meetings and be involved. ATFE's stated mission is "to conserve, preserve, protect and restore the environment, natural and cultural resources within the Mohawk territory of Akwesasne in order to promote the health and survival of the sacred web of life for future generations and to fulfill our responsibilities to the natural world as our Creator has instructed."[43] The New York State and U.S. federal governments had procedures in place for working with the federally recognized SRMT, but in a politically complicated community like Akwesasne, this meant that a number of stakeholder voices were not being formally included. ATFE was developed to reach across these different political lines to create a united front, a unified community voice, that would represent the best interests of all Akwesasro:non. As one of the founding members, Dave Arquette, explained, "We had to come together as one or we would lose everything."

Because ATFE is removed from the political process, it can both advocate for community-based solutions to environmental issues and ensure that researchers do not "take advantage of intra-tribal differences."[44] As described in greater detail in chapter 3, ATFE has also established its Research Advisory Committee and developed the Good Mind Research Protocol to ensure that any research conducted in Akwesasne is to the benefit of the residents there. As a community-based institutional review board, the ATFE RAC has set the groundwork for several other community organizations seeking to gain better control over the research being conducted on their members. In 1995, ATFE became incorporated so that it would be able to apply for grants, conduct its own research, and eventually have control over the use of its own data; another goal was to ensure that grant money received for work in Akwesasne is spent to benefit the community.

While the community was coalescing to develop grassroots organizations that could operate outside the political system, the SRMT government was also working to improve its own capacity to deal with the environmental situation. As noted in chapter 1, the SRMT Environment Division grew out of a single position sponsored by the federal Indian Health Service, through which an environmental health technician was hired in 1977. The technician's primary duties at the time included testing water at residences and seeking out funding for septic systems.[45] Jim Ransom, who was one of the first to hold this position, remembers that among the program's initial concerns were child car-seat safety and animal bites—it was a basic program aimed at ensuring the health and safety of the community in relation to the environment. He described how that all changed on December 9, 1981, when the *Watertown Times* ran an article stating that the GM plant site was contaminating the groundwater with PCBs, which could be migrating into the Saint Lawrence River. Suddenly Jim was no longer just worrying about basic environmental safety—he was researching PCBs, collecting and testing samples, drafting press releases, learning about legal issues, and negotiating with industry. "It was just amazing what we were doing and I think a lot of it was because nobody told us we couldn't do it, and nobody else was doing it for us. So we learned hands-on how to do it ourselves and we found a lot of allies along the way who were there to transfer knowledge to us about how to collect water samples" and were able to lend equipment.

Beginning a Study

While regulators as well as tribal departments and organizations were working to understand the extent of the contamination, one midwife was developing concerns about the potential health impacts of this contamination. As someone who was intimately connected to the women in the community through her midwifery practice, Katsi Cook began hearing concerns about the numbers of miscarriages among young mothers around the same time that the contamination was being discovered. Katsi also felt that she was seeing an unusual number of birth defects, especially of an intestinal nature. One child was born with no intestines. Another had a torsion of the intestines that had to be surgically corrected, and another was born with the stomach and intestines on the outside of the abdomen. When Katsi began to do literature searches, she found that female beagles exposed to PCBs produced puppies with intestinal abnormalities. This caused her to become concerned about the babies in her community who were similarly being exposed to this contaminant. She noted, "I don't have an environmental engineering degree, I don't have anything like that, but what I do have as a midwife and as a Mohawk woman moving through the small world webs of the community, I would hear this one had a miscarriage, that one over here is sick with this." This "situated knowledge," as Donna Haraway describes it, gave Katsi insight into a portion of the community that had been overlooked by previous studies and by health professionals.[46]

In January 1984, as she began an undergraduate degree in biology and society in the School of Human Ecology at Cornell University, Katsi met medical sociologist Lin Nelson, who assisted her with further literature searches about PCB contamination. These searches led her to articles written by NYSDEC wildlife epidemiologist Ward Stone, who had reported on samples of owls and turtles he had found along the Saint Lawrence River that were convulsing or already dead and had high levels of PCBs in their livers and brains. Katsi also discovered papers by Brian Bush, a chemist at the New York State Department of Health, about breast milk studies he had done in Oswego, New York, a town about 150 miles southwest of Akwesasne, on the shores of Lake Ontario.[47]

As women in Akwesasne learned more about environmental contamination, they became especially concerned about the top of the food chain: the breast milk they were feeding their infants. The Krook and Malin study and the Mount Sinai research had collected various samples across Akwesasne, leading to a heightened consciousness in the community about contamination. However, breast milk had not been sampled, and this frustrated Katsi and the mothers she worked with. Katsi recalled how staff from the Band Council's Department of Environment and the Mount Sinai researchers did presentations at the office of the *Akwesasne Notes* newspaper and at the Akwesasne Freedom School, detailing how and why people should sign up to take part in the study. At one of these meetings, Katsi asked if they would be including breast milk in their samples, to which the researchers responded that this would not be necessary since they would be doing fat biopsies. She recognized that in reality they would have had a difficult time collecting milk samples from women in the community, because most of the researchers were men. But as a midwife promoting breast-feeding, Katsi was faced with concerns about the safety of this practice as more was being discovered about the extent of the contamination. As she described in her 2005 interview with Joyce Follet:

Mothers in my care who also lived in some of these geographic areas of our communities that were under special focus of the Mt. Sinai study because they were practicing traditional subsistence lifestyles—raising their own food, raising their own animals—and so the scientists were taking samples of ducks, of cattle, of vegetables, and the mother, who's ready to have her baby at home, is saying, Gee, Katsi, these scientists are coming to my home taking samples of everything but me. Is it safe to breastfeed? And I said, "You know what? I don't really know. I wish I did."

And so, the Akwesasne Mother's Milk Project began as an effort to find that out.[48]

In order to try to answer some of these questions, in April 1984, Katsi, sociologists Lin Nelson and Doug Brown, and environmental scientist Janet Rith-Najarian from Cornell University met with Brian Bush about constructing a breast milk study at Akwesasne. As Bush laid out in a letter to a fellow doctor in April 1984, they set out to "obtain as much data as possible of previous epidemiologists' work done on the cohort," "commence location of nursing mothers at Akwesasne," "prepare questionnaire in collaboration with Dr. Fitzgerald, after reference to Dr. Selikoff's questionnaire," and "prepare sampling kits for Mrs. Cook."[49]

With that work under way, Katsi also met with Ward Stone at his office that fall and invited him to come to Akwesasne and test the wildlife there. He did, and with startling results, which he began announcing throughout the summer of 1985: A snapping turtle taken from Raquette Point registered 835 parts per million (ppm) of PCBs, which was seven to twenty-eight times higher than levels found in turtles taken from the upstream Thousand Islands region the year prior. Chicken containing more than 3 ppm of PCBs is considered unfit for human consumption, and substances containing more than 50 ppm qualify as toxic waste. High levels of PCBs were also found in frogs, mice, and shrews taken from the area.[50] A masked shrew found 150 feet from the GM dump had 11,520 ppm PCBs.[51] The level in an owl was 2,290 ppm, and 190 ppm were found in a duck, 11 ppm in a sturgeon, and 3,067 ppm in a male snapping turtle.[52] The results, which Stone shared directly with the community, had immediate resonance, due in part to the painful connection between the contaminated turtles and the Mohawk creation story. Recall that in the creation story, Sky Woman falls from a hole in the Sky World and is saved from the watery world below by a turtle who offers its back as her resting place, and as the birthplace of humanity. Turtle is also one of the three clans of the Mohawk Nation, further demonstrating the animal's cultural significance.

After finding high PCB levels in ducklings found near the GM site, Stone described Akwesasne as "the worst place in the world to be a duck," a designation that some interviewees felt influenced how outsiders, as well as Mohawks, viewed their homeland.[53] While he was criticized for the statement and later censured by NYSDEC, the Mohawks, including Katsi, took an immediate liking to Stone, giving him the name Rahontsiohares, meaning "he who washes the land."[54] Much to the chagrin of NYSDEC, as Stone moved through his investigations over the years, he reported results to the Mohawk, and to the local press, as soon as he found them, and he was not shy to point out the local industries as the sources of the high levels of toxic substances he was finding. The head of NYSDEC, Thomas Jorling, ordered Stone to follow due process and report to the agency prior to announcing results to the public. Stone did not comply, and, according to the Post Standard, Jorling "clipped the wings of Ward Stone, the free-flying environmentalist in his department with an uncanny knack for pouncing on hazards that no one else had detected. Now Jorling has bound Stone in miles of red tape and stuffed a gag in his mouth."[55] Jorling persuaded the governor of New York to withhold extra funding that the state legislature had approved for Stone's wildlife pathology lab and shifted Stone's lab to the Division of Environmental Enforcement, where Stone would be required to have all investigations and the public release of results approved by the director of the division, the technical bureau chief, and the assistant commissioner of public affairs.[56] While the state justified these moves as a means of strengthening the NYSDEC team, to reporters and Mohawks, it appeared that the state bureaucracy was out to stifle the one person they felt was helping Akwesasne.[57] Stone, for his part, sided with the Mohawks and worked to embarrass his agency, declaring that his colleagues were guilty of "scientific malpractice" for not finding the contamination sooner and asserting that the cleanup costs for GM and neighboring Reynolds would have been consider-ably lower if NYSDEC had been doing its job a decade prior.[58] But while Stone remained a thorn in the side of his agency, the results he was reporting directly to the Mohawk community were crucially important. According to Jim Ransom, who worked for the SRMT En-vironment Division at the time, "Without Ward, we'd still be think-ing groundwater was the major concern. It's not. It's the wildlife and the fish. And the food chain. Stopping the pollution becomes even more urgent."[59]

Finding contamination in the food chain also highlighted the ur-gency of determining the contaminant contents of breast milk. One woman who lived on Raquette Point at that time described to me con-versations she had with Katsi, who delivered four of her children in her home. She recalled asking, "Well, if everything is so bad around here, what about our milk, the mother's milk? I mean, if I'm drinking the water here, what's happening to our milk?" In 1985, with a small grant from the Need More Foundation, the Mother's Milk Project began. Katsi presented a proposal to the Saint Regis Mohawk Health Services and to the Mohawk Council of Akwesasne's Department of Health, and then began collecting samples of breast milk:

> The first thirty or so samples I collected myself, beginning with clients, women that I had delivered their babies, and then extended out into the broader base of Mohawk women who were nursing. And it was fun. I'd go to their homes and hold their babies, visit with them, talk about their birth stories. They'd go take a warm shower, their milk would let down, and the next thing I knew, we had a milk sample of 500 mills [ml]. You know, piece of cake. (laughter) And those would get fro-zen and shipped, and attached with it a legal document, chain of custody, so that we could be assured that nobody in between was messing with those samples.[60]

Katsi has described this work as "barefoot epidemiology," with Indig-enous women developing their own research projects based on com-munity concerns and then collecting their own data.[61]

With Stone's encouragement, and because of her own distrust of New York State, Katsi initially sent the samples to a private lab in Wisconsin rather than to the NYSDOH lab in Albany:

I wanted to use a private lab in Wisconsin that I had located, because none of our women would believe in the Health Department of the State of New York. I mean, we have always fought with New York State, ever since New York State created itself. And there was just no trust for it. I mean, my child was born on a day when New York State sent its SWAT teams to close up the reservation. So, there was no trust in New York State.

So we sent them to a private lab and we got the initial samples and it was in the milk. There was PCBs in mothers' milk. And not only PCBs but agricultural products: Mirex, which is a flame retardant, all kinds of—hexachlorobenzene—different chemicals that at that time, it astonished me.[62]

Despite the Mohawk's distrust of the state, in May 1985 samples were also sent to Brian Bush at the NYSDOH Wadsworth Laboratory, and Bush analyzed them for "chlorinated pollutants, PCB and TCDD [dioxin] systems." He agreed that "PCB, DDE [dichlorodiphenyldichloroethylene], Mirex, fat content and protein content data will be returned to you within a month of sampling in the form, normal or abnormal. . . . I understand that you need a turnaround time of one month for this process to maintain credibility with the women you have motivated to participate in the study."[63] In a letter to Katsi in November of the following year, Bush sent back the results from seven milk samples, none of which he considered to have dangerously elevated levels of PCBs (they ranged from 6.7 to 38.08 ppm). He wrote, "You will be glad to note that the present levels are well below those of the 1979 suburban Americans."[64] Although Bush did not feel that the levels were dangerously high, he did believe that the results warranted further investigation, as levels appeared to be connected to fish consumption.

The discovery of PCB-contaminated waste leaching from the General Motors plant into the Saint Lawrence River led the SRMHS to issue an advisory in July 1986 recommending that Mohawk residents not eat more than one fish meal per month, that lactating women and women of childbearing age not eat any fish, and that everyone consider fish from the Saint Lawrence to be contaminated.[65] This advisory further damaged the local fishing economy, which had previously supported a number of Mohawk families and had already begun to diminish after the Band Council's 1978 fish advisory. In order to more fully quantify levels of PCBs in Akwesasne women's breast milk, and to investigate connections with fish consumption, Bush approached epidemiologist Edward Fitzgerald. The two had worked together on other PCB projects, and Bush felt that he needed assistance on the epidemiological aspect of designing a human health study and recruiting participants. After the requirements for a health risk assessment had been negotiated by the state, federal, and tribal governments and GM, Fitzgerald and Katsi Cook began work on designing a full-scale breast milk study at Akwesasne.

Health Risk Assessment: Fish, Wildlife, and Breast Milk

In October 1986, the Superfund Amendments and Reauthorization Act added Section 126 to the Comprehensive Environmental Response, Compensation, and Liability Act, directing the EPA to treat qualifying tribal governments substantially the same as states for specified provisions of CERCLA. A qualifying tribal government is one that is federally recognized, has a governing body with authority to protect the health and welfare of tribal members and the environment, and has jurisdiction over the site where CERCLA actions are contemplated.[66] Under this law, the SRMT now had authority over the contamination that had left the GM site and flowed onto tribal land.

During the summer of 1987, representatives from the Saint Regis Mohawk Tribe Environment Division sat down with representatives of the EPA, NYSDEC, and General Motors. Jim Ransom, who represented the SRMT Environment Division at the time, described how they sent the GM delegates out of the room, and then Jim and a chief from the Tribe discussed their options with the government agencies. When the agencies acknowledged that GM was not likely to pay for the entire health risk assessment the Tribe was requesting, Jim responded, "Well, I think they are responsible for all of it, so I think they should pay for all of it. But if you are telling us that you can't force them, then I want a commitment from you to make up the difference." The agencies agreed. The GM representatives were then called back into the room, at which time they agreed to pay for 80 percent of the cost of the health risk assessment (meaning GM would pay $370,000 of the full $461,300 price tag); the remaining

20 percent would come from the NYSDEC Conservation Fund.[67] GM agreed to pay for all of the wildlife study and the breast milk study, but the company did not feel that it was responsible for all of the PCBs in the river, as it had been discovered that the Reynolds plant had also been leaching PCBs; therefore, GM would not pay for all of the fish study.[68]

In 1987, when the Tribe was negotiating the health risk assessment studies, more effort was needed to secure funding as well as to hire additional staff. The Tribe hired a lawyer to seek funding that would support programs aimed at improving the air and water quality of Akwesasne. Through negotiations with the EPA, the Tribe was able to create two programs that specifically dealt with water and air quality.[69] The Tribe needed to have its own environment division because, according to Jim Ransom,

> we were treated the same as they were treating the fish in the water, and the turtles and the wildlife and the plants. We were just viewed as not being human in a sense of "yeah, it's a minor problem, don't worry about it, it's all under control." We had to make the case that it was a problem and that it was much more serious than that, and it took us years to do that, but we were successful.

From a single environmental health technician funded by IHS, the SRMT Environment Division developed into a larger unit funded in part through the EPA.

HEALTH RISK ASSESSMENT RESULTS

The three-part health risk assessment examined contaminant levels in fish, wildlife, and breast milk.[70] In order to develop an assessment of the health risks associated with the fish species utilized by the community, researchers collected 343 fish from twelve locations in the vicinity of Akwesasne and analyzed the samples for several organic chemicals and heavy metal contaminants. Fish from all of the locations exhibited PCB levels in their lipids above the NYSDOH criterion for the protection of fish-eating wildlife, and above the federal tolerance of 2 ppm.[71] Researchers also collected specimens of nineteen wildlife species from eighteen locations and found detectable levels of PCBs in waterfowl, but not in deer—the most frequently eaten of all wild game in Akwesasne.[72]

The third part of the study built off of the pilot breast milk samples that NYSDOH chemist Brian Bush had analyzed as a favor to Katsi in 1986–87, which had indicated that fish consumption correlated with higher levels of PCBs in breast milk. To recruit additional eligible women to the study, the outreach department at SRMT Health Services, the local Women, Infants and Children (WIC) nutritional program, and local physicians contacted new mothers either before they delivered or within one month after their children were born. Katsi served as a liaison between the mothers, tribal leaders, and project personnel, who were Mohawk women that Katsi insisted NYSDOH hire to collect the samples. Sixty-five nursing mothers were identified at Akwesasne, and fifty-three completed the study, with an additional four samples included from the first pilot project. Comparative data were obtained from the WIC clinics of Warren and Schoharie Counties to the south of Akwesasne, from 109 women who had given birth during the same period. Project personnel interviewed participants at home within two to four weeks postpartum, collecting information on sociodemographic characteristics; height and weight; health conditions; use of medications; occupational, reproductive, and residential histories; cigarette smoking; alcohol and coffee consumption; sources of drinking water; and diet.

The results showed that among participants from 1986 to 1989, Mohawk women with the greatest estimated lifetime exposure to PCBs through consuming local fish had twice the concentrations of PCBs in their milk as the controls or as Mohawk women who did not report eating local fish.[73] This was especially true for the PCB congeners found in fish taken from near the GM site, as well as for mirex. However, among the women who participated in the study in 1990, these differences were no longer apparent, probably as a result of the decline over time of fish consumption in the community, especially during pregnancy. This was evidenced in the sharp decrease in reported number of fish meals between the Mount Sinai study's dietary surveys in 1979–80 and the dietary portion of the interviews conducted with these women participants.[74] Although actual concentrations were low, the Mohawks did have significantly higher levels of 2,5,3′-trichlorobiphenyl (a lightly chlorinated congener present in Aroclor 1248, the PCB mixture used at GM) than the control group.

This congener is not typically found in human milk because it is easily metabolized and excreted, so this finding pointed to a local and continuous source of PCB exposure.

Upon receiving the results from the breast milk study, the Akwesasne Task Force on the Environment issued a press release on May 12, 1992, titled "Mohawk Mothers Responsible to Their Future Generations; Tell Local Industries: Now It's Your Turn to DO the Right Thing!" The release quoted a group of mothers:

> "Our traditional lifestyle has been completely disrupted and we have been forced to make choices to protect our future generations. We feel anger at not being able to eat the fish. Although we are relieved that our responsible choices at present protect our babies, this does not preclude the corporate responsibility of General Motors and other local industries to clean up the site," said the mothers. The Mohawk mothers were congratulated for leading healthy lifestyles and drastically reducing the amount of fish they eat. "Why do we have to be the ones to make the adaptations? Our traditional economic base, our very culture has suffered severe impacts from industrial hazardous waste. Our children are growing up with pollution, they see it every day. . . . In spite of reassurances from the scientists, we are concerned about our babies who are breastfeeding now and those who are about to be born. The only reason our milk levels are not higher is because we were responsible enough to do the right thing, not because GM did the right thing."

As illustrated by this press release and the following excerpt from an article written by Akwesasne community members, the scientific community's reactions to the results of this health study were different from those of the mothers themselves.

> In speaking about Akwesasne, a prominent health researcher suggested that the community should be considered a success story because Mohawk people had eliminated their exposure to PCBs and other toxic substances. Mohawk people, however, have argued strongly that eliminating the consumption of local fish, wildlife, and plants is no solution to the problem of

> environmental contamination. Unfortunately, the voice of the
> community is not heard as often as that of prominent govern-
> ment scientists. To suggest that Akwesasne is a success story is
> to suggest that it is acceptable for the victims of environmen-
> tal contamination to continue to pay the price for pollution.[75]

By decreasing what had been traditional levels of fish consumption
in order to reduce their PCB body burdens and protect their infants,
Mohawk women had shown that exposure to the contamination was
in some ways avoidable. In this sense, the health studies and fish consumption warnings were a success. However, at the same time, this
avoidance of a traditional and nutritious food was unacceptable from
a cultural, health, and justice standpoint. Fish advisories are based
on risk avoidance, in which risk bearers are encouraged or required
to change the practices that expose them to contamination; true risk
reduction, in contrast, would reduce contaminants and make the
fish safe to eat.[76] The avoidance of fish may have helped to prevent
further PCB exposure, but the community lost a primary source of
protein and other nutrients such as iron, calcium, zinc, and essential
omega-3 fatty acids. This further exacerbated chronic diet-related
health problems in the community, such as diabetes and cardiovascular disease.[77] Also not considered when these fish advisories were
declared as successful in protecting human health was the social and
cultural damage sustained by the community (a topic discussed in
greater detail in chapter 4). As scholars of tribal health risk evaluation Stuart Harris and Barbara Harper explain, among most tribal
people, individual and collective well-being comes from being part
of a healthy community with access to heritage resources and ancestral lands, which allow community members to satisfy the personal
responsibilities of participating in traditional activities and providing
for their families. According to Harris and Harper, "Because tribal
culture and relation are essentially synonymous with and inseparable
from the land, the quality of the sociocultural and ecocultural landscapes is as important as the quality of individual natural resources
or ecosystem integrity."[78] These factors were not taken into account
when avoiding fish consumption was offered as the answer to PCB
exposure. However, faced with contaminated fish and a Superfund
cleanup that would take decades to address the problem, this was

the only answer available to Akwesasro:non at the time, the only way they could protect their health and that of their children.

Superfund Basic Research Program Studies, Round 1: 1990–95

After the completion of the health risk assessment breast milk study, David Carpenter, a researcher at the SUNY Albany School of Public Health, where Fitzgerald also held an appointment, thought that a continuation of the study would make a good topic for a project under the Superfund Basic Research Program (SBRP), which had been developed by the National Institute of Environmental Health Sciences (NIEHS).[79] The team decided to design a number of investigations around the PCB contamination at Akwesasne, continuing the human health studies and adding toxicology experiments, engineering studies to find the best ways to remediate PCBs, and studies examining how PCBs degrade in the environment. The SBRP application was first submitted in 1988, and the project was not funded. In 1990, however, NIEHS program director Bill Suk informed the SUNY researchers that additional money had become available, and the project would receive funding. As Fitzgerald recalled:

> They were most interested I think in the fact that this was a Native American population and they have a mandate, you know, from Congress, to help fund the research on environment contamination and minority groups. There wasn't a lot, at least at that time, not a lot going on about environmental contamination among Native peoples. So I think that is where his interest was in that regard. They thought this would be an important addition to their portfolio and they can show Congress not only are they doing good science but they are also looking at environmental problems and Native Americans.

The SUNY team was funded from 1990 through 1992 to continue the breast milk studies, and then the project was renewed in 1992 for a three-year period, with Fitzgerald as the principal investigator for the human health component and Carpenter as the lead principal investigator on the entire grant. After the grant was renewed in 1992, the researchers expanded the focus beyond nursing women to examine all pregnant women and the men related to or affiliated with the women, since there was concern that men ate more fish and were not following the advisories as strictly as women were. Breast milk and blood samples were collected from pregnant women, and blood samples were taken from their male partners and relatives. Some men and women underwent a caffeine breath test that allowed the researchers to look at the activation of P450 liver enzymes, which are the first biological response to exposure to PCBs and other chemicals. Detailed interviews were also conducted, with the aim of determining how PCB levels were related to fish consumption and other avenues of exposure. In addition, samples of air, soil, local produce, meat, and dairy products were collected to further illuminate the routes of exposure to contaminants.

The Mother's Milk Project founded by Katsi morphed into the First Environment Research Project (FERP), named in recognition of the fact that mothers are the first environments experienced by all humans. Mohawk fieldworkers and their director were paid by SUNY through the SBRP grant, but they worked together under FERP. The First Environment Communications Project, an offshoot of FERP, worked to educate the community about environmental health issues through health fairs, workshops, a radio show in the Mohawk language, and a publication. As described by ATFE members Alice Tarbell (who was also a FERP employee), and Mary Arquette (DVM, PhD), the communications project "provide[d] the community with information on how to cope with contaminants by using culturally relevant strategies. For example, an alternative proteins workshop provided information and training on how to prepare meals using alternative sources of proteins."[80] This came in the form of *First Environment*, a periodical publication, and a series of videos on preparing protein-rich PCB-free foods like tofu.

With funding from the Agency for Toxic Substances and Disease Registry (ATSDR) and NIEHS, the research team carried the breast milk study into a second phase, collecting additional samples in 1991–92, which brought the total number of participants up to ninety-seven. For breast milk samples taken between 1986 and 1989, there was a positive association between estimated lifetime exposure to PCBs from consumption of local fish among Mohawks and their milk PCB concentrations. During this period, Mohawk mothers had

*Painting by Akwesasne Mohawk artist Shirelle Jacobs Tahy
titled* Mother and Daughter, *which illustrates how "woman
is the first environment." Image provided by Fyl Tahy.*

twice the PCB level of control women.[81] Beginning in 1990, there
was no significant difference between the Mohawk mothers and the
women in the control group, due to the Mohawks' decrease in fish
consumption after the fish advisories were issued. Women who had
nursed previous children had lower milk PCB levels; they had excreted more PCBs from their bodies through milk fats because of the
longer time they had spent breast-feeding. Concentrations of PCBs
increased with maternal age (older women had consumed more fish
over their lifetimes) and alcohol consumption during pregnancy, due
to the adverse effects of alcohol on the liver's ability to metabolize
PCBs.[82]

During this period, new techniques were also being developed, including a "fingerprinting" method to identify the point sources of PCB exposure by matching congener patterns found in breast milk samples with those in fish. While the concern and assumption had been that PCBs would migrate from the General Motors site to the fish in the Saint Lawrence, and then into Mohawk bodies, Fitzgerald and his team were able to show definitively that this was in fact what was happening. Analyses of local fish found that those collected near the GM site were contaminated with the same lightly chlorinated congeners as the sediment collected offshore from the plant. The primary contaminant found was Aroclor 1248, the commercial mixture used by all three industries near Akwesasne on the New York side. Fish taken from other locations not near GM contained the more heavily chlorinated congeners characteristic of Aroclor 1260, a ubiquitous contaminant more typical of Lake Ontario, the source of the Saint Lawrence.[83] Tests found that the breast milk of the Mohawk women who ate the most local fish had a congener pattern that more closely resembled that of perch caught near the waste site or average sampled fish caught near the reserve, compared with Mohawk women who ate less fish or the women in the control group.[84] These results were significant because they demonstrated that PCBs could be definitively traced as they migrated off-site from industrial sources to the fish and from the fish to the women. These studies made tangible a sentiment Katsi expressed when the results from the first breast milk studies came in: "I began to realize, We're part of the dump. If this is in the river and in the GM dump, then the dump is in us."[85] Residents often refer to how in the past the Saint Lawrence River was the lifeblood of the community; through its pollution, Mohawk bodies were directly contaminated as well.

Another new technique that was developed and field-tested enabled the analysis of PCBs in the urine of Mohawk mothers and their infants.[86] Low levels of PCBs were detected in the mothers' urine, with half of the Mohawk and control mothers having reported concentrations. In contrast, all of the five infants tested had detectable PCBs in their urine that was ten times higher than that found in their mothers. There was also a significant association between PCB concentration in the urine of the infants and how long they were breast-fed, which confirmed that nursing infants are exposed to PCBs from breast milk. While this sample was very small, this transfer of PCBs from mother to child demonstrated that contaminants had worked their way up the food chain to the community's most vulnerable members.

PCBs were also found in blood samples taken from community members, at levels similar to those in women who had taken part in other studies who had no unusual exposures to PCBs. Levels of PCBs were found to be related more closely to fish consumption than to residing near the GM site.[87] Fish consumption also affected the PCB body burdens of men in the community, as men who ate the most fish had a congener pattern similar to the pattern found in those fish.[88] Among the men sampled, there was evidence of lighter congeners that may have been breathed in from PCBs volatilizing from the GM site, but those were only visible in men who did not eat a lot of fish, as the heavier congeners from the fish tended to drown out evidence of the lighter congeners.[89]

For the purpose of understanding the implications of research results like these, scientists compare contaminant levels found across different study groups to determine a toxicity threshold. This approach is based on the idea that, as the Centers for Disease Control and Prevention (CDC) states, "the presence of a chemical does not imply disease. The levels or concentrations of the chemical are more important determinants of the relation to disease, when established in appropriate research studies, than the detection or presence of a chemical."[90] That is, it is taken as a given that environmental chemicals and their breakdown products are always present in the human corpus. We all have thousands of chemicals in our bodies, many of which we are powerless to do anything about. For many Akwesasne residents, participation in these studies was their first real exposure to concrete representations of their precise toxic body burden. For some of the participants, it was not satisfying to hear that their PCB levels were comparable to those found in people in other communities who had also had the dubious honor of being studied.

In nearly all of the papers they published on their findings, Fitzgerald's team highlighted that the PCB levels in participants at Akwesasne were not elevated in comparison to those found in other studies. The levels found at Akwesasne were similar to those seen in a variety of populations—nursing mothers in North Carolina, people in Atlanta, Georgia, and people from two communities in Ontario—and lower than those in populations that ate more fish, including the

Ojibwa people of Wisconsin, Lake Michigan charter boat captains, and the Inuit of Hudson Bay.[91] In each case, the levels in Akwesasne were found to be comparable to or lower than those found elsewhere. While these studies could not tell Mohawks what the numbers meant for their health, they could confirm that they were in good company, faring better than some and not much worse than other communities that had been studied.

One of the problems that residents saw with the first round of studies was that they only determined numbers that represented the amounts of contamination present inside of them—they did not offer concrete predictions for their health or confirm a correlation between the illnesses they saw in the community and the contamination. Such outcomes were not considered possible due to the small size of the community and the lack of scientific understanding about how PCBs actually affect the human body through chronic low-level exposure. The first round of studies quantified specific contaminants in blood and breast milk, recorded numbers to stand in for people, and then compared them to numbers in other similar studies. Because these studies found congruence regarding levels of toxicants present in different populations, the numbers were not considered alarming. On the other hand, several Akwesasne community members expressed that "zero would be a good level" and spoke against assuming that the presence of contaminants is normal just because it is seen across multiple populations.

After Brian Bush returned the first seven milk samples to Katsi in 1986, he wrote to her, "You will be glad to note that the present levels are well below those of the 1979 suburban Americans." Yet Katsi continued to press for more studies, more research. I asked her if receiving Bush's letter made her feel any better, and she replied that she was used to science "poo-pooing" the Mohawks' concerns, and felt that the problem ran deeper than that. She did not think that Mohawk women were like 1970s housewives, physically, culturally, politically, or environmentally, and so was not comforted by the information that they had levels of PCBs in common, even if nothing else. She drew a parallel between that comparison and the fact that most science, including the determination of acceptable exposures to contaminants, is based on research conducted on young white men. Katsi was also trying to drive home the concept that while everyone was discussing the Mohawk subsistence lifestyle, breast milk is the most important part of that subsistence. In addition, she was beginning an "empowerment model of research," as she calls it, designed to gather information to answer community questions, a concept she continues to carry on today in her push for "centering pregnancy" programs in local clinics.[92]

The researchers compared the Akwesasne data with data from other studies in order to situate each of their published papers within the scientific literature, but at the same time, by reporting Akwesasne residents' results alongside results from other communities with similar or higher levels of PCBs, the general impression they conveyed was that one should not be too concerned. Even within the research team, there was no clear consensus as to the level of hazard the Akwesasne community was facing. One of the researchers from SUNY Albany, David Carpenter, who has been known to take an activist stance toward community health issues, recalled:

> I remember long arguments about what we say, about what levels were dangerous. We tried to avoid that as much as possible. I'd still tend to think it's more dangerous than some of my colleagues do. I think time is proving me right but, you still—there's no benefit by frightening people and they can't do anything about [the PCB levels].

In the articles they published, Fitzgerald's research team qualified their efforts to normalize reported PCB levels by comparing the levels to those in other study populations, making statements such as the following: "Caution must be exercised regarding health implications, and the possibility of subtle, long-term effects such as disruption of the endocrine system cannot be ruled out."[93] While the results they found in Akwesasne may have been similar to those found in other communities, this did not necessarily mean that the levels of PCBs in Akwesasne did not pose potential future health risks. Several of the health studies participants expressed frustration at receiving numbers back that represented levels of PCBs in their blood but not gaining any sort of understanding of what this meant for their personal health or the steps they should take to rid their systems of these contaminants—other than the continued avoidance of local fish.

Other environmental health research studies have found that for their participants, a "perception of 'average-ness' allayed concerns of health risk."[94] This was not necessarily the case in Akwesasne. For some participants, having their results normalized on the basis of being similar to those seen in other studies did not make them feel better about their own results; rather, it made them concerned about the "norm." One woman, Leona, was worried about her breast milk and wondered in regard to her infant daughter at the time, "What am I passing on to her? Is she going to be all right?" She was surprised when the results letter informed her, as she put it, "well, you're about equal to everybody else. So it's like, holy! What kind of world are we living in!? [laughs]." Her expectation was that as a woman living on Raquette Point, considered to be one of the most contaminated regions of the reservation, her levels would be dangerously high. The fact that they were comparable to the levels of other Americans made her feel concerned for those other Americans more than it made her feel relieved for herself. Another woman, Jean, and her husband received results that indicated that they were in the normal range, but they felt that the range must have been pretty wide for them to be considered normal—they expressed concern about what defined the "normal range" at the same time that they were somewhat relieved to be considered within that range.

Despite the comparisons of Akwesasne results to average PCB levels, when I directly asked some community members if they worried about contamination in their bodies, more responded yes than no.[95] Of those who were concerned, many cited either their own past health concerns—including battles with cancer, thyroid disease, and fertility issues—or what they saw as elevated rates of diseases like cancer in the broader community. Among those residents who were not concerned, for two of them this was specifically because they use traditional medicines to cleanse their systems, in order to ensure that they do not have to worry about the presence of contaminants in their bodies. In many ways, the political bodies that were supposed to ensure that these contaminants did not find their way into their individual bodies in the first place (the federal and state governments, which set regulations regarding pollution emissions, and the agencies that were supposed to police these industries and ensure thorough hazardous waste cleanup) have failed them. In light of this, these individuals have taken it upon themselves to eliminate the contaminants from their own bodies. Another man, Jake, who said that he was too concerned about the scope of environmental issues in general to be worried about contamination in his own body, joked later outside of the interview that he was afraid to lose weight because then all the PCBs in his fat would enter into his bloodstream. For some who were not concerned about contamination in their bodies, the study results they received informing them that their contaminant levels were relatively low contributed to their lack of concern. Two of these women happened to be FERP employees who were initially subjects of and also later worked on these studies. Having closer contact with the scientists who ran the studies and witnessing the work that went into the research could have played a part in establishing their trust in the study results. Another woman thought for a moment when I asked if she worried about the contamination in her body and then replied, "No, I don't worry about it. I'd rather be at peace," indicating that the other option was to give in to a sense of powerlessness that went along with worrying about test results.

Superfund Basic Research Program Studies, Round 2: 1995–2000

In 1995, the SUNY SBRP researchers received a renewal of their grant to continue to conduct studies at Akwesasne. Fitzgerald left the project at this time because his time was stretched thin over too many other research commitments. David Carpenter continued to serve as the lead principal investigator, and he was joined by Lawrence Schell, jointly appointed to SUNY's Anthropology Department and Epidemiology and Biostatistics Department, and Joan Newman from the Educational Psychology Department. Together they developed the Mohawk Adolescent Well-Being Study (MAWBS) to examine the effect of PCBs on adolescent development. Azara Santiago-Rivera and Gayle Morse in the Counseling Psychology Department began a project to examine biopsychosocial well-being among adult residents. Maria Schymura in the School of Public Health ran the Epidemiology/Biostatistics Core (Epi-Core), which oversaw all data collection activities, and additionally examined the effects of PCBs on older adults.[96] The second round of studies not only reported on measurements of PCBs found in Mohawk subjects but also linked PCB levels with potential health effects. While earlier research had sought to quantify the amount of PCBs in Akwesasro:non bodies relative to other exposed populations, this round of studies sought to create a more nuanced image of the types of PCBs present in these body burdens and to examine the potential health impacts caused by them.

During this time, the science around PCBs continued to develop, allowing for a deeper understanding of how different types of PCBs might affect human health differently. As mentioned previously, the category of PCBs includes 209 different congeners. All PCBs contain between one and ten chlorine atoms attached to two benzene rings connected by a carbon–carbon bond at the 1,1′ position, resulting in a biphenyl. During the process of manufacturing PCBs, chlorine atoms are attached to the biphenyl with chlorine gas. Within biological systems, the toxicity of any PCB congener is dependent on both the number and the position of each chlorine atom on the biphenyl ring. Greater toxicity is generally associated with a higher number of chlorines—higher chlorinated congeners tend to last longer in the body and are most frequently acquired through eating contaminated food or occupational exposure.[97] Lower chlorinated congeners are lighter, more volatile (and thus breathed in), and more water soluble, and are more quickly metabolized from the body. Their presence in samples indicates more recent exposure. However, in addition to the number of chlorine atoms present, their position on the benzene ring also determines their toxicity. PCBs with chlorines in the ortho positions of each ring (positions 2, 2′, 6, and 6′) are less toxic than non-ortho or mono-ortho PCBs. Non-ortho PCBs, also known as coplanar PCBs, bind to the aryl hydrocarbon receptor in the body and are capable of producing dioxin-like effects similar to TCDD, causing health impacts such as cancers and immune suppression.[98] Coplanar PCBs have a greater biological toxicity than non-coplanar PCBs and are the most stable and resistant to degradation.[99]

Aroclor 1248, the commercial mixture used by GM, contained fifty individual PCB congeners, each of which has a different physiological impact on living organisms, depending on its shape and weight.[100] Because of this, as the technology became available it became important for the SUNY SBRP researchers to measure the different individual congeners of PCBs present in samples, to determine the correlation between health impacts and higher versus lower chlorinated PCBs and non-ortho (dioxin-like) or ortho-substituted PCBs.

The second round of SBRP studies sought to determine levels and types of PCBs and their impacts on health in both adults, through the Bio-Psychosocial Adult Well-Being Project and the Epi-Core, and youth, through the Mohawk Adolescent Well-Being Study. MAWBS included 271 youth ages 10 to 16.99 years, who had been born between 1979 and 1989—some before and some after fish advisories had become prevalent. The youth had been exposed to PCBs in utero through their mothers' blood, which brought nutrients to the developing fetuses. They had also been exposed through breast milk, as the lipophilic contaminants bound themselves to the high-fat liquid. In addition, the youth were exposed as they grew up—both through eating fish, although this became less and less common after fish advisories were issued in the 1980s, and through inhalation, as lighter-congener PCBs volatilized from contaminated sediment and soil. As a result of these myriad exposures, the adolescents tested in these studies fell in the ninety-third percentile for PCB burden in the United States.[101] These levels were considered consistent with chronically exposed groups, but lower than those associated with severe food contamination.[102]

Data were collected from more than 750 adults during this second round of research, although most of the individual studies drew from smaller, specific subsets of this group.[103] In general, men tended to have higher levels than women—the men were more likely than the women to be occupationally exposed and were also less likely to follow fish advisories. In addition to being more likely to follow the advisories (which specifically listed "women of childbearing age" among those who should avoid fish entirely), women could shed PCBs through childbirth and breast-feeding. Older Mohawks had higher levels than younger, as they had been accumulating these persistent pollutants over longer periods. Samples taken from Mohawk participants included PCB congener profiles that represented Aroclor 1248, from GM, as well as Aroclor 1254, believed to have come down the river from industries on the Great Lakes.[104]

The various research projects conducted during the second round of SBRP studies found that higher PCB levels were linked to thyroid problems and cognitive impacts in youth and adults, as well as issues involving sex hormones that could potentially affect reproductive capabilities. The researchers also linked higher PCB levels to greater rates of diabetes and heart disease, illnesses more frequently attributed to poor diet and exercise. These impacts likely compounded the effects of the unhealthy diet that the researchers noted in dietary surveys, contributing to obesity.[105] Below, I present a summary of the results of these studies, but I recommend that readers seek out the research papers themselves for much greater detail and more nuanced explanations of the results.

One of the main foci of MAWBS was the impacts of PCB body burden on participants' thyroids. The thyroid is important for regulating metabolism, growth and development, and body temperature.[106] An overly simple summary of the findings from a decade of work by Schell and his team is that exposure to PCBs can have negative impacts on thyroid function; further, there is likely a prenatal window in which this damage can occur. Additional postnatal exposure can then contribute to the development of autoimmune thyroid disorders.[107] The relationship between serum levels of PCBs and reduced thyroid function appeared to be stronger in adolescents who had not been breast-fed, even though adolescents who had been breast-fed had higher serum PCB levels and greater levels of persistent PCBs.[108] Schell's team concluded that prenatal exposure to PCBs alters thyroid function in a long-lasting manner.

Their follow-up Young Adult Well-Being Study with the youth (by then 17 to 21 years old) showed that persistent PCBs were associated with an elevated level of anti-thyroid peroxidase antibodies (TPOAb).[109] TPOAb, which are produced by the immune system and may attack thyroid cells and damage thyroid function, are often used as a diagnostic marker for some autoimmune diseases. Chillingly, this study indicated that the PCB levels in the youth were lower than those found in other studies, suggesting that "PCB exposures at levels commonly found in the U.S. population and elsewhere could promote autoimmune disease if exposure occurred during a critical window. . . . Exposure to background levels of PCBs may in fact increase the risk of acquiring an autoimmune disease."[110]

Thyroid issues were also observed in Akwesasne adults: the researchers examined the health records of patients at the Saint Regis Mohawk Health Services who presented from January 1992 to January 1997 and found that hypothyroidism and diabetes showed higher age-specific prevalence than in the general U.S. population, especially in postmenopausal women.[111]

PCBs were also found to affect sex hormones in both adolescents and adults. While the specific mechanisms of the effect of PCBs on reproductive function are not known, "modification of the hypothalamic-pituitary-gonadal axis has been proposed as a likely means of action."[112] The researchers also found that higher levels of certain estrogenic PCB congeners found in Mohawk girls led to earlier menarche among those girls by about half a year.[113] Among adult men, testosterone concentrations were found to be inversely correlated with total PCB concentrations, but especially with the congeners found in fish, leading to the conclusion that exposure to some but not all PCB congeners was associated with lower concentration of circulating testosterone in males.[114] Similarly, among adolescent boys, the researchers found that exposure to the more highly persistent congeners of PCBs in particular was associated with lower testosterone levels.[115] During a community presentation, SBRP principal investigator David Carpenter joked with the audience that if the men had to take Viagra, they should blame PCBs, although he quickly followed that by saying, "Is this significant enough change to really be a disease? No! But it's a way that PCBs interfere with our normal bodily functions."[116] In addition, a study currently being conducted by Schell and his colleagues is examining the impact of PCBs on reproductive hormones in adult women. Preliminary results indicate that higher levels of PCBs decrease the likelihood that a woman will have the type of regular menstrual cycle necessary to enable her to conceive and maintain a pregnancy.[117]

PCBs were also found to have cognitive impacts in both adolescents and adults. Negative relationships were found between PCB levels and two separate measures of long-term memory, and between PCB levels and a measure of comprehension and knowledge.[118] In examining whether certain types of PCBs were more likely to affect test scores, the researchers also found that almost all congeners associated with cognitive outcomes were non-dioxin-like and ortho-substituted.[119] Using a test of general intelligence involving nonverbal multiple-choice measures, they found that the scores were negatively associated with levels of dioxin-like congeners of PCBs, a result that attests to the neurotoxic effects of PCBs. For auditory processing, scores were negatively related to levels of the persistent (highly chlorinated) congener group. Low scores on delayed recall, long-term memory retrieval, and comprehension/knowledge were associated with the nonpersistent congener group. Joan Newman's team also conducted a study examining the possibility of a relationship between PCB levels and behaviors related to attention-deficit/hyperactivity disorder, but did not find any relationship.[120] Newman noted that on visual processing tests, Akwesasne adolescents scored much higher than the average in the United States, something she described as not surprising considering the amount of beautiful artwork produced by members of the community.[121]

Among the adults studied, the researchers found that after age, gender, and education were controlled for, PCB levels above a threshold of 2 parts per billion (ppb) were significantly related to executive functioning, motor function, and memory.[122] Results appeared only in the thirty-seven to seventy-nine age group. At levels between 2 ppb and 25 ppb, significant deterioration was observed in two of the three variables that make up the executive functioning cluster. In addition, the researchers found a similar threshold effect, largely among the older group, for a test of fine motor behavior and finger dexterity required to manipulate pegs on a grooved pegboard test. Finally, they observed a weaker, but discernible, threshold effect of PCB exposure on a measure of logical memory.

While Newman's research team emphasized that, overall, "the data indicate that the participants in the study were functioning cognitively, on average, similar to comparison adolescents in the normative groups," and Haase et al. noted that "even the poorest level of performance on these variables does not rise to the level of clinical concern," Carpenter stated during a community presentation, "We showed that the increased PCB exposure was associated with reduced mental function in both adolescents and adults, and from my judgment, that is one of the most serious things, because one's whole ability to hold a good job is a function of the brain, and you don't want something messing with your brain."[123] Describing the impact of PCBs on cognitive functioning of Akwesasne Mohawks became a delicate dance between emphasizing the injustice of experiencing any kind of decrement because of contamination and not stigmatizing the community or overemphasizing a loss of cognitive function among residents.

The relationship between metabolic disorders and PCBs was also explored in this round of research. Diabetes and heart disease are prevalent in Akwesasne—the community's rate of heart disease is almost three times that of the general U.S. population.[124] While illnesses like diabetes and heart disease are most frequently attributed to poor diet and lack of exercise, or to genetic predisposition, the SUNY research team found that PCB body burden could contribute as well. Even after age and body mass index (BMI) were controlled for, individuals with higher levels of PCBs (of all types) tended to have higher levels of total serum lipids. The researchers concluded that PCB exposure stimulates liver function, as the P450 enzymes are produced to rid the body of the contaminant, and this causes the overactive liver to synthesize excessive amounts of cholesterol and triglycerides, which can then contribute to heart disease.[125]

The researchers also found a significant association between serum PCB and pesticide levels and diabetes, even after age, sex, BMI, serum lipid levels, and smoking habits were controlled for.[126] Although they noted that these results do not establish cause and effect, the researchers pointed to a growing body of evidence that exposure to persistent organochlorine compounds is associated with elevated rates of diabetes. In continuing to analyze these data, Carpenter's team has found that people with higher levels of the more lightly chlorinated (non-dioxin-like, less persistent) congeners had significantly elevated risks of developing diabetes.[127] These findings point to the health impacts of breathing the volatilized PCBs coming from the GM site.[128]

The findings from the second round of the SUNY SBRP research began to be published in the early 2000s, and some articles are still in process as this book goes to press. The community's response to these results, the format of the studies and the results report-back, and the timeline of the broader research and publication of the findings are discussed in detail in chapter 3.

Superfund Site Cleanup

Over the past three decades ATFE, the Saint Regis Mohawk Tribe Environment Division, the EPA, and NYSDEC all worked, in various ways and in varying levels of agreement, to have the General Motors Superfund site cleaned up, in order to prevent additional contamination from entering the surrounding environment and the bodies of Mohawk people. The cleanup process consisted of a series of compromises, in the end dominated by "the ironies of science, corporate power and neoliberal governance" that are endemic to what environmental anthropologist Peter Little describes as "mitigation politics."[129]

Under EPA oversight, GM placed a cap on the Industrial Landfill in 1987 to prevent further migration of contaminants while the fate of the site was being decided. Because the GM site was so large, the cleanup process was addressed in stages. In 1990, the EPA issued a Record of Decision that divided the site into two "operable units," designated OUI and OUII. OUI pertained to the cleanup of the settling lagoons, the North Disposal Area, and the contaminated river sediments. The ROD called for the excavation of all soils on the GM site contaminated above 10 ppm, dredging of contaminated river sediment, pumping and treating of the groundwater, and on-site treatment of the contaminated sludge and soil. A 1999 amendment to the ROD allowed for the waste to be transported off-site to be disposed of in a landfill elsewhere.

In 1980 and 1984, the EPA adopted official Indian policies that aimed to allocate more responsibility for the development of environmental standards to qualified tribes.[130] These were then followed by amendments to federal legislation. In 1986, as noted earlier, amendments were made to CERCLA that directed the EPA to treat qualifying tribal governments substantially the same as states when it came to establishing cleanup standards on tribal lands.[131] In 1987, amendments to the Clean Water Act allowed the EPA to delegate programs for establishing water quality standards to tribes, and 1990 amendments to the Clean Air Act allowed similar reallocation for air quality standards.[132] Because of this series of amendments, when it comes to cleaning up Superfund contamination on tribal lands, tribal "applicable or relevant and appropriate requirements" (ARARs) are treated consistently with state requirements—meaning that if a tribe adopts standards that are stricter than those put in place by the federal government, the portion of cleanup that affects reservation land must meet the stricter standards.[133]

In 1989, the SRMT developed ARARs for PCBs of 1 ppm for soil and 0.01 ppm for sediment, numbers far lower than the state and federal standards that were applied on land outside the Tribe's jurisdiction (1 ppm for sediment and 10 ppm for soil).[134] In reflecting on the process through which the Tribe chose the standard, Jim Ransom stated: "When we set the Tribal ARAR for PCBs, we recognized that it had to be scientifically and technically achievable. Our preference would have been zero. However, our lawyers advised that this would not meet technological requirements." Instead, after consulting with Ward Stone and other scientists and considering the standards in other states (such as Washington), the SRMT chose standards that were both achievable and strict enough to deliver the desired results for the community. As Ransom explained:

> We decided on the numbers based on our community's reliance on the natural world to support subsistence lifestyles. Our hope was that by setting on-reserve cleanup standards that were more stringent than state or federal, it would help lead us back to the natural world. It fits in with our seven generations philosophy that states we have to have confidence that the people seven generations from now can look back and say we made the right decision in evaluating the decisions we make today.[135]

Because of the SRMT's status as a federally recognized tribe, and thereby a sovereign entity, the EPA was bound by law to follow the stricter standards for cleanup on Mohawk land.[136]

That the Mohawks were pushing for stricter standards than those applied to the general public was a recognition of the differences between the average American and the Mohawk tribal citizen. As members of ATFE note, Akwesasne's cries for environmental justice were brushed aside by government agencies that stated that Akwesasne was not being treated any differently than any other community, ignoring that Mohawk people and culture are "unique." They write:

> Akwesasne, like many other Native communities, needs additional consideration and more stringent remediation. Standards and regulations have been tailored to meet the needs of industrialized society, not subsistence cultures and endangered peoples. These standards are often minimalist in nature and do not begin to address special tribal rights. Conventional risk assessments which drive remediation are severely limited in their application to Native peoples because they fail to adequately value cultural, social and religious factors as well as sovereignty, treaty rights and issues of self determination.[137]

For this reason, the SRMT Environment Division worked to enforce stricter cleanup standards than the EPA would ordinarily impose.

The position taken on the cleanup by residents of the neighboring town of Massena was diametrically opposed to that of the Tribe. The Tribe called for the landfill to be excavated to prevent any further exposure of Mohawk people in the future, but Massena residents called for it to be capped, concerned that too great a financial hardship would cause GM to lay off more workers. During a public meeting held in Massena on April 25, 1990, several Massena residents bristled at statements made by Akwesasro:non and the descriptions given by EPA staff, arguing that their town should not be described as "an industrial wasteland," "a chemical wasteland," or "an environmental wasteland."[138] Frank Alguire, director of the Massena Economic Development Council, called for a "factual, scientific and objective approach to the issues. We need to, if we can, separate emotion and politics from our task at hand," which he saw as remediating the site in the least economically detrimental way possible.[139] Since their livelihoods had not been disrupted to the same extent as those of their Mohawk neighbors downstream, but rather relied on the presence of employing industries in the area, Massena residents downplayed, and took offense at, the characterizations of environmental contamination.

Contention grew as the EPA formulated the cleanup plan for OUII to address the East Disposal Area and the Industrial Landfill, which covered twelve acres and contained waste that was buried between ten and twenty feet below the surface of the landfill. During a meeting hosted by the EPA in Akwesasne on June 26, 1991, to present the plan for remediating this second operable unit, Akwesasro:non were displeased with the EPA's plan to contain, rather than excavate and treat, a great deal of the contaminated materials. The level at which contaminated material would be capped rather than excavated and treated changed from 10 ppm to 500 ppm, which made the cleanup more affordable for GM. This change was imposed because the EPA had produced a document to guide the treatment of PCB contamination for all industrial sites in which the EPA was involved, and that document called for less rigorous standards than those the EPA, NYSDEC, and the SRMT had agreed upon for the original GM remediation plan. Jim Ransom responded angrily on behalf of the community:

> It is obvious to me that EPA has prepared their PCB guidance document so that they can justify to themselves circumventing

the Superfund law and selecting remedies that are not permanent. The message that you are sending is that "if you are going to pollute, do it on a large scale and you won't have to clean it up. We'll let you cover it up." After the cap on the GM landfill is finished, EPA should erect a monument in honor of their failure to enforce the Superfund law, and of their failure to protect Mother Earth.[140]

Other Akwesasne residents at this meeting similarly stood up and commented that the EPA was pandering to the corporation rather than protecting the environment or Mohawk health. As Wesley Laughing stated: "EPA has chosen to follow the cleanup directives of the corporation, General Motors, instead of residents of Akwesasne. Mohawks feel that we do not have a chance with the EPA or General Motors. . . . GM's high-priced lobbyists and consultants had persuaded the EPA to lower it's standards."[141]

In 1992, the plan for OUII was officially released, and as the Mohawks had feared, it reflected the financial interests of the industry, stating that GM was to excavate materials from the East Disposal Area in excess of 500 ppm (rather than 10 ppm as in the OUI decision) and then cap the area. For the Industrial Landfill, the EPA chose to upgrade the cap and continue to collect and treat groundwater. NYSDEC and the SRMT were outraged and refused to sign the consent decree because it was not stringent enough.[142] In addition, GM threatened legal challenges to the 1990 remedy, and in 1995, under GM's influence, the EPA proposed that the treatment levels associated with the OUI decision be raised from 10 ppm to 500 ppm, meaning that any waste with concentrations below 500 ppm would be contained on-site rather than excavated. This change would mean that GM would have to dredge and/or treat only 54,000 cubic yards of soils instead of 171,000 cubic yards, saving $15 million.[143] During a public session regarding GM's request to alter the remediation levels, Mohawks cried "environmental injustice," "genocide," and "environmental racism," lamenting the continued impact the PCBs would have on their ability ever to eat muskrats or fish out of the river.[144] After much additional public outcry, the EPA withdrew the plan.

In the fall of 1995, GM completed the dredging of PCB-contaminated Saint Lawrence River sediments. The cleanup goal was not met in all areas, so a multilayer cap was placed over the sediments. Dredged sediments were shipped by rail to a hazardous waste disposal facility. The cap has proved problematic—according to members of the SRMT Environment Division with whom I spoke in 2007, the engineers initially did not believe their assertions that ice scouring (damage inflicted on the cap by sharp chunks of ice) would be a problem, but ice scouring has occurred in shallower parts of the river, necessitating the application of additional layers of rock to protect the cap.

From July 2000 to August 2004, GM worked on the remediation of the two inactive lagoons at the facility. Contaminated sludge and soils surrounding a 1.5 million-gallon lagoon and a 350,000-gallon lagoon were excavated, stabilized, and shipped to an off-site facility. From August 2002 to September 2003, GM remediated the Raquette River bank soils and sediments, meeting the goals of 10 ppm PCBs for soils and 1 ppm for sediments. In the fall of 2003, GM completed removal of contaminated soils at the top of the slope of the Industrial Landfill, which reached out toward Akwesasne. From October 2004 to March 2005, GM remediated Turtle Cove, now known as "Contaminant Cove." Here Tribal standards were applied: 1 ppm for soil and 0.1 ppm for sediment. Groundwater remediation is currently ongoing.[145]

Despite Massena's efforts, the 2008 U.S. financial crisis affected the viability of General Motors Corporation, and the GM Central Foundry in Massena was closed in 2009. In April 2009, the U.S. government gave GM $49.5 billion in bailout money, but the company filed for bankruptcy that June and spun off a holding company, Motors Liquidation Company, to handle its idle properties. When it emerged from bankruptcy, General Motors LLC was freed of responsibility for rehabilitating dozens of toxic waste sites in thirteen states where it had manufacturing plants.[146] In the spring of 2011, the RACER (Revitalizing Auto Communities Environmental Response) Trust assumed ownership of eighty-nine former General Motors properties. This $773 million trust is tasked with completing remediation and ultimately selling off dozens of former GM properties left behind after the bankruptcy.[147] The Massena factory was dismantled and shipped away by rail, and its hazardous materials were taken to a hazardous waste dump in Indiana. The new GM, freed of its old liabilities, has reachieved success in the auto market, while the residents of Massena who fought to shelter the company from high cleanup expenses are left without jobs and the Mohawk are left living adjacent to a landfill that they suspect will continue to pollute their environment. According to the EPA's 2010 report about the GM site, "institutional controls" like fish advisories recommending that Mohawks do not eat contaminated fish are considered, when combined with the remedial actions that have been completed, as measures that "address unacceptable exposure pathways."[148] This report takes for granted that fish advisories are an acceptable tool for preventing human exposure, similar to a cap on the river bottom that isolates contaminated sediment.

The twelve-acre landfill of PCB-contaminated waste now sits under a cap of clay, geotextile, and grass. The EPA has plans to move the landfill 150 feet from the border of the reservation, but many residents, as well as scientists like David Carpenter who have worked with them over the years, think the landfill should be removed entirely away from the reservation.[149] As Carpenter noted after his recent presentation to the community that included information on how volatilized PCBs were contributing to diabetes rates, as long as the material remains so close to the reservation, there is a risk of Mohawks being exposed.

The Thompson family property is immediately adjacent to this landfill. Dana Leigh Thompson calls the actions of GM "environmental genocide" and a continuation of George Washington's 1779 order to colonial troops to lay waste to their settlement.[150] Her husband, Larry Thompson, decided to take matters into his own hands, and in August 2011 drove his backhoe through the fence surrounding the site and began digging up the landfill himself. Thompson was arrested, and when he was arraigned in Saint Lawrence County court in February 2012, he entered the courtroom wearing traditional Mohawk attire and refused to answer the court's questions regarding a plea "because he doesn't recognize the court's jurisdiction or NYS Law, and wouldn't abide by American law, but instead Tribal law."[151] On December 11, 2012, he returned to court and entered a guilty plea to a reduced charge of criminal mischief for his deeds, a fourth-degree misdemeanor in New York, and agreed to a five-year order of protection barring him from the site.[152] For now the landfill cap has been repaired and the site continues to be slowly deconstructed, although its possibilities for reuse, as well as the extent to which it will continue to pollute the Akwesasne community, remain up in the air.

Civic Dislocation, Environmental Governance, and Community Action

Many Mohawk people went into the experience of advocating for the cleanup of the contaminating industries with a distrust of state and federal (and in some cases tribal) governments and their accompanying agencies and academic institutions. Throughout the cleanup process, their interactions with the state and federal agencies reaffirmed for members of the Akwesasne community their impression that these entities were not working in their best interest. In many instances Mohawks experienced what Sheila Jasanoff calls "civic dislocation," which she defines as

> a mismatch between what governmental institutions were supposed to do for the public, and what they did in reality. In the dislocated state, trust in government vanished and people looked to other institutions . . . for information and advice to restore their security. It was as if the gears of democracy had spun loose, causing citizens, at least temporarily, to disengage from the state.[153]

The dislocated state is characterized by a breakdown in communication between the government and its citizens, and a distrust that the government is playing the role it should of protecting the public "against the complex uncertainties of the modern condition."[154] Without the ability to assure the public of this protection, public institutions lose legitimacy, and other entities sometimes step in, or are created, to ensure safety.

Akwesasro:non have had a contentious relationship with New York State and the U.S. federal government for more than two centuries, and this was further compounded by the lack of support they felt they were receiving for the cleanup. Of the Akwesasne community members I interviewed, several articulated a general distrust for the state and federal governments, and others took the view a step further with the belief that these entities were actively working to undermine Akwesasne. One man, Loran, asserted that there are spies on the reservation paid by the state, federal, and county governments. When I asked him what kinds of things these governments are so interested in learning about the community that they would pay people to be informants, he replied, "Well, if we are going to start a march to go and shut down that plant they want to know so that they get their police ready. Is it a violent protest, is it a peace protest, is it somewhere in between? All of that stuff. They put their information feelers in there." Another man, Henry, expressed the belief that Mohawks have their current status because the federal government never defeated them. "If they got the opportunity they'd come in, shoot people, and declare the Mohawks defeated. Then the state would have control of the place." Hearing about the lack of institutional support from the state and federal environmental agencies for a thorough cleanup, in some cases to save GM money, further entrenched many Mohawks' feelings that these agencies were not just failing to protect them; according to some, the agencies were actively working to harm them.

Like other communities fighting for environmental justice, Akwesasne suffered through mitigation politics, fighting against a powerful corporation whose main goal was to protect its bottom line, and working both against and alongside state and federal agencies— agencies that were in many cases underfunded, understaffed, and mired in bureaucracy, and whose interests were sometimes influenced by industry. What made Akwesasne different from other communities fighting similar corporate powers was that as a tribal nation, the Saint Regis Mohawk Tribe had federally ensured rights and powers to dictate cleanup levels on tribal land, and to have a seat at the table negotiating the site cleanup. Given the previous two and a half centuries of history in which Mohawks clashed with settler colonial powers regarding jurisdiction over and governance of the Akwesasne Mohawk community, that they were able to develop and assert their own environmental governance, and then collaborate with entities in New York State, is indeed impressive and important.

This level of advocacy and environmental governance required a combination of resource-based and relationship-based forms of tribal organizing. Cherokee scholar Clint Carroll argues that a resource-based approach is necessary in order for American Indian nations to take control over tribal resources that have been mismanaged by the federal government. He goes on to state that the establishment of tribal environmental programs has been an important contribution to the assertion of tribal sovereignty, but this has been accompanied by the need to maintain complex bureaucracies that are often impediments to the utilization of traditional environmental relationships, values, and practices. Many traditional Native people believe they have a responsibility to maintain relationships with nonhuman beings in a way that acknowledges the agency of those beings. In many ways, the relationship-based approach has been absent in much of tribal policy, since the development of bureaucratic tribal departments is based on U.S. federal models.[155] In Akwesasne, the SRMT Environment Division now has departments devoted to air quality, brownfields, solid waste management, water resources management, wetlands protection, Natural Resource Damages Assessment, hazardous materials, and Superfund oversight. As former Environment Division employee Lorni Swamp notes, "Driven by necessity, the Environment Division has become one of the most advanced tribal environment programs in the country, partly due to its experience with the severe contamination from the aforementioned industries."[156] But at the same time that this resource-based environment program was developing, the broader community of Akwesasne was also forming relationship-based organizations (like MASH and ATFE) geared toward transgressing tribal political divisions and bringing together the members of the collective community to advocate for themselves and their nonhuman relatives.

Contending with the industrial contamination in Akwesasne required the community to interface not only with state and federal environmental agencies but also with research- and health-based institutions. After experiencing a health study conducted by Mount Sinai researchers that left them feeling uninformed and disempowered, Akwesasro:non prepared themselves to take greater initiative in the second large health study to come to Akwesasne. Women had watched as scientists collected fat samples from fish, livestock, and humans, but they were not convinced that this necessarily informed them about whether the community's most basic form of subsistence, breast milk, was safe for their infants. Intent on finding out, they overcame ingrained distrust toward New York State and initiated a partnership with NYSDEC and NYSDOH, and eventually with researchers at SUNY Albany. The resulting health studies were valuable in that they supplied the information that Mohawk mothers were initially seeking—they learned that the levels of contaminants in their milk were low enough that it was considered more beneficial for them to continue to breast-feed than to switch to bottle-feeding. The studies also demonstrated a mechanism by which Mohawks could decrease further exposure: the unjust and highly inconvenient remedy of decreased fish consumption. What the studies were not able to answer were participants' questions about their individual health, at present or into the future. It took a decade of academic papers before the members of the SUNY research team were able to potentially link levels of PCBs with conditions in the community, illnesses that some community members were certain were caused by contamination. The residual effects of these studies in the community vary from person to person. Individuals who served as fieldworkers on the studies still have strong opinions about how things were done, and how they potentially could have been done differently; I discuss their views in the next chapter. Many others only remember that they are not supposed to eat the fish because that is where you are exposed to PCBs, and PCBs are bad for your health. Others, like MCA Department of Environment employee Henry Lickers, point to the fact that "just the mention of PCBs, whether seen as high or low, is enough to scare people and screw everything up." Critiques of how the study results were communicated and suggestions for research going forward are presented in the next chapter.

CHAPTER 3

"We're Not Going to Be Guinea Pigs"
Lessons from Community-Based Participatory Research

In December 2014, I sat in the packed dining room of the Tsi Tete-watatkens Saint Regis Mohawk Senior Center along with more than one hundred community members who were there to hear what the scientists from SUNY Albany had to say. The researchers were to report on all of the studies they had completed in Akwesasne, concluding with a study that Lawrence Schell's team had recently completed in collaboration with the Saint Regis Mohawk Health Services clinic to determine the impact of PCBs on women's menstrual cycles. Dana Leigh Thompson, a vocal and politically active community member whose relatives live directly adjacent to the General Motors dump, coordinated the event, advertising it on the radio and in the local newspaper. Everyone seemed surprised by the turnout; in contrast to past years, when researchers' community presentations were attended by more scientists than audience members, the room was packed to capacity. For many of the scientists, this was a homecoming of sorts—while Schell had been in the community the year before to report on the progress of the recently completed reproductive health study, some of the other scientists who were presenting remarked on how good it was to be back a decade after they had completed their research projects.

The event was opened and closed by a student from the Akwesasne Freedom School reciting the Ohen:ton Karihwatehkwen (Thanksgiving Address), a long prayer in the Mohawk language that acknowledges the relatedness of Mohawk people to the Creator and the natural world. The prayer was offered, as it is at any significant event in Akwesasne, in recognition of the cultural importance of the gathering as well as the growing body of young Kanienkeha (Mohawk language) speakers. After the prayer, Dana Leigh and the local tribal environment directors, Henry Lickers from the Mohawk Council of Akwesasne and Ken Jock from the Saint Regis Mohawk Tribe, described the history of the contamination and the research studies and expressed gratitude for the amount of time the SUNY scientists had invested over the years. As Henry noted:

> To have a group of people like this, who have the tenacity to stay with us for as long as they did, is amazing. You know, if we had to do consulting work this way, we would've been long broke, but now we have people who really do want to continue to work with us, so I thank you very much [claps].

A majority of the community members in attendance stayed for the entire three-hour presentation, getting up periodically to fill plates of food, occasionally murmuring comments to their neighbors, and then asking questions of the scientists, ranging from questions about concerns regarding the fate of the GM dump and the reproductive future of Akwesasne to basic questions about what PCBs are and whether they can be flushed from the body.

The scientists spoke of "contaminants"—specific PCB congeners and pesticides found in samples that should not have been there, substances that were inadvertently released and are now found where they do not belong. Community members in turn referred to "poisons," indicating that these were not merely substances out of place, but rather chemicals with the ability to injure, impair, or even kill, which had been allowed to permeate their homeland. "Poisons" are toxic substances used to intentionally cause harm. This difference in language use demonstrated the divergence in thinking between researchers educated in toxicology and members of a community that has felt under threat by outside forces for centuries. The presentation concluded with Dana Leigh's insistence that there would be more such meetings, and more research: "We have all the evidence that our people are really suffering because of what's happened, so I thank you for coming, and hope that you continue to come out and help and find the solution. Together, we've gotta find the solution." Despite two decades of intensive research and the feeling of being "studied to death," many Akwesasro:non expressed an interest in continuing to pursue research into the impact of PCBs on their health.

This meeting came at the culmination of more than twenty years of environmental research partnerships between Akwesasne and SUNY Albany, and reflected the salient themes of communication, report-back, and partnership that pervaded this research process. In part, this chapter focuses on the process of studying environmental health, examining the impact of this research partnership not only on the community but also on the scientists themselves. The anthropological study of various forms of Indigenous knowledge has been a staple for the discipline, but it is only in recent years that this lens has been turned on laboratory science.[1] This is what Tim Ingold describes as anthropology *of* science, or what Laura Nader has called "studying up"—turning the ethnographic lens on those in society who wield the power.[2] In addition, recognizing that science, like any other form of cultural knowledge, is, as Paul Nadasdy notes, "embedded in larger social processes which give it meaning," Ingold describes the need for an anthropology *between* science and society, examining the impacts of scientific knowledge and practices on social life and how people have responded to them.[3] Scholars of science and technology studies have argued that science is fundamentally a social endeavor and have demonstrated that scientific knowledge is the outcome of culturally situated practices.[4] Native studies scholars who have interfaced with science and technology studies, such as like Kim Tall-Bear, Gregory Cajete, Kyle Whyte, and Robin Kimmerer, similarly challenge the view of science as objective, arguing that what counts as science is culturally relative, that Indigenous knowledge should be better incorporated into what counts as science, and that it is important that Indigenous interests are protected in the production of scientific knowledge.[5] As TallBear notes, "The exercise of indigenous sovereignty in the twenty-first century depends in no small part on how indigenous peoples account for the roles of technoscientific knowledge production."[6] This chapter focuses on this important issue by examining how one Indigenous community worked to control the ways in which scientific knowledge was produced with and around the community's people.

In examining the lay/scientist divide, other scholars argue that rather than trying to place science more firmly within society by revealing that it has a culture, just like everything else, it is more beneficial to bring society into science, making science more accountable to society.[7] In this context, we have witnessed the rise of ethical monitoring in Western knowledge institutions, with scientific proposals increasingly judged by the explicitness with which they identify both the usefulness of their research (to society) and their provisions for ethical monitoring.[8] As I argue in this chapter, another way to bring society into science is through community-based participatory research, which strives to blur this divide somewhat by making researchers and the communities they study partners in defining and implementing research projects. Social scientists' call for democratizing science and environmental policy turns natural scientists' call for focusing on "public understanding of science" on its head, suggesting that scientists incorporate the insights of the public rather than just critique the public's grasp of scientific facts.[9]

There is also a social justice component to the call for CBPR. After decades of traditional health and environmental research that left many studied groups—especially low-income communities and communities of color—feeling disempowered, community involvement in the production of science is being heralded as necessary for the achievement of environmental justice.[10] Many Indigenous communities are beginning to speak back to years of research exploitation and are now insisting on a community engagement component to any research conducted with their peoples.

The discussion in this chapter is based on a subset of the interviews I conducted while I was working on the research for this book. In March 2008, I traveled to SUNY Albany and the offices of the New York State Department of Health to interview seven scientists who had conducted health studies at Akwesasne from 1986 onward. While dozens of scientists worked on the Superfund Basic Research Program studies, I spoke only with those who conducted health-related research and had direct contact with community members. In the interviews, they spoke about their experiences in organizing the studies and in working directly with Akwesasne community members, and they shared their ideas about how they might conduct the studies differently if they were to do them again. Then, from June through November 2008, I interviewed sixty-four Akwesasne community members, thirty-two of whom had been involved in the environmental health studies in some capacity.[11] These interviews pertained to the health studies, perceptions of change in the health and environment of the community, and participants' suggestions for improvement of future environmental health research.

In this chapter, I examine the benefits to both the local community and the researchers of being part of the first major CBPR project conducted in an Indigenous community, a project heralded by CBPR scholars and Indigenous communities alike as an example for others looking to conduct similar research in communities affected by environmental contamination.[12] In addition, I discuss some of the challenges faced when two groups of people with very different histories and cultural paradigms come together to work collectively, yet from very different seats of power.

Community-Based Participatory Research

Under the umbrella of citizen science—broadly defined as science conducted by scientists and laypeople (nonscientists) working in partnership—there are varying levels of public involvement in the initiation of a research project, research design, data collection and analysis, and dissemination of results. Human health impacts are often identified through local citizen science, in which laypeople engage in research design, data collection, and analysis.[13] "Street science" and "popular epidemiology" are approaches utilized in community-driven projects in which laypeople employ scientific methods to answer questions about or draw attention to issues in their communities, often working independently of research institutions.[14]

Street science is a practice of knowledge production that embraces the coproduction framework and combines local knowledge with a scientific approach to achieve better solutions for environmental health problems.[15] A subset of street science is popular epidemiology, a "process by which lay persons gather scientific data and other knowledge and resources of experts in order to understand the epidemiology of disease. . . . It involves social movements, utilizes political and judicial approaches to remedies, and challenges basic assumptions of traditional epidemiology, risk assessment, and public health regulation."[16] These approaches reverse the order of a traditional contributory citizen science model—in which the public just collects data—and resemble more of a cocreated project, entailing the initiation of research by community members, who also gather the scientific data and, if necessary, recruit scientific professionals.[17]

Popular epidemiology and street science are often utilized to initiate more formal community-based participatory research projects. CBPR is an approach that focuses on conducting research with—rather than on—communities. It is "a collaborative process that equitably involves all partners in the research process and recognizes the unique strengths that each brings. CBPR begins with a research topic of importance to the community with the aim of combining knowledge and action for social change to improve community health and eliminate health disparities."[18] CBPR is not a method but rather an orientation to research that takes "a more democratic and ecological approach to scientific study."[19] This approach has been embraced by the public health field as a means of creating more inclusive and effective public health interventions, and by social scientists as a means for achieving broader community input and greater community acceptance of research projects.

CBPR has received considerable attention in the past decade as an important alternative to the previous model of research that separated the researchers from the researched and applied a top-down model of scholarship. Chavis et al. use the term "experimental colonization" to characterize the traditional relationship of scientists to many host communities, where subjects are often left feeling exploited and believing that they will not benefit from the research.[20] The main tenet of CBPR is a reshaping of the research process to redistribute some of this power by including community members as coproducers of knowledge rather than as passive subjects. Schell et al. note that part of the ongoing postmodern critique of how knowledge is produced within the sciences is a "critique of the essentialized and disempowered research subject. This critique reconceptualizes the people who we study, or the researched, from passive objects/subjects of our research to one of active agents, or participants in research who have their own interests, priorities, and agendas."[21] Reconceiving of study *subjects* as active *participants* requires a dismantling of barriers between the researcher and the researched, a sharing of power, and an emphasis on colearning and dialogue. This shift in power dynamic inherent in CBPR can help to reduce the understandable distrust of research on the part of communities that have historically been the "subjects" of such research.[22]

Among the many principles of CBPR (which have been reviewed extensively by scholars such as Minkler and Israel), one of the most important is recognizing the community as a unit of identity and building on the strengths and resources in the community.[23] CBPR also facilitates collaborative equitable partnership in all phases of the research and promotes colearning and capacity building among partners. Rather than providing the sole source of design for the research project and educating the community with the results, the researchers are expected to elicit and incorporate community suggestions while being open to learning along the way. CBPR also emphasizes the local relevance of public health problems and ecological perspectives that recognize and attend to the multiple determinants of health and disease. In addition to balancing power dynamics within the research process, the rationale for conducting CBPR includes the need to improve the quality and validity of research itself by engaging local knowledge and local theory based on the lived experiences of the people involved.[24]

An important element of CBPR is the requirement that researchers report results to the community of study and include the community in the analysis of these results.[25] Knowledge is power, and thus all partners involved should be able to use the knowledge gained through research to direct resources and influence policies that can benefit the community.[26] Decisions about reporting community-level information, as well as about whether and how to report results to individuals (a topic discussed in greater detail below), should be based on four principles: autonomy (right to know), beneficence (potential benefits to participants), nonmalfeasance (avoidance of the potential for results to cause fear, worry, or stigma), and justice (distribution of benefits and harms).[27]

In recent years, community–academic partnerships using a CBPR approach have played an important role in bringing attention to and addressing situations of environmental injustice.[28] In the rest of this chapter, I explore how the Mohawk community of Akwesasne utilized popular epidemiology and CBPR to determine the health impacts of environmental contamination on tribal members, the benefits and challenges of this research, and ultimately what is still to be gained.

Native American Communities and Research Studies

For a number of racial and ethnic minority groups in the United States, mistrust of research is rooted in a general mistrust of mainstream society, where exploitative or unethical treatment remains a serious problem.[29] Historically, research conducted on Indigenous peoples has served to advance "the politics of colonial control," which is often obsessed with classifying and labeling Indigenous peoples in an attempt to "manage" them.[30] Research studies conducted on Native Americans have often been exploitative and have not contributed to community empowerment. In many cases, researchers have entered with predeveloped projects, failed to ask for community input, pressured people into taking part, treated Native people as subjects or informants and not as colleagues, sensationalized problems in the communities in their publications, and used Native people's blood samples for unauthorized projects.[31] In some cases, the confidentiality of community identity has been violated, attracting negative attention and creating difficulties. In one situation, a reservation was identified in a study on syphilis; in another case, a community received adverse credit ratings after being identified in a study on alcoholism.[32]

Frequently, as discussed in chapter 2 in regard to the Mount Sinai research study, results are not properly reported back to the community. This has led to the belief that researchers cannot be trusted. Among the negative views that community members have expressed are that researchers receive career advancement from their studies of tribal communities, while the communities themselves get poorer; that researchers are disrespectful of cultural practices; that research studies are actually designed to harm Indians; that participation in disease studies may cause the disease to manifest in one's family or the community; and that the benefits of studies rarely reach tribal members. Many complain that results are not shared with the tribal community, or, if they are, they are presented in a way that is too technical to understand.[33] Overcoming this legacy of past research projects is one of the difficulties that researchers now face when they embark on studies to explore and address community problems.

Many of the problems associated with research in Native American communities boil down to issues of power: traditionally, the researchers coming into the community have had most of the power over the research project, and the Native subjects have had very little. Much of the literature on community-based research connects the issue of trust directly to that of transforming the power imbalance between the researcher and the community under study through properly implemented CBPR. Mohawk scholar and Native studies professor Marlene Brant Castellano recalls sitting at a community meeting at which Indigenous people were complaining that they had been "researched to death" (a comment I also heard, verbatim, more than a few times at Akwesasne). One elder spoke up and declared, "If we have been researched to death, maybe it's time we started re-searching ourselves back to life." Castellano notes that "researching ourselves may mean self-initiated action or it may mean entering into effective partnerships."[34] Creating the appropriate framework for these partnerships has become one of the central issues in the development of CBPR for Native communities.

Language of Science and Power

Citizen groups often seek to utilize science because of the power that scientifically derived results have to either reassure community members or give them cause for concern about their health. Such results can also prove that what community residents already feel to be true is indeed true. As noted in chapter 2, Katsi Cook went to the New York State Department of Health looking for numbers that could help Mohawk women decide if they should continue to breast-feed; she also hoped to find out whether some of the reproductive effects she had been seeing could be attributed to the contamination. Scientific results are also a necessary component of efforts toward policy change or legal recourse, especially in battles with polluting industries, where simple observations of environmental destruction or poor health are often considered insufficient evidence.

By virtue of their relation to state power, some ways of convey-ing information are legitimated as "official" or "formal," while oth-ers are suppressed.[35] The people of Akwesasne found it difficult to describe and draw attention to the environmental contamination in the community because they were not using the language of scientific study results. Mohawk science, based in generations of observations and interactions with the physical environment, could not provide sufficient legal evidence regarding the changes in and destruction of this environment. In discussing the difficulties Mohawks faced in telling their story of the effects of pollution on their territory, Akwesasne Mohawks Alice Tarbell and Mary Arquette note, "There is not even a word for pollution in the Mohawk language."[36] Indigenous legal scholar Rebecca Tsosie describes this as epistemic injustice, in which Indigenous peoples have been harmed by the domestic legal system in their capacity as "givers of knowledge" and in their capacity as "subjects of social understanding."[37] Similarly, Arquette et al. describe how

> vastly different languages, cultures, and worldviews present real barriers to effective communication. At Akwesasne for example, elders, mothers, children and other community members have presented eloquent testimony about social, cultural and health effects they have experienced as a result of contamination of area ecosystems. The presentations of effects such as these have been met with resistance, a few yawns, and overt eye-rolling, and deemed "nice stories" with little relevance to scientific discussions of risk-based scientific decision making.[38]

It was only when a sufficient number of wildlife, sediment, and breast milk samples were demonstrated to contain high enough levels of PCBs that some action was taken, although still not at the level that Mohawk people would prefer. The method of conveying concern about the impacts of contamination had to conform to the requirements of the linguistic field of the audience, which in this case was made up of environmental health scientists. As anthropologist Paul Nadasdy notes in his work describing interactions between Kluane First Nations people and wildlife biologists in "comanaging" natural resources, the production of knowledge is an inherently political process. The political context in which knowledge is produced and legitimated has a direct effect on this process by placing constraints on what can qualify as knowledge and the uses to which that knowledge can be put. Struggles over knowledge are not waged on an even field, as the terms under which these struggles take place tend to favor certain conceptions of knowledge over others. Indigenous people are free to construct and produce environmental knowledge according to whatever cultural criteria they wish, but if they want to see that knowledge actually used in negotiations, they must express it in a way that conforms to those criteria specifically sanctioned by state power.[39] In short, in communicating with the scientific, political, and legal communities—whether in the context of resource co-management and land claims, as Nadasdy describes, or in the case of Akwesasne establishing environmental damage—the public needs to take on the language of science and use scientifically sound methods to demonstrate levels of contamination discovered and numbers of community members ill. To acquire this language, community groups often engage in popular epidemiology or other forms of citizen science to gather scientific data, understand the epidemiology of disease, and conduct risk assessment.

However, with the language of science, and specifically epidemiology, comes a difficult set of principles, many of which may run counter to a community's beliefs about life itself. In their discussion of the Agency for Toxic Substances and Disease Registry's interactions with the public over sites of environmental contamination, White et al. note:

> Accepting language of epidemiology along with its principles requires reconceptualizing things like death. Epidemiologic principles and terminology routinely accepted by researchers can be complex or controversial in the community setting. For instance, the concept of "expected" deaths or the "significance" of an event can connote something different to a resident than it does to a researcher. Training can be provided to help community residents become more informed users of epidemiology, but this training should be tailored to local needs.[40]

Note that training is recommended for community residents only to help them overcome the shock of this use of language. As purveyors of the language of power, the epidemiologists in this case can speak of concepts like "expected deaths" while suggesting training as a solution to reduce community members' alarm about the language. "So how many people have to die?" asked Lloyd, a former Mohawk Council of Akwesasne chief. "We don't have that many around here to decide that." This sentiment was expressed several times in Akwesasne as people wondered how many of their community members had to pass in order for the numbers to be considered significant, noting that in their families each death from illnesses like cancer felt incredibly significant. However, in order to garner the support necessary to take political or legal action against the polluting industries, the community had to engage with science, observing the "forms and formalities of that field," in Nadasdy's words, and at least tacitly accepting some of its assumptions.[41]

CBPR in Native American Communities

Because of the current necessity of utilizing this language of power—that is, scientific results—tribal communities continue to engage in research projects. But for such projects to be successful, the appropriate approach needs to be taken. Because of past research abuses in Native communities, CBPR is seen as necessary in many places. Whether the research is ethnographic or concerned with health promotion or community water quality, as Potvin et al. note, programs "can no longer be applied as universal technical solutions to local problems without being transformed by the context," namely, the wishes of the community they are intended to serve.[42] CBPR is being heralded as useful for reducing health disparities and ensuring delivery of health care that is culturally appropriate and relevant to Native communities, whether the issue of interest is children with chronic disabilities, cancer prevention, or myriad other health issues.[43] In discussing the importance of CBPR for research in Indigenous communities, Cochran et al. note that "the way researchers acquire knowledge in indigenous communities may be as critical for eliminating health disparities as the actual knowledge that is gained about a particular health problem."[44] CBPR can not only encourage a greater level of participation by tribal community members but also build community capacity and the tribe's ability to carry out its own health research and program implementation.[45]

Important to note is that while CBPR is seen as a necessary method for working with ethnic minority groups, a tribe is not simply another ethnic minority group; tribes are also sovereign nations, with their own governments, courts, laws, health care systems, and citizenship rules.[46] In many Native communities, tribal police enforce tribal laws and patrol borders. Health care for tribal nations is generally delivered through tribal clinics, primarily funded by the Indian

Health Service, or by traditional healers. Tribal institutional review boards (discussed below) determine whether or not research can be conducted in some Native communities. Recognizing that CBPR cannot be conducted in exactly the same way in tribal communities as in other communities, researchers in the fields of cancer research, public health, psychology, and environmental health have laid out key principles for conducting CBPR in Native communities.[47] While the eight key principles that are frequently noted in the CBPR literature are important to apply to work in Native communities, researchers must also consider these communities' particular contexts and histories. [48] In addition to applying the eight key principles, researchers should (1) acknowledge the community's historical experience with research and with health issues, (2) work to overcome the negative image of research, (3) recognize tribal sovereignty, (4) differentiate between tribal and community membership, (5) understand tribal diversity and its implications, (6) plan for extended timelines, (7) recognize key gatekeepers, (8) prepare for leadership turnover, (9) interpret data within the cultural context, and (10) utilize Indigenous ways of knowing.[49]

CBPR is a useful approach for conducting research in Indigenous communities, but it is not without its challenges for researchers. These challenges include navigating tribal politics, as a turnover in tribal government can affect support for a research project.[50] Adhering to research timelines and maintaining sufficient funding to sustain a project to the end—which includes interpreting and disseminating data in conjunction with the tribe—can also be challenging.[51] Coordinating tribal oversight, employing culturally specific assessment and intervention methods, and incorporating community involvement necessarily lead to longer timelines than are usual for conventional research studies, and budgetary considerations can be complicated, as a portion of project funds must be devoted to including community members.[52] Many researchers also find the shift in researcher–community relationships in CBPR challenging, as control over the decision-making process is less unilateral in this research than it is in conventional studies.[53]

Today, CBPR is seen as the gold standard for research in Native communities, a necessity if research is to continue after decades of research abuses. However, the community members of Akwesasne (including ATFE members and FERP staff) and the researchers from

SUNY Albany were navigating CBPR at the beginning of the movement, before most of the currently available literature on the subject
was published. As such, the Akwesasne experience makes an interesting case study in the development of CBPR in the Native community—a case that is cited today as one of the pioneering efforts
in this work.[54]

Tribal IRBs

One of the ways in which Indigenous communities have tried to
codify the relationships between researchers and communities, and
to ensure that the research conducted will benefit the communities,
is by developing tribal institutional review boards. For more than
three decades now, universities and other institutions conducting research on human subjects have been required to have IRBs to screen
research projects. Past unethical research projects like the Tuskegee
Syphilis Study, conducted by the U.S. Public Health Service, led to
the National Research Act of 1974, which created the National Commission for the Protection of Human Subjects of Biomedical and Behavioral Research. This commission developed the *Belmont Report*,
which outlines the primary ethical principles for research involving
human subjects, including respect, beneficence, and justice.[55] Any
institution receiving federal research money is required to have an
IRB to review human subjects research to ensure that research protocols adhere to the principles of the *Belmont Report*.

For some tribal communities, it was not enough that the institutions desiring to work with them approve of their own research
projects. U.S. federal regulations reflect a society that values individual autonomy, yet some cultures place a higher or equal value on
family, clan, or other identity group. Drawing from this, if individual
rights are to be protected, so too should cultures or communities that
may have different needs or may be affected differently by research
than are individuals.[56] As sovereign entities, some tribes (like the Navajo Nation, the Mi'kmaq, the Kahnawà:ke Mohawk, and the Akwesasne Mohawk) have begun developing their own IRBs to control the
types of research that are conducted in their communities and to take
agency over how the results are disseminated. This is an important
step, as a survey of federally funded "community-engaged research"

projects in 2009 found that having a tribal agency in place to approve research studies was associated with more control over and a greater share of resources for communities, as well as and a higher level of formal agreements about data use and research dissemination.[57]

The Akwesasne Task Force on the Environment, composed of members of the community and the staffs of tribal environmental agencies, was formed in 1987 to contend with environmental problems at Akwesasne. The ATFE Research Advisory Committee was formed in 1994 to develop and review proposals for research that affects the people of Akwesasne.[58] The ATFE RAC developed the Good Mind Research Protocol under three main guiding principles: skennen (peace), kariwiio/kanikonri:io (good word/good mind), and kasatstenhse:ra (strength). These three components of a fair and successful research process reflect the idea that from peace comes respect, from a good mind comes equity, and from strength comes empowerment.[59] A research proposal submitted to the ATFE RAC needs to demonstrate that the planned study will respect the culture and needs of the community, that the resources and power derived from the research will be shared with the community, and that the project will empower the community by hiring and training community members and by providing useful information back to the community. The goal of the advisory committee is to help ensure that the proposed research will benefit the whole community, give the people of Akwesasne opportunities to be involved in decision-making processes during the research, and empower those involved through education, training, and/or authorship.

As detailed in the Good Mind Research Protocol, a research team must begin working with ATFE in the earliest stages of study planning, so that community members have sufficient time to thoroughly review and understand all aspects of the proposed research. The research team must submit a synopsis of the project that includes information about the methods that will be employed, how the project results will benefit or harm the community, how confidentiality will be protected, how data will be stored, and how study participants and the community at large will be fairly compensated through grant money and shared authorship.[60] If the project is approved but the researchers then fail to meet protocol's stipulations, ATFE reserves the right to (1) withdraw consent for the researchers to use or release information and/or prevent the publication of data that are unauthorized or sensitive, that misrepresent or stereotype Mohawk people, or will harm the health, safety, or welfare of the Mohawk people of Akwesasne or their environment; (2) deny the researchers (and future researchers from the same university or institution) the opportunity to conduct further research in Akwesasne; and (3) withdraw approval for projects, in which case all information and copies of data must be returned to the community.

ATFE formed the RAC and published the Good Mind Research Protocol at the halfway point in the SUNY SBRP studies. Some of the SUNY researchers felt that they had been working with the community in an equitable and empowering way, and they were surprised to be presented with this document. David Carpenter, the lead principal investigator on the project, described the research experience and his response to the protocol:

> It hasn't been necessarily easy or without a lot of bumps in the road but we did negotiate very directly about what the respective roles would be and who would do what. . . . At the last moment, after we had pretty much done all these—what they issued was not the joint document we had expected but a "this is the way it will be" kind of document which was fairly irritating for a number of our people. I mean I sort of understood it. I didn't get terribly upset about it.

The SUNY team agreed to abide by the terms of the protocol and continued to work with community members, collecting data and publishing results.[61]

First Environment Research Project

Part of what made the research conducted at Akwesasne a CBPR project was the Mohawk community's insistence that the SUNY research team hire and train local residents for the project, as opposed to employing professional researchers or graduate students. This was an important means of promoting equity and empowerment, as laid out by the Good Mind Research Protocol, but it was also seen as necessary for recruiting study participants. As Katsi Cook has described:

At the very outset, I demanded that the only way we're going to work with Mohawk women in the precious intimacy of Mohawk mothers' milk and our relationship to our young is to ensure the mothers that they are co-investigators in this study. There's not going to be any one of you researchers that stand taller than the Mohawk mothers. We're all of the same height, which is a traditional principle in our longhouse. That we're not going to be guinea pigs. You're not going to run back to your funding agency with our analyses before you tell us. Those are our tissues. That's our data. It doesn't belong to your funding agency first. We want control over how this happens.

And so, in fact, in the generations of research that followed from that, we were able to position fluent Mohawk women speakers to do the field work, to go collect the samples.[62]

Katsi began the First Environment Research Project as a means of organizing Mohawk women fieldworkers and coordinating the data for the health studies. As described previously, she collected most of the samples for the pilot study in 1986. She also recruited women whose babies she had delivered at home—like Trudy Lauzon, a bright woman who is fluent in Mohawk and has an extensive network of relatives, which was helpful in identifying who was going to give birth and could be recruited into the study. When Katsi became pregnant with twins, she suggested that the scientists hire Trudy to take her place. She said the initial response from the scientists was "She doesn't have a degree." To which Katsi replied:

Why does she need a degree?! Train her in venopuncture, train her in the protocols, you don't have to be—this is not rocket science, this is human interaction to get a milk sample. The women have got to know you, got to trust you. You've got to know what it feels like to nurse a baby, what it means when—to know how to recognize when your milk lets down. How to problem solve in that visit. "I can't get a sample," well you know what, let's take it easy, let's make tea, go have a hot shower, I will watch the baby. Don't you know, they've got to trust that you are not going to be doing something weird to their baby while they are in the shower. You know, it has got

139

to be complete trust, and who are you going to have that for, except someone you have known all your life.

Trudy, whose milk Katsi had collected in the pilot study, ended up working on all of the SUNY SBRP human health studies in the follow years, work that she described to me as a very rewarding eleven-year job.

FERP staff members had an office in Akwesasne, but they were hired through the Epi-Core of the SBRP at Albany. The researcher at the head of the Epi-Core explained that since the fieldworkers were to become research foundation employees, SUNY had to follow its usual hiring processes (with the exception of Mohawk preference in hiring), advertising positions and conducting interviews. The fieldworkers were all trained in the necessary methods, including how to collect blood and breast milk samples, and for some studies they learned how to conduct cognitive assessments, take body measurements, and administer nutritional surveys. They were periodically videotaped while collecting data, so that the SUNY scientists could make sure that all the standardized procedures were being maintained. Fieldworkers were also retrained at regular intervals in order to prevent measurement drift—that is, to ensure that they were following procedures in the same way for the whole five years of each study. A fieldworker might visit a participant's home three or four times: once to secure participation and set up future visits, then a return visit to collect biological samples and, for some participants, to conduct a psychological evaluation or a dietary survey (or, for some studies, several interviews), and then often another visit to collect samples or conduct surveys again to see if there were any changes. While some of the fieldworkers recalled the job as being difficult (going door to door trying to recruit participants, getting up before dawn to collect fasting blood samples), most of the five women I interviewed about their experiences reported really enjoying the job and learning a lot from the experience. The data these women collected were sent to Albany for analysis, and eventually the SUNY researchers sent letters back to the participants explaining their individual results.[63] The SUNY researchers also hosted retreats at Akwesasne, where they gave presentations to inform the broader community about the progress of the studies.

Benefits and Challenges to CBPR in Akwesasne

Akwesasne community members and the SUNY scientists came to take part in these studies with slightly different motivations. Members of ATFE and FERP wanted to gather the necessary data to determine the health impacts of neighboring industries, with the goal of either allaying the concerns of residents or confirming their fears, forcing the industries to clean up, and achieving financial compensation for damages. The SUNY researchers took part in these studies not only to further their own professional and academic careers but also to help the Mohawk people and other communities affected by PCB contamination better understand the potential health impacts of PCB exposure. The outcomes included forty-seven peer-reviewed publications (which had collectively been cited 863 times as of May 2014) based on the research conducted, which helped to answer some, but not all, of the questions held by participating parties.[64] There were benefits as well as challenges for both sides, many resulting from the negotiations among all parties and the limitations of the types of questions the studies were able to answer. In addition, this extensive project led to some capacity development, both for the FERP fieldworkers as individuals and for Akwesasne as a community, as well as for some of the scientists who participated. Below I discuss the benefits accrued to and the challenges faced by all those who took part in this project, including the benefits and challenges around the understanding and communication of the limitations on the types of answers the research process could provide.

BENEFITS FOR THE COMMUNITY

Akwesasne benefited from the SBRP studies through the information gained from the research, the education and job skills gained by the FERP fieldworkers, and the grant money spent in the community. These benefits resulted in part from the intentions of the academic partners, but they also came about because of the stipulations of the Good Mind Research Protocol.

Because of the requirement that results be reported back to individual study participants, the participants benefited from the information they received about the levels of contaminants in their bodies. Many of the participants I spoke with remembered being surprised when they received their results, expecting that they would indicate higher levels of PCBs and pleased when they did not.[65] For example, one participant who had her breast milk tested told me: "I was thinking it was going to be horrible, but it wasn't. So I was really happy about that." Many of these participants described limiting their fish consumption after fish advisories were issued and before these tests were done, which in all likelihood helped to ensure that their levels were not elevated.[66]

In most conventional research, the academics conducting a study receive salaries while people from the community doing the work are volunteers. In describing successful health research with Native American communities, Burhansstipanov et al. note that a CBPR project in Indian Country rarely succeeds if it relies on volunteerism from communities of poverty, and so it is important that tribal staff members receive competitive salaries.[67] At Akwesasne, the SBRP grant provided tangible benefits for the community through the full-time employment of ten community members, as well as support for local businesses from the SUNY researchers, who purchased everything locally for their conferences. In addition, SUNY offered two classes on research methods and testing measurements, so FERP employees received college credit while training for their jobs. The skills they gained from the training they received in phlebotomy and the administration of various tests had the potential to help the women acquire jobs in hospitals. One of the fieldworkers, Agnes, who is now a community health worker, gained her first practical experience in this field through working at FERP. She expressed that she "got a lot out of it. I was in the community, I had a job, I felt I was doing something." Similarly, another FERP employee, Trudy, described her time with FERP as "the best job I ever had." When I asked her why, she replied, "Because it was so easy to approach people and I was always welcomed into these homes."

Beyond these concrete skills, and in line with the broader principles of CBPR, Lawrence Schell from SUNY noted that "a lot of people involved in the Task Force did get some greater exposure to science, to the industry of science, how papers are produced and so on, and to methods of analysis and questions that scientists have." In addition to helping the community to *understand* science, Schell noted, the researchers wanted the community to be *empowered* by these skills. One of the researchers' aims "was that people in the community would have skills for research methods so that when other researchers would come in, they would be able to say 'We have expertise too.' That was kind of the goal."

Many research needs have been identified in Indigenous communities—areas of interest include environmental degradation, epidemic health threats, and the need for culturally appropriate economic development.[68] Akwesasne Mohawk scholars highlight that "the need for better site- and Nation-specific data emphasizes an important area of research for Native Nations."[69] Often, communities do not have the capacity to carry out the research that they see as needed. Significant disparities exist between tribes and their academic partners in levels of training and resources.[70] For the FERP employees who received training, for the ATFE members who consulted, and for the participants and community members who learned from the study process and results, involvement in the studies was a step toward community capacity building. Mohawk professionals and paraprofessionals gained experience working in the community and were able to go on to seek local employment versus moving away.

Community health scientists Goodman et al. propose two complementary definitions of community capacity: (1) "the characteristics of communities that affect their ability to identify, mobilize, and address social and public health problems," which emphasizes community capacity as an outcome or a characteristic of a community; and (2) "the cultivation and use of transferable knowledge, skills, systems, and resources that affect community- and individual-level changes consistent with public health–related goals and objectives," which focuses on the process by which capacity is created.[71] Reflecting the first definition, determined members of the Akwesasne community—like members of ATFE—possessed these characteristics as people who were used to having to be vigilant in the protection of their land and sovereign rights. They were able to help identify public health hazards and mobilize their own community, as well as the research community, to work to better understand these hazards. Regarding the second definition, CBPR emphasizes capacity building of community members (i.e., ensuring that participants are better off after the process), improving relationships among community members and between community members and "outsiders" (e.g., representatives of government agencies, academics, other professionals) and incorporating local knowledge into the research process.[72] Part of this capacity building is the creation of conditions that will enable community members to to embark on future research that they see as necessary.

To create such conditions, Chavis et al. advocate that scientists and community collaborators form linkages and partnerships in research that will help the people help themselves, a trait that ATFE labels "empowerment."[73] These partnerships must involve more than just returning the study results to community members; they must also help to build a community that is more knowledgeable about research methods and is more self-sufficient. In reflecting on the research conducted at Akwesasne, Schell et al. note, "As we trained research partners in data collection and management, they became better informed about specific research methodologies, and, more importantly, about the conduct of a logistically complex operation."[74] This type of experience, combined with an increase in the number of Akwesasne community members who are acquiring scientific degrees, can eventually lead to an empowered community better able to conduct its own research projects.[75] One of the FERP fieldworkers noted, "That's why I think the Task Force really started going with their incorporation, so we could do research the way we wanted to." She envisions a day when all of the scientists for research projects involving the community will come from the community. One participant, Randi, expressed that because she lives in Akwesasne and took part in the health studies, she has a greater awareness of chemicals that affect the ecosystem and her body. She told me that being a participant in the health studies and a resident of Akwesasne during this pivotal time in its environmental history gave her the vocabulary both to understand and to speak about environmental contamination in a different way than she would have if she had not been exposed to this form of education. In recent years, Akwesasne has had a number of tribal members return with college educations in the sciences and become active in working with the SRMT Environment Division and the health services in the community. In short, engaging in CBPR can benefit tribal nations by increasing both individual and community capacity to conduct research.[76]

BENEFITS FOR SCIENTISTS

The benefits to the scientists involved in this CBPR project with Akwesasne included access to a community that will no longer allow research to be conducted without community members' input and better recruitment than they likely would have obtained without the help of Mohawk fieldworkers. FERP employees and ATFE members worked with the SUNY team to ensure that surveys issued in the community were appropriate, in order to avoid offending people and thus maximize participation. Schell expressed that CBPR-framed studies provide better results for the scientist:

> I really believe that it works better when it involves a community; it's better scientific work. And one reason why it is, is because you often get better interviews and of course you're probably going to get more cooperation in terms of people wanting to be in the study that they're getting asked [to participate in], especially . . . if they're being asked by someone they know and hopefully trust.

As one of the fieldworkers, Trudy, noted, "I believe that's why our projects were so successful. It's because they took somebody from here that knows everybody and they sent them out." Trudy felt that because she is related to so many people in the community, she had an easier time getting potential participants to agree to take part in the study. Working from the randomly generated list of houses, she started by approaching those where members of her family or extended family were living and then branched out from there. She collaborated with one of the other fieldworkers who also had a large family, and if someone was hesitant to participate in the study at the request of one woman, he or she would often agree to participate at the request of the other. Another woman reported that "we had to appeal to people personally to help us with the study," especially since census takers had come through the community with the long form of the U.S. Census at the same time the fieldworkers had been trying to recruit participants. Someone without the personal connections of FERP employees would likely have had a far more difficult time recruiting participants.

Bidirectional education was another benefit accrued through the research relationship. Schell told me that he learned a lot from working on this project, and when I asked for specifics, he mentioned that, among many other things, he learned to listen more, to talk when necessary, and how to communicate better. Another researcher who was in the room during my interview with Schell, and who had worked with him on the project, remarked, "They taught me a lot about their culture and taught me how to look at and perceive things in a different light, in a different point of view." This two-way education is highlighted in an article cowritten by Schell and FERP director Alice Tarbell, in which they describe the university–community partnership as "an opportunity for researchers to learn as well as teach."[77]

In addition to community members' gaining greater capacity to take part in and conduct future scientific research, the SUNY researchers increased their capacity to conduct future community-based research through their experience of working with the Akwesasne Mohawk community. Schell, who led the thyroid studies in the Mohawk Adolescent Well-Being Study portion of the second SBRP project (as well as the follow-up Young Adult Well-Being Study), went on to conduct an additional study with the Mohawk community centered on reproductive health in women (2009–13). Describing the progression of his research career from traditional health studies to CBPR work with the Mohawks, he has noted: "In the future, it seems likely that community willingness to participate in research may not be assumed. Many communities and populations that human biologists want to work with . . . are politically galvanized and expect more from research that is conducted in their backyards."[78] David Carpenter, who worked on both SBRP grants, went on to conduct CBPR with the Yupik on Saint Lawrence Island in Alaska.[79] At a conference organized by Katsi Cook that brought together environmental health scientists and members of Indigenous communities affected by environmental contamination, the Yupik women present thanked the Mohawk women for "training David so well" in how to work with Native communities.[80] Their experiences with the Akwesasne community have positioned both of these scientists, and many of their colleagues, well for future CBPR work with Indigenous people.

In addition to the beneficial aspects described above, there were difficulties in the collaboration that the scientists and the community members had to work to overcome. These included some disagreement about the amount of time various aspects of the study should take, as well as issues of control over what data were collected and how. Such conundrums are common in CBPR work, as well as in CBPR in Indigenous communities, but some of the challenges in this case were specific to this particular community, given the Akwesasne Mohawks' previous experiences with researchers and the state of New York in general.[81]

CHALLENGES OF TIME

The extra time required to utilize CBPR methodologies in a research study can prove challenging, both for researchers attempting to adhere to grantor and publication schedules and for community members who want their results back as soon as possible. In interviewing community participants and SUNY researchers about their experiences in the Akwesasne studies, I found that both groups raised issues related to the amount of time it took to accomplish certain things. The SUNY researchers noted that, because this was a collaborative project, with community input required every step of the way—including in the authorship and approval of research projects—the project took more time than others they had worked on. Joan Newman stated that the project took quite a while because it was important "that we work with the community to develop it rather than do what the scientists think we should do. Which was a different focus and it takes a little longer to put together a project that way." Maria Schymura expressed that even though they had better recruitment because of Mohawk fieldworkers, the process was still much slower than she had experienced in other projects. Newman also admitted:

> It was hard doing research there, much tougher than with any other population I have worked with because—I guess we were so careful, so careful to collaborate at every stage of this. . . . I mean, like you have a deadline for something but you have to go through them. They have a meeting. It's not that week, you know it is slow so it really meant that output from the study in terms of publication and presentations has been slower than it might be from another population because

of all of these necessary steps. I recognize the need for them, but it's been slow.

FERP staff also mentioned time issues that they found problematic, but these concerned the amount of time it took to return study results to participants. Nearly all of the FERP interviewees mentioned that the participants they worked with complained about waiting for their results, which for many subjects were meaningless by the time they were returned. As Trudy noted, "They want answers, but like within a month, they don't want to wait for three years down the road to get the answers." Because of the difficulties of setting up a lab that was certified to return results to participants, some of the samples were held up in the first few years of the study. As Alice Tarbell, the FERP director, described:

> Sometimes it was years before people got their results back, and it was embarrassing. . . . [The results were] irrelevant, and it was embarrassing to us. We would go to the post office, we would go to the supermarket, and people would run into us and say, "Where's my results?" Our hands were tied.

While the scientists conducting the research were willing to adapt to the need for community report-back, this did not mean that the labs they were sending their samples to were prepared to process them any more quickly. For example, the lab in Albany that was set up to test for PCBs was not able to process samples for clinical measures, like cholesterol tests, immediately, and this caused delays. For another study, several labs were involved in the analyses, and so the results came in pieces; also, one of the labs refused to process samples until it received more money to run the tests. When I relayed this information to the FERP employees during their interviews, they suggested that future studies get their labs in order before the researchers collect samples from individuals. In this particular situation, the clock was already running on the time frame designated by the grant for data collection, and so putting off the sample collection could have led to other time issues. But in general, this experience made both the scientists and the FERP employees aware of the necessity of establishing lab specifications at the inception of a study. In addition to the time lag in the processing of samples, fieldworkers and participants mentioned that they had been hoping to gain information about what everyone's results actually meant in terms of health trends in a much more timely fashion. When it came to analyzing the data, Alice noted that they had five years to collect the data for the SBRP, and then at the end of five years, the funding ran out. The researchers still needed to analyze the data, but this was done at a slower pace, because the money was gone and the scientists took on other projects. As a result, the analysis "wasn't happening as fast as the collection period was," and some community members were "waiting and waiting and waiting and waiting," as Alice put it, to see what would come out of all of the data. As noted in chapter 2, even though data collection for most of the studies ended in 2000, and that for the Young Adult Well-Being Study ended in 2003, papers linking the community's PCB levels with potential health effects did not begin to be published until 2004, with a majority appearing after 2007, and more still being written.

One of the researchers, Joan Newman, addressed this, recognizing that the research process takes longer than most people realize, with often a delay of years between when the data are collected and the reports are produced. While this community, like many other communities engaged in CBPR, insisted on the importance of the community seeing the results before publication, Newman felt that the scientific peer-review process was important for ensuring that the results and analyses reported back to the community were sound and valid:

> The way in science that you accept that something is valid is you go through the peer-review process and you have experts review what you have written and say, "Okay, your conclusions are warranted." The whole process is incredibly long and not to mention that you have to do your analysis and write it up and submit it and resubmit it and such. . . . It wasn't that we wanted to keep it from them [the community]. We wanted to not be just giving, you know, things that were going to be proven invalid, because we knew people's lives were impacted. So it was long, so I'm sure they must have felt at some point, and maybe still do, that we didn't give them all the results back. We are still doing that, I have still got students analyzing the stuff and writing it up, and I am doing it, so it is still

coming and it is eleven years later. So I don't see how they
could understand that, you know, not being part of the professional community, the academic community. So I hope they
don't feel that we've done that.

From this scientist's perspective, delays in giving study feedback to
the community are part of the reality of the scientific peer-review
process and reflect the importance of this process for assessment of
the validity of results. The scientists did not want to return results
to the community until they knew those results would stand up to
scrutiny—learning that there was something wrong with the results
after sharing them with the community and then having to retract
them would have had negative impacts. However, from the community's perspective, the wait for information about their health was
too long.

Issues of "ownership" by researchers over particular data can
also slow down the rate at which papers reporting the research are
published. Maria Schymura from the SBRP Epi-Core explained to me
how none of the adult thyroid data had been analyzed or published
because one particular graduate student was using the data in his
work on his doctorate in public health, and "we wanted to wait until
he was done so I am envisioning some papers coming out of that."
Carpenter also noted his regret that he, as the principal investigator,
allowed individual research projects to hold on to "their little pots
of data" for too long in an effort to respect their concerns about authorship. "Everybody's always going to write the paper and analyze
the data tomorrow. Well, I waited six years. . . . And the problem is,
of course, when the funding ends people get other jobs," and then it
is even more difficult for them to publish on the data. He expressed
regret that he now has less money to employ students to look at the
data, but he feels that he has an obligation to the community to learn
all that he can from it.

At the same time, ATFE saw value in the production of articles
about the community's case. In writing about their research experience at Akwesasne, Schell et al. have described how, at the inception
of the adolescent study, they discussed with the community what
the product of the research would be, and "we agreed that peer-
reviewed publication would be of value to the community. A part of

the community's interest focused on the utility of such publications in furthering legal attempts to redress the impact of pollutants in the community."[82] Attempts at litigation against General Motors to date have not been successful because lawyers for the community were not able to prove an absolute link between the contamination and community health. With some of the more recent publications, some community members are again taking up the issue. If further connections between PCB levels and health are found as additional data are analyzed, that information could also be potentially helpful in this cause.

CHALLENGES OF CONTROL OVER DATA AND DISTRUST OF ITS USE

Another area of contention between the research partners was deciding what data would be collected, by whom, and how. Although they understood it was necessary, the scientists found it difficult, and contrary to their training, to give equal control over the data to the community. Schell, who is an anthropologist and epidemiologist, described how FERP field staff would go and collect all of the data: "It was very unlike anthropology, having someone else do your data collection. Would you have someone do your interviews? . . . We had to do that. . . . It's a kind of letting go. You can't be a control freak. You have to really channel that control."

Even beyond relinquishing control of the data collection, the Good Mind Research Protocol states that if members of the community feel that harmful data are being collected, they reserve the right to retrieve those data and keep them within the community. This happened in relation to a cultural affiliation scale that one of the research projects used. Some community members became uncomfortable with the scale and demanded the cessation of its use and that all data collected with this scale be returned to the community. One woman remembered the scale as eight questions, and from these "they could determine how Indian you were, and we didn't like that at all [sarcastic laugh]. We made them return them all, and I think they were destroyed. . . . We didn't think it was their place to determine people's heritage. And that kind of thing could be used against you. It just didn't serve a good purpose."

This distrust toward the possible use of results extended not only to cultural information collected but to the use of blood as well. Two of the SUNY scientists I spoke with related that when they began to develop a continuation plan for the Superfund project renewal grant, the Mohawks refused to allow for genetic study of any kind. Because genetics were a hot issue at the time, and their renewal grant proposal did not include a genetic component, the SUNY team's grant was not renewed.[83] The scientists respected that these were the wishes of the community, but they never fully understood why the Mohawks were so opposed to genetic testing. When I was interviewing FERP employees, I asked them why they thought the community was so resistant to this form of study, especially after being party to so many other types of research. The answers were similar to those about the resistance to the cultural affiliation scale described above: it was feared that the government could and would use and distort any genetic information gathered to "prove" somehow that Akwesasne Mohawks are no longer Indians. The community's past experiences, especially with the state government, supported this concern.

One of the fieldworkers, Loralee, described the scenario in terms of government programs that non-Native people think the Mohawk no longer deserve on the basis of being a distinct population:

> The big concern among the staff is that there's always been this big push to prove that Mohawks aren't Indian anymore . . . because the big thing that people would say is "Oh, you're not anything special. You've been mixed up with all these other races for so long that there's no such thing as a Mohawk anymore."

She pointed out that it would be difficult to do any kind of genetic analysis based on the data they collected anyway, because some of the people who took part in the study were not Mohawk by blood. Some couples who participated included non-Native partners who had been living in the community for more than twenty years: "We figured they are just as exposed as everybody else here. They're eating the same food, drinking the same water so we let them take part too." The inclusion of non-Native family members was natural if the point of the study was to determine the health impacts of contamination on all community members, but that inclusion also meant that not all samples represented "Mohawk blood."

Community concerns about the misappropriation or misinterpretation of samples and data by New York State were a theme throughout the studies. As described in chapter 2, Katsi Cook sent the first blood samples to an outside lab, because she did not trust that the NYSDOH lab would give her accurate results. After the SBRP project began, the first batch of blood samples that were sent to Albany, to the Wadsworth Lab, were stored for an extended period of time but not analyzed, and that caused the community to become nervous. Alice, the FERP director, described the concern in the community: "They weren't letting us have the blood samples, and there was a fear at the time that New York State, the Department of Health, Wadsworth Center is going to use those blood samples for genetic testing. At the time, the Human Genome Project was a big thing and they really wanted Native blood to look at." As the community became increasingly anxious and distrustful, FERP decided that the best thing to do would be to bring the samples back to Akwesasne. The FERP office had a freezer that was capable of keeping the samples preserved until a course of action around analysis could be set. More than two hundred samples were stored there until an epic ice storm struck the community. There was a power outage, but Alice managed to secure a generator to keep the freezer operating. She was eight and a half months pregnant at the time, but she and another worker, Agnes, took turns going down to the office three or four times a day to make sure the generator had enough gasoline and oil. It was imperative that these samples be preserved, because if the fieldworkers went back and collected new samples from the participants, the samples would not match the interview data, and an incredible amount of time would be lost. They kept the generator going for five days before making an arrangement with researchers at SUNY Albany to meet them in Lake Placid, New York, where they handed off the samples and the documentation of chain of custody. Shortly after that, the lab was able to begin processing the samples. This anecdote illustrates the fragility not only of the samples but also of the entire research process and the maintenance of relationships in this type of research.

Once the samples began being processed, since the serum was the only part of the blood analyzed, the Mohawks insisted that anything left over be destroyed. As Loralee explained, this was "so somebody couldn't come in and say, 'Oh, well, you're not using these red blood cells, I'll just take them for my study,'" and then conduct research with Mohawk blood that the community might not approve of and that could prove detrimental. The Mohawks' fear of having their blood misappropriated for unauthorized testing is not unfounded: the Havasupai Tribe in Arizona took part in a study focused on diabetes only to learn later that participants' blood samples had been used in research on schizophrenia and consanguinity, as well as in research on migration theories. The community felt deeply betrayed that their blood, which they had allowed to be collected for a project that was supposed to help them, was then used without their permission in other studies. But rather than punishing the scientists who participated in this betrayal, the system rewarded them. The geneticist who was the key person responsible for the misuse of the blood samples was awarded the Presidential Award for Excellence in Science, Mathematics, and Engineering Mentoring, followed by a million-dollar NIEHS grant.[84] A similar betrayal happened to the Nuu-chah-nulth, who agreed to take part in a study on rheumatoid arthritis; the samples collected were then sent around the world, without the participants' knowledge or approval, and were used in research on human migration as well in studies that resulted in hundreds of academic papers on controversial topics, such as the spread of lymphotrophic viruses by intravenous drug use.[85]

To some scientists, especially those convinced of their own ethics and good intentions, the fears of the Akwesasne Mohawks may seem like paranoia. Akwesasne is clearly a Native American community, culturally, ethnically, linguistically, politically, and, as the membership records with blood quantum requirements show, "racially." But Akwesasne has a long-standing and well-founded distrust of New York State and the neighboring industrial plants. History has demonstrated that in most cases, the state has operated against the community's best interests. Episodes of direct conflict between Akwesasne Mohawks and the state government are still recent in the community memory, and so the possibility that they could be maltreated at the genetic level as well does not seem farfetched to many Mohawks.

The final major challenge faced by the scientists and community members, the challenge of communicating the results of the research, is discussed below within the context of the growing body of literature in environmental/medical sociology and public health concerning the reporting of health study results to study participants.

Report-Back of Study Results

One of the greatest ethical challenges facing researchers in biomonitoring studies involves report-back, or the communication of study results to study participants.[86] Whether and how results are reported to participants has been controversial because researchers worry about giving participants information that may have uncertain health or intervention implications; critics of report-back have understandable concerns about the emotional and psychological stress for participants who might receive data that do not paint a clear picture of health implications or outcomes, or how to reduce exposures.[87] For this reason, some university IRBs have been hesitant to grant approval for projects to report back individual results, reasoning that they are trying to protect subjects from the stress of uncertainty.[88] Many IRBs have traditionally allowed aggregate reporting of study results while discouraging researchers from conveying individual information.[89] For this reason, some researchers who support a "right-to-know ethic" have complained that there are few models for reporting personal exposures to study participants.[90]

However, participants often want to know their results, and some researchers have argued that individuals have a *right* to know their results, asserting that it is "ethical to return information to the 'owner' of that information."[91] Despite the concerns about stress associated with receiving ambiguous data, researchers who advocate for results report-back have found no evidence of harm to participants from receiving this information. On the contrary, they have found that individual report-back can contribute to environmental health education, stimulate behavior change and public involvement, and serve as a tool for public health advocacy.[92]

For the SUNY SBRP studies conducted at Akwesasne, the general procedure was as follows: A fieldworker, often collecting data for a specific project, would approach a house that had been randomly selected and ask the appropriate resident to take part in the study. If the resident agreed, the fieldworker collected the individual's information and biological samples (usually breast milk or blood) over the course of a series of visits. The data and samples were then sent to SUNY Albany, where the samples were tested in one of the labs and the cognitive tests were analyzed. Each study participant eventually received a letter in the mail with that person's individual results. As Schell et al. describe:

> Participants received results from individual testing (toxicant profiles, hormone levels, cognitive assessments, and growth assessment). Each participant received several letters relaying these results back to him or her as they became available. The letters were carefully crafted in tandem with the community partners, and in accord with community values and concerns. Special attention was paid to translating results into layperson's terms and providing an explanation of the available toxicant standards, so that participants could better understand their individual results. This may be one of the most significant steps in the research process from the community's perspective, as it represents the delivery of "product from research" back to the community.[93]

Periodically, the SUNY SBRP scientists would also host retreats at Akwesasne, where the full team of more than sixty scientists would spend a weekend, camping in local cabins. During these retreats, they would offer presentations for the entire community in which they would describe the progress of the studies as well as aggregate findings.

As part of understanding the "exposure experience" of Akwesasro:non study participants, and as way of gathering feedback for those who executed the studies, I asked study participants about their reactions to receiving their results, as well as about any recommendations they might make regarding how future study report-back should be handled.[94] Many of the answers I received reflected a community in political and environmental flux, where people were working to process complex scientific information about their individual bodies as well as the community body.

CHALLENGES OF SUCCESSFULLY COMMUNICATING STUDY RESULTS AND THE LIMITATIONS OF SCIENCE

Some participants told me that when they received the letters with their individual results, they either did not understand the information or were disappointed because they had expected a great deal more information to come from their results. This disconnect between what they expected to receive and what they actually received arose from a combination of a need for education (some needed more accessible language and additional information around basic science) and expectations that could not be met (some anticipated that the study would deliver information that was simply beyond the limits of science at the time).

Six of the participants told me that they did not really understand what the results stated in their letters meant. As Rob put it, "There were a lot of words describing the toxins and stuff like that, levels that I didn't really understand." He was generally able to understand that his levels were not considered high, but others did not gain even that much understanding. One woman who took part in a study with her daughter did not understand the results at all: "They gave the results but they didn't give me reference to what was normal. Just my results." When I asked her how the results made her feel, she said, "Well I was trying to figure out, but I had nothing—I had no idea. They didn't do anything." Another woman did not understand her results at first, but then asked some questions of the woman who took her blood, and "a few years after" came to understand what those results meant. Joyce described how she received her daughter's results but thought that the paper sent in the mail "doesn't really tell you very much. You know, they talk like co-genitors [sic] and things like that. I don't know if that was in particular to my daughter's blood sample . . . some of the concepts that they used were, you know, I misunderstood them until somebody took me aside and explained it to me." As a well-educated woman, she was concerned, because if she had trouble understanding the results, other community members must have as well. Another woman received the results of her breast milk sample but was angry because

> they didn't say "this is what this means." . . . I lost it [the paper with the results] because what does it mean to me? I don't

157

know what a triglyceride level is or whatever or this is really high. How do I know? . . . It made me feel worse. You get something and people don't help you, don't tell you about it. So it makes me feel bad because what you expect is that somebody is going to show this to you. You participate in this study and then they're going to say, "This is what this means, this is what you should do. This is our advice." So you got none of that so it makes you feel bad . . . like a waste of time. You participated in a study where you don't have the proper follow-up, and they didn't follow up. You know what I mean? You have value as a part of a statistic, but not as an individual.

Between her expectations that she would receive more personal feedback and recommendations about actions to take and her difficulty understanding the technical information contained in the letter, this participant in early health studies felt disempowered by the research process.

Many of the individuals who told me that they did not understand their study results felt that in future studies, results should be better explained to participants, in simpler language. The report-back letters changed gradually as the SBRP studies progressed, as the SUNY researchers took some of these issues into account. One of the FERP fieldworkers who was herself in one of the earlier breast milk studies felt that the level of clarity of the results letters sent to participants improved over time, as each successive study learned from the one before.

In addition to the report-back letters, the SUNY researchers organized information sessions for the entire community in which they described basic study details and results. At the beginning of each study, these community meetings were well attended, but as the years passed attendance decreased significantly, despite efforts on the part of the researchers and FERP staff to recruit a community audience. Newman recalled that one meeting held to report information about the adolescent study was attended by just one community member. Another scientist who worked on the adolescent study described a couple of meetings, sometime between 1995 and 2000, "where there were more scientists in the room than community people." Carpenter laughed about how "our public meetings would have ninety people from Albany and maybe two or three people from Akwesasne [chuckles]. It wasn't always that bad, but the funniest time was only two people showed up," and it turned out one of those men was at the wrong meeting. They all laughed about it, and the man stayed for the presentation. Carpenter concluded that "now, I have no criticism for how the community reacted to what we were doing," but he was curious about why there was such a lack of attendance when the community had insisted that the scientists conduct these meetings. The fieldworkers I spoke with were also puzzled by the lack of attendance. "It was like we tried everything. They had meetings; they didn't show up. We gave you your letter. We did everything we possibly could," noted one FERP employee. Similarly, Trudy said:

> I think they tried everything just to give the information back to the participants, but it always seemed like the timing was never right or there wasn't enough interest to find out what the results were. . . . Oh my God, I remember we tried everything. We would be there at different areas and different—like we put everything out there. They had a projector there with the overview and everything. We just didn't get the participants to come back. There was not enough interest out there.

Alice also noted: "A lot of people got their paper in the mail. They don't know what it means. So we did try to hold some information sessions, and those rarely go over well."

When I posed the question directly to study participants as to why the presentations were poorly attended, many people reflected a concern, perhaps based on reactions to the letters, that the meetings would be boring or the researchers would speak in scientific language that they would not understand. As Joyce asked, "If the community can't understand it, then why go?" Leona, who took part in the breast milk study, attended some of the meetings, but just wanted to know "is the turtle good or bad? I think they've got to bring it down to our language. . . . People felt intimidated by the language that was used." Agnes, one of the FERP staff, said that when she went to the meetings, "there was a lot of big words used. They're a little dry."

But in addition to language issues, part of the reason some participants did not understand the results was that they had been expecting the report-back letters and the community meetings to give them information that the researchers were not able to provide at the time—an assessment of their health, not just numbers that held no meaning on their own. Joyce kept mentioning that she was looking for the results to give her "an assessment, overall assessment of what does it mean? You know, what are the long-term effects? . . . What's the impact long range on our family? Or, you know, our grandchildren?" Some of the scientists told me that this was one of their greatest frustrations—that the community wanted them to be able to spell out what the contamination meant for the health of individuals and the community, and they could not.

One of the SUNY/NYSDOH scientists who worked on the earlier studies expressed to me an understanding of these frustrations in the community, noting that one of the most dissatisfying things about the science that came out of their work with the community

> was our inability to really be able to determine scientifically and statistically the health impact of the PCB exposure on the community. My work was able to tell that they were exposed at least in the past and that exposure had some biological impact as indicated by those P450 enzymes but—and I said that in turn might indicate some cancer risk, but—I wasn't able to address what I think is their primary health, primary question which is you know "How have these PCBs affected my health?" I think I have alluded to the primary problem there was that the Mohawk population is relatively small, so I'm just not going to be able to statistically demonstrate excesses of cancer, but even if you do, be able to relate it to PCB exposure, see, that was the basic problem, and also those kinds of studies are very expensive.

Alice, the director of FERP, expressed similar frustrations with the limitations of the ability of science to answer the community's questions. She noted that the studies "opened up a lot more concerns and questions without answering some of the basic things." Some of the concerns she mentioned involved the levels of cognitive delays that could be attributed to PCBs and the potential effects to people's metabolisms and reproductive systems. Unfortunately, with these kinds of questions, "technology, at the time, couldn't answer them. I'm not sure we're really ready to be able to understand what that meant."

This was frustrating to the community because the studies "raised more questions than we can even answer initially. It kind of shook my faith in the system. I really put my heart and soul into wanting this project to work and to mean something." Alice personally believes that people's health has been affected by the contamination, but, she asked,

> How do you pinpoint exactly what caused it? . . . Yes, I think people's health [is] affected. But to what extent, we still can't prove it. You can't make that direct connection, and that's what people wanted to find out, how it's directly affecting themselves. The level of PCB or lead or whatever they had, if you have this then you should have this. I think that had a lot to do with the limitations of technology then. I don't know if they can even do that now or ever. But that was one of the limitations we really couldn't get around.

Henry Lickers, who directed the Department of Environment for the Mohawk Council of Akwesasne for decades, reiterated the scientists' hesitancy to make definitive statements during a community meeting:

> Being a scientist, I believe that if we are going to speak to our people, we have to speak with some certainty about what we're saying. And that's very difficult for a scientist to do, because certainty to us is a very big word. So when somebody says, "This is impacting on something," whether it's a person, or an individual, or an animal, and we say that we're certain this has been occurring, well, that's a big statement.[95]

Beginning with the Mount Sinai research, Akwesasne community members were looking for these big statements, but many of the scientists were reluctant to make them based on the information at their disposal. Environmental anthropologist Peter Little and the Health Investigations Communications Work Group both found similar issues among ATSDR scientists regarding the challenges they faced when community members misinterpreted the actual ability of environmental health science to create "clean, useful, and evidence-based theories of causation."[96] White et al. note that to avoid this disappointment, a

> considerable amount of work is needed to help community residents understand what a health study can and cannot do, and this effort needs to occur during the planning phase. If this interaction does not occur, community residents may feel that they have been misled when the results and conclusions are presented. Of course, investigators also need to understand the needs and concerns of community residents so that studies can be tailored to address these needs.[97]

Many of the papers resulting from the second round of research, which are beginning to show possible connections between PCB levels and health issues, have been published only very recently (several after I conducted these interviews). In addition, while they note trends, all of these research papers also caution that the researchers cannot definitively say that PCBs cause any of the illnesses studied, and they cannot make predictions for anyone's individual health.

"Family Meetings": Alternative Suggestions for Report-Back

While some interviewees told me that they were perfectly happy with the way their results were conveyed back to them and were grateful to receive the information (especially after previous studies had neglected to provide any), others shared their reflections on how information could be conveyed back to participants in the future in ways that would be more reflective of how community members choose to communicate with each other.[98]

Some participants and field staff suggested that a more personalized delivery of results would be helpful; staff could go "visiting" or speak to family gatherings about the study. As noted previously, visiting is a valued form of social interaction in this community. My interviews with participants were often treated as visits over coffee, and community members joked that they were envious that I had obtained a grant that allowed me to spend several months visiting with people. Informative visits by health study field staff were suggested as a means of providing participants with the opportunity learn about the study and their results at a level each individual could understand.[99]

Interviewees saw the potential for such visits to be used as a way of delivering information in settings where study participants would feel comfortable asking questions and as a way of spreading information through the community through family groups. One woman who was a participant in the breast milk study and whose daughter took part in the adolescent study noted that they had received letters with their results, "but I think it would have been nice if they put as much into dispensing that information through the results as they did in trying to get us involved." Two of the fieldworkers also noted that they thought it would have been more effective for someone to go back to the participants and deliver the results individually, so they could be sure that each participant understood the results. Trudy commented that the participants "just need that personal touch instead of getting a letter in the mail and it's all scientific, plus they can't understand it. . . . I think if you went back and try to explain that [the numbers] to an individual face-to-face, I think it would probably have made a difference." Agnes similarly noted that community members "like the one-on-one thing or let's go to their house and sit down and have coffee." She pointed out that like the larger gatherings SUNY tried to host, tribal meetings are also poorly attended: "Out of ten thousand there are twenty people at the tribal meeting and the same thing goes for the other side of the so-called reservation. The same thing there, you have a district meeting, there would be ten people there."

While the study report-back targeted individuals and the broader community as a whole, some community members suggested that reporting to family groups might have been more helpful. One woman, Brenda, who is a member of ATFE and helped Katsi coordinate the data in the early breast milk studies, described how the public meetings were held in large conference rooms, and people in the community are unlikely to attend such events. She suggested that if you want to educate people about something like a health study,

> you go to their homes and say, "Can we have a family meeting?" The family all comes and they sit and they talk because families are not going to go out and get the information. If you want to tell somebody something, you go to them. That's the

way it is here. They'll come together. They'll have the snacks, they'll have the beverages and whatever. They'll ask the questions.

She noted that people were unlikely to raise their hands and ask questions in larger meetings "because they don't want to feel stupid, but in a family setting, in a family environment, they'll ask questions." The woman quoted above who participated in the breast milk study and whose daughter took part in the adolescent study suggested that small focus groups would have worked better than trying to bring the whole community together for meetings. Because of the numerous political, spiritual, and regional divisions in the community, as a whole it does not always function as an efficient social body. The most efficient social bodies within the community are extended family networks, and targeting these groups for meetings and presentations could have been effective. Some Akwesasro:non suggested that, rather than sending letters to the individual bodies from whom the samples were collected and attempting to educate the entire community of Akwesasne through large gatherings hosted by scientists, report-back should take place within an intermediate social body, the family gathering—a setting in which community members are very comfortable interacting.

Conclusion

In addition to contributing to the capacity development of the scientists and community members who worked together on these health studies, environmental health research at Akwesasne contributed to the development of science more broadly at a time when CBPR was just beginning to become a standard of community research. Science and technology studies scholars Ottinger and Cohen offer a theory of how science and engineering can change through "ruptures" in the routines of scientific practice. Because they are often viewed as static, scientific knowledge, institutions, and experts are sometimes excluded from accounts of the transformative nature of environmental justice work, but "environmental injustice is an important source of ruptures in technical practice, and thus a powerful force for the transformation of science."[100] Creating a more dynamic research environment and relationship in which community members shape study design as well as data collection and analysis and continue to provide feedback and ask questions allows for "transformations" that "grow out of routine ruptures in everyday technical practices, where scientists and engineers have room to make new choices about how to do their work."[101] By having members of the affected community contribute directly to study design and data collection, the Akwesasne SBRP studies altered the status quo of environmental health research. By refusing to remain on one side of the researcher/subject divide, Akwesasro:non brought environmental health research into discussions about tribal sovereignty, forever changing how this type of work will be done in this and other tribal communities.

The case of Akwesasne also gives us the opportunity to consider what "citizen science" means in a tribal community. Who constitutes the "citizen" in citizen science has generally not been considered critically. "Citizens" have been conflated with volunteers, amateurs, or "members of the general public."[102] Ostensibly, this is anyone who is not a scientist. The noble intention behind many citizen science projects is to create a nation with a more educated citizenry, which will then in turn support scientific principles and projects. But what does it mean to be a "citizen," as distinct from a professional scientist, and what about when citizen scientists do not necessarily feel they share nationhood and citizenship with the scientists with whom they are working? As described in chapter 1, citizenship at Akwesasne is complicated. Many of these citizen scientists are tribal citizens first. The Akwesasne Task Force on the Environment worked to bring together people from all of the various political entities in the community to form one grassroots organization that would govern research at Akwesasne. The Mohawks who founded this organization, which includes both professional scientists and amateur scientists, sought to work toward the broader goal of a healthier community and a cleaner environment. They fought against the distinctions of "citizen" and "scientist"—as noted above, Katsi insisted that women did not need to have degrees to be trained in data collection, and "there's not going to be any one of you researchers that stand taller than the Mohawk mothers." The binaries between citizen and scientist, between subject and researcher, were blurred through this research process (as Katsi insisted, "We're not going to be guinea pigs"). This is just one more way in which Akwesasne as a case study in CBPR and citizen science leads us to intentionally consider the social, cultural, and political processes that structure research in an Indigenous community.

Political scientist Kevin Bruyneel refers to this resistance to existing solely inside or outside the system as a "third space of sovereignty."[103] Similar to Indigenous nations that have for centuries demanded rights and resources from the settler state while also challenging its impositions on them, Mohawks resisted the binary of researcher/subject, citizen/scientist, to create a third space of sovereignty in the context of research, in which they refused the subjugated role to which communities under study are commonly relegated. Through the creation of the ATFE Research Advisory Committee, Akwesasne community members took a position of authority in the research process. They did not reject the institutions of science altogether, recognizing the need for this type of knowledge. But neither did they agree to a conventional research study. Instead, they created the ATFE RAC, a new community governance body, and developed a hybrid research model that has in recent years been emulated in increasing numbers of community-based research projects. Within this third space, Mohawks and SUNY researchers created room for a new research culture at the beginning of the CBPR movement.

CHAPTER 4

Contamination, Convenience, and a Changing Food Culture

During the first week of May 2015, almost one hundred Akwesasne youth completed the Ohero:kon rites of passage, a seven-year ceremonial program that culminates each spring in a fast. Youth in the program fast for one, two, three, or four days and nights, with the time increasing as they progress. Over the course of four days the cohorts are taken out to their fasting sites, and then they are all brought back in together on the last day to rejoin the community. Family members and friends prepare a feast to welcome them back. On this warm spring afternoon, there were three long tables of food filling the Tsionkwanati:io Heritage Center, and the range of dishes was emblematic of the food culture in Akwesasne.[1] One table was filled with pots of corn soup, a Haudenosaunee traditional food containing Iroquois white corn that has been boiled in hardwood ash as well as beans, meat (usually pork), and turnips (the inclusion of which is unique to the Mohawk version of this soup). Dense rounds of boiled corn bread—made from ground white corn with kidney beans—also sat on the table, along with corn mush sweetened with berries and maple syrup. There were also dishes of meat in gravy—moose, venison, and beef—and pans of baked and fried fish and fried chicken. There were local vegetables like winter squash (smashed, with maple syrup), string beans, and potatoes, both boiled and mashed. Dozens of casseroles, many of which were drenched in cheese and creamy sauces, crowded together on the tables. Some people brought green salads in an effort to encourage the community to eat healthier. Fluffy, greasy fry breads, some made with maple syrup (a local touch), were snapped up quickly. The dessert table featured strawberry drink (made from water, smashed frozen strawberries, and maple syrup) and sliced-up fruit as well as doughnuts, homemade cakes, and store-bought cookies and cupcakes. Enough food to feed an army was laid out, featuring both homemade dishes and items purchased at the Walmart or the Hannaford supermarket in the next town. Some ingredients were produced locally, like some of the white corn, the beans and squash, the maple syrup, some of the fish, and some of the potatoes and turnips. Others came from store shelves, from cans, from bricks of commodity cheese. As at any big family function centered on food, people compared plates, commented on their favorites, and went back for seconds.

This feast is representative of what Akwesasne food culture once was, what it has become more recently, and where it is heading. Over the past generation, the diets of most Akwesasro:non have undergone some fairly dramatic changes, from a time when most families procured a majority of their food locally through farming and fishing to the present, when much of that local food has been replaced with store-bought or fast food. A variety of environmental, social, and economic factors have led to these changes, including concerns about environmental contamination as well the adoption of a modern, convenience-based lifestyle. These shifts, as well as the maintenance of aspects of what some identify as a traditional diet, are connected to complex narratives of risk assessment, trust, culture, and relationality. At the same time, there is currently a push in the community for members to begin eating healthier, to return to some of the foods that many no longer eat for various reasons.

This chapter explores the changes in the Akwesasne food system that have occurred over the past half century. The shifts have come in two stages, first with the diminishment of fishing and farming in the community and then with the replacement of these locally procured foods by what interviewees described as "fast food" and "junk food," eaten on the run rather than in family meals. Some see the changes in food culture as the inevitable products of more fast-paced lifestyles, in which families are tied to the wage economy and kids are involved in sports and other activities. For others, the changes came about almost entirely because of the contamination from local industries, which led to the issuance of fish advisories and concerns about whether planting gardens was safe. This shift in diets has trig-gered anxiety about the health of the community but also about the preservation of Mohawk culture. Food is more than nutrition; it is bound up with social relations, culture, and meanings of health.[2] As Jean Anthelme Brillat-Savarin's oft-quoted aphorism declares, "Tell me what you eat and I will tell you who you are."[3] French food scholar Claude Fischler argues that food is "central to individual identity, in that any given human individual is constructed, biologically, psycho-logically and socially by the food he/she chooses to incorporate."[4] In Indigenous communities, food is also central to tribal identity, as it connects family and community members through the cultural prac-tices necessary to procure and prepare the food, as well as through the time together spent consuming the food. Food can also be central to political identity, as political claims to Indigeneity, treaty rights, and property rights are often anchored in subsistence food produc-tion.[5] As Dian Million notes, "'Food' profoundly organizes a sense of Indigenous polity; thus, any discussion of food is always a profoundly political one."[6]

The move by members of recent generations away from the diets of their parents and grandparents has raised anxiety for some Akwe-sasro:non, not only about maintaining the community's health but also about maintaining Indigenous culture in a community affected by environmental contamination and pressures from outside forces. These concerns are reflected in conversations around food—what people are able to eat, and who they choose to eat it with. The prac-tices that Indigenous people engage in within their food system are part of the environmental identity of that community, embodying its ecological, religious, and nutritional beliefs. These practices also lend a significant feeling of belonging to the place from which they derive sustenance.[7]

Fish Consumption

As noted in the preceding chapters, fish was an important part of the diet and environmental identity of Akwesasro:non for centu-ries. Akwesasne is located at the confluence of the Saint Lawrence, Saint Regis, Raquette, and Grasse Rivers, which provided rich fish-ing grounds for the inhabitants of the region for eons. Almost ev-eryone I spoke to in the community had some kind of connection to fish or fishing. People reminisced fondly about fishing with their fathers and grandfathers on the river, helping them prepare fishing equipment, and working with their mothers to clean and cook the fish. Species like sturgeon, perch, walleye, and bullhead were mentioned most frequently; they were eaten smoked or fried. Fish was eaten several times a week at ordinary dinners, and it was consumed in large quantities at "fish fries" held to celebrate special occasions and family gatherings.

Aside from supplying a dietary mainstay, fish and fishing, according to community members, constituted a livelihood, a lifestyle, and a culture. The processes involved in catching and cooking fish out of the river were at the root of many of the interviewees' childhoods, and these processes connected them to the original residents of the area. People in their fifties, sixties, and seventies recalled with youthful excitement their childhood experiences of going to their families' fish boxes—which held captured fish submerged in the water on the shore of the river—to pull out each night's supper.

For nearly forty years, Akwesasne has been grappling with the need for fish advisories, notices aimed at curtailing fish consumption to protect residents from exposure to environmental contaminants. Health studies that demonstrated how contamination moved directly from the industrial sites to Mohawk bodies by way of fish led to these advisories, which continue today. As a result of the advisories, as well as a general concern about the perceived presence of contamination in local food, more recent generations of Akwesasro:non have begun to eat less fish or have cut it out of their diets entirely. The dietary surveys conducted as part of the early Superfund studies with both Mohawk women and men documented a self-reported decrease in fish consumption in response to the fish advisories that had been issued.[8] Community members who were not involved in the health studies also reported a general decrease in fish consumption. Visible changes in fish, the advisories, and the information coming out of the health studies—coupled with a rapid decline in the fish populations—led to this decrease in fish consumption. Nonetheless, some community members have maintained their levels of fish consumption, and others who had stopped eating fish have returned to it after reconciling their choices with the available information.[9]

Of the people I interviewed, 74 percent told me that they had decreased their fish consumption or cut fish out entirely, even though for most of them it was previously an important part of their diet. For some, eating fish had become an infrequent activity, reserved for special occasions, as opposed to regular meals. Some said that they would occasionally eat fish, but then feel concerned, like one woman who commented, "When you are eating the fish, you know in the back of your mind that you're going to be glowing [laughs]. You know what I mean? You know it is there, the fear is still there." Even though the fish advisories targeted women of childbearing age and children in particular, men I spoke with said they assumed that if it was bad for the women, they should not eat it either. These interviewees reported that this was predominantly the case for the rest of their family members as well—they had either severely reduced their fish consumption or cut fish from their diets entirely.

Even prior to the announcement of fish advisories, residents began noticing visual clues that fish were not safe. Interviewees reported finding fish with "humungous tumors on them," with "funny-colored eyes," with black spots, with bugs inside them, with sores on them, with black spines, with "globs of green," and with holes in their sides—all features that they attributed to the effects of contamination. Studies have shown that PCB concentrations in fish can lead to increased lesions and tumors; the black spots that residents were describing in fish were likely caused by parasites in the Saint Lawrence, and the holes in the fish were probably caused by lamprey eels.[10] Since the levels of the river became regulated during the building of the Saint Lawrence Seaway, which directly preceded the building of the industrial plants, it is likely that fish would have begun contracting parasites in this slower-moving water around the time when General Motors began contaminating the river. This is also the time when the invasive lamprey eel—with its round mouth full of razor-sharp teeth, used to latch onto marine life—was making its way upriver with the ships. The river changed in myriad dramatic and subtle ways at the same time the industrial plants were depositing pollutants, leading to the impression that all abnormalities could be traced to the contamination, even if they were more likely to be the results of parasitism or other nonchemical factors. As Tony David from the SRMT Environment Division noted, "I think when you have a large traumatic event like the discovery of contamination here, it tends to stick in people's mind as a benchmark. It affects people's perception, it affects your ability to interpret what you're seeing." One community member I spoke with, Brenda, asked if the PCBs could be affecting the immune systems of fish, making them more susceptible to parasites and pathogens. This is a possibility that some environmental scientists have found evidence to support.[11]

Problematically, not all contaminated fish showed such visual cues. In 1986, Ward Stone took samples from a sturgeon caught by Mohawk fishermen in order to test it for PCBs. When he came back with the results, which showed the fish to contain levels of PCBs above what the EPA considered safe for consumption, he was aghast to learn that the fishermen had already eaten the sturgeon.[12]

Because it is difficult to tell from just looking at a fish whether it is contaminated, many community members who still wanted to eat fish but were concerned about those procured locally began to rely solely on outside sources of fish. Some got their fish from as far away as British Columbia, sent by family members; others obtained fish from nearby communities, like Tyendinaga. One man I interviewed, Robert, explained how he would get his perch "out of Upper Canada, where they're not polluted yet," with the "yet" indicating his skepticism that communities up north will be able to avoid Akwesasne's fate. Some interviewees realized the irony of the likelihood that they were still consuming contaminants, just contaminants they knew less about. Chris described how "people think that if the fish comes from someplace else rather than right here, then it is okay. They don't realize every Great Lake dumps into the next Great Lake, which dumps into the Saint Lawrence River. It is one big sewer." Some also told me that they would only eat fish from a store. As Alice put it, "So we end up being supermarket Indians, buying tilapia from Hannaford's, not so much perch or walleye."

Other community members never stopped eating fish, some because they felt a cultural obligation to continue eating it or because they were not concerned about the warnings. Still others had recently gone back to eating fish after giving it up, because they had come to feel that eating it was no longer a problem for their health. Some said that they trusted the environmental remediation process. One woman who is a member of the Akwesasne Task Force on the

Environment and was a fieldworker in the SBRP health studies described how her family continued to eat fish, saying that her kids "love it. They eat it whenever they can get it. I know that the area has been remediated and the fish isn't that bad anymore. So I hadn't told them not to eat it. So we just continue." Another ATFE member, Joyce, described how "the levels with the fish going down, the PCB levels going down . . . I feel more comfortable eating fish now. So I don't think I'm going to pick up that much contamination with PCBs anymore." Randi, whose relatives worked on the health studies and who was herself a participant, noted that many people in the community had vilified the consumption of all fish, especially for pregnant women, reacting in much the same way toward pregnant women who ate fish as they would toward those who smoked or drank. She was disappointed that the only lesson that people seemed to take away from the health studies was not to eat fish:

> I feel like sometimes I could try to educate people about what fish is good for you and what is bad for you, but sometimes it is just, why bother? You know my 30-second conversation is not going to undo twelve years of ingrained messages—"Don't eat any more fish." . . . So I don't fight it too much, I just eat my fish in private.

She laughed at the idea that people who eat fast food felt they could criticize her for eating fish.

There are also probably some in the community who still eat fish but report that they do not because of the expectation that they should avoid it, given the fish advisories. Henry Lickers, who works for the Mohawk Council of Akwesasne Department of Environment, described how when he first arrived in the community thirty years ago, when he went visiting, he found that 90 percent of the people were eating fish. Then as the fish advisories became more prominent, people began changing their behavior. When he would stop by a house at dinnertime,

> suddenly, the old man or whoever was cooking the fish would put it in the cupboard and shut the door. And then they would be cooking something else, you know. "Well, you know, Henry

has been talking about this. And you don't want to show him that you don't believe what he's talking about, because I really like fish, you know. And besides, I'm over sixty, and it's not going to hurt me. And I don't want to have any more kids, so I'm okay." But you got funny things like that occurring.

Henry told me that he no longer eats fish because he feels that he has a responsibility to set an example: "I don't eat fish from the Saint Lawrence. I believe the same way, if people saw me eating, then they would say, 'Oh, then we can go back.' And I don't think that that's responsible. If I'm going to tell them not to, well then I better not too." At the same time, he recognizes that some people do still eat fish, even if they do not admit it openly.

For others, the continued presence of elders who always ate fish served as proof that fish consumption couldn't be that harmful. Nelson expressed skepticism at the fish advisories because "we've been fishing all of our lives and we're still here. And my aunt, we just buried her last week. My great aunt was 102." Agnes similarly described how "we were brought up by the river and on the river. We were brought up to fish, we were brought up to swim in the river, and we were brought up on a boat. I don't have no fear of contamination. It was just a part of my life." She still eats fish as well.

For some Akwesasro:non, the traditional relationship with fish, as described in the Ohen:ton Karihwatehkwen, or Thanksgiving Address, necessitates a continuance of respectful consumption. Richard noted the traditional connection and responsibility that Mohawks and the fish have to each other, saying that for this reason, he continued to eat fish. As he related, the Creator put the food in the water, and

> we give thanks for that food and we have to use it. . . . I mean it doesn't make sense scientifically, but it makes sense spiritually and mentally that you should eat that, you know. You can't just put it aside and say, "Well your work is not good enough" or something, you know? [The fish are] still given out what their original instructions were, and it's us that are at fault, it's our fault that they're like that, you know.

Richard believes that even though as a Mohawk he is not responsible for the contamination that has affected the fish, as a human being he is implicated in the problem, and therefore it is even more important for him to work to maintain this relationship with the fish.

Generational Differences

To some extent, the choice of whether or not to eat fish has become divided along generational lines in the community. In several families, younger women who were planning to have children would not eat fish, but older women would. And even though some older residents had gone back to eating fish, they did not raise their kids to do so because of the warnings, and so the younger generation "didn't develop a taste for it," as Joyce put it. These older residents told me that their children and grandchildren have no desire to eat fish now and would not likely show an interest in it even if it were determined to be clean at some point. As Agnes said, "They weren't brought up with the fish so they're not going to turn around and change their ways."

With this generational loss of fish, many of the Akwesasro:non I spoke with felt that they had lost more than just omega-3 fatty acids and other beneficial nutrients; another part of their culture was being eroded by outside influences. As Henry Lickers pointed out, the language and culture around tying knots in nets, as well as the social interactions that occur around the process of creating these nets, are lost when there is no longer a use for the nets. Similarly, the language used to name and describe certain fish is lost. As one older gentleman said about these losses: "A lot of that has been forgotten, and the fish names in our language. Because a lot of the fishermen when they go fishing they talk about their Indian names to them, there is no English part of it, but that has been sort of forgotten now." An article written by members of the ATFE RAC emphasized that "everyone in the community must engage in culturally important activities, not just talk about them. Pollution discourages young people from spending time on the river and engaging in subsistence activities so important to the culture."[13] The cessation in fishing has not only had negative impacts on health but also has gradually diminished aspects of Mohawk culture.

Aside from the issue of contamination, some community members expressed the opinion that the fish population is too low to support the rates of consumption that previously existed in the community. As Joyce, whose father was a fisherman, noted, "There isn't enough of a fish population to make a living off of anymore." Ernie, an elder who witnessed the coming of the Saint Lawrence Seaway, described how the fish spawning grounds were destroyed as channels were dredged and rock ledges in the river were blasted. The dams and locks that were added to the seaway to make ship traffic and hydroelectricity possible also prevented fish from returning upriver and spawning as they once did. In addition, the cormorant, a voracious bird that is new to the area, has been decimating fish stocks, especially the perch populations.

While some Akwesasro:non have maintained their usual levels of fish consumption or have returned to eating fish after giving it up for a period of time, the amount of fish eaten in the community has decreased—as a result of concerns about contamination, because fish stocks are too low, and because younger generations have not been raised to eat fish. The other main sources of locally procured foods, farming and gardening, have also diminished over the past generation or two, for similar as well as divergent reasons.

Farming and Gardening

Horticulture has always been an important part of Mohawk culture, as demonstrated by the description of first foods in the creation story and the history of Haudenosaunee settlement patterns. Farming has been a significant part of the economy of Akwesasne since the area was resettled in the eighteenth century. The 1890 census notes a number of farms on the Saint Regis Reservation, and according to Haudenosaunee anthropologist Arthur Parker, "the Indians at St. Regis" were "progressive enough not only to use all their own lands but to rent from the whites."[14] Early in the twentieth century, agricultural production was one of the main economic activities of Haudenosaunee communities in New York State, important enough that the Cornell University Agricultural Extension Services implemented an Iroquois white corn breeding project to generate varieties of this type of corn suitable for mechanized harvest.[15]

It was not uncommon to hear "I grew up on a farm" while I was interviewing Akwesasne community members, followed by descriptions of the animals and crops raised. For some, farming was a casual venture to provide food to supplement other income the family was receiving, whereas for others it was the sole source of sustenance. Solomon Cook, who received his PhD in agriculture at Cornell in 1950, was proud of his scientific knowledge on the topic and spoke of his preference for "super" hybrid seeds and purebred animals, as opposed to his father's "subsistence" way of farming. Solomon taught classes in agriculture and was proud to report that he passed along to his students his appreciation for well-bred animals, particularly registered Holsteins. Another octogenarian, Howard, also reminisced about growing up on a farm, raising horses and milking cows. His family would take the milk to the neighboring town of Cornwall to sell, and this income sustained them for several years. A number of others spoke about raising pigs, chickens, dairy cows, and beef cattle, and living off the products they produced, bartering with neighbors, and selling the surplus for income. Despite these nostalgic recollections, very few of the people I spoke with, or their families, were currently living on farms or raising any farm animals. In the latter half of the twentieth century, farming began to decline in Akwesasne, as well as in other communities across upstate New York.

In 1989, a team from Cornell University visited New York State's Haudenosaunee communities to measure how much land was still in agricultural production. At Akwesasne, they found that while about a third of the community still had gardens, only nine families ran full- or part-time farms. Currently, most of the remaining farmers in Akwesasne, of which there are only a handful, are focused primarily on selling hay. The Cornell team also found a decrease in the amount of land being farmed on the other reservations they visited (Onondaga, Oneida, Allegany, Cattaraugus, Tuscarora, and Tonawanda), as well as in the numbers of families involved in farming. On many reservations, white farmers who rented the land were doing a good portion of the cultivation. The Cornell team further found that when Iroquois people were running farms, they were using modern practices involving chemicals on commercial crops in their fields but traditional practices in their home garden plots.[16]

This decline is not unique to Native-run farms; small farms have diminished in number all over the country, and indeed the world, with the growth of multinational agribusiness. In the United States, federal policies have had devastating effects on family farms, many of which were driven out of business in the 1980s.[17] At Akwesasne, the desire for wage labor, the cost of modernization, and the impacts of environmental contamination have driven farmworkers to nonagricultural jobs.

While not all food production operations in Akwesasne could be defined as farms, almost everyone I spoke to said that they had grown up tending large gardens.[18] Several people stated that "everyone" had substantial gardens when they were growing up. As Gina described, "I mean we had rows and rows and rows and rows of fields and fields of corn, potatoes, string beans, cucumbers, tomatoes." Emmy reminisced how "the gardens used to be a mile long." A few people described how when they were younger their families grew all of their own food, buying or trading for only such things as sugar and flour. People nostalgically recalled the corn, beans, squash, potatoes, tomatoes, and cucumbers. A few also mentioned turnips, carrots, onions, beets, raspberries, blueberries, and apples. Many told stories of working in the garden all morning before they were allowed to swim in the afternoons. Others recalled hours toiling in the garden pulling weeds or plucking bugs from the plants, and said they did not miss these activities. Mothers would can the produce, especially tomatoes and string beans, "putting up food" for the winter in glass jars. Some Akwesasro:non told me that they found the younger generation's lack of knowledge regarding how to "put up a garden" lamentable.

While the gardens in Akwesasne have diminished in number and size over the past generation, gardening has remained common, unlike farming. Small backyard gardens are seen as a manageable means of producing a little extra food for the family and maintaining the cultural and familial connections to planting. Despite the challenges described below, Akwesasro:non continue to grow food—some have always maintained gardens, and others are just now embarking on the project. For some who have always gardened, maintaining a family tradition has been an important part of their motivation. As one older gardener explained: "As far as the gardening, I still do it because it always fed me and the farm has always fed me. . . . I was brought up that way and that's the way I live today." For others continuing to garden was a matter of principle, or they they did it because they felt the fresh food was important, even if they did have some concerns about their soil. One woman who lives on the eastern end of the community stated that she gardens because she wants to know what is in her food, and she wants to provide for her family: "I really want to know what I'm feeding my kids. And also, we don't have a lot

Gardening across four generations: Gina Jacobs gardens with her mother, Lenora David, and her granddaughter, Laney Tahy. Photograph by Elizabeth Hoover, 2008.

of money so it would help us. I like the idea of providing for my family and to know that I did that, I grew that, and it feels really good."

In addition to gardening to supplement their families' diets or continuing to garden because it was something they had always done, Akwesasro:non emphasized that growing food was important to the identity of the community. Many of the longhouse ceremonies are based on the agricultural cycle, and several people mentioned to me that to understand and be a fully active participant in Mohawk ceremonies, people need to have experience in planting. As Joyce expressed, "If you look at all the ceremonies, all the ceremonies are based on the natural world, and they're based on thanking that natural world for whatever it provides for us." Katsi stated, "We all had a garden. You can't be traditional unless you have a garden." One elderly gentleman who has always kept a garden spoke disapprovingly of people who, rather than garden, live "payday to payday, that's not the real, that's not the traditional way to live." He added, "My way is to store your nuts for the winter and we'll always have food ahead."

Another man, Rob, after choosing to become sober in his mid-thirties, became involved in longhouse culture and found a mentor there who taught him that "growing your own food is a big thing in our culture. Taking care of yourself with the earth is the biggest thing and I found it very, very satisfying." Rob expressed his belief that the future of Akwesasne "really hinges on a few people that are going to keep going and live off the land again and save the culture," because he predicts there will come a time when the government is going to come to Akwesasne and demand to see evidence of Mohawk culture. "And if we can't produce anything then they're just going to say, 'Well, we declare this the township of Saint Regis.'" To him, the fate of the Akwesasne as an Indian community relies on the efforts of individuals like himself and his mentor who are trying to preserve this particular aspect of Mohawk culture. Traditional varieties of vegetables like white corn are staples in longhouse ceremonies, and many of the gardeners quoted above cultivate those varieties. Sodi, who was cultivating white corn with members of the community farming organization Kanenhi:io Ionkwaienthon:hakie, spoke of its importance in teaching young women about Mohawk culture. Sodi used some of the corn they harvested to teach the adolescent girls going through the rites of passage ceremony about how to properly lye the corn, grind it into meal, and then make mush or corn bread, which is distributed to participants during ceremonies.

The importance of horticulture is also connected to the theme of responsibility to food mentioned earlier in the context of fish; Mohawks see themselves as having a reciprocal relationship with seeds, especially heritage seed varieties. One October afternoon, I sat beside a pile of Iroquois white corn ears with Dean, a man who has been involved with gardening projects in Akwesasne for a number of years. We were peeling back the husks, tearing off all but three sections, and then weaving the remaining parts of the husks into a braid, working in new ears the way one would French-braid hair, until we each had a braid several feet long. These braids were then hung from barn rafters to dry. While we were braiding, Dean described how back in the beginning of time, people had corn, beans, and squash readily available to them. However, the people began to neglect these plants, failing to harvest them properly, and the food rotted into the ground and was eaten by animals. When the Creator saw this, he became angry, and he decided that from then on the people would have to work for their food. The people asked forgiveness and burned a pure white dog as a sacrifice. In contemporary ceremonies, a pure white basket decorated with ribbons is burned instead. In working with youth, Dean tells them that they need to be grateful for what they have and work hard to maintain gardens, or they will lose the plants completely. As he finished his story, he looked down at the pile of corn we were braiding and expressed sadness that this was something that most people are not doing anymore.

One of the women I interviewed, Brenda, who was part of an effort started by the Mohawk Nation Council of Chiefs to increase the preservation of heritage seed varieties, also expressed the need to recognize the responsibility that Mohawk people have to the maintenance of traditional crops:

> As Onkwehonwe this is your responsibility, because every time you plant those seeds you're giving thanks to the plants of the world and you're showing them respect.[19] That you remember them every year and you're asking them to come back every year. You're giving thanks for everything that they've given you. That's part of our responsibility, because when we stop doing that—and that's the big thing with that heirloom seed project—because when we stop, the plants will go back to the Sky World because they volunteered to come to the earth and help man to survive. And so when they don't hear us say those words anymore or care for them, they may think that their job here is done and they go back to the Creator.

Note the reciprocal nature of this responsibility: the plants have fulfilled their end of the bargain by sprouting every spring and bearing seeds every fall. It is then up to the humans to meet their responsibility by planting them, maintaining them, and giving proper thanks. Otherwise, the covenant between the two groups is broken, and humans, especially Onkwehonwe, will suffer as a result.

Tsí Yotsihstokwáthe Dakota Brant, a Mohawk woman from the Six Nations reserve northwest of Akwesasne, has also described this responsibility:

> The relationship between corn and Our People can be regarded as the first treaty of this land; between Natural Law

*Braid of Iroquois white corn hanging in the Kanenhi:io
Ionkwaienthon:hakie greenhouse to dry. Photograph by
Elizabeth Hoover, 2008.*

and the human being in the Americas. It is the place where the
offerings of life, medicine and sustenance from nature have
gone beyond just natural offerings to a place where human
beings have a hand in the crafting of food plant and medicine
life, forging a type of relationship that embodies every con-
notation from basic nutritional values, the cropping of it, the
ceremonies and songs involved with it, the whole cycle of life;
all represented by this one plant.[20]

Beyond just worries about whether community members have become lazy or overly reliant on store-bought food, some Mohawks are

concerned about the implications of a lost relationship with special heritage seed varieties. As Brant makes clear, this relationship goes beyond just nutritional value to an understanding of ceremony and the whole cycle of life. The loss of this relationship will have negative impacts not only on the seeds and heirloom varieties but on the sociocultural health of Mohawk people as well.

While the longhouse culture is an important component of the Akwesasne gardening movement and culture, most residents belong to other faiths (most are Catholic, but the community also includes Methodists, Baptists, and Jehovah's Witnesses) and still consider gardening to be an important aspect of community identity. One Catholic woman described to me seeing a vision of the Virgin Mary in her garden while she was out weeding one evening, demonstrating how the garden is an important and often spiritual place for people of a variety of faiths in Akwesasne. Akwesasne supported itself for most of its history through gardening, hunting, and fishing, regardless of the predominant religious faith practiced by the community, and most residents still see participating in these activities as important rights. Yet despite the importance of gardening in this community, food production has diminished in Akwesasne for a number of complex reasons.

Modernization of Farms

Most of dairy farms that had been operating in upstate New York closed during the latter half of the twentieth century, as farmers became unable to compete with large agribusinesses. In his study on the decline of family dairy farms across upstate New York, sociologist Douglas Harper found that expensive modernization, as well as an increase in industrialized wage labor, "drew agricultural labor from small farms, hastening both industrialization and the demise of small operations."[21] Similarly, many farmers at Akwesasne were unable to afford the changes in technology that accompanied the modernization of farms in the United States. Before recent health and sanitation requirements were put in place, cows were hand milked, and the milk was placed into steel milk cans. These cans were put into cookers to kill potential bacteria and then placed into boxes that used well water to chill the milk. About thirty years ago, many farmers began switching to bulk tanks, sterilized containers that receive milk directly from pipelines connected to mechanized milkers; all of this equipment is very expensive. This mechanization began in the 1970s, at the same time the fluoride contamination was affecting Akwesasne farmers. In addition, while many off-reservation farmers were able to secure loans to purchase the new costly equipment, banks would not give loans to Indian farmers, whose farms could not be taken as collateral.[22]

Many older former farmers in Akwesasne conveyed their own experiences and those of friends who had difficulty securing the loans they needed to sustain their farms. One elderly man, Solomon, went to the bank as a young man to try to borrow money to purchase a farm. The treasurer of the farmers' cooperative told him that the cooperative did not lend money to Indians. However, when he realized that Solomon had gone to school with his son, he considered this education and his son's friendship as the appropriate backing, and he lent Solomon $10,000 to buy the farm. Most farmers were not that lucky. Ernie relayed the story of Mose Cook, who retired to the family farm and set about to restore it. He rebuilt the barn and put in a herd of more than a hundred dairy cattle. He then paid cash for milking machinery, new tractors, and new conveyers in the barn. He was selling his dairy products but having a difficult time paying for all of the improvements. A health inspector then came and recommended additional new equipment to maintain the necessary sanitation standards. Mose went to an equipment dealer to purchase the machinery, but because he had been paying cash for all of his improvements, he had no credit history, and the company refused to provide him the equipment on credit. Despite the small fortune Mose had invested, it was not enough, and he went out of business. The farm has since been divided into smaller plots, none of which are currently supporting cattle. Other farms similarly folded and were divided up.

WAGE ECONOMY

After World War II, Haudenosaunee communities experienced drastic changes. There was a general move toward a wage-based economy, and people left reservations to take jobs or to attend school. Beginning in the late 1950s, many farmers in Akwesasne decided that joining the wage economy was a more practical way to support their families. Howard, an elderly farmer who lives on Cornwall Island, blames the seaway for initially bringing wage labor to the region, and thus contributing to the demise of farming in Akwesasne.

> There were farmers with cattle before the seaway. After the seaway, it ruined everything. The money was there to work. They all went to work and then they gave up the farms. Terrible. There were a lot of big farms, a lot of cattle. Now there's only two farmers left.

Howard complained that kids got away from the farm and "got the taste of that money. You tell them, and they don't want to do nothing. I can't even get anyone to pick berries. And that's not a hard job." Howard's establishment consisted of a series of raspberry and strawberry patches and large vegetable gardens. Despite suffering from diabetes, undergoing triple bypass surgery, and having experienced a stroke that left him nearly paralyzed on one side and walking with great difficulty with the help of a cane, Howard still drove his tractor and tended his crops. His adult children and a few hired helpers assisted him in the gardens, but he had trouble attracting enough hired help because community members were not interested in this type of work. Because he had trouble with his balance, he rigged a platform with a lawn chair to the back of his tractor so that he could sit and hoe his vegetables, and then pull it a little farther down the row to sit and weed some more. He was proud of the fact that he was able to persist in his farm work, but he lamented the lack of assistance.

By the 1970s and 1980s, ironwork and other construction, service, and factory jobs became the main economic activities in many Haudenosaunee communities.[23] Mohawk scholar Rowen White notes that during this era fields in Akwesasne went fallow, and "serious social and cultural disintegration resulted from the migration of these traditional peoples off the reservation in search of such work. With many of the younger generations leaving the reservations in search of better economic opportunities, agriculture within Six Nations has taken a hard hit."[24]

In recent years, the prospect of steady wages and an eight-hour workday has proven more popular with Akwesasro:non than the farming lifestyle. Farming is, as one woman pointed out, "a twenty-four-hour job." Her sister chimed in, "twenty-four, seven days. No vacations." "The cows don't say you can go," the first woman agreed, laughing. Another woman, Judy, described the financially tenuous state of farming:

> Farming is out. I don't think even if they raise horses or pigs or cows, I don't think there is enough money in it. Not when you can go out and make twenty-five dollars an hour doing something else you know, that's guaranteed. Something happens to your animals, you haven't got a dime.

Even on farms that were once fairly successful, the members of the next generation in line to inherit have tended to not take an interest in the business, either "splitting for the city," as Richard put it, or dividing up the land among family members to build houses on. One elderly farmer, Henry, has resigned himself to the fact that his children, most of whom have moved to Syracuse, are not interested in carrying on his farm: "They are all working their ways, and they don't even know squat about cows. They're scared of them." At this his wife, Sarah, laughed hysterically—and then exhaled a resigned sigh. For this elderly couple, and others with farming operations, the fate of their farms when they become unable to work the land is uncertain.

While most people saw the shift from farming to wage labor as an issue of income and convenience, others suggested that this move was part of the government's broader plan to make the Mohawk community less self-sufficient. Loran, who has lived in close proximity to the General Motors plant for most of his life, saw the introduction of wage labor as a deliberate method of drawing Indian people off the land:

> There was a decision made in government and corporate structure to put those plants on the outskirts of Indian reservations, to pull the men off the farms on the reservations because as long as the farms were there, they could argue, the Indians could argue their points and stand together. But if you pull the men out of the farms on the reservation and pull them into the plants and the workforce, they would be the taxpayers that would assimilate the rest of the people.

Rob expressed a similar opinion, describing this perceived attempt at assimilation as a slightly more subtle approach than "when they were burning longhouses and killing people."

Even the lure of pay will not entice many community members to work in gardens or on farms, because they can find less labor-intensive jobs that pay just as well or better. Some older people complained that they could not even find youth who were willing to work in their gardens for pay. Solomon explained, "So that's why I'm shorthanded, this happened too with our youth, they're getting easier jobs than to be pulling weeds." Mark stated pointedly that he could not hire someone to help in his garden or cut the grass because the wages he could offer could not compete with what kids could make smuggling. "I mean kids can make a couple thousand dollars a week running goods across the border. Who is going to mow my lawn?" he exclaimed, throwing his hands in the air.

Some interviewees said that it was hard for them to maintain even small gardens, much less farms, while they were working full-time jobs. Judy pointed out that even the traditional longhouse people, who in her mind were most affiliated with gardens, "are not too successful either, because how are they going to work in the garden? How are they going to plow fields when they have to look for a job to support themselves? They can't do it, unless they do it on weekends." With all of the adults in a household working outside the home, some families find it difficult to make the time for gardening, even if they are interested.

For many community members, the time spent working at jobs provides a more comfortable material life than they could have if they attempted to subsist entirely from family farms or gardens. When people can put a cash value on their own labor time, they start to find that it makes economic sense to buy things that take a lot of time to produce. In Akwesasne, some of the people I interviewed said that it is just easier to buy vegetables than to grow them, especially if they work all day and their free time is at a premium. One older farmer objected to this attitude, noting, "It's too easy to just go to the store and buy whatever you need. Who's going to raise—because some people would just say, 'Well it's easier and the food is very cheap,' and that's why people just live from payday to payday." As Alice reiterated in regard to shopping for vegetables rather than growing them, "We're just busy. We're supermarket Indians."

Laziness and Responsibility

The observation that many residents would rather buy food than grow it was made by several gardeners who felt that many people in the community had become too lazy to work a garden now that they had been exposed to less labor-intensive ways of procuring food. As one man said, "Years ago everybody planted because they had to plant. But now, we got the option and we always pick the lazy way out of it." Edith expressed a similar sentiment: "Everybody is just lazy now. . . . When I ask people how come you don't have a garden, they always say that 'I did that when I was growing up and I am never going to do it again.' . . . It's just laziness." Faced with the prospect of trying to teach the next generation how to garden, another woman sighed and said, "Kids are lazy today, real lazy."

Some even disbelieved those people who said they did not garden because of environmental concerns. Rob, who had recently made gardening a priority in his own life, stated that "using the environmental issues is usually an excuse not to do anything." Another avid gardener, Nelson, declared, "They can't blame it on the soil. They can't blame it on the—it's lazy." He pointed to the pile of white corn sitting in his driveway, which we were busy husking, as proof that the soil is fine. "There's nothing wrong with the soil. There's nothing wrong with it because we have a proven fact right here in this soup corn that there's nothing wrong with that ground. And it's 106 days to grow that stuff to look like this. And it's beautiful. And the people been eating it." While he had no challenges in finding people to eat his produce, finding enough help to plant, care for, and then harvest the food was another story.

Lack of Land

In addition to the motivation of individual farmers and gardeners, planting food is contingent on the practical requirement of adequate space for crops. As more land has been developed to accommodate the growing population at Akwesasne, the feasibility of large farms and gardens has diminished. Mohawk writer Doug George-Kanentiio describes how the population of Akwesasne "doubled from World War II to the 1960s, and doubled again a generation later. Operating large farms was not possible, given the high demand for housing.

The hay fields and cow pastures were converted into single-family lots upon which homes designed by federal agencies rose by the hundreds."[25] A number of the people I spoke with about gardens at Akwesasne mentioned that part of the problem was that there is not enough land available in the community for everyone to have a garden. Ernie noted that on Cornwall Island "in fact there's quite a bit of acreage that was spoiled for gardens by the dredgings that came out of the river, and then they didn't have any other place to put it, so they put it down on the land, and the part of the island where they had spread it out lost quite a few acres." The contaminants and heavy clay soil that came up with the river dredging have made these areas unsuitable for gardening.

However, the main factor affecting land availability is the growing population of the reservation. As Jean mentioned, "Nobody has land. Nobody has any land to have any sizable gardens. Everybody has these one-acre lots; it has to have their house, their garage, all the necessities of a family, all that stuff." Unless there is success with pending land claims, the population is on pace to outgrow the current land base. Many people who reminisced about gardens of the past noted that the land where they gardened now has houses on it. As Joyce said, "Where my mom's garden used to be, there's now two houses. You know, there goes the garden." Housing is currently difficult to find on the reservation, and people predict that new houses will continue to be built. Beatrice described the situation: "Like when you have five kids and I only have one acre. So how am I going to house all these children or how am I going to get land for these children to even have a garden, because oftentimes a garden is the perfect size for a house to be built on. . . . We're running out of land to even have gardens."

CONTAMINATION AND THE DEMISE OF FARMING AND GARDENING

While farming began to diminish in Akwesasne for many of the same financial reasons that led to decreased farming throughout the Northeast, one of the main differences between Akwesasne and other farming communities was the presence of environmental contamination. As noted earlier, Akwesasne is downwind and downstream from the PCB-leaching General Motors Central Foundry and the fluoride-emitting Reynolds (now Alcoa East) and Alcoa (now Alcoa West) plants. The fluoride emissions had an especially dramatic effect on the dairy cows grazing in the vicinity of the Reynolds plant. On Cornwall Island, the deaths of cows from fluorosis during the 1960s and 1970s led to the complete collapse of the dairy industry by the mid-1980s.[26] To this day, the memories and stories of these events affect how Akwesasne residents think about farming. They spoke to me in painful detail of cows losing their teeth and then failing to thrive. A former farmer from Raquette Point recalled how they could not keep the cows "for more than two years, because they would be contaminated from the fluoride pollution." As one woman whose family used to farm noted, "It's made people think twice about doing anything with farm animals or farming." Memories of suffering animals, both on their own farms and on those of their neighbors, still color people's perceptions of the viability of maintaining farms at Akwesasne.

Interviewees also cited concerns about contamination as a reason for the decrease in the number of gardens being planted in the community.[27] Louie, a Snye resident, described how the effects of the fluoride emissions on cattle continue to influence people's feelings about planting: "I mean if the grass is poison to that extent you wouldn't want to be planting a garden either." Gina, who lives on Cornwall Island directly across the river from the GM foundry, said that "they told me not to plant a garden anymore because of the plant, and Reynolds is right there and . . . they told me to check my plants in the morning and see if there's that white powder and there was. There's a white powder on my car, white powder on my plants." New York State has since forced Reynolds to install new scrubbers on the plant's smokestacks to cut down on fluoride emissions, but this still leaves some people to wonder what residuals lay in their soil, and if they should bother planting food. As another woman who also lives on Cornwall Island noted:

> You're hearing all the stuff is landing on the island. So then I'm thinking, so I plant these plants, I canned them, I give them to my family so they can eat fluoride. Why would I do that? So I stopped. This is big and abrupt for me. All of a sudden my life growing vegetables stopped. Next year I got no heart to plant.

So I'm not going to plant because I'm planting poison food. Why would I do that?

For these island residents, the history of contamination from neighboring factories, visible from their front porches, was enough to discourage them from continuing to plant gardens. Since the point of gardening is supposed to be to nurture one's family, why grow "poison food"?

Other Akwesasne residents, even many from other parts of the community, were discouraged from gardening by uncertainty about whether the food they grew would be safe. As one woman who lives at the opposite end of the reservation from the industrial sites stated, "I think people have stopped putting in gardens because they feel that the soil is contaminated. They might grow food, but you don't know what's in it. Some people have stopped." As respected community leader Jake Swamp described:

> People are now afraid to go and plant crops anymore and also to make a living off of the land because you don't know what's there. That's the hard part about it, is not being sure, not being certain anymore, what you're eating or what you're coming in contact with. . . . The whole community just came to a complete stop, especially during the early seventies, because the information that they were getting is that the whole area is contaminated. So these guys would think, well if I plant crops, will I be eating contaminated food? So it was the fear that was driving us.

Even in areas that might be safe, the concern remains when people consider planting. As Henry Lickers noted, "There's that inkling in the mind—is it good stuff? Is it good food?"

For some who were concerned about contamination in their gardens, any strange growth of vegetables was attributed to this threat. Residents from Cornwall Island and Raquette Point described lettuce that grew strangely, broccoli with odd sprouts that didn't taste right, tomatoes in strange shapes with pockmarks on them—oddities they assumed must be the results of environmental issues. In other cases, blights that might be considered somewhat ordinary in other gardens were attributed to the contamination when they appeared on Cornwall Island or Raquette Point. One woman said, "You get a tomato out of your garden and there is little black dots on there, but didn't understand what it was, so right away, you know, you didn't want to eat it, because you think it is the contamination, contaminated right away." Nelson described his brother's garden on Cornwall Island: "If you grow potatoes it's not so good . . . they look like they're moldy or something. They get white spots on them. It's got to be the soil." Nelson is an avid gardener, and he has complete confidence in his own soil because he lives on the opposite end of the community from his brother. Just as they did with the anomalies found in fish, many of the people I spoke with attributed any incongruities in plant growth to contamination—they saw contamination as the cause of anything wrong or out of place in the natural environment.

Soil Tests

While community members were concerned about the potential for contamination in their soil and produce, scientists in the community were much less so because of the results of soil testing conducted by both SUNY scientists and SRMT Environment Division scientists. Soil tests conducted from the early 1990s through 2008 determined that most soil in Akwesasne, when considered in the context of scientifically based standards, is safe for gardening.

In the early 1990s the SUNY Albany team collected soil samples from around the entire community, and the only samples that registered greater than or equal to 0.1 ppm PCBs were those collected on Raquette Point near the GM site and on Cornwall Island on the shore that faces the GM dump site.[28] Similarly, Hwang et al. reported on 119 surface soil samples and found that, in general, all results were within background ranges for upstate New York.[29] The samples with the highest levels were in Saint Regis Village (0.215 ppm) and on Raquette Point (0.886 ppm), and these levels were still below the action level of 1 ppm set by the Tribe (as described in chapter 2).[30]

The team also collected and tested eighteen vegetable samples and found that for the most part they did not contain PCB levels that could be detected.[31] The only produce in the study that contained significant levels of PCBs was obtained from a garden directly adjacent to GM.[32] I noticed this garden when I went to interview the resident,

Loran. The corn stalks made a stark picture, the length of a football field from the base of the GM landfill, which rose ominously behind them. I asked Loran why he planted a garden so close to a landfill, and he replied that he had just started it up again that year. "I just started again because I want to check to see just how true the Environment [Division in] Akwesasne is keeping tabs with it because they say that nature has cleansed the surface. That's what they tell me. Well, when you plant corn, the fine hairs go down into the ground a long ways and others go down further. So we'll see." He sent some of the vegetables he grew to a lab for testing, but he had not yet gotten the results at the time I spoke with him.

The elevated PCB levels found in vegetables near the dump probably reflect atmospheric and vapor-phase deposition rather than uptake through the plant roots, given the lipophilic nature of PCBs.[33] The SUNY team also analyzed blood samples they had taken to see if residing on Raquette Point or eating food grown there resulted in higher PCB blood serum concentrations, and they found that none of these factors were related.

Soil testing for PCBs commissioned by the SRMT Environment Division in 2007 found similar results. All of the samples taken from sixteen different gardens had PCB levels more than one hundred times lower than the Tribe's action level of 1 ppm. According to the report on the testing, even at the 1 ppm level, if someone ate 400 milligrams of this soil per day for thirty years, his or her chances of developing cancer from the PCB exposure would be just three in a million.

Because fluoride is also still a concern in the community, the SRMT completed a "fluoride report" in 2008. The researchers found that even consumption of the vegetables containing the highest amounts of fluoride, combined with the ingestion of fluoridated water, led to a daily dose for a 70-kilogram (154-pound) adult of only 0.077 milligram of fluoride per kilogram per day, which is below the safe level of 0.12 milligram of fluoride per kilogram per day set by the EPA. They concluded that "the risk of adverse health effects from fluoride exposure via the consumption of home grown vegetables is likely below the level the USEPA considers to be safe."[34] In describing this study, an employee of the SRMT Environment Division reflected, "I think you'll find out from the fluoride study. I think that people kind of got carried away and I think the gardens are not really a problem. Maybe the ones that are just immediately adjacent, but the air emissions, whatever is in the air drops off pretty quickly." He explained that dust settling on vegetables planted close to the industrial plants could contain contaminants, but as long as the dust was washed off before the vegetables were consumed there would not be any problems. "But as far as the soil, we tested the soils in the Raquette Point area, and like I said in the whole area and they were quite clean. . . . Accumulation [of these contaminants in the soil] is so minuscule that, I don't know, it would take maybe hundreds of years before anything accumulated. And the way you work soil, you turn it over all the time, you know." According to this Mohawk scientist, and the scientific evidence more broadly, the vast majority of Akwesasne residents should not be worried about PCBs or fluoride in their gardens.

But for many, concerns still abound. At a December 2014 community meeting, a gentleman in the audience asked SUNY researcher David Carpenter, "There's still a lot of us that depend on those gardens and you're talking about air pollution and stuff like that, do you still recommend sticking to the gardens?" Carpenter replied:

> Absolutely. Gardens are pretty safe. Now, you can't find anything that doesn't have some PCBs on them. Wash your lettuce. Wash the dirt off your carrots. But PCBs dissolve in fat, so they're very unlikely to be present in high concentrations in vegetables, because they don't have any fat, pretty much. Now, in fact, people have shown that zucchini and cucumbers, they have a lipid layer on the outside, that can accumulate PCBs. So I would peel them, if you're concerned about that peel your cucumbers and zucchini, but in general, there's not a problem with PCBs exposure from any vegetable. It's the animal fat—you can't have a Big Mac without getting PCBs. It's in butter, it's in whole milk."

Ironically, as will be discussed later, some people moved to processed foods like Big Macs in order to avoid consuming contamination.

Soil tests have not been enough to convince some people that the soil is not hazardous. Because the Akwesasne Freedom School is on Raquette Point, staff and parents there have been extra concerned about the possibility of contamination in the school's gardens. Hawi, a former employee at the school, told me that they had testing done there, which came back with heartening results: "We had soil testing done and the soil is fine. It's not contaminated so we can actually take the food out [of the gardens] and eat it." One of the Freedom School staff members, who has advanced degrees in toxicology, explained this to the parents, but, according to Hawi, some were not willing to trust the soil reports and still did not want their children planting food in the school's gardens.

Among the people I interviewed, there were different responses to and feelings about the findings of the same studies and soil tests. One person who works for the traditional medicine program described how they did tests on the plants they were picking to ensure they were safe. "We did a GPS on the areas that we picked to see the contaminants of the soil, to see if we are not going to damage the people more. . . . So we had all the soil tested . . . and later on we got back the results, and stuff was very, very low, just a touch of it, so it was really good areas that we pick." In contrast, another former employee of the same program told me, "When I was in traditional medicines, what we did was we went to all the different districts and we tested the soil and the plants. Every one of them came back with carcinogens, dust mites, PCB, all these things in the plants." Whereas the first respondent was relieved to find that if the plants did contain levels of contaminants those levels were very low, the second respondent was upset and alarmed that the plants contained *any* level of contamination.

For one woman in the community, Alice, it was the soil tests that she assisted with that allayed some of her concerns about gardening. "We did collect soil samples from different gardens from different parts of the reserve. It didn't seem to be as bad as we feared. So that kind of made me feel better." Many people also suggested soil testing to me as something that would set their minds at ease about planting gardens on their properties. This desire for further testing indicates that either these people had not been informed about the tests that had already been done or they were hesitant to apply results derived from samples taken anywhere but on their own properties.

Trust, Politics, and Relationships

My juxtaposition of the findings of scientific tests with persistent community concerns is not intended to diminish or disprove those concerns. In addition to reflecting a lack of access to the latest scientific information in many cases, the concerns expressed by community members are evidence of the damage sustained to relationships between them and government agencies—specifically, the "civic dislocation" that has resulted from outside government forces seeking to disrupt self-governance in Akwesasne and the failure of environmental and government agencies to protect Akwesasro:non.

These issues arose in my discussions with interviewees about what it would take for community members to trust the environment again as a safe source of food. To get an indication of what it would take to rebuild people's confidence in fish in particular, I asked, "If the Environment Division announced tomorrow that they had done tests and the fish were safe, would you go back to eating them?" Interestingly, many people's answers were more reflective of their opinions of the Environment Division and the SRMT, and their distrust of any level of government, than of their feelings toward fish or local food.

Several people told me that they did not think that community members would go back to eating more local fish because they did not trust the Environment Division to give them accurate information. When I prompted them to explain why they did not trust the division, even though it appeared to me that individual employees of the division were well liked and well respected in the community, most of these interviewees stated that the Environment Division was run by the Tribe, which was too closely connected to the state and federal governments, politically and financially, to be trusted. One woman said that eventually people would go back to eating fish if this announcement were made, but ultimately,

> I think the issue would be, can we trust the Environment Division? [laughs] That's all, you know. It ultimately goes back to, sadly, people's trust in Tribal government because the Environment [Division] is a branch of the government here, so you know I think there is that nagging suspicion all of the time for anything that might be good for you or bad for you, that ultimately it is going to come down to can we trust the Tribe to tell us.

One man felt that any results announced by the Environment Division were not trustworthy, because "I think they can be bought, you know, if you have enough money. It's like the tests they do on all kinds of drugs, you know? You can skew the results any which way you want, you know, and I am just safer if I don't eat it." When I asked him who he thought would pay off the Environment Division to say that the fish are safe, he replied, "Who knows. Someone with a lot more money than me."

When I posed this hypothetical scenario to Jake, a respected community elder, he paused and then explained:

> Over the years we have an issue of trust with the people that had done the studies. Mainly because they're always differing in opinion and it's not real clear how [the results of the studies are] put out. So when you look at that then it makes you nervous if that's really true or is it not. So I imagine if that were to happen, that they would issue a statement saying you can go back and eat fish, I would probably tend to be careful, not really jump into it and jump in the air. I'd probably take a time out and go into it slowly.

In this case, the response had less to do with the reputation of the division itself than it did with how the scientific process does not always provide one definitive, trustworthy answer to be immediately acted upon. In light of this, Jake felt that he would need additional sources of information. Later in our conversation, he mentioned, "People are starting to go back into their gardens. I think the fear factor is probably going away a little bit at a time because . . . they get reports that things are starting to get better. So I guess people tend to trust that and they go back into it slowly." In some cases at least, time, in addition to studies, can help make people feel more comfortable with their surroundings.

Other interviewees wanted multiple sources of information and proof of multiple studies, not just the word of the Environment Division. As one woman said, it would not be enough for community members to hear the Environment Division saying the fish were safe, because "they'd probably be too suspicious right now." She felt the division would need the backing of the fishermen in the community also saying that they thought the fish were safe. Another woman similarly reflected, "You would have to make sure that there was no sores on the fish. I mean, the pollution studies can say one thing, but the physical says another." Both these women felt that if the fishermen and the Environment Division worked together to spread the message, people would be more likely to believe it. Some interviewees were less directly critical of the Environment Division but also said that they would need evidence of results from multiple studies, and then they might still wait a few years to see if opinions changed on the matter. For example, Mark stated:

> I would need more than one individual announcement and I would need some proof, you know, and I don't know what form that proof would take but I know that unless there has been an ongoing process to clean up, you know, it doesn't reverse itself overnight. So I would need more information than just a public announcement that it's okay.

Jann, also a Raquette Point resident, reflected on people's likely skepticism:

> It would be nice to hear, but I think people are a little bit more skeptical and maybe they'd say, "Well, what was the study? What did the study consist of? How come it changed? What was done all these years?" Because we hear about the bottom dwellers and the bottom feeders and things like that, so what changed in our system that now it's okay? But it would be nice to hear again.

As a community, and especially in the region of Raquette Point, these residents have been exposed to more scientific studies than most communities, and accordingly they have grown savvy and skeptical of any results, not quite willing to trust them until that trust has been earned through confirmation from multiple sources. Even though many people prefaced their opinions with "I'm not a scientist," they seemed to have gained enough experience through this process to know when they needed more data.

Among some of the people I spoke with, these suspicions extended not just to a hypothetical announcement of safe fish but to any information coming from the Environment Division. Two of the women I interviewed thought that any information from the division was tainted because of division employees' concerns about keeping their jobs. One woman described an incident that took place during the construction of the hotly contested casino, when the water table was contaminated with salt. She recalled that between the first and second community meetings held about the issue, the representatives of the Environment Division went from describing how high the levels of salt were in people's water to saying "'no it's not correct; that first meeting we had wasn't right.' I don't like it when people are so afraid of their jobs that they can't give the right information and treat people the way they should." When I told another woman about some results of soil sampling that I had learned from an employee of the Environment Division, she replied: "I know, he has got a good-paying job. Those are always factors . . . don't tell you too much because it could jeopardize his job. It's a funny game, it's a funny world, it's a funny thing." Another woman was skeptical about any information coming from the division "because their hands are tied to the Tribe and the state with the funding they get, so they're limited in what they are doing."

In his book *A Social History of Truth*, sociologist Steven Shapin points to the centrality of trust relationships in the development of modern science. Much of what we count as knowledge comes to us secondhand, through the reports, testimonies, and writings of others, and, according to Shapin, we assess information based on our moral estimates of those upon whom we depend for the information. For Shapin, knowledge rests on trust and is inseparable from social relations: "Knowledge is a collective good. In securing our knowledge we rely upon others, and we cannot dispense with that reliance. That means that the relations in which we have and hold our knowledge have a moral character, and the word I use to indicate that moral relation is trust."[35] With this in mind, "the identification of trustworthy agents is necessary to the constitution of any body of knowledge."[36] Evaluations of the expertise as well as the trustworthiness of persons or institutions that are the sources of information are important to people in deciding whether to accept information. Often the evaluation of the trustworthiness of an information source will outweigh the level of expertise accorded to the source when it comes to whether or not a person decides to believe the information.[37] For some people at Akwesasne, although they would not necessarily question the expertise of SUNY or Environment Division scientists in conducting soil sampling and testing, they nonetheless question whether they can trust the final published results. They also question whether other interests—namely, the industrial plants and the state of New York—have somehow insinuated themselves into the final written products. For some, a lack of trust in the political process has led to a lack of trust in the scientific results.

Even though some residents described the SRMT as untrustworthy, and the Environment Division as part of this institution, they often spoke highly of individual employees of the division. One woman, who had earlier in our conversation disparaged the division, later described having a friend who works there: "She, you know, gives me inside scoops. She's devoted to her job. They are doing a good job." I consistently see other employees of the division contributing to community events and programs in their roles as trusted friends, educators, and family members. When I asked interviewees whom they rely on for information about the environment, a majority responded that they rely on the Environment Division.[38] My point in this section has not been to disparage the efforts of hardworking individuals in this division but to highlight what Clint Carroll has observed in his own work with environmental programs in the Cherokee Nation—that the appropriation of state forms of government by tribes is challenging and frequently challenged by tribal members who do not trust outside government entities. Carroll cites Taiaiake Alfred, who argues that Indigenous leaders, in accepting statist institutions as part of their political aspirations, inevitably legitimate a colonial framework and the subordinating relations that this framework demands.[39] But at the same time, Carroll argues, tribes have used these state forms to counteract injustices—such as when the SRMT Environment Division set its own standards regarding environmental contamination. Considering the political and environmental history of Akwesasne, the development of trust between the community and government and scientific agencies will be a long process.

Return to Gardening

Despite all of these challenges and concerns, the Akwesasro:non I interviewed highlighted the importance of growing food and the need for efforts to encourage it. Some people who remembered planting as part of their childhoods had recently begun cultivating gardens again.

One woman, who lives across the river from the GM and Reynolds plants, told me that she had initially stopped gardening because she was concerned about contaminated vegetables, but recently she had gone back to keeping a small garden, using imported topsoil.

For some Akwesasro:non, a renewed interest and involvement in traditional culture has brought them back to growing food. As Kenny described:

> Well, ever since we're little we always planted gardens, we always used the fish heads, we kind of saved the seeds, and my mother was always canning and making food that we planted out of our garden. And as the years went on, different food and commodities became my next favorite thing to eat so basically it wasn't until I started listening to Ohen:ton Karihwatehkwen and what it really meant. And Ohen:ton Karihwatehkwen is our opening address that we do that has to do with the natural world around us. And in there is a particular part about kakwahshona, the food, that they all have spirits and that they all need to be acknowledged and to have gratitude towards them. And I started to understand that a little bit more and that our community that we come from is based on food, traditional food that we used to eat. That's what keeps our communities healthy and we've gotten away from that and I was guilty of it. So because of Ohen:ton Karihwatehkwen I started to investigate why we have blue corn, why we have white corn, why do we give dates to the beans and the strawberries and the maple trees, and what is their role and what is my role.

Because of the Akwesasne Freedom School and programs like Ohero:kon and Ase Tsi Tewa:ton (described in the conclusion), there are increasing numbers of Mohawk speakers in the community, and many of them are learning from the Ohen:ton Karihwatehkwen and, like Kenny, considering how it can structure their lives.

The Transfer of Gardening Knowledge

One of the challenges to reviving the planting culture, in addition to those mentioned above, is that knowledge around gardening is not being transferred from one generation to the next as it once was. Now

Tahawisoren Kenny Perkins and Karahkwino Tina Square selling vegetables from the Ohero:kon garden at an Akwesasne Freedom School fund-raising event. Photograph by Elizabeth Hoover, 2016.

that parents are too busy or are not inclined to maintain gardens, the members of the next generation are not learning the necessary skills to take it up themselves. Moreover, when this knowledge and the habit of gardening are not passed along, it becomes increasingly difficult to convince young people to take up gardening. As Jim explained:

> What happens is all it takes is one generation of stopping it and suddenly you have got a whole new generation that doesn't even know how to garden, doesn't appreciate growing your own vegetables, and now it certainly becomes convenient to just say, "Well I am used to going to the supermarket so I will continue doing that."

Gina similarly observed:

> So that generation is not helping the next generation now because they don't know—they don't know the importance of

planting, they don't know the importance of culture, they don't know the importance of having a child dig their own potatoes, or do the hard work, they don't know that—and it's sad. It's sad because there are only a handful of people that know that. . . . Because they don't know, they haven't been taught, their parents don't know so they haven't been taught.

The generational differences became especially apparent when middle-aged and older residents spoke about the difficulties of trying to interest younger relatives in planting gardens and the effort that would have to go into educating a cohort that had not been exposed to these practices. An older man who prides himself on working a nine-to-five job and also maintaining a large garden told me, "This generation, I don't think they know how to plant a garden. I don't think they know how to take care of a garden." For this reason, Elizabeth said, a solution is "going to come very slow because there's like a whole generation or two that haven't been taught how to work. They watch TV, play video games, ride their four wheelers. They don't work. It's so hard to get them out there. It's sad, isn't it?" Henry mentioned the younger generation's preference for more mechanized forms of entertainment with frustration as well: "It's going to be hard to teach them over. Kids come over they go right to the TV or right to a machine and you try to talk to them and it's like, 'Hey, I'm trying to talk to you!'"

Once that knowledge has not been passed on and the family falls out of the gardening habit, it is particularly difficult for the family to become reinvolved in food production. As Jean stated, "Hardly anybody I think gardens anymore anyway. That's why it's so—this garden that's going up here [the community garden] is so difficult for people to get going, is because nobody's done that—they don't have like a pattern every year of doing this stuff, like we've been doing it every year since we've been married." As can be seen in the frustration of these community members, the skills involved in planting and taking care of food are viewed as important, and as time passes, it will become increasingly difficult to pass these skills on if they are not handed down from generation to generation. The lack of gardening skills could also complicate efforts to reverse the diet changes described in the next section.

Jean and Henry Laffin, my other parents, at their farm. Photograph by Elizabeth Hoover, 2016.

Processed, Fast, Junk, Commodity Foods: "What the Hell Am I Putting in My Body!?"

The diminishment in fishing as well as in farming and gardening in Akwesasne has led to an increase in the consumption of purchased foods. These include what the community members I spoke with often called "fast foods" or "junk foods" (with the most frequently referenced being McDonald's and pizza), defined as much by their content (lacking in sufficient nutrients while being high in fats, sugars, and carbohydrates) as by the lack of social connections that go into procuring, preparing, and eating them.[40]

While some community members began to avoid local foods like fish and garden produce in an effort to reduce their exposure to contaminants, some also recognized that the processed foods they turned to contain other unhealthy ingredients, unknown ingredients that consumers do not particularly understand. Jean noted that people stopped eating local foods because of concerns about contamination, but

> I don't know why because we don't know where the hell this other food is coming from, and we're eating it, or how they're processing it. . . . They put these things in their mind that you can't do this because our foods are poisoned or whatever, so we eat other stuff which we have no idea where it comes from.

Howard similarly lamented, "Then again, we don't know what's in the food now today." He went on to point out that all the canned goods in the stores have salt and preservatives. "What I've been seeing, stuff in there isn't good." Others felt that they did know what was in these processed foods, and they were working to avoid these ingredients. Beatrice, who helps run an alternative healing center, had been working to make people "more aware about the additives, preservatives, things that are inside manufactured food that you buy [in] grocery stores and stuff like that." She was trying to encourage people to buy more organic foods as a way of avoiding pesticides and preservatives, which have "higher cancer causing rates and it accelerates your diseases." She also expressed concern about the growth hormones in meat and dairy products, particularly the effects they can have on young girls, who she sees as physically maturing too fast. Chris, who was working with a community gardening organization at the time, said that "processing is taking the nutrients out of your foods and it is adding stuff to keep it good on the shelf. You know, like nitrates and sodium and all these other chemicals and preservatives." He conjectured that the community might counter consumption of such foods "if you could get the people out of that and get them back, little by little start steering them back to the garden, you know, whole foods, whole grains, you know, and get rid of all this processing."

Concern about contaminants in local fish prompted some Akwesasro:non to turn to processed foods as a safer choice, but some of the interviewees described giving up contaminated fish for fast food as a lateral move, rather than one that was protective of health. Randi, who has continued to eat a moderate amount of fish because she considers it a healthy food, described feeling irritated that people "can be sitting there eating McDonald's telling you how bad it is to eat fish, and it just doesn't make any sense, and you can't really make people understand that." Her sister-in-law had been one of those people. While I sat at the sister-in-law's kitchen table, she realized midconversation—as she was talking about how she does not eat the fish because in doing so she does not know what she is putting in her body—that eating McDonald's is not really any better. "What the hell am I putting in my body!?" she exclaimed, laughing. A few minutes later, her husband walked through the door with a sack full of fast food for her lunch. "Here I am talking about health," she laughed, as she pulled a container of fries from the bag.

The complicated risk assessment undertaken by eaters in Akwesasne is demonstrated by some community members' staunch avoidance of fish in favor of processed foods that carried some guarantee of safety through their commercial packaging. Food anthropologist Pat Caplan writes that people live in a complex landscape of relative risk and are thus led both to believe and to disbelieve the health messages around food, becoming "skeptical eaters."[41] She notes that people will continue to eat high-fat foods even when they know about the risk of heart disease, but they will quickly abandon foods that are connected with immediate dangers, such as when salmonella cases are tied to eggs. Many people in Akwesasne have responded similarly, abandoning fish because of the frightening and somewhat mysterious implications of PCB contamination, yet continuing to consume high-fat and high-sugar foods that are known to have more banal, yet serious, consequences for health but come with the relative guarantee that they are free from chemical pollution.

COMFORT FOOD AND EATING AS A "SOCIAL EXERCISE"

People I spoke with recognized that even if they were preparing food at home, they were eating more energy-dense foods than they should be, especially in social situations. Emmy, who runs the Thompson Memorial Wellness Center, described how she was doing better with her diet and eating healthier, but the summer had seen several deaths in the community, and with all of the wakes she had been assisting with, she was surrounded by "comfort food." This, combined with summer cookouts "and the big dinners that our community has and the feasts and stuff like that," led her astray from a diet that she perceived as more healthy.

Randi similarly described the struggle to buy and cook healthy food in her own home, saying that in such a tight-knit community, it is difficult to

> combat the birthday cake and the parties and just Sunday dinner and Saturday dinner and bingo night. You know it is like a constant—and I don't want to say it is like a constant trap, but it can feel that way if you are trying to avoid food. If you are trying to avoid food that is high in sugar, high in fat, it's like it can drive you crazy. . . . You know, just being around my grandparents' house for the past three weeks very intensively—I've eaten more eggs than I ever have in such a small period of time and—it's just, and I would never do it at home, but at grandma's you just put a big old teaspoon of butter in the pan before you cook your egg and it just seems right because that's way they do it there. Even though at home I would probably be disgusted by that, and that is how it is, it's—"God I would never make this cake and I would never eat this," when you go to grandma's and it like feels so good you know. It makes you feel good, yes. So it is all these feel-good things and this is why we are so close with our families, you know, part of it because of the food, we like to eat together. So I don't know, I think any solution that is going to come has to start there.

Sharing food and taking part in meals brings family members together, and rejecting that food in an attempt to eat "healthier" as an individual raises concerns about isolation and offending relatives. As Randi suggested, it is likely that any change in diet in her family will have to emerge as a group choice.

In any culture, food serves to express personal and group identities and to cement social bonds.[42] The Akwesasne culture of communal eating has sometimes served to illuminate differences between Mohawk people and visitors. In looking back on her experience with the first large group of health researchers to descend on Akwesasne, Katsi Cook described how the differences between the Mount Sinai researchers and Mohawks became especially apparent at mealtimes. She recalled a time when, during a lunch break, Mohawks sat down together to eat their ham sandwiches and mashed potatoes, while a researcher stood with an apple looking out the window. The researcher turned from the window to tell the Mohawks, "Oh, what you're eating is really unhealthy. No wonder you have such diabetes and heart disease," and then went back to staring out the window while eating the apple. Katsi continued:

> You know, the dynamics of eating and food are very culturally ingrained, and our people like to sit and visit and eat as part of that social—eating is a social exercise as well as to nourish your body. And here is the outsider, the scientist, telling people how they should be, and how they, you know, eat by yourself, looking out a window, which, to me, is not a healthy thing to do.[43]

In this case, definitions of "healthy eating" go beyond the nutritional content of the food being consumed to include the atmosphere and the relationships among the eaters. In accordance with the "one dish, one spoon" philosophy (discussed in the preface), the social sharing of food is central to a smoothly functioning Haudenosaunee society. Concerns about the shift in diet of many Akwesasro:non in recent years centers not just on the nutritionally poor food being consumed but also on the consumption of this food as a rushed, thoughtless process, rather than as part of social or family settings.

As noted above, any successful event in Akwesasne is accompanied by food. As Henry put it, "If you feed Mohawks, they're happy." To which his wife Jean replied, "That's the problem with my culture, everything involves food." This is a problem, as defined by Jean, in recent years because of the expanding waistlines of Akwesasro:non. Using "visiting" as a social science methodology in Akwesasne to collect the stories for this book meant that I did a lot of eating—I often had to find a way to eat more than one lunch or dinner in a day, and at the very least had to share in coffee and snacks, to avoid offending the people who had invited me into their homes. My slightly underweight frame concerned some people, prompting them to want to feed me more (one man referred to me as "skinny Liz" to differentiate me from another Liz). Drawing attention to my thinness was not a compliment but rather a marker of concern that I was not being properly nourished, that I had not received enough hospitality, and a reminder that thinness was not the average or expected body type.[44]

This cultural expectation of the communal enjoyment of food helps place into context the anxiety over the diminishment of shared meals in busy families. It also means that the individualistic attitude toward dieting held by most Americans will not necessarily work in a community like Akwesasne. As Randi noted, healthy eating is going to have to start at grandma's house. At the same time, the new dietician I spoke with at the Mohawk Healthy Heart Project described efforts to help clients eat better, teaching them how to make healthy snacks. Many of the grandmothers in her program were worried that their grandchildren were not going to like these snacks, preferring chips and candy. Evidently, for change to come about, the entire family needs to come together under the opinion that the collective diet needs to be healthier.

No Time for Meals

The lack of time necessary to cook a full meal was among the reasons given for the rapid change in diet of many Akwesasro:non. As one older woman, Sarah, explained, people began to consume more fast food "because it's so easy for you to go out and get it. It's better than making it in the kitchen. It is easy, huh. . . . 'Cause it takes time to prepare and some people don't have time." Half a dozen other community members echoed her thoughts, describing how making home-cooked meals was especially difficult for working mothers, who were trying to balance their own schedules with those of their families, shuttling children to sports and taking care of their households. As one of the nurses at the clinic noted, "Every kid is doing something, which is really good except that they're never home. So they don't eat at home, so they don't cook, and they eat out a lot, so obesity is rampant in the community for adults and for kids." While intensive sports like lacrosse, which is very popular in Akwesasne, develop healthy athletes, the athletes' families are eating take-out food while shuttling to and from practices or eating stadium food in the stands during games. Interviewees emphasized that people need to start making their own meals at home again, although, according to Chris, "a lot of people will balk at it because of the convenience of the fast food. You know it has just totally taken over everything."

In addition to concerns about the nutritional implications of fast-food meals on the go, community members expressed anxiety about the loss of shared family meals. In "eating without meals," eating has been desocialized. The social relations that would be fostered by communal meals have taken on a new form as the structure of meals has dissolved into a pattern of "grazing" on snacks.[45]

IMPACT OF THE CHANGES IN DIET: GASTRO-ANOMY

Food scholars have described anxiety over the loss of shared family meals and people's alienation from the processing of their own food as "gastro-anomy." As anthropologist Claude Fischler argues, without meals to structure food choices, and without a connection to the process of creating, harvesting, and preparing food, people are left without clear sociocultural cues as to what their choices should be, and when, how much, and how they should eat, which leads to a collective sense of anxiety.[46] At the same time, consumers feel anxiety because of their lack of understanding about what is in the processed foods they are now consuming. As food preparation has moved from the kitchen to the factory, the processing of food no longer seems to guarantee symbolic purity—people no longer fear biological corruption of food, but rather corruption by chemical additives and excessive processing.[47] In contrast to the products of the fishing and farming culture that dominated Akwesasne's food scene until the current generation, the foods now consumed out of boxes or cans, or procured through drive-up windows, are relatively devoid of cultural and family connections. As Fischler reflects, "If one does not know what one is eating, one is liable to lose the awareness or certainty of what one is oneself. How do modern foods transform us from the inside?"[48]

In Akwesasne, this gastro-anomy cuts two ways. Some residents have given up local foods that connected them to their families, ancestors, and culture because of concerns about contamination, which cannot necessarily be detected by the naked eye, leaving them, as Fischler notes, "effectively unable to trust the sensory messages given off by any given food product as a reliable guide to its actual nature."[49] Fish that might look and taste fine could potentially be contaminated, and so was not to be trusted. At the same time, the processed foods that replaced the fish also came to be seen as suspect as people learned more about the preservatives and other unhealthy ingredients they might contain.

Return to Traditional Food

As food anthropologist Gillian Crowther describes, this gastro-anomy was "unleashed" on society by the industrialization of food, and especially fast food. She notes, "The often proposed antidote is a return to traditional eating practices, regarded as rooted in local cuisines."[50] Many Akwesasro:non that I spoke with felt that it was especially important to move toward reincorporating traditional Mohawk foods into community members' diets. Foods that are considered traditional include wild game and garden staples that Mohawks have been consuming for centuries, such as venison, fish, corn, beans, squash, and berries. At the conclusion of most longhouse ceremonies, participants are fed corn bread; soup that contains corn, beans, and squash as well as meat (usually venison, buffalo, or pork); and strawberry drink. The Ohero:kon rites of passage ceremonies focus as much as possible on the consumption of traditional foods.

Traditional foods are considered to have health-providing medicinal qualities that Mohawk people are intended to consume. As one man stated: "We have to get more back to our natural way of eating. Corn, beans, and squash—that also is a medicine. It's not just a food. It's a medicine too." Another man told me that when he eats his traditional corn, beans, and squash, his blood sugar stabilizes, and he feels healthy. When he strays from this diet, he gets sick. John Mohawk describes how Haudenosaunee people spent a great deal of time developing and cultivating foods that came together to form a balanced diet that kept them healthy past one hundred years of age. He contrasts this with modern American society, where "I've been in a hospital and they'll kill you from the kitchen. They clearly don't believe that food is a medicine."[51]

The traditional foods most commonly referred to as medicinal are traditional varieties of corn, beans, and squash, the "three sisters," considered important for cultural reasons in addition to being more nutritious than some conventional vegetable varieties. These plants grow symbiotically: beans fix the necessary atmospheric nitrogen for the corn, which in turn provides structure for the winding bean plant, while squash keeps weeds and herbivores away. Similarly, these foods complement each other as a meal. The basic building blocks of protein are amino acids, nine of which the human body cannot make and so must be consumed in the diet. Both corn and beans are low in some amino acids, but each is short on amino acids abundant in the other, which dramatically increases the protein quality of the combination. Corn is low in the water-soluble B vitamin niacin, but a dietary combination of corn and beans avoids the problem of niacin deficiency (which can lead to diseases such as pellagra) because beans are good sources of niacin. Haudenosaunee corn is treated with lye or wood ash before it is eaten, a process that also makes more niacin available for absorption, as well as increases the calcium content of the corn. Traditional varieties of corn, from both the Northeast and the Southwest of North America, are higher in protein than modern corn varieties, which have been bred for their sugar content.[52] A corn, bean, and squash diet is high in complex carbohydrates and low in fat. Beans also have a low glycemic index, which means they are helpful for moderating blood sugar. Thus, corn, beans, and squash form a complete diet. Katsi Cook has commented on the cultural importance of these foods:

> They say corn is the breast milk of the Mother Earth, and it is very true. Complemented with the beans and squash they create the perfect protein. . . . The very act of husking the corn, is like seeing a newborn baby, my how beautiful it is! . . . In Mohawk the word for bundling a newborn baby is "putting the husk back onto the corn" so every one of these babies that comes to us is an ear of corn![53]

White corn is the traditional variety that has persisted to the greatest extent in the community, as it is necessary for foods like corn soup, corn mush, and boiled rounds of corn bread.

Community organizations that are working to promote traditional foods face a double challenge: in addition to getting more people to garden, they need to get Haudenosaunee seeds into community members' gardens. In her 2002 dissertation about heritage seeds at Akwesasne, Mohawk seed keeper Rowen White notes:

> Community members mostly eat non-traditional food from the grocery, allowing themselves to prepare traditional foods and

Young Mohawk gardener Ionawiienhawi holding ears of Darwin John Calico corn (a Haudenosaunee heritage seed variety) in the Kanenhi:io Ionkwaienthon:hakie garden. Photograph by Elizabeth Hoover, 2008.

crops for special occasions. This not only has severe personal health implications for Haudenosaunee people, but also affects the genetic integrity of their heirloom cultivars. When they are taken from daily life and placed into a more "ceremonialized" forum, they too lose part of their life and dynamics.[54]

Organizations like the Akwesasne Task Force on the Environment, Kanenhi:io, and the Ase Tsi Tewa:ton Cultural Restoration Program (described in this book's conclusion) are working to make these seeds more available to gardeners.

Muskrat was once a well-loved and frequently eaten food in Akwesasne that people have uniformly given up since the issuance of the fish advisories. Gina described how people used to eat muskrat all the time, saying, "That used to be medicine because muskrat lives on our roots," which would transfer their medicinal qualities to the meat of the muskrat. Unfortunately, because of concerns about contamination, people avoid muskrat now. Snye, the region of the reservation located in the lowlands on the banks of the Saint Lawrence River, was an area where people were especially reliant on muskrat. Henry remembered that when he was a kid, when he would go visit people in Snye, "every house you used to go to had a pot of muskrat." His wife, Jean, reminisced with sad fondness about "muskrat cheeks," a dish she has not had in decades. She remarked, "When all this pollution and the don't-eat-the-fish came, and can't eat the muskrat because they're all polluted, too. They still don't eat muskrat. But they started to eat fish again, but nobody eats muskrat." Howard, the elderly farmer from Cornwall Island, also reminisced about catching and eating muskrat, adding, "Now I don't dare to eat them even though they might be clean. A lot of change in life." Although some people, as noted previously and discussed below, have gone back to eating local fish, there has not been a movement to return to eating muskrat. One woman noted:

> When you start seeing people eating muskrat again, then you'll have an idea that we're getting back to where we were. Now, I mean, a whole generation has gone without eating muskrat. So to think of eating a muskrat—"Ew!" you know. But we did, and they were good. And people knew how to cook it. And that's another thing, is to be able to use them again before people forget how to cook them, you know. Or we'll be going to the white man for recipes.

Tony David, an employee with the SRMT Environment Division, has done testing on beaver and muskrat, and except for one, all samples showed undetectable levels of PCBs. As he noted, muskrats are herbivores, and plants do not tend to uptake PCBs. He lamented that muskrat consumption is "a prime example of something that was given up that was unnecessary," and now "there's a generation gap because people gave it up for thirty years, and now nobody knows how to cook it." The Ase Tsi Tewa:ton Cultural Restoration Program, described in this book's conclusion, is working on reteaching community members how to trap, skin, and cook muskrats.

Conclusion

In criticizing the conventional risk assessment model, Akwesasne community members Alice Tarbell and Mary Arquette note that sometimes the greatest health effects are seen outside of chemical exposures and are thus not included in risk assessments.[55] The environmental contamination at Akwesasne had negative impacts on the cultural, social, and physical health of the community beyond those directly related to the ingestion of fish. Fear of exposure to contaminants led to the replacement of this low-fat source of protein and other important nutrients with high-fat and high-carbohydrate sources of food, which in turn led to increases in diabetes (discussed in the next chapter) and the interruption of traditional food systems. Despite these impacts, the SUNY researchers who conducted health studies in Akwesasne have stated that the reduction of fish consumption has been more beneficial to community members' health than continued fish consumption because of the risks of contaminant exposure. In a paper published in 2012, Schell et al. assess the benefits of consuming less local fish (lower PCB levels in the youth they tested) versus the costs (cultural losses and higher rates of diabetes and obesity).[56] While they do not go so far as to recommend what community members should do or eat, they conclude that regulatory agencies should give more consideration to the holistic risk-based environmental decision-making model proposed by ATFE members Arquette et al.[57] They also suggest that biologists should give more attention to the nonnutritional components of many foods, such as persistent organic pollutants. David Carpenter has argued that, especially since some studies done at Akwesasne have connected PCB levels with potential health effects, the cessation of fish consumption was the best option for Mohawks, although more should have been done to help people find healthier food substitutes. Carpenter has also questioned whether the touted benefits of fish consumption are enough to counterbalance the potential impacts of the contaminants.[58]

At a community meeting the SUNY researchers hosted on

January 11, 2012, to discuss the results of more than a decade of research, questions arose around whether the issuance of fish advisories had been the best course of action, considering the unintended health consequences, such as obesity and diabetes, that have been linked to a more modern diet. The researchers acknowledged that their data demonstrated that youth born before the Tribe's fish advisory (1985) had higher PCB levels than those born after, demonstrating the effectiveness of the advisory in lowering PCB body burdens.[59] One participant pushed further—what about now, after the remediation work that had been done? In the discussion that followed, the general consensus was that more testing needed to be done on local fish populations to determine current contaminant levels. The new fish advisory that has since come out of this work by the Environment Division is discussed in the conclusion.

In another community meeting almost three years later (December 11, 2014), Ken Jock, the director of the SRMT Environment Division, stated:

> Fish are clean enough to eat in certain areas, and to me, that's something we really need to do. We need to go back to the river, we need to go back to hunting and trapping, raising our own gardens, because that's the food that's best for us. That's the food that we're meant to eat, not the food that you get at a grocery store that you buy, processed. Macaroni or whatever. The food we need is the food that lives out here, that we can catch.

Later during that same meeting, when community members asked David Carpenter what they should do to protect their health, he replied:

> You can't avoid some exposure, but you can hold the feet to the fire of the industries and the government to have them not just cover [the contaminants] up, but get them out of here. You can take reasonable steps to—don't eat highly contaminated fish. Pay attention to these new fish advisories. Just use some common sense, and of course it's always absolutely critical to balance your culture, the benefits of cultural lifestyle, against the harm of the contaminants. And nobody can answer that but each individual person.

In a community where many food choices are made collectively and are influenced by the myriad factors described throughout this chapter, this is not an easy set of recommendations to follow. As Katsi noted at an environmental health conference, food insecurity as a result of reduced choices could "amplify adverse environmental reproductive health effects at the individual, community, and collective levels."[60]

In my discussions with community members about changes that have occurred in Akwesasne around fishing and farming, a number of common themes arose, including a sense of responsibility to these local foods, concerns about the lack of transmission of cultural knowledge related to the diminishment of local food procurement practices, and issues of trust and risk assessment that come with relying on government agencies for information on whether or not foods are safe to eat. On many levels, the anxieties that interviewees expressed relative to these issues boil down to the interruption of systems of responsibilities, what Kyle Powys Whyte refers to as the "relational responsibilities" that are necessary for a tribe's "collective continuance."[61] Whyte notes that a tribal community's capacity for "collective continuance" and "comprehensive aims at robust living" are hindered when the relationships that are part of traditional food cultures and economies are disrupted.[62] Even though most Native communities are no longer reliant on subsistence production of food, Kirk Dombrowski notes, taking part in traditional food production helps provide Indigenous people with a "sense of uniqueness and participation in a community which . . . provides an important sense of belonging."[63] In his work, he has found that while most Indigenous communities are deeply embedded in the wider political economy, Native people "continue to emphasize the central place of subsistence in their mutual relations and the 'sense of place' that these practices and relations create."[64]

Environmental contamination, industrialization, and modernization have all affected the food culture of Akwesasne. As environmental psychologist Michael Edelstein notes, toxic exposures may disrupt the lifescape, "a term that refers to our fundamental understandings about what to expect from the world around us. The lifescape reflects not only our own unique interpretive framework, but also the shared social and personal paradigms used for understanding the world."[65] By necessitating advisories recommending that Akwesasro:non limit or cease fish consumption to protect their health, and by raising fears about the safety of local gardening because of a general perception that the land is tainted, environmental contamination from the GM, Reynolds, and Alcoa plants interrupted the lifescape of Akwesasne—the shared social and personal paradigms that had structured Mohawk life for generations.

In considering a political ecology of eating, factors beyond environmental contamination that have influenced Akwesasne food culture also need to be taken into consideration: diminished local food production because of a switch to wage labor, a lack of land for gardening, youth who are more interested in digital entertainment than in manual labor, mothers who are too busy to garden and cook meals, and a preference for the convenience of store-bought and fast foods. Jessica Hayes-Conroy and Allison Hayes-Conroy note that "in terms of how to make healthy foods more 'available,' we need to begin to recognize the question of motivation itself as a question of access. Indeed, if the emotive/affective, visceral impetus to eat a certain food does not exist in the first place, then access is necessarily about much more than the distance or price of the food, or even its cultural meaning."[66] They describe food access in affective/emotive terms, as a whole network of forces that influence bodily movement, desire, and drive—many of the same forces that political ecologists study in terms of ecological struggle. The work of Akwesasne community organizations that focus on a return to traditional food is about more than just battling for environmental cleanup (although this is still a serious issue); these organizations are also working to reintroduce Akwesasro:non to an emotive/affective attachment to traditional foods and the culturally important means of procuring them.

CHAPTER 5

PCBs and Thrifty Genes

Broadening the Scope of Illness Explanation

One sunny afternoon, I sat with Mohawk elder Howard David on the front porch of his house on Cornwall Island, in the northern part of Akwesasne. As we sat overlooking his garden, and in the distance the Saint Lawrence River, he spoke about how his father used to take him fishing. He told me that the water in the river was so clean that when they got thirsty, they would lean over the side of their boat and dip a can into the water and drink from it. Then the industrial plants were built along the river.

> Ever since then they started up pollution. I do believe this is where we're getting our diabetes too, lot of pollution. I've been diabetic, I just found out there two years back now and that's what brought a lot of disease, a lot of stuff from these pollutions. And the fish we used to eat, I know one guy used to catch sturgeon, I'd go every spring and then take one and have a good feast. And the muskrats, we used to eat them too. Now I don't dare to eat them even though they might be clean. A lot of change in life.

Later in the conversation, after we had talked about his work on the Saint Lawrence Seaway, the effects of fluoride contamination on his neighbors' cows, and the vitamin regimen he used to cleanse his body of any contamination, I asked him, "Do you think that this contamination has affected people's health in Akwesasne?" He replied:

Yes. See, I didn't see that when I was a kid and like it wasn't that bad. Ever since all this pollution coming in, it got worse and worse. The first thing I found out, diabetes. Everybody has it. After I got it, I find out that everybody's getting it. I know when you eat the wrong food, that's what causes it. Then again, we don't know what's in the food now today. Yeah, we used to have our own milk and our own beef, our own meat, pork, everything. Now we don't keep nothing no more. . . . We cut back a lot, not much beef no more. Mostly, well for me now, chicken and fish. My diet for diabetes, and a lot of green vegetables.

Howard has lived along the river since before the seaway came through, and he has seen the dramatic changes in both the diet and health of his fellow community members and the quality of the environment, what Harris and Harper call the "eco-cultural system," for Mohawk people.[1] In our conversation, he blamed diabetes directly on the pollution, which he saw as having "brought" the disease to the community, like an unwelcome guest or an unwanted gift. He reinforced this by offering diabetes as an example when I asked him about the effects of contamination on health. In the same breath, he said that diabetes is caused by eating "the wrong food," although all foods are somewhat suspect because "we don't know what's in the food now today." He also mentioned the changes in farming practices brought on by environmental contamination, which have contributed to the diet changes. This snippet of my conversation with Howard captures much of the ambivalence that many of the residents I spoke with felt about the root causes of diabetes in the community. The blame is diffuse: it does not rest long on the diabetes sufferer, who may be at fault for eating the wrong foods, but who also cannot trust any food these days, and who has been subjected to a half century of pollution.

Community members blame a vast majority of the other illnesses they mentioned directly on the industrial plants, and, as demonstrated in chapter 2, some of the recently published papers by the SUNY SBRP team support some of these concerns. Opinions on the root of the diabetes "epidemic" proved to be slightly more complicated, weaving together issues of individual responsibility and the problems of living in an environment altered by contamination. In voicing their opinions about why the community suffers from high rates of diabetes, some interviewees agreed with the common biomedical explanations of poor diet and lack of exercise, coupled with factors related to genetic makeup, whereas others explicitly challenged these explanations.

Conversations around diabetes and other illnesses commonly came up when I asked Akwesasro:non interviewees to broadly "rate the health of the community," with the understanding that "health is not some absolute state of being but an elastic concept that must be evaluated in a larger sociocultural context."[2] This was represented in the narratives interviewees presented. When I asked Akwesasro:non to rate the health of the community, most gave negative responses: "poor," "very poor," "terrible," "It sucks," "There's something wrong with everybody that I know," "a lot of health issues," "so-so," "worse than the average American suburbia guy I guess," "A lot of people are not well," "not very good," "not the best," "Oh, there are so many issues," and "like that big river in Africa—in de-Nile." A few people had more positive opinions, including "pretty good," and "fair, but it's getting better, it's improving." Three people independently offered to rate community health on a scale from 1 to 10, with 1 being the worst: two of them gave it a rating of 6, and one gave it a 5. The reasons they gave for these generally low ratings had to do with the preponderance of illnesses that community members mentioned: diabetes, cancer, heart disease, respiratory ailments, thyroid disorders, rashes, reproductive issues, cognitive issues, autoimmune disorders, emotional issues, headaches, digestive disorders, unidentifiable illnesses, and allergies. They attributed most of the illnesses the community is facing (85 percent of the preceding list) to contamination from the local industrial plants, while they attributed some aspects of diabetes, cancer, and heart disease (the top three ailments mentioned) to lifestyle choices by some members of the community.

Interviewees' explanations for the prevalence of diabetes—the most frequently mentioned health problem—both diverged from and converged with common biomedical explanations in interesting ways, as community members placed differing weights on self-care versus uncontrolled exposure to contaminants and had differing images of what it meant for the community to suffer from this illness. Below I discuss specifically how critical medical anthropology has shown diabetes to be an illness with roots that are much more complex than just lack of individual compliance—roots that Native American studies scholars link to settler colonialism and that political ecology scholars find in environmental, political, and social disturbance—and how Akwesasro:non, with their distinct etiologies for this illness in their community, contribute to efforts to broaden the scope of illness explanation beyond the biomedical.

Diabetes

First, a brief discussion of the conventional biomedical etiology for type 2 diabetes, also known as adult-onset diabetes and non-insulin-dependent diabetes mellitus, is in order. Insulin, produced in the pancreas, is necessary for the body to break down sugars and starches into glucose for energy and then transport the sugar from the blood into the cells. In a person diagnosed with diabetes, either the body does not produce enough insulin or the cells ignore the insulin. As a result, glucose builds up in the blood rather than being transported into the cells, and the individual is described as having elevated blood sugar. People with diabetes are now often considered to be what medical anthropologist Juliet McMullin describes as "failed bodies and unhealthy others," bodies that the medical community perceives as having not maintained the health that nature has given them and are not disciplined in the knowledge of health.[3]

Upon being assigned the diagnosis of diabetes, individuals are instructed by their doctors to amend their unhealthy behavior; they are told to alter their diets to include more vegetables, fruits, and other healthy sources of fiber and to decrease their consumption of sugars, fats, and refined carbohydrates. Fiber is capable of slowing down the digestion and absorption of carbohydrates and increasing the sensitivity of tissues to insulin, thereby preventing a rise in blood sugar. Foods that are high in simple sugars and low in fiber have a high glycemic index, meaning they break down quickly during digestion and raise blood sugar rapidly. Foods that are high in saturated fats interfere with the pancreas's insulin-producing capabilities and are also to be avoided.[4] In addition, since adiposity is considered a contributing factor to the disease, people with diabetes are told to get more exercise, which can improve their metabolisms and assist in weight loss. If their blood sugar levels do not go down as the result of changes in diet and exercise, their health care practitioners will know that they have been "noncompliant"—that is, they have not followed the prescribed diet and exercise regimens. Their physicians may prescribe oral insulin agents to help their diabetic bodies better process the sugars in their blood. If this is also unsuccessful, insulin injections will be prescribed.

Diabetes is the seventh leading cause of death in the United States and is a major cause of heart disease and stroke. Other outcomes of diabetes include blindness, kidney failure, nervous system damage, foot ulcers leading to amputations, gum disease, complications in pregnancy, and susceptibility to other diseases—for example, people with diabetes are more likely than those without the disease to die from pneumonia or influenza. Measures recommended to prevent these complications include glucose control, blood pressure control, and control of blood lipids, generally through diet, exercise, and insulin therapy.[5]

DIABETES IN NATIVE COMMUNITIES

Prior to the 1940s, diabetes was practically unheard-of in Indian Country. Now it is an all-too-common illness that affects most Indigenous communities around the world that are experiencing dramatic shifts in diet and lifestyle. During World War II, when Denis Burkitt was serving as a physician in Africa, he noticed that chronic degenerative diseases seemed to follow in the wake of a diet that closely matched that of industrialized countries; he labeled these "Western diseases."[6] He noted that as populations around the world adopted a Western diet and lifestyle, Western diseases emerged in a distinct order, with obesity among the first to appear, paralleled closely by the rising incidence of type 2 diabetes and cardiovascular disease.[7] Diabetes was first documented among Native Americans around the mid-twentieth century, and anthropologists first studied diabetes in this population in the late 1970s.[8] Medical anthropologist Dennis Wiedman found in his research with Cherokee people in Oklahoma that within ten years of a dramatic demographic, technological, and cultural transition, there was an increase in rates of diabetes. The transitions he noted included the shifts from subsistence agriculture to a cash economy, from self-produced to energy-dense store-bought foods, from vigorous household activities to the comforts of labor-saving appliances, and from active walking to riding in trucks and cars.[9] Wiedman points to the association of the critical juncture of modernity with the initiation of metabolic disorders.[10]

Large disparities exist in the rates at which different populations suffer from diabetes. The population designated as "American Indian or Alaska Native" by the U.S. Department of Health and Human Services has been found to have twice the number of overall cases of diabetes as the white non-Hispanic U.S. population.[11] American Indian or Alaska Native adults (16.1 percent) are more likely than black adults (12.6 percent), Hispanic adults (11.8 percent), Asian adults (8.4 percent), or white adults (7.1 percent) to have ever been told they had diabetes. These rates vary by region, from 5.5 percent among Alaska Native adults to 33.5 percent among American Indian adults in southern Arizona.[12] Similarly, rates of diabetes among Indigenous populations in Canada are three to five times higher than the rate in the general population.[13]

COMMUNITY PERCEPTIONS OF DIABETES AT AKWESASNE

As noted above, when I asked Akwesasro:non to describe the current health of the community, diabetes was the most frequently mentioned health problem. People quoted figures, stating that between 25 percent and 70 percent of community members suffer from diabetes. The upper range of their estimates is much higher than research and clinical estimates, but it serves as in indicator of community concern and the extent to which this illness has affected some people's families. Janine Rourke, director of the Tsitewatakari:tat/Let's Get Healthy program, which serves residents with diabetes, told me that 13–16 percent of community members have diabetes, while another 7–10 percent go undiagnosed, for an estimated total of about one-fourth of the community. It is clear that the personal impact that diabetes has on many residents' lives has made the problem seem even more immense and ubiquitous than it is, as reflected by the interviewees' estimates.

In 1989, Charlene Martinez, a family nurse practitioner at the Saint Regis Mohawk Health Services, and Karen Strauss with Indian Health Services conducted a survey of the Saint Regis Mohawk Reservation (the southern portion of Akwesasne) and found that the age-adjusted prevalence of diabetes in the Mohawk population was two times the national average. There was a high prevalence of diabetes among New York Mohawks under forty-five years of age (21 percent), compared to rates in the U.S. population as a whole (17 percent).[14]

In reviewing records from the tribal clinic from 1992 through 1997, SUNY Albany researchers Negoita et al. also found that diabetes showed a higher age-specific prevalence among Akwesasro:non than in the general U.S. population, the age being lower than the national average among young Mohawks and higher among older Mohawks.[15] Janine noted that the largest increases in the incidence of diabetes in Akwesasne have been in the thirty-five to fifty age group, but also, "we're definitely seeing and feeling the impact of the twenty-five-year-old coming in, the twenty-eight-year-old coming in, and the twelve-year old." Health studies conducted by SUNY Albany researchers found that Akwesasne girls and boys are in the eighty-fifth and ninetieth percentiles, respectively, for body mass index among youth in the United States.[16] Similarly, women taking part in a reproductive health study were found to be above average in weight: 24 percent were overweight, and 58 percent were obese.[17] But while many of the residents I spoke with were in agreement that diabetes and obesity pose serious challenges to health in their community, not everyone agreed on the sources of these problems.

Etiology of Disease

Biomedical explanations for diseases tend to focus on pathologies within the individualized body—illnesses brought on by exposure to germs or viruses, organs or cells malfunctioning as a result of maladaptive lifestyle practices or exposure to chemicals. Epidemiology seeks to quantify numbers of people within a social body who suffer from the same affliction, to determine if those numbers are above what should be expected for that population. Social scientists—and here I will be referencing mainly critical medical anthropologists—explore patients' or sufferers' own explanations for the sources of their afflictions, which often point to influencing factors beyond their own individual, seemingly maladaptive, lifestyle choices. In addition, social scientists explore the historical, political, economic, and environmental factors that are implicated in a network of disease causation, which extends from political and social bodies down to the individual body. Medical anthropologist Sherine Hamdy notes that in exploring how power inequities produce and distribute illness, she came to understand that patients were formulating "political etiologies," extending the pain of their illnesses beyond the diseased body to implicate corrupt institutions, environmental pollution, and inadequate food as the cause of their ill health.[18] Often these etiologies find their root in what Nancy Scheper-Hughes refers to as "everyday violence" and Paul Farmer calls "structural violence"—the normalized suffering, disease, and premature death found in certain marginalized populations.[19] This structural violence leads sufferers to "interpret their bodily states, seek care, and fashion themselves according to prevailing moral notions" that are often based in an individualized, neoliberal idea of who deserves to be healthy and how they should become so.[20] In contrast, exploring the historical, political, economic, and environmental factors behind illness in Native communities "shifts the medical gaze from the diseased body to a diseased colonial and post-colonial history of genocide, the collective experience of trauma reproduced in many 'small wars and invisible genocides' practiced against Indigenous Peoples to this day."[21]

The importance of exploring diverse disease etiologies lies in the potential for such investigation to produce knowledge that will support the creation of prevention programs and strategies that can "transcend the exclusive biomedical focus on the physiological body, so as to include aspects of the social and political bodies as well."[22] In clinical interactions with patients, physicians are the "architects of meaning and explanations" about disease.[23] Considering patients' perceptions about the causes behind their illnesses allows them to build on their own meanings and explanations to create interventions that are more effective.

By highlighting the social, political, and environmental factors in disease etiology, I do not mean to dismiss the contribution of lifestyle factors in the prevention and treatment of disease. Rather, my aim is to demonstrate that traditional biomedical explanations and statistics do not tell the whole story of affliction or its causation. As Scheper-Hughes notes, to say that a condition like diabetes is a "sociopolitical pathology" is not to deny the medical model of disease

> but rather to search for ultimate, rather than immediate, causes and to recognize that what medical anthropologist Margaret Lock calls "local biologies" . . . emerge out of distinctive and collective experiences and histories of embodiment and risk, producing local and even culture bound symptoms and experiences of supposedly universal illnesses and disease.[24]

Below I discuss how the roots of diabetes are more complex than they are often assumed to be, involving much more than just individual behavioral choices. I also address how Akwesasro:non, with their distinct etiologies for this illness, contribute to critical medical anthropology's efforts to broaden the biomedical scope of illness explanation.

RACIAL/GENETIC EXPLANATIONS: POOR DIET AND THE "THRIFTY GENE"

The dominant epidemiological paradigm (DEP) for type 2 diabetes highlights genetic and behavioral risk factors.[25] The Centers for Disease Control and Prevention lists "race/ethnicity" among the factors that can contribute to type 2 diabetes (along with behaviors like "physical inactivity," traits like "obesity," and dysfunctions like "impaired glucose metabolism").[26] Frequently cited biomedical reasons for why Native people might be especially susceptible to this disease range from lifestyle factors such as poor-quality diet and lack of adequate physical activity to genetic theories about a "thrifty gene." First proposed by geneticist James Neel in 1962, the thrifty gene was thought to protect the bodies of hunter-gatherers against starvation in times of great seasonal fluctuation, but it became maladaptive with modern patterns of food consumption, leading Native people to store unhealthy amounts of fat.[27] Thirty years later, Neel tempered his theory, emphasizing that the high frequency of type 2 diabetes among American Indians was not attributable solely to an ethnic predisposition, but rather was predominantly a reflection of lifestyle changes.[28] But the thrifty gene hypothesis has taken on a life of its own—it has been cited in popular press accounts of the diabetes epidemic among Native Americans and incorporated into Native community members' own understandings of diabetes etiology.[29]

Genetics: "We Have a Completely Different Medical Makeup"

Despite debates around the utility of the thrifty gene theory, some Indigenous people have come to embrace it or otherwise use genetics as a metaphor for expressing vulnerability in the face of a challenging history.[30] Some of the Mohawks I interviewed had the impression that diabetes is something that is inherited, something that emerges,

Sculpture by Akwesasne Mohawk artist Natasha Smoke Santiago,
depicting a traditional Mohawk woman made from corn husks, insulin
bottles, and hypodermic needles. This piece represents the rapid increase
of cases of diabetes in the Akwesasne community, with the corn husks
symbolizing the traditional foods that the artist wants her relatives to
return to in order to regain their health. Photograph by Jessica Sargent.

as luck would have it, from one's family tree. As we stood in his living room, Robert rattled off a list of family members, some of whom
had diabetes and some of whom never did. "See, it's hereditary. It's a
hereditary thing. My sister didn't get it. My mother and father didn't
have it. I got it from my father's mother, my grandmother. So that
stinks. And it killed my two older brothers." Robert described diabetes as if it functions like a recessive gene—like the gene responsible
for blue eyes—that can emerge at random from one's lineage.

Other community members saw diabetes not just as a sur-
prise waiting in one's genetic makeup but as the result of a mis-
match between what Mohawks were designed to eat and what they
are currently eating. Henry, a biologist with the Mohawk Council of
Akwesasne, explained to me that the way Haudenosaunee bodies respond to alcohol or sugar "shows that we have a completely different
medical makeup. And when you say that, everybody goes, 'Ooh what
do you mean?' Well, you know that's been called—what was it—the
thrifty gene, the survival gene. But it does have a really serious impact on the metabolism." He went on to give an elaborate description
of how the Haudenosaunee body breaks down and stores sugars and
carbohydrates differently from the European body, and how the traditional Haudenosaunee diet, with crops bred to be high in protein
and complex carbohydrates, was better suited to the Mohawk metabolism than the more modern diet. Agnes, while citing diet change as
the main culprit in diabetes, also made a genetic link between Mohawk bodies and their traditional foods: "You know, going back to
diabetes, [fish] is a key protein missing in our diet right now. That's
got something to do with it. We're genetically made to have that in
our bodies. And now we're just eating McDonald's, Kentucky Fried
Chicken." The genetic need for fish is being met with an inferior
food, and that is triggering illness.

Beatrice, who helps run an alternative medicine center in Akwesasne, went a step further, not just condemning "junk food" but
describing the genetic preference of the Mohawk body for traditional
foods specifically of this region. She expressed her belief that "any
of the foods that have been produced in the northeastern part of our
country were specifically made for that people." The foods grown in
other territories, like the fruits imported from South America, were
designed for people from those regions:

But now because of our plants and everything are not being
grown healthily around here anymore that we are forced to
eat bananas, fruits, and things all year around, and our bodies
weren't built to eat that. We were only made to eat strawberries in the springtime. That was it. We weren't supposed to
have that kind of fruit through our diets and to our nutrition
and the bread that we're eating and stuff, we're not supposed
to have that. We were supposed to just have corn because corn

is a part of the thing that we've had here all through the generations. So all that food that we have available here—the fish, we were supposed to eat fish, muskrat, all that. We were supposed to. But because of the way that society has changed, the way the [industrial] plants contaminated the soil, and the sickness that goes on in our community and stuff, people are buying at the grocery store. It's coming all the way from the South, which our bodies were never built to eat anyway because our genetic makeup tells us that we have to eat the food that's here, and we can't anymore. So now what's happening to us as a society?

Her codirector at the center took the conversation even further, including intermarriage as another factor contributing to Native people's genetic difficulties in processing foreign foods.

Our genes are not made to mix with another breed. The immune system goes down. . . . So the genes of a Native person cannot digest all the white processed foods. Then when you're mixing the genes together, it makes the immune system of that person even weaker. We start developing all these different illnesses like stomach problems and stuff like that. . . . You can see it happen with our people now because we all have mixed.

Some of these lay conceptions of genetics may not always fall within the parameters of biomedical definitions, but they reflect broader social concerns about food production, environmental pollution, and intermarriage, and they provide insight into the ways these individuals have made sense of the social, environmental, and health changes that have accompanied diet changes in the community. As Indigenous science studies scholar Kim TallBear has explored in her work, some Native people have come to adopt the language of genetics to illustrate the deep physical connection they feel to cultural features. TallBear notes that in researching conceptions of Native blood and DNA, she found a trend in recent years among Native people of using language indicating that particular things are "part of our DNA" or "our genetic memory," things that would have previously been referenced more generally as "in our blood." She writes,

"This sense of inexplicable inheritance would not have been chalked up to genetics twenty years ago. It would have been spoken of in the language of blood."[31] Now that the language of genetics has become more popular, some community members are using it as a means of explaining their anxiety over decreased access to traditional foods and how this has affected community health.

Political Ecology of Diabetes

Although a genetic factor provides a convenient explanation for the disproportionate rates at which Native Americans suffer from diabetes, a number of scholars have spoken out against this explanation. While noting that genetic variation has much to do with the risk of becoming obese, geneticists have been unable to locate an actual thrifty gene and argue that epigenetic events (i.e., environmental factors that can affect gene expression) need to be taken into consideration.[32] Social science scholars argue that the notion that Indians carry a maladaptive gene is "scientific racism."[33] Scheper-Hughes asserts that the idea of such a gene suggests that "Indigenous blood carries a taint—the threat of passing on an inherited risk of diabetes."[34] There is also concern that the message that being Indian can lead to being diabetic promotes an "attitude of surrender" that disempowers individuals and communities, leaving them to feel as though there is nothing they can do to avoid the disease.[35]

Focusing on a primarily genetic cause for diabetes masks the underlying structural inequities that cause people of color to be more susceptible to the disease.[36] By placing "race/ethnicity" on a list of diabetes causes without qualifying why it is there, the CDC neglects the underlying root cause—that race/ethnicity is often associated also with class, education, levels of stress, and access to health care and fresh foods. The presence of low-income Appalachian whites among the ranks of the populations at high risk for diabetes is proof of this.[37] The correlation between race and diabetes becomes an "individual fallacy," a spin on the concept of "ecological fallacy," where a researcher makes an inference about an individual based on the aggregate for the group.[38] Chaufan argues that to counter the focus on the medicalized aspects of diabetes, which has led to the individualization and depoliticization of the issue, a political ecology framework needs to be applied to the disease, one that is concerned with the social, economic, and political institutions of the human environments where diabetes is emerging.[39] Such a framework would highlight how diabetes rates among Mohawk people are influenced more by changes in the natural environment and home environments than by genetic makeup.

Diabetes as "Directly Related to the Contamination"

Residents blame the industrial plants adjacent to Akwesasne for a number of the health and social problems in the community. Along these lines, about a half dozen interviewees stated that the high rates of diabetes in Akwesasne could be directly attributed to the environmental contamination from neighboring industries. When I asked Judy how she would rate the overall health of the community, she replied, "I think it sucks. Probably I would say 60 to 70 percent have diabetes, now a lot of it is inherited but a lot of it is caused by pollution also, certain amount, I don't how much exactly, but I am sure some of it is." Similarly, Brenda told me, "I think a lot of the health problems we have are directly related to the contamination. I think the diabetes, hypothyroidism, all of your endocrine disorders is a direct correlation and we can't prove it." The environmental health research conducted by SUNY Albany at Akwesasne is beginning to bear this out. One study concluded that in Akwesasro:non subjects, elevated serum levels of PCBs, dichlorodiphenyldichloroethylene (DDE), and hexachlorobenzene (HCB) were positively associated with diabetes after all potential confounders were controlled for.[40] The researchers state, "Although these results do not establish cause and effect, there is a growing body of evidence that environmental exposure to persistent organochlorine compounds is associated with elevated incidence of this disease."[41] In continuing to analyze the data, the SUNY team found that people with higher levels of the more lightly chlorinated congeners of PCBs had a significantly elevated risk of developing diabetes (for people whose levels of lightly chlorinated PCBs fell in the top 25 percent of the sample, the risk of developing diabetes increased 7.5-fold).[42] Some of the community members I spoke with were aware of this research; others intuited the connection between diabetes and PCB exposure based on their own experiences.

Unfortunately and ironically, the presence of diabetes in the community has now led to a new source of contamination. During a public meeting in December 2014, former director of the MCA Department of Environment Henry Lickers described how an increasing number of pharmaceuticals had been found in fish sampled from local rivers. As he reported to community members:

> The last study we did on fish in the river, we were able to find, for example, metformin. Any diabetics here, might be what you take is metformin. You don't use it all up in your body, when you go, it goes straight through the sewage system, right out into the river. So what is the impact of that drug on fish? We know that Prozac will do the same thing. So there's many of those pharmaceuticals that we're now finding in the water, and again, we don't know what the influence would be.

Some Akwesasro:non point to industrial contaminants as contributing to diabetes, and many of these contaminants have made their way into Mohawk bodies through fish eaten from the river or have discouraged people from eating fish from the river. In turn, the resulting diabetic bodies are now contributing pollution back into the river.

Individual Responsibility: "It's Your Choice"

Congruent with the dominant epidemiological paradigm, diabetes is commonly attributed to bodies that have begun to malfunction due to poor behavior. Some interviewees expressed that Akwesasro:non needed to take responsibility for their own behaviors and diets, and work to improve their health and individual bodies. One woman spoke of diabetes as an issue of control: "Diabetes is so high on our reservation here. I believe that it has nothing to do with the contamination. It's really their eating habits; it's about control of their weight." Later in the conversation, while she was describing cancer and other "long-term diseases" that had resulted from environmental contamination, she reemphasized that "I think diabetes could have been—that's all your food intake—it's your choice, right. So I think that's just out of control." Another woman also paused in the middle of a description of cancer as an environmentally caused disease to specify, "I don't know if diabetes resulted from contamination. I just think that's the lifestyle of the people." This lifestyle was something that people were expected to manage if they were to become and remain healthy.

Among this group of interviewees, discussions around diabetes centered on accepting blame for one's poor health. In describing the community health trajectory, which he saw as steadily declining once residents reach their fifties, one young man bluntly stated, "A lot of it is self-inflicted. I know better than to eat at McDonald's, I do anyway." He also pointed to smoking as another self-destructive behavior that people knowingly engage in. Others similarly expressed that Akwesasro:non need to move beyond blaming outside entities for their poor diets and health. As one woman stated, "It is somebody else's fault that we had to find another diet. You know, and the diet that we choose, we choose it, it's not very good. So whose fault is that?" In her view, even if the environment constrained the choices Akwesasro:non could make, they were still ultimately responsible for themselves. Another man told me that he wished that people would move beyond

> always saying, "Oh, the white man this, the white man that." It can't be about that anymore, you know, you have to—there is the blame there and there is the obstacles in your path, it's enough, you know, you have to say, "Well, I can do this, I can do that," you know, and the sooner we realize that, the sooner we'll be healthier.

A brief article published in 2008 in the Saint Regis Mohawk Tribe newsletter by the Tsitewatakari:tat/Let's Get Healthy program draws on both cultural connections to healthy ancestors and people's individual responsibility to follow a lifestyle similar to that of their ancestors in an effort to raise awareness of the connections between Mohawks' diet and modern sedentary lifestyle and their diabetes. The article states:

> Our elders didn't always have diabetes or high blood pressure. They grew up working hard, gardening, gathering, trapping, farming and fishing. Every day they had to work to eat. Indian country today fills up on pizza, poutine, and chicken wings.

> Many people only cook a full meal once or twice a week. Does this sound like you or anyone you know?[43]

This is one example of fellow residents asking Akwesasro:non to take responsibility for their own diets and health. While many community members, as discussed below, attribute their current poor diets to fears of contamination in local food, the individuals quoted above (none of whom had diabetes) all talked about the need for residents to move beyond blaming outside entities for their poor health and begin taking steps to improve their health.

"It's Like a Chain Reaction": Contaminated Environment, Changed Diets, and Diabetes

In reflecting on their research in the Mohawk community of Kahna-wà:ke, Macaulay et al. note,

> In Aboriginal communities, chronic diseases such as diabetes are considered indicative of the negative socio-cultural changes, the long term results of colonization, disempowerment, decreased land base, loss of traditional ways, social stressors, and a lifestyle that is increasingly mechanized and no longer includes the former high level of physical activity for daily living.[44]

None of this complex picture is captured in a biomedical model, which points only to the "faulty gene" or noncompliant behavior of an individual suffer of diabetes. As Ta-Nehisi Coates writes, "The purpose of the language of . . . 'personal responsibility' is broad exoneration" of the larger structures and systems that are implicated in illness.[45] Dennis Wiedman describes these negative sociocultural changes and structures of disempowerment as "chronicities of modernity," which produce everyday behaviors that limit physical activities while promoting high caloric intake and psychosocial stress.[46] These limiting, containing, and recurrent cognitive, social, and material processes restrict the decisions, alternatives, and agency that individuals can take to improve their well-being and become embodied in the physiology and metabolism of the body. In reflecting on why there are high rates of diabetes in Akwesasne, some community members described disease etiologies aligned with Wiedman's "chronicities of modernity" theory, linking diabetes to diet and lifestyle choices, but expressing that those choices had been limited for them because the free healthy foods to which they once had access were now perceived as unsafe to eat.[47] The issue that some people took with biomedical explanations for diabetes at Akwesasne was that individuals were often implicated for their poor diets, and they saw this as an oversimplification. Henry Lickers noted that these explanations do not point to the contamination that ruined the fish, they point to the person who changed his or her diet: "Again, epidemiology isn't pointing to the contaminant, it's actually pointing to the person and saying that you've changed your diet to a high-carbohydrate diet. Therefore, what's the cure for that? Ah, insulin. And again, the medical people go back to the treatment of the symptom, not to the source cause." This ties back to the political ecology of health theory discussed earlier—taking into account all of the social, political, and environmental factors that lead to individual and community food choices.

Most of the scholarly articles that have been published by members of the Akwesasne Task Force on the Environment concerning diabetes have connected the rising rates of the disease in the community with the forced change in diet spurred by the contamination. For example, Tarbell and Arquette, two ATFE members, argue that environmental risk assessments need to more broadly take into account the cultural viewpoints and lifestyles of Indigenous residents as part of determining what levels of exposures are acceptable. They draw a direct line from the contamination of the environment by industrial plants to the rapid change in diet and lifestyle of Mohawk people to the current rates of diabetes in the community—an unplanned outcome of the cessation of fish consumption. Tarbell and Arquette note:

> Sometimes the greatest health effects are seen without any exposure and thus would not be included in risk assessments. At Akwesasne human health has been affected by toxicants even without the ingestion of fish, wildlife, or water. For example, Mohawk people have customarily relied heavily on fish and wildlife as low-fat sources of protein, vitamins, and other

important nutrients. Many health care providers at Akwesasne fear that rapid changes in diet associated with the fish and wildlife advisories may be leading to diet-related illnesses such as heart disease, hypertension, stroke, and diabetes. The loss of fish in their diets represents the loss of an excellent source of protein. Thus, many Mohawks must turn to unhealthy, high-fat sources of protein, such as those found in fast-food places. Recent reports indicate that diabetes is on the rise because more people no longer eat traditional foods and no longer participate in cultural activities that once provided healthy forms of exercise.[48]

Similarly, in each of their articles reporting results of the SUNY Albany Mohawk Adolescent Well-Being Study, Schell and his team include a paragraph indicating that the diminishment of fishing that followed advisories against consumption of local fish at Akwesasne altered traditional subsistence patterns. This, they state, had a profound effect on the preservation of Indigenous Mohawk culture, as avoidance of foods and activities that may expose people to PCBs means that traditional activities are not performed, and social bonds forged between generations through the transfer of culture are not created.[49] In addition, while they might have diminished their fish-borne contamination exposures, community members have lost a primary source of protein and other important nutrients, such as calcium, iron, zinc, and omega-3 fatty acids.[50] The replacement of fish with cheap foods has had the effect of "further exacerbating chronic, diet-related health problems in the community, such as diabetes and cardiovascular disease."[51] All of these authors point to the collateral damage caused by the contamination: even when residents avoid contaminated food to prevent exposure to PCBs, they still suffer negative impacts to their health.

Many community members attribute the diabetes problem in Akwesasne to a diet high in sugar and fat and a lack of exercise, but rather than placing the blame on individuals for poor diet choices, they expressed the opinion that the contamination of natural food sources forced this change in diet on them. As Trudy said:

I think right now with the changes that they have nowadays, where they tell you, "You can only consume so much fish."

It's all substituted with all these fast foods. This is where our diabetes comes in. It's like a chain reaction. . . . You change over from fish to what? Pizza and wings? Of course, it's going to change things.

Richard estimated that more than half of adult males in Akwesasne are diabetic. "That's mostly based on diet. There's a lack of healthy food here. I mean, used to be we'd get bullheads out of here for consumption. I wouldn't touch them now." Jim, who worked for the SRMT Environment Division at the time when the contamination was discovered, expressed mixed feelings about the fish advisories that strongly encouraged people to change their diets: "The problem we didn't anticipate, though, was the change in the diet and the change in lifestyle we feel has contributed to the diabetes in the community and to the other illnesses in the community that has occurred since then. So that concerns me." In contrast, as noted earlier, SUNY researcher David Carpenter has argued that, especially as more recent studies have connected PCB levels with potential health effects, the cessation of fish consumption was the best option for Mohawks, although more should have been done to help people find healthier substitutes.

Some people were especially sensitive to the implication that individuals should be held responsible for their dietary choices and diabetic conditions. As one woman told me:

I don't think everybody knows yet what are all the reasons that cause diabetes. Of course they're going to say, "Well, you stopped growing a garden and therefore you did less exercise and you ate less fresh fruits and vegetables." Well that's true. But it sounds like it's your fault, and that ain't all it is.

She went on to describe how, before the creation of the seaway, she and other people in the community lived off the land and out of the river. After she found out about the fluoride emissions from Reynolds settling on the island where she raised her garden, and about the PCB contamination of the fish in the river, she stopped eating local food and turned to the grocery store. But whereas she could eat almost for free prior to the contamination, food at the grocery store

Diving board on the shores of the Saint Lawrence River. Photograph by Elizabeth Hoover, 2016.

was very expensive, and her purchases were limited to inexpensive, unhealthy foods.

Some interviewees who connected the increase in diabetes with changes wrought in the community by contamination mentioned not only the changes in food consumed but also the loss of activities that were once required to acquire those foods. After describing how she thinks the community is "in a crisis with diabetes" and its related complications, Barbara continued:

> Why are we diabetic? Because our lifestyle has changed and our food has changed. So we don't spend three hours a day in a garden, and we don't make sure our children are out there weeding and doing things like that, and we don't have the big gardens. We don't have them trapping in the spring and whatever. We don't have them out in the woods picking nuts and stuff like that. So a lot of things, you know, we've changed. And so, yeah, our environment has changed. We don't swim in the rivers anymore. And that's where everybody used to swim,

whether it was on the Saint Regis River or the Saint Lawrence River, that's where there were swimming holes. And people don't swim there anymore. They have pools.

She saw the shift in lifestyle not simply as the result of changes that came to the community over time, but rather as an outcome of fear: people became afraid to interact with the environment as they once had, and now, even though the immediate threat may have passed, they are used to a different way of living.

To some extent, linking the suspected contamination of food sources to diabetes has become an accepted part of community rhetoric because it serves to reduce the blame placed on those with diabetes and their families. One woman, after I commented that her kids seemed healthy, replied:

> Well, my son just got diagnosed with diabetes so I can't say they are that healthy you know. I think he got diabetes because we can't eat the food out of the garden; we can't make juice from the apples that are growing here. So you've got to run to the store and buy the canned jars of food. Right, so that processed foods—we can't make a garden you know, so you buy processed foods.

Just an hour before this conversation, she and I had walked to her neighbor's house to pick bags full of pears, which were then sitting at our feet during the interview. We sat at the kitchen table, with her mother's garden in full view through the sliding glass kitchen door. Earlier in the interview she had described to me her own small garden. When I asked her whether she thought these details went against the reasoning she had just laid out, she thought about it for a moment and then replied that we did not *really* know if those pears were safe. And people might still plant gardens, but they are not the big gardens they used to plant. They still plant because it connects them to their ancestors—in her case, it made her feel closer to her deceased father. This is not to discredit concerns that this woman may have about the safety of foods grown in her community, but rather to point out that some residents, in attempting to find explanations for illnesses like diabetes, may reach for explanations that have been laid out by community leaders, that both reflect their anger toward the industrial plants and deflect some of the blame that can be placed on those who have "failed" to help their families maintain health.

Diabetes Programs at Akwesasne

Akwesasro:non have access to a number of programs that address diabetes through the Saint Regis Mohawk Health Services, an IHS clinic in Hogansburg (in the southern half of the community), and through the Kanonhkwat'sheri:io Health Facility in Saint Regis Village (in the northern portion of the community). In their study of diabetes at Akwesasne published in 1997, Hood et al. found that community members had knowledge about healthy lifestyles but lacked confidence and social support for bringing about desired changes.[52] One of the outcomes of this study was the founding of the Tsitewatakari:tat/Let's Get Healthy program to support diabetic patients in improving their lifestyles. In 1998 the program began to operate out of the SRMHS, funded by grants from the federal Special Diabetes Program for Indians; it has since resulted in what director Janine Rourke calls the "diabetes clan," a group of programs that work to educate people about diabetes.

In 2005, another track of funding came out of the special federal program, and it was used to create a demonstration project called the Mohawk Healthy Heart Project. This program uses a model of case management for people with diabetes, specifically to reduce or prevent heart disease. Each participant works with a case manager, a registered dietitian, a fitness staff, and a lifestyle coach. Originally intended to be a four- to five-year demonstration project, Mohawk Healthy Heart has continued to be extended, and as of August 2009, when I interviewed the director, a little over one hundred people were enrolled. The project coordinates with researchers at the University of Colorado for the collection and analysis of participant data in terms of IHS standards of diabetes care.

One of the projects currently run by Mohawk Healthy Heart involves the building of raised-bed gardens for participants. This effort is aimed at making produce more available to participants, especially those on fixed incomes, while circumventing any concerns about soil contamination. Mera, the director of Mohawk Healthy Heart, and Janine, the director of Let's Get Healthy, developed the idea of building raised-bed garden containers for program participants and filling them with topsoil brought in from outside the community, so that no one would have to worry about even the *possibility* that the gardens might be contaminated. As Janine reported, they labeled the project

> Raised Bed Gardens, primarily because of the issues, we wanted to knock down the wall of contamination. We knew going in that that was the fear and anxiety of many people, so we figured Raised Bed Gardens would help alleviate that or will move them forward to doing this, plus it had the element of physical activity and tending to something and seeing success and seeing harvest.

In its first year, the project established thirty-two gardens, each approximately four feet by four feet by ten feet. The boxes were built from rough-cut lumber, to avoid concerns about chemicals leaching from treated wood, and then filled with topsoil. Tomato, cucumber, zucchini, and pepper plants were then given to the participants because, as Mera noted, "people don't want to wait for seeds." In the second year, the number of gardens in the program grew to forty-two. When I spoke to Mera during the summer of 2008, project workers had just finished building five new boxes and delivering fresh soil to thirty gardens established in previous years. The project also helped six people who were not worried about contamination build their own gardens in the ground. Mera related: "We told them to call the Environment Division for soil testing, but their theory is that 'we don't know where the store vegetables are being grown, can't be any worse here on our own land.' The soil looks wonderful there." In addition to the gardening project, the Let's Get Healthy program started cooking classes to show participants how to turn their fresh vegetables into meals. Janine explained: "I thought that was an important—both cultural and traditional—way of putting that into a very clinically designed program. It's turned out to be very rewarding in a lot of ways."

The Tsitewatakari:tat/Let's Get Healthy program began seeing patients in the newly constructed Diabetes Center for Excellence in late 2013. The $3.6 million building contains a gym, yoga rooms, pool, and kitchen for cooking demonstrations. Funds for the center came "from a lot of different pockets," as Janine put it, including federal grants, construction grants, housing grants, and grassroots fund-raising events, including the Seven Generations Walk and golf tournaments.

In the northern half of the community, the Kanonhkwat'sheri:io Healthy Facility hosts the MCA Department of Health and Department of Community and Social Services. They in turn host a diabetes program that includes group exercise, cooking classes, and participation in Green Food Bag, a regional program through which community members can get access to discounted produce. In this program, which began in Akwesasne in 2011, produce is bought in bulk and then divided up and placed in reusable shopping bags, which are sold to program participants for ten dollars each.

I mentioned to Janine that people I had spoken with tended to attribute the high rates of diabetes in the community to three main causes: contamination, forced changes in diet due to contamination, and lifestyle choices. She was pleased that people had considered lifestyle as a cause of diabetes and thought that maybe Let's Get Healthy and other programs had helped to inform them about this: "The fact they're thinking of lifestyle change in preventing diabetes makes me feel really good." When I asked her what her program's participants said about the root causes of their diabetes, she replied that while they might have different notions about the causes, their job at the program is not to spend a lot of time on the "why," but rather to work as quickly as possible to control or reduce complications and the risk of heart disease and other diabetes-related illnesses. "So we actually just don't get into that conversation because we're providing direct caring now. So it's like let's deal with your blood sugar right now, and stuff like that. So clinically, we're just not opening that door whether it is a contamination issue." She went on to say that, generally, most of the program's participants know they are at risk because family members have diabetes:

> Some of them are to the point of saying that "it is because of what I ate, because of what I failed to do." Some people are saying that in terms of exercise and lifestyle. There is a sense of, there's still contamination issues, but where we are right now is we're like dealing with real term, we're dealing with "what can we do for you now." . . . That's where our thinking

is. So that's not to say we don't think that there are other reasons why they're crossing our door, but that's for other people to think about. We're the medical managers.

Thanks to the efforts of dedicated staff, programs are becoming increasingly available in Akwesasne to help individuals amend behaviors that might be contributing to their illness, even as other factors, as discussed earlier, will be more challenging to address.

Suggestions for a Healthier Community

In addition to asking community members to describe the health of the community, as well as the etiologies they perceived as best explaining prominent health conditions, I asked them what they thought the community could do to become healthier. Some answers focused on individual education and capacity building, while others tended to align more closely with the "chronicities of modernity" theory, which shifts the emphasis of metabolic syndrome interventions away from individual education, counseling regimens, and medications and toward efforts involving community, national, and global institutions.[53] Interviewees' suggestions reflected the need for a balance among three levels, related to the three-bodies model discussed in the introduction: individual agency, the community working collaboratively, and tribal government and agencies providing resources and structure to create a healthier living environment for residents.

INDIVIDUAL AGENCY: "WE CAN START PICKING OURSELVES UP AND DO SOMETHING"

To become healthier, some interviewees suggested, community members need to do more than just "prepare foods the proper way" or eat more traditional foods—they need to go beyond that to shift their way of thinking and take agency. According to a young man named Rob, this would require people to get sober and achieve better mental health, and then pull themselves into better physical health from there. Richard stated that, rather than looking to someone else to help them, people need to "wise up and stop blaming people, and say, 'Well, what can I do?' You know, they've got to make that statement to themselves because the more you blame somebody, the more of that power goes to them, you know, you are lessening yourself." Brenda similarly expressed how, when she would attend meetings where the SUNY scientists described their research findings, she started feeling down. "So I said to the group, 'We've got to start looking at survival. How do we get beyond this? We can study ourselves to death and feel down, or we can start picking ourselves up and do something.'"

One young man discussed the need for people to take greater responsibility for their own health, and not rely on the clinics and programs at Akwesasne to tell them how to improve their behavior. "Right now they basically bribe you. They give you a free gym membership. They make you feel bad about being fat, but it's okay to have a positive body image. They don't just say, 'Fat fuck, get off your ass and eat less and you won't be fat.' It really comes down to that, uh?" While his approach would probably not go over well with most community members, his opinion is clear: people have been coddled too long and need to take action on their own behalf.

Structural Inputs: Education, Programming, and Environmental Cleanup by Political Bodies

Several interviewees' suggestions involved steps that the community's leadership could take to help improve health, such as banning things that are considered unhealthy (like cigarettes and poutine), ensuring the cleanup of the contaminated environment, and (most frequently mentioned) providing educational programs and the facilities necessary to help community members lead a healthy lifestyle. Several mentioned that education was needed in the community—about diet (as Robert explained, people need to be "taught to eat a balanced dinner"), exercise, and cultural knowledge that would support a healthy lifestyle. This was framed as "reeducation" of the community by Beverly, who was a nurse at the SRMHS clinic, with the understanding that cooking and exercising do not require entirely new knowledge; rather, these are things that people have to be reminded to do in these changing times.[54]

People pointed to active sports programs in the community and the proliferation of diabetes prevention programs as eliminating some of the barriers to achieving physical health. At the same time, one woman expressed frustration at the fact that to join the

Tewathahita Walking Trail, located adjacent to the Diabetes Center for Excellence. Photograph by Elizabeth Hoover, 2016.

gym, "if you're not low income, you don't have diabetes, you spend like forty dollars a month." She had already spent five hundred dollars on gym memberships so far that summer for herself and her family. She noted that it was a problem that gym membership was offered for free only *after* someone became fat and diabetic, as opposed to being offered as a preventive measure. Some interviewees pointed to a need for more facilities to help community members get more exercise—suggestions included a community pool, more sports facilities, and a walking path. Walking for exercise can be tricky in rural communities. Usually, the people seen walking down busy Route 37, the main road through the southern half of the reservation, are walking because they do not own cars and they could not get rides from friends or relatives. People seeking physical activity do not want to be seen as falling into that category. In addition to traffic, which can make walking dangerous, as on many reservations, "rez dogs"—large mutts who often roam in packs—are seen frequently along the roadsides in Akwesasne (as I can attest, having been chased by them several times when I was jogging). Joyce King, in her role as director of the

MCA Department of Justice, has worked to educate the community about the need to leash their dogs so that people are not discouraged from taking walks for fear of being bitten. Interviewees suggested the construction of a walking path as an intentional space for people to gather to exercise in a socially supportive setting that could also be monitored for stray dogs. In 2012, such a path was created: the Tewathahita Walking Trail, located near the senior center and the new diabetes center, now provides a walking space for the community.

COMMUNITY COOPERATION: "WE ALL HAVE TO WORK IN A CONCERTED EFFORT"

Many interviewees felt that for any improvement in community health to come about, cooperation would be required—among family members, among community members, and among the various governments in Akwesasne. This would be no small feat in a community divided politically, spiritually, economically, and geographically, but some interviewees had solid suggestions for family- and group-based health models.[55]

Working together among family members was a notable suggestion. Randi, who described the predicament of trying to diet when the rest of your tight-knit family is still eating calorie-dense comfort food (see chapter 4), suggested that all family members need to work together and cooperate for individual diets to improve. In the United States, advice about dieting and particular weight-loss plans are targeted primarily toward individuals—to entice them to buy certain plans and certain foods. In a community where eating together is an important communal activity, individual diet change is not going to be effective—the family as a unit needs to be involved.

Principles of social support would be beneficial to explore in a family setting before the onset of diabetes. Along this line, midwife Katsi Cook and her cousin Beverly Cook began a "centering pregnancy" model at the SRMHS clinic. Rather than each woman going through her pregnancy as an individual, meeting with the doctors and nurses by herself to receive information about the gestation process, this model brought together a cohort of women to support each other through their pregnancies. This model of group care could be applied to diabetes prevention and care as well. Studies have shown that women who develop diabetes during pregnancy are more likely to have children with diabetes, continuing the cycle.[56] In her review of obesity and diabetes programs in Native communities, Halpern notes that the problem with many attempted interventions is that they catch the kids too late—after they are already set in their diets, already obese, and already predisposed.[57] By beginning with pregnant mothers through interventions like the centering pregnancy model, a community may help the next generation to avoid diabetes.

Taking this a step further, Joyce suggested that cooperation among families, children, and schools could help to improve children's diets. A program with this aim was enacted in a neighboring Mohawk community: the Kahnawake Schools Diabetes Project provided outreach to students and their parents and limited the types of foods that students were allowed to bring to school in an effort to diminish the rates of obesity and diabetes the community had been witnessing.[58]

Other interviewees felt that all of the leadership in Akwesasne should come together and cooperate to promote health in the community. As noted previously, there are three tribal governments within the community, as well as two health clinics and two environment divisions, each supported in part by a different external federal government. A number of people noted the absurdity of having to keep these departments separate when they could be working more effectively together. Unfortunately, federal funding issues necessitate their operating separately, at least for the foreseeable future. One woman stated that cooperation among the leadership was necessary for an improvement in health because "when leadership battles, the rest of the people don't know what to do, so they battle. They don't know what to do so the next generation battles, so that to me is the fix, it can't be anyplace else." She talked about how this stress is passed from one generation to the next, and people do not even know why they are stressed. Generations of conflict have been passed down since the formation of all the separate governments.[59] Barbara also expressed that the community needs the leadership to come together and say, "There needs to be a change here. And we all have to work in a concerted effort to make those changes." She recognized that this would not happen overnight, noting that it took the past forty years for the health of the community to reach its current condition, and so it could potentially take that long to improve.

Conclusion: Health Revisited

Understanding a condition like diabetes in a place like Akwesasne necessarily entails examining the ecosocial history of the community. Ecosocial theory posits that how

> we develop, grow, age, ail, and die necessarily reflects a constant interplay, within our bodies, of our intertwined and inseparable social and biological history. . . . Taking literally the notion of "embodiment," this theory asks how we literally incorporate biologically—from conception to death—our social experiences and express this embodiment in population patterns of health, disease, and well-being.[60]

At Akwesasne, community perceptions of health reflect an understanding of the embodiment of environmental and social turmoil in the community. The views of Akwesasro:non regarding the etiologies of current health issues like diabetes and obesity reflect a generalized understanding of how the biomedical health world perceives these conditions, as issues of diet and lifestyle. However, they also incorporate a history of environmental contamination and the changes that have come as a result. Understanding community conceptions of this intertwined "social and biological history" is important because, as Juliet McMullin notes, examining the intersections of health, identity, family, and the environment helps to "denaturalize biomedical definitions of health and moves us toward including knowledge that is based on a shared history of sovereignty, capitalist encounters, resistance, and integrated innovation."[61] The inclusion of this knowledge can lead to the crafting of interventions that community members see as addressing the root causes of their health conditions and promoting better health. Akwesasne community members Arquette et al. describe the community's view of health:

> Health, then, has many definitions for the Mohawk people of Akwesasne. Health is spiritual. Health is rooted in the heart of the culture. Health is based on peaceful, sustainable relationships with other people, including family, community, Nation, the natural world, and spiritual beings. Health is supported by the solid foundations of a healthy natural world. To support

249

Illness	Number of people who mentioned this illness
Diabetes	37
Cancer	34
Heart disease (including high blood pressure)	21
Respiratory illnesses (mostly asthma)	18
Thyroid disorders	17
Rashes (eczema, photosensitivity rashes, impetigo,unidentified rashes)	12
Reproductive issues (1), miscarriages (7), problems with ovaries (2), birth defects (1)	11
Cognitive issues (2), learning disabilities (3), attention deficit disorder (2), bipolar disorder (2), Alzheimer's disease (1)	10
Arthritis	11
Autoimmune disorders (rheumatoid arthritis, scleroderma)	4
Emotional issues	3
Headaches	2
Digestive disorders	2
Unidentifiable illnesses	2
Allergies	1

The main health concerns of Akwesasro:non interviewees.

healthy communities, empowerment is an essential component of any assessment, action, or intervention.[62]

In the context of this model, health can be achieved only through individual, community, and political/structural cooperation.

Rather than focusing solely on the maladaptive behavior of individuals as the root of a disease, it is important to take into account perceptions of what has led to the individuals' choices—the social, economic, political, and environmental constraints that have created or limited these choices. At Akwesasne, some community members focus on the environmental contamination either as the direct source of diabetes or, more commonly, as the reason they can no longer eat traditional and local foods, which has in turn led to diabetes. Many Akwesasro:non believe that changes in diet and lifestyle, including more physical activity and a return to a more traditional diet, can help to reverse or prevent conditions like obesity and diabetes. But they also believe that such changes will not be possible without supportive family groups, remediation of the environment, and the cooperation of community governance institutions.

Highlighting Resilience

Individual, Social, and Political Resurgence and Survivance

On a sunny afternoon in August, I sat in a coffee shop on Cornwall Island with Brenda, who has been active in movements and organizations around health and the environment in Akwesasne for decades. She had been part of the efforts of the Akwesasne Task Force on the Environment as well as the environmental health studies conducted in collaboration with SUNY Albany, and she has coauthored articles on issues of health and the environment in Akwesasne.[1] She is now mostly retired, working as a consultant on issues of Indigenous governance.[2] As we sipped our coffee, Brenda reflected on the traumas her community has been through, as well as the strength and resilience that Mohawks have shown in fighting for the protection of their environment and health. She described how when people focus only on the negative history of environmental contamination, it draws the energy out of them. Conversely, when people speak about positive things and focus on ways they can bring about change, it lifts the energy:

> You see how the energy changes? Like when you talk about the contamination and the losses and you could feel the energy go down but when you start talking about these things the energy goes up, and you can feel that energy, and you can feel that energy go up. I think that's more important than the contamination, that we start to gain and recover and reassert our own who we are in spite of what's around us.

In the spirit of Brenda's insistence that we "bring the energy back up," in this conclusion I not only reflect on the ways that Akwesasro:non have framed and understood the environmental and health crises facing their community—through a framework of "three bodies"—but also consider proposed solutions put forth by community members and highlight the work currently being done that could serve as an example for other communities facing similar struggles.

Three Bodies

As laid out in the introduction of this book, the framework I have used to structure comments, suggestions, and understandings around the impact of environmental contamination and other health issues, as well as the actions that community members suggested for addressing these issues, centers on three bodies: the individual body, the social body, and the political body.

Individual Bodies

The individual body is often seen as the locus of control and the entity to be addressed in health research and health promotion. When the SUNY scientists and their Mohawk counterparts completed the environmental health research studies in Akwesasne, they were careful to inform participants of their individual results. Past studies had not done this; rather, they had aggregated data and left study subjects without a clear understanding of their individual body burdens. Receiving their individual results affected participants in different ways, as described in chapter 3. Some were happy with their results, as learning that they had relatively low levels of contaminants set their minds at ease. Others were upset—they did not understand the information in the letters they were sent, or they did not think it was properly contextualized so that they could decide for themselves whether or not to be worried. Still others were frustrated with the general limitations of a health study: the results could give them numbers that represented certain levels of contaminants in their bodies, but no one could definitively tell them what those numbers meant for their health. And while some were happy receiving individual letters, others thought a different form of report-back, one that addressed social rather than exclusively individual bodies, would have been more suited to the community.

Discussions around individual bodies also came up in the context of diabetes. As described in chapter 5, there are different understandings among community members about the reasons for the diabetes epidemic, and how and whether it is connected to local environmental contamination. The dominant epidemiological paradigm for diabetes points toward faulty bodies, which are often malfunctioning as a result of individual behavior that is noncompliant with health care workers' advice. Some interviewees agreed with this viewpoint, arguing that Akwesasro:non need to take responsibility for their own behaviors and diets and work to improve their own health. Others described more nuanced etiologies, pointing to the influences of the environment, family, and the broader community, and the ways in which the community needs to address these in order to empower individual action and change.

Social Bodies

The social bodies of Akwesasne were evoked when interviewees discussed how "the community" was healthy or ill. This concept of social bodies also came out when Akwesasro:non shared their thoughts on how both environmental health research and health care could be conducted differently. As noted in chapter 3, some interviewees thought that holding "family meetings" would be a better way to deliver study results to people than individual letters, because this would educate a broader range of people about the research and create opportunities for people to ask questions. Similarly, discussions around changing people's diets and combating diabetes considered the social body. As described in chapter 4, Randi pointed out that it is nearly impossible for one family member to go on a diet because Mohawks like to eat in social settings. Any change in eating habits, she suggested, was going to have to "start at grandma's house" and involve the whole family. Similarly, as discussed in chapter 5, interviewees described a need for diabetes-related programs that involve the entire family, not just the family member officially diagnosed with the condition. As John O'Neill notes in his reflection on how to address less-than-healthy food habits, "We must insist, then, that

Ionawiienhawi receives help from her father, Josh Sargent, and her uncle, Scott Martin, in setting up her fasting lodge for her second year in the Ohero:kon ceremony. Ohero:kon provides community and family support for youth as they enter adolescence. Photograph by Jessica Sargent, 2016.

the family should be a thinking body, whose common sense should be fostered in any healthy community and by any practical means."[3]

This notion of group-based care has been enacted at the Saint Regis Mohawk Health Services clinic in the form of the centering pregnancy program, begun in early 2010. Women join the program when they are fourteen to sixteen weeks into their gestation and attend ten prenatal sessions with a cohort of half a dozen expecting mothers. At the beginning of each session the women have the opportunity to see the health care provider. During the two-hour session, the women chart their own vital statistics and then take part in group discussions. These meetings give the women the opportunity to network and support each other through relationship difficulties, health issues, and challenges like breast-feeding. Older mothers are able to give advice to those experiencing their first pregnancies, and in a way the connections that are formed help to replace the close kinship networks that some of these women no longer have access to. This is a model that can also be applied to other health conditions, as Katsi noted, "whether it's cardiovascular disease, pregnancy, aging, diabetes, centering health care can be applied to all of these different contexts," something she is working to make possible.[4]

Conceptions of the social body also extend outside human communities in some cases. ATFE has been critical of conventional risk assessments and their applicability to Native communities because of the lack of consideration of this extended social body. ATFE members have expressed that "all peoples, including plants, animals and the earth herself must be included in defining environmental justice."[5] Health risk assessments conducted in Akwesasne have found that with a decrease in fish consumption, body burdens of PCBs also decreased. From the perspective of toxicologists, this defined a success, but from the perspective of Mohawks, they were being forced to make necessary concessions to protect their own health while their environment and the fish, in particular, were still suffering. As two ATFE members describe, "In classical models of toxicology, there is no risk if there is no exposure. Conventional risk assessments are severely limited in their application to Native peoples because they fail to adequately value cultural, social, subsistence, economic, and spiritual factors."[6] Whyte's work also highlights the relational responsibilities between human and other communities that are not valued or taken into consideration in conventional assessments.[7] As these authors demonstrate, Mohawk philosophy espouses a more precautionary approach that is protective of a wider range of "community members." Conventional risk assessment did not take into account the sociocultural impacts of the cessation of fish and wildlife consumption in Akwesasne, or the health conditions resulting from this rapid shift in diet.[8] To better anticipate such impacts, Arquette et al. suggest, a metadisciplinary approach is called for:

> Social scientists in the fields of anthropology, history, education, ethnography and sociology have been developing and using socio-cultural assessment methodologies for many years. By crossing and bridging disciplines and using tools that are specific and relevant to the community of study, social science research strategies can be modified to address environmental health issues as well.[9]

A metadisciplinary approach would allow the addition of more holistic and comprehensive evaluation of all impacts on health to the often-incomplete scientific data on human health and ecological impacts. Overall, ATFE suggests a new paradigm of holistic risk-based decision making that would bring together community health, risk assessment, and environmental restoration. This approach would entail the use of community-specific, culturally informed definitions of health, risk, and restoration, which would be more inclusive than just conceiving of health as the absence of disease or injury. ATFE also recommends including concepts of wellness that integrate physical, mental, social, and ecological well-being. This more inclusive model would contribute to the development of environmental policy that would recognize a wider definition of "community" and thus better prevent contamination and ensure more thorough cleanup of contaminated sites.

POLITICAL BODIES

A multitude of political bodies (state, federal, tribal, traditional) affect the social and individual bodies of Akwesasne. Each of these political bodies seeks to control some aspect of the fate of Akwesasro:non, and most elicit some level of distrust from community members. This was especially apparent when interviewees described not trusting departments in the Tribal government because of their affiliation with the federal government, but then described their affection and respect for individual employees of those departments. The contentious relationship that Akwesasne has had with outside political bodies, as described in chapter 1, has colored perceptions of who can be trusted.

At the same time, when I asked people what could be done to improve the health of the community, many gave answers that focused on what the tribal governments and their agencies could do. Some suggested that additional testing and outreach by the SRMT Environment Division could let people know whether their land was safe to plant on and if local fish were safe to eat. (The latest fish advisory, described below, may help ameliorate some of those concerns.) As described in chapter 5, others said that the Tribe should do more to support and expand programs like Let's Get Healthy and should provide additional exercise resources. Several interviewees also suggested that they would like to see educational programs developed, especially for the youth, around nutrition and traditional subsistence activities like gardening. One mother cited a lack of good after-school and summer programs, and felt that the schools and the tribal governments should work to fill this void with educational programming that would create a healthier cohort of youth. Some wanted the tribal governments to help provide the community with greater access to fresh food by supporting local farmers and by developing a farmers' market or tribally run grocery store. The tribal agriculture program described below may be a step in that direction.

In short, many people felt that the best way to address health changes in the community would be for political bodies to help the social bodies of Akwesasne work together to improve diet and exercise through education programs and farming organizations. In addition, interviewees wanted to see a broader consideration of who is included in the social body of the community, through more culturally appropriate and inclusive impact assessment methods and through greater financial and institutional support from relevant political bodies.

Boundary Crossing

This tension that arises when community members challenge political bodies while simultaneously demanding that they address the issues of the community has been theorized by political scientist Kevin Bruyneel, who describes how for centuries Indigenous political actors have demanded rights and resources from the American settler state while also challenging the imposition of colonial rule on their lives. He calls this resistance a "third space of sovereignty" that resides neither inside nor outside the American political system, but exists on the very boundaries of that system.[10] Mohawks have created this third space in a variety of forms and settings, building tribal governmental departments and programs, as well as community grassroots entities, designed to give Akwesasro:non greater control over the management of the industrial contamination that affects their land. These entities (which include ATFE, the SRMT, and the First Environment Research Project) have moved community members from the role of passive subjects or consumers of research and regulation to the role of active players, taking part in the utilization of grant moneys and in the cleanup process. They have influenced environmental regulation and cleanup standards. Through their efforts, they have reshaped how science is conducted and created a third space where the subjects and community are also part of the research process. In creating this third space of sovereignty, Mohawks have encountered myriad forms of boundary crossing, some of which they have challenged and others of which they have encouraged.

Akwesasne, even more so than most Indian communities, is constantly battling boundaries and borders that appear in many facets of life. From the moment non-Native settlers arrived in the region, Mohawk people have had to guard the boundaries of their land, while at the same time arguing that their use of land in this region should not be bounded at all. This is what Audra Simpson refers to as a "refusal to recognize," which "involves using one's territory in a manner that is historically and philosophically consistent with what one knows. . . . Mohawks refused to consent to colonial mappings and occupations of their territory."[11] As illustrated by the land claims that both the Saint Regis Mohawk Tribe and the Mohawk Council of Akwesasne are currently fighting, land speculators and settler colonial nations chipped away at the boundaries of land designated for Mohawks. Passage through Mohawk land became complicated when the Treaty of Paris (1783) drew the boundary between British North America and the United States directly through the community of Akwesasne. This imaginary geopolitical line, meant to pass "eight feet over the head of the tallest Indian," has complicated travel between different portions of the community ever since.[12] The Raquette Point standoff in 1979 began in reaction to a boundary delineation project that traditionalists felt would symbolically weaken Mohawk claims to traditional territories.

But Akwesasro:non also speak of more nuanced boundary transgressions. The PCB-laden fluids that coursed through the machinery at the General Motors plant, which were flushed into leaching ponds and then buried in a landfill, did not stay on GM's property. The fluids overflowed the ponds and bled out of the landfill and made their way into the Saint Lawrence River and into the groundwater. At a community meeting in Akwesasne hosted by the EPA on April 25, 1990, representatives of the agency attempted to describe how the EPA defined the site. The project manager on the site, Lisa Carson, stated, "EPA defined the site as where we find the contamination."[13] Earlier in the meeting, her colleague George Pavlou, associate director for the EPA's New York programs, stated, "We define the site as solvent contaminated soils, lagoon sludges, river sediments, wetlands and groundwater that have been contaminated by previous disposal practices at the plant. The boundaries of the site are defined as the end of the contaminated medium."[14]

But the contamination migrated away from this defined site—beyond soils, sludges, sediments, and groundwater. From the river, the PCBs were taken up by fish that were then eaten by Mohawk people. From dinner plates, these PCBs made their way into Mohawk bodies, into their fat, into women's breast milk, which was then passed on to the most sensitive members of the community. In her book *Tainted Milk,* Maia Boswell-Penc notes that breast milk is "symbolic of the most essential human connection," and when breast milk is contaminated, that "should be a wake-up call."[15] Boswell-Penc demonstrates "how child sustenance becomes a figure for the oppressive frameworks at work in any historical juncture," and this is seen in Akwesasne, where Indigenous women have been instructed to abandon their traditional food practices in order to prevent accumulating more PCBs that would then be transferred to their children.[16] As Julie Sze notes, "Polluted babies are troubling creatures because they collapse the boundaries of the bodily and the natural with the technological, the man-made, and the synthetic."[17] Tests done decades later would connect the PCBs still carried by youth to health impacts like thyroid disorder. Heavier congeners of PCBs, which have a half-life of thirty to forty years, are passed from mother to daughter for generations. Through the consumption of fish, a traditional food for Mohawks for eons, women's bodies, wombs, breast milk—a baby's first environment—and those of subsequent generations became part of the GM Superfund site.

PCBs continue to volatilize from the site, making their way into air currents, traveling not only over Mohawk land but also north to the Arctic, where they continue to affect Indigenous people. With this in mind, where do the boundaries of the Superfund site end? When Katsi Cook received the lab results on the first breast milk study samples and discovered that they contained PCBs (as well as mirex, hexachlorobenzene, and other contaminants), she later told an interviewer, "I began to realize, We're part of the dump. If this is in the river and in the GM dump, then the dump is in us."[18] So how, then, does one delineate the borders of the contaminated site? Julie Sze, thinking through Donna Haraway's *Simians, Cyborgs, and Women,* describes how "we are already hybridized and cyborgian through our pollution exposure," because "technologically polluted bodies . . . are a fusion of things living (human bodies) and nonliving (chemicals, plastics, pesticides), human and nonhuman, early and synthetic hell created out of our culture's desire to engineer the natural through the technological."[19] So while General Motors and other industries were forced to meet the terms of the Natural Resource Damages Settlement, they are responsible for toxic trespass on Mohawk bodies as well, regardless of the number of quantifiable health impacts that can be definitively connected to that contamination.

The blurring and crossing of boundaries also took place as Akwesasne community members negotiated with scientists over their roles and positions in the environmental health studies. As opposed to previous studies, which drew distinct lines between the scientists and the community members who served as subjects of study, the research conducted collaboratively between SUNY Albany and Akwesasne shifted the status quo of community-based research by disrupting the researcher–subject dyad. Community members became collaborators, data collectors, and, to some extent, data interpreters and disseminators. These "ruptures" in the scientific process changed how this and many other communities would choose to take part in environmental health research going forward.[20]

As demonstrated in this case study, Mohawks resisted the binary of researcher/subject, citizen/scientist, creating a third space of sovereignty in which they refused the subjugated role to which communities under study are commonly relegated. Through the creation of the ATFE Research Advisory Committee, Akwesasne community members took a position of authority in the research process. They did not reject the institutions of science altogether, recognizing the need for this type of knowledge, but neither did they agree to a conventional research study. Instead, they operated within a third space of sovereignty, helping to create a hybrid research model that is now being used with increasing frequency in community-based research.

Community Efforts to Address Environmental and Health Issues

In recent years, both grassroots organizations and tribal governments have moved in a number of ways to address Akwesasne's environmental issues and community access to healthy, traditional, and locally produced foods. These efforts have put Akwesasne on the map as part of a broader movement among Indigenous communities to reclaim gardening and traditional food procurement methods.[21]

ATFE AND GARDENING

In addition to pressing the governments at Akwesasne to push for the most stringent environmental cleanup possible and publishing scholarly articles about the effects of the contamination on the community's culture, the Akwesasne Task Force on the Environment has supported a number of agricultural projects. As described by one of the organization's principal members, Dave, many of ATFE's efforts have been aimed at getting people off subsidized foods and back to growing and eating healthy traditional foods. ATFE started a community garden in conjunction with the longhouse and also started a greenhouse project on Cornwall Island, although that project ran out of funds and ATFE was unable to maintain it. From the early 1990s to 2009, ATFE was funded principally through the American Friends Service Committee, which gave money to support the black ash restoration project, the growing of fruit trees, the establishment of sustainable agriculture, environmental education projects, and the ATFE web page. That funding is no longer available. As Dave stated, "You live by the grant, you die by the grant. But the work continues, it just falls on a chosen few," primarily Dave, his wife, and his brother.

For a number of years, ATFE has been working on a sustainable agriculture program that includes support for organic gardening projects through annual seed, plant, and tree giveaways. Each spring, ATFE provides free seeds to community members for their gardens, so they can grow squashes, zucchini, carrots, string beans, corn, cucumbers, and more. The organization also gives away tree seedlings, providing red and silver maple, red and white pine, white spruce, red oak, black oak, and burr oak. There are also heritage seeds available, mostly for different types of Haudenosaunee beans, like Cranberry, HiYo, Yellow Gonyea, Desoronto Potato, and Six Nations beans. Several people who spoke to me about heritage seeds (see chapter 4) have worked with ATFE's heritage seed efforts.

In addition, each year for the past couple of years ATFE members have planted a garden at the Tsionkwanati:io Heritage Center, a complex that includes a nineteenth-century house and barns. The property where the center is located formerly belonged to an Indian agent and is rumored to have been a stop on the Underground Railroad. Currently the property, with adjacent fields, is owned by the Traveling College, a cultural organization based in Akwesasne. Some years, the children from the Akwesasne Freedom School help with the planting at the center, and some of the garden's vegetables are then used in preparing their lunches. ATFE has also worked to help maintain food projects at elders' homes, including an apple orchard at Solomon Cook's house and strawberries at Howard David's farm.

Kanenhi:io Ionkwaienthon:hakie

Kanenhi:io Ionkwaienthon:hakie (We Are Planting Good Seeds) is a grassroots organization at Akwesasne dedicated to helping families with agricultural projects.[22] The organization got its start in 2007 with funding through Heifer International, which went toward constructing a community greenhouse, buying seeds and equipment for a community garden, repairing a building for use as a community kitchen, and sending members to training sessions and food conferences, where they were able to learn about permaculture and network with other Indigenous farmers. In the beginning, Kanenhi:io supported individual food projects at members' homes. Upon officially joining the organization, each member would fill out a form describing the project he or she wanted to work on, the amount of money it would cost, and the way in which he or she planned to repay the group for funding the project. Members could pay the group back either by selling the fruits of their labor and giving the money directly to Kanenhi:io or by donating their labor to group projects. Home projects have included keeping egg-laying chickens (with accompanying fencing and coop), raising pigs, growing white corn, and constructing fencing for buffalo. The members of Kanenhi:io are particular about where their funding comes from and have elected to not pursue funds connected to any state or federal entities, including the tribal governments. This has placed some limits on the group's ability to support projects, but members feel that their ultimate goal of making the community, or even a few families, more "food sovereign" cannot be achieved through collaboration with colonizing entities.

Kanenhi:io has partnered with the Intensive Prevention Program for youth, the Ohero:kon rites of passage program, and the Freedom School on various gardening projects and is now closely connected to the Ase Tsi Tewa:ton Cultural Restoration Program described below, through that program's master gardener. Most of Kanenhi:io's current work centers on the community cannery—where members butcher chickens and preserve vegetables—and a shared garden on the site. While several members also still garden at home, I have found that the communal aspect of working together in the cannery or in the garden is what brings people to the organization—both people who think they do not have the knowledge or resources to do the work by themselves at home and those who feel as though they have knowledge to contribute.

ASE TSI TEWA:TON: CULTURAL RESTORATION

While the EPA is working to remediate the contaminated sites upstream from Akwesasne, this cleanup does not necessarily restore the natural resources lost to the community or repair the damage caused by the cessation of traditional activities. To address this impact, the community undertook a claims process to seek compensation for the injuries to natural resources.[23] As part of the CERCLA process, a Natural Resource Damages Assessment (NRDA) is conducted to collect, compile, and analyze information that is then used to "assess the extent of injury to a natural resource and determine appropriate ways of restoring and compensating for that injury" and to "make the public whole" following the release of hazardous substances.[24]

The NRDA in Akwesasne examined three aspects of loss: ecological injury and the loss of natural resources, human-use and recreation loss, and cultural injury—that is, injury to natural resources that in turn affects significant cultural use of those resources. The natural resources trustees in the case were the SRMT, the U.S. Fish and Wildlife Service, the National Oceanic and Atmospheric Administration, and the New York State Department of Environmental Conservation. The final settlement based on the results of the NRDA, reached in 2013, includes $1.8 million in restoration funds from the 2011 GM bankruptcy settlement and $18.5 million from Alcoa and Reynolds Metals. The total settlement of $20.3 million is to be divided up among projects aimed at ecological restoration, fishing/boating access, and cultural restoration for the SRMT.

Akwesasne Freedom School students Tekaherha and Niiokohontesha examine a sturgeon with Norman Peters, the master fisherman in the Ase Tsi Tewa:ton Cultural Restoration Program. Photograph by Jessica Sargent, 2015.

Approximately $10 million of the settlement will be spent on ecological restoration projects. In the NRDA, ecological injury was quantified using a habitat equivalency analysis, which calculated past and future injury inflicted by contaminants to determine acre-years of habitat loss to birds, fish, mammals, and benthic organisms. Projects chosen to amend this provide similar acre-years of habitat gain and include land conservation and enhancement and restoration of wetlands, fisheries, and wildlife habitat.

Because of advisories discouraging the consumption of fish from the Grasse and Saint Lawrence Rivers, local communities suffered lost recreational fishing opportunities. The NRDA team calculated "lost" fishing trips between 1981 and 2030 using a random utility model. A total of $2 million from the settlement will be dedicated to projects aimed at replacing lost fishing and other recreational opportunities, with the current focus on shoreline fishing and boat access on the Grasse and Raquette Rivers.

While the other two parts of the restoration program are intended to benefit all residents in the region, the third, focused on cultural injury, is specific to the Mohawk community. To assess cultural injury, a team led by Mohawk professor Taiaiake Alfred formed a community advisory committee and conducted interviews with elders and other knowledge holders to understand what elements of Mohawk culture had been negatively affected or lost due to contamination and to identify appropriate restoration projects.[25] Based on these and other studies, $8.4 million from the Alcoa/Reynolds settlement went to the SRMT to support traditional cultural practices through the Ase Tsi Tewa:ton Cultural Restoration Program. The four-year program seeks to restore land-based cultural practices and traditional economic activities while also promoting the Mohawk language. With eight master teachers, sixteen apprentices, two language specialists, and three administrative staff, the program focuses on four areas of traditional cultural practice: fishing and use of the river, medicine plants and healing, hunting and trapping, and horticulture/basket making/traditional foods. Because the interruption of the cultural use of natural resources had a negative impact on Mohawk language use and transfer, all participants in the program take or teach language classes, with the overall goal of increasing the number of fluent speakers in the community. In addition to the development of this new program, settlement money earmarked for the remediation of cultural injury has gone toward supporting four preexisting institutions that were already conducting work parallel with the mission of cultural restoration: the Akwesasne Freedom School, Ionkwa'nikonri:io Cultural Youth Camp on Thompson Island, the Kanatsiohareke Strawberry Festival and workshops, and the Mohawk Healthy Heart Raised Bed Gardens program.

Kenny Perkins was selected as the master teacher of horticulture for the Ase Tsi Tewa:ton program. In discussing his goals for the project, he told me:

Where we come from in Akwesasne, we have a very big need for agriculture because our whole system is based upon our

Dr. Mary Arquette (doctor of veterinary medicine and PhD in environmental toxicology from Cornell University) works for the Ase Tsi Tewa:ton Cultural Restoration Program as a teacher of four adult apprentices in the area of horticulture and traditional foods. She has been an administrator at the Akwesasne Freedom School and participated on the Akwesasne Task Force on the Environment. Here she holds a Buffalo Creek squash, a Haudenosaunee heritage variety. Photograph by Elizabeth Hoover, 2016.

food. And we can't really call ourselves sovereign unless we can feed ourselves—and I've heard that over and over but today I know what that means. And I try to as best that I can incorporate that with the language, with the growing techniques, old and new, and the traditional styles that we use today. It's fascinating how our ancestors used to grow our white corn, the amount of it, and who it used to feed. I mean we fed nations and we were very strong at one time. So I'm trying to reintroduce that in this cultural restoration program that I am involved with now as the lead horticulturist and teaching four apprentices the different techniques that we used and some of the new techniques because of the changing weathers. We can't always grow according to the moon cycles, which we used to. So we need to figure that part out and that's what we're doing today.

Alfred argues that if environmental contamination had not affected the community, and if Akwesasro:non had an intact land-based cultural framework, then they would have maintained food production culture, adapting it to new technological conditions. In his view, the Ase Tsi Tewa:ton program is a positive step toward addressing the cultural harm that has been identified as a direct result of the contamination.[26]

TRIBAL AGRICULTURE PROGRAM

Efforts are currently under way to establish a tribal agriculture program to develop food policies for the SRMT, support farmers, and develop plans for expanding farmland in Akwesasne. In a letter to the SRMT in 2015, Tom Cook, agriculture consultant for the Tribe, stated that his goal for such a program would be to establish "a nonprofit structure with for-profit activities supporting a mission of food sovereignty and community engagement."[27] This idea was developed into a three-year pilot program, managed by Wallace Ransom and championed by Chief Eric Thompson, which began in March 2016. The program's stated mission is "to stimulate interest in consuming naturally grown foods and to awaken the spirit of producing healthy food in Akwesasne." The program offers tilling services to home gardens and has also offered to "possibly provide soil testing," because attendants at a community meeting expressed concern about putting what could be contaminated land into production.[28] In one of the program's projects aimed at both providing food and training students in agricultural production, ten students were trained in how to raise chickens and market organic eggs. One thousand egg-laying hens were purchased and are currently being taken care of by the students and the program. Another project is focused on the revitalization of farmland in Akwesasne, much of which has become overgrown and some of which has been flooded because drainage ditches have been blocked by beavers. To promote the potential increase in agricultural production, Tom Cook convened the first meeting of the Akwesasne Farmers Co-op in August 2016, bringing together families with farmland to advocate for the improvement of their land through the maintenance of ditches and to encourage them to combine their production power so that they can fulfill bigger contracts for produce than they would be able to fill individually.

New Fish Advisories

In addition to the increase in programs and interest around growing food in Akwesasne, recent community efforts have focused on encouraging safe fish consumption. The fish advisories issued in the 1980s were blanket warnings against eating most local fish. Tony David, Water Resources Program manager for the SRMT Environment Division, noted that encouraging zero consumption is "the easiest for management. It's not the easiest on the people who have given up fishing, but it's certainly the simplest message. Crafting a more nuanced message requires a lot of time and resources and expertise." More recently however, the Environment Division collaborated with the New York State Department of Health to produce a new, more nuanced fish advisory based on information gathered through community interviews and testing of more recent fish samples. As Environment Division director Ken Jock noted at a community presentation on December 11, 2014:

> The river is getting cleaner. Over the last twenty years, the sources have been slowly cut off, and so the river is cleaning itself gradually. Just this past year, Tony David and others in our office were working with the New York State Department

of Health, and we have the new fish consumption advisory in place for actually telling people in the community that you can start eating fish again. Fish are clean enough to eat in certain areas, and to me, that's something we really need to do.

This was a dramatic change from a conversation I had with Ken in his office six years earlier, at which time he was hesitant to say whether people should eat local fish or not. While there has been no improvement in some areas of the river—particularly "Contaminant Cove," directly in front of the GM site—as Ken noted, other areas are getting cleaner.

The development of the new fish advisory is a good example of the community's increasing leadership role on environmental issues. Tony David spearheaded the project in his position as the Environment Division's Water Resources Program manager. In a recent interview, he highlighted how in his own family, fish consumption had dropped off with each successive generation after the first fish advisories were issued. "I think that's a common story, that there's that loss of knowledge within a family, and that's a direct result of these advisories. One part of the project [to develop the new advisory] was to encourage consumption and share recipes and sort of highlight ways to make fish and game taste good."

Tony David worked with Tony Forti from NYSDOH to obtain a Great Lakes Restoration Initiative grant, which supported their work over three years to determine which fish were safe and to craft a new advisory, in the process collaborating with health programs at Akwesasne like Let's Get Healthy as well as with the EPA and NYSDEC. Fellow Mohawk and Cornell graduate Mary LaFrance, who was hired onto this project with Tony, sent out fish consumption surveys, canvassed community events, and conducted in-depth interviews with twenty-four community members.

The result of their work is a glossy pamphlet titled *Akwesasne Family Guide to Eating Locally Caught Fish* that features photos of people catching, filleting, cooking, and eating fish. The pamphlet includes a brief history of the local environmental contamination; an explanation of the two major contaminants of concern (PCBs and mercury); information on how to catch, prepare, and cook the fish; and optimal portion sizes (three to four ounces). At the center of the pamphlet is a map of the waters of Akwesasne, color coded to indicate the areas where the fish are and are not safe to eat. For example, the Grasse River is colored a putrid brown on the map from the Alcoa site in Massena north to where the river joins the Saint Lawrence by the former GM site; according to the caption, this color corresponds to the recommendation "DO NOT EAT ANY FISH." The pamphlet also includes a color-coded chart of fish species, with American eel and carp in a red "Do Not Eat" box at the bottom. Above that is an orange box featuring species that are safe to eat once a month (e.g., sturgeon, pike, and bass), and above that is a yellow "up to four portions a month" box, featuring smaller bass and trout. Finally, at the top a green box features species that can be eaten up to eight times a month, including yellow perch and brown bullhead.

Tony noted, "In my experience, Native people are visual learners, so shying away from heavy text was a way to draw people's attention, to capture their attention and keep it." The colorful chart is significant because it shows clearly that many of the favorite species that people told me in 2008 they no longer ate, like perch and bullhead, are now safe to eat again. The purpose of the pamphlet, as Tony noted, is to empower people to make informed decisions about eating fish or not:

> The intent is to try to get people to concentrate on the better choices of fish, the better species, for lack of a better term, the "cleaner fish." And just give them that knowledge so that they could make those decisions. They don't have to. If you don't want to eat from the green category, which is the "cleanest" category, you don't have to, but at least you can do that with the knowledge of what you're doing, and to have a little bit of confidence in your decisions.

Part of what made this project, and the subsequent fish advisory and brochure, a success in the eyes of the Environment Division was the level of control that Mohawks had in steering the research and design of the outreach materials. Tony noted:

> The Department of Health made it known from the outset that this was the tribe's message to give. We really had the final say on what the message was going to be. And I think that's a rare

relationship to have with a state agency, and it was something that was built on a good deal of trust. And if we wanted to scrap the advisory and start over, they would follow our lead and do that. And we also had the control over the final say in which fish to list and which fish not to. So that was—it gave us the confidence of just knowing that we weren't going to lose the sense of self in putting this out. . . . This trust, these relationships, they happen over time, they don't happen overnight. It's about connecting with people professionally and personally. I value the time that we spent with our colleagues at the Department of Health; they learned a lot about our culture, and we learned a lot about their culture. We exchanged ideas and we exchanged food, we had great conversations with them, so I think that went a long way. I'd almost say that if you don't have that level of involvement, maybe your relationship isn't as good as you think. I think if you have to deal with Native communities, you sort of have to get that involved, you really have to roll up your sleeves and get to know the people that you're working with. Otherwise you're not going to get the whole story.

Mary LaFrance credited NYSDOH with giving the Mohawks design leeway to make the pamphlet something that would appeal to the community:

New York State Department of Health gave us a lot of freedom in the design. . . . There was a lot of opportunity, if we wanted to, to include cultural imagery. On the cover of both of our booklets, there's a segment from the Ohen:ton Karihwatehkwen, right on the front of the book, to kind of tie it into the culture, which really made it personal to this community.

Mary also noted that it was important to tie this project into work that was already being done in health programs in the community:

I think that was very instrumental, because they've already been sharing messages about health, and we had realized that we wanted to make our messages in line with the way the community was already receiving them, so that influenced a big part of the booklet, where there's a picture of a hand and the size of a fish, because a lot of the nutritionists were using the visual images of the hand, of the palm.

Despite the level of control that the SRMT Environment Division had over the creation of this new fish advisory, Tony and Mary both acknowledged that some community members were bound to be distrustful because the project was funded by a state agency. But Mary felt that

> because of the methods that we used to roll out this project, being very community driven, there was a much better level of acceptance, because the people who participated, who asked the questions, we came back with our drafts and asked them, "Is this clearly understandable to you?" So it feels more like the community has ownership over the project and they're more willing to take the advice, even though with everything else, it's still against New York State, and Tribe, and they're more willing to open up with our project because of the way we did it.

Tony agreed, describing how community members interacted with fellow Mohawks employed by the Environment Division while they were out collecting interviews and data and designing the materials. Even if the project was funded by NYSDOH, he noted, the agency "was not out in front, they were in a support role. They followed our lead."

Tony also mentioned another concern: "Where you have gaps of information, I think people from the public will draw their own conclusions." To avoid this, Tony and Mary worked hard to have conversations with community members to find out what types of fish people like to eat, and how they prepare and cook them, so that they could be sure to collect data on those kinds of fish. While the earlier fish advisories "cast a wide net," as Tony put it, discouraging most people from eating a majority of the local fish species, this new advisory offers a more nuanced message, giving people the information they need to make their own decisions about how much and what types of fish to eat.

Conclusion

Brenda, whose words open this concluding essay, wanted to make sure that I would highlight the resilience of her community. As she observed: "The struggles we have undergone have not buried us. We have stepped back, assessed, brushed ourselves off, and adapted through positive, forward-thinking measures. Surprisingly, we are quite a resilient population." My goal in this book has been to describe the issues that Akwesasro:non are up against and the challenges they see going forward, but I have also sought to highlight the resistance and resilience that Mohawks have demonstrated in adapting, maintaining, and refining who they are as a community.

Along these lines, Aleut scholar Eve Tuck has called on us all to suspend damage-centered research, which focuses on documenting pain or loss in an effort to explain underachievement or failure. While Tuck acknowledges that it makes sense to look to historical exploitation, domination, and colonization to explain contemporary brokenness such as poverty, poor health, and low literacy, she warns that the danger of this type of research is that it is a "pathologizing approach in which the oppression singularly defines a community," even when the construction of damage narratives is used as a strategy for correcting oppression.[29] The alternative to damage-centered research that she lays out involves the use of a desire-based framework that is "concerned with understanding complexity, contradiction and the self-determination of lived lives" and does not fetishize damage but, rather, "celebrates our survivance," to borrow a term from Gerald Vizenor.[30] This survivance moves beyond "basic survival in the face of overwhelming cultural genocide to create spaces of synthesis and renewal"—gardens, if you will.[31] Taiaiake Alfred refers to this as "regeneration," acting against ingrained and oppressive fears. He calls on Indigenous communities to "self-consciously recreate our cultural practices and reform our political identities by drawing on tradition in a personal and collective sense."[32] Continuing this line of thought, Kyle Whyte notes that Indigenous resurgence involves supporting and promoting political movements that assert Indigenous visions of ecologies and support Indigenous collective capacities.[33] Jeff Corntassle argues that resurgence requires acting in ways that will "reclaim and regenerate one's relational, place-based existence by challenging the ongoing, destructive forces of colonization."[34] This

A message left in chalk on a bridge railing where a rally in support of Attawa-piskat took place in 2016. Photograph by Jessica Sargent.

type of community regeneration and resurgence is what the programs and projects described above are working toward: rebuilding relationships between Akwesasro:non and their environment, their food, and each other. This work will continue at Akwesasne, despite political, social, and environmental challenges, into and beyond the next seven generations.

Acknowledgments

First and foremost, I thank the people of Akwesasne who generously shared their time and lives with me. I would especially like to thank Katsi Cook, who set me on the path of the topics covered in this book. She sat with me in her living room, in coffee shops and restaurants, in tipis, on planes, in hotel rooms, and in cars and spent countless hours on the phone and over e-mail discussing relevant issues. Thanks also to her brother Tom, who dreams big and doesn't mind sharing those dreams with me. I also extend a special thanks to Mama Jean and Henry Laffin, my "other parents" who took me in as their daughter and have fed and sheltered me for years now—and to Lori, for sharing them with me.

I am grateful to Josh Sargent and Natasha Smoke-Santiago and their family (my dear niece Ionawaiienhawi, as well as Shoienkwaronwane, who have grown up so fast, and now little Ronkwaientiio!). These dear friends, always up for late-night coffee-fueled conversations on everything from permaculture to tribal politics.

Niawen:kowa to Elvera Sargent, who patiently answered my many Kanienkeha language questions (any errors are my own). And many, many thanks to Jessica Sargent, my photography consultant, whose beautiful work is featured in this book. Hugs to Sarah Herne Rourke, who has always been there, asking how she can help.

Many thanks to the members of Kanenhi:io Ionkwaienthon:hakie with whom I worked over the years: Lorraine Gray, with whom I first planted seeds in Akwesasne as she strove to get

277

Kanenhi:io off the ground; Dean George, who shared hours of gardening knowledge and who still takes me on garden tours every time I'm back; Kenny Perkins, my gardening buddy and pickle-making, basket-weaving, gourd-painting, wood-chopping friend; and many others. Special thanks to Gina Jacobs, who first educated me about the gardening situation at Akwesasne as we stood in her yard on Cornwall Island, and to her daughter, Shirelle (whose art is featured in this book), Shirelle's beautiful daughters, and their father Fyl Tahy.

I am grateful to the members of the Akwesasne Task Force on the Environment, especially Dave Arquette, Craig Arquette, Mary Arquette, and Brenda LaFrance, who were very helpful in guiding this project over the past several years, ever since Joyce King first handed me a copy of the Good Mind Research Protocol. Thank you to Brenda for serving as the community editor of this book. Many thanks to Jim Ransom, who lent me his collection of newspaper articles spanning more than twenty years, which covered the discovery of environmental contamination at Akwesasne. Les Benedict and Ken Jock at the Saint Regis Mohawk Tribe Environment Division and Henry Lickers and Richard David at the Mohawk Council of Akwesasne Department of Environment also provided a great deal of valuable information.

I thank Bear Clan mother Wakerakatsiteh (Louise McDonald), who has been a teacher and an auntie and a friend, and whose tireless effort inspires me. She gave me the wonderful experience of becoming involved in many of her projects, programs, and ceremonies, and she has guided me through ceremony and fasting, through love and life, and through a draft of this book's preface.

A special thanks to the ladies of the Akwesasne Library, who were always helpful and encouraging when I would spend many hours with my laptop in my "other office." And a big niawen:kowa to all the people who shared their time, homes, stories, and food with me as I conducted the interviews. My apologies to the ten who passed away before they were able to see this book in print. Mark, Ernie, Salli, Louis, Solomon, Howard, Jake, Judy, Jann, and Barbara—you are missed.

I thank the SUNY Albany Superfund Basic Research Program researchers who took time out of their busy schedules to speak candidly about their research experiences. I especially thank Lawrence Schell and David Carpenter, who have taken time over the years to read drafts of chapters in this book and explain science to me.

I owe a special debt of gratitude to Phil Brown, who patiently guided me over several years as his research assistant, student, and postdoc. He has been an extraordinary mentor and a model for how to blend scholarship, community activism, and teaching. Thank you also to my fellow members of the Contested Illness Research Group, especially Laura Senier and Rebecca Altman, and to members of the Social Science Environmental Health Research Institute at Northeastern University, who read through drafts of chapters 3 and 5.

Upon returning to Brown University as an assistant professor in American studies, I discovered I was in the most supportive department a junior scholar could hope for, and that helped to drive the completion of this book. I am grateful to all of my colleagues at Brown, but I owe special thanks to my department chair, Matt Guterl, who pushed me and supported me in myriad ways and saw this project through to the end. Many thanks also to the Brown University Rockefeller Library staff, especially to the interlibrary loan department, for years of tracking down sources for me. I am especially grateful to Bruce Boucek, who worked with me to create the two maps of Akwesasne in chapter 1.

Many thanks to Jason Weidemann, the very patient editor at the University of Minnesota Press who was a great support in this process. Thank you to both of the readers selected by the Press, who together provided the most helpful feedback I have ever received on my writing.

A very special thanks goes to my dearest friends, Jennifer Edwards Weston, Jamie Spears Vanderhoop, and Honor Keeler, who held me up during my entire Brown education and were there for me when I returned to Rhode Island as faculty. Pilamayaye, kutâputush, and wado to them. And to Sammie White Rossi, who has been there for me since the first grade. Their constant support, humor, and companionship brought me to where I am today.

Last and most important is my foundation: thank you to my immediate family, who supported me unconditionally even as they wondered why a person would want to stay up so late reading and writing all the time. To my parents, Anita Ovitt and Robert Hoover, who raised me to love learning, gardening, powwows, and talking to people, and who gave me the confidence to pursue my educational goals and the resilience and determination to finish what I set out to accomplish. To my stepmom, Karen, who has provided the support and patience that only a family member could and continues to serve as my guide to the English language (although she can't be blamed for any errors in this book). And love to my sisters, Rebecca, Amanda, and Tina, who have grown into wonderful, responsible human beings with senses of humor I can't find anywhere else, who love me unconditionally, and who remind me not to take myself too seriously.

This project was made possible through funding from a Ford Foundation Postdoctoral Fellowship (2014–15), a Ford Foundation Dissertation Fellowship (2009–10), a National Science Foundation Cultural Anthropology Dissertation Improvement Grant—Award Number 0819535 (2008–9), a Switzer Environmental Fellowship (2008–9), a Brown University Graduate School Fellowship (2008–9), a Swearer Center Dissertation Award (2009–10), and a Lynn Reyer Tribal Community Development Grant (2008–9).

Notes

Preface

1. In tracing the roots of the name Iroquois, Dean Snow describes how Basque fishermen came to know the Algonquian-speaking people who lived along the northeast coast of North America, from southern Labrador to New England, including the shores of the Gulf of Saint Lawrence. A pidgin language developed so the two groups could communicate. One of the words that survived referred to a feared nation of Indians who lived far to the interior and sometimes came down the Saint Lawrence River to trade. The local Algonquians and Basques called them by the pidgin Basque name Hilokoa (the killer people), thus they became known through an unflattering secondhand description provided by rivals. The Algonquian language lacked the *l* sound, so the name became Hirokoa to Algonquian ears. By the time the French followed Jacques Cartier's earlier route into the Saint Lawrence in the late sixteenth century, they had adapted the name from the Algonquians, revising the spelling to fit their own language; thus it became Iroquois. Canadians still pronounce the name closer to its original sound (ir-o-kwa), but speakers of New York English have long since changed the pronunciation, as with other French words, and so it now rhymes with Illinois. Snow, *Iroquois*, 1–2. Similarly, according to Taiaiake Alfred, the name Mohawk comes from an Algonquian term meaning "cannibal monster." For this reason, and loyalty to the Indigenous name, he prefers Kanien'kéha:ka. Alfred, *Peace, Power, Righteousness*. Throughout this book, I most frequently use the names Mohawk and Haudenosaunee, as these were the names used most often by the people with whom I spoke in the community.

2. There are no official versions of these stories, and the full telling of most of them can take days. For example, myriad versions of the Haudenosaunee creation story have been published, and where it should

start and whose version should be codified are widely debated. See Mohawk scholar Kevin White's "Rousing a Curiosity in Hewitt's Iroquois Cosmologies." The version I've given is just a small portion that starts in the middle of the story. What I present here are merely short summaries of the various stories, crafted to give a general idea of the cultural elements that many Akwesasro:non would like to see used as the basis of policy and practice. Many thanks to Wakerakatsiteh (Louise McDonald), who assisted me with this.

3. Ohero:kon translates to "under the husk," in reference to a period in the creation story in which children were kept apart from the general public.

4. Gray and Lauderdale, "Web of Justice"; King, "Value of Water."

5. The work of Mohawk scholar Laticia McNaughton has highlighted the role of food throughout the Confederacy's formation story, from the Peacemaker's convincing Jigonsaseh to stop feeding war parties and instead accept a position as one who feeds those taking part in treaty negotiations to the insistence on feeding negotiating parties before any treaty discussions began. McNaughton, "Tetewatskà:hons ne Sewatokwà:tshera."

6. In the late 1960s and early 1970s, a group of Haudenosaunee known as the White Roots of Peace traveled around the country carrying the message of the Great Law of Peace.

7. In recent years, there has been a push within Native American and Indigenous studies to "normalize" Indigenous language terms by not treating them as "foreign" and italicizing them in English-language text. Throughout this volume, Mohawk words are not italicized.

8. King, "Value of Water."

9. The Tuscarora Nation became the sixth nation to join the Confederacy in 1722. The original founding date of the Confederacy is contested; most Iroquoianist scholars' estimates date to the sixteenth century. See Tooker, "League of the Iroquois." Based on oral histories and eclipse tables, Mann and Fields estimate August 1142 as the founding date. Mann and Fields, "Sign in the Sky."

10. Tooker, "League of the Iroquois," 422.

11. Fenton, "Leadership in the Northeastern Woodlands."

12. I have taken the spelling of these terms from King, "Value of Water." The following synopsis is influenced by Hewitt's papers, published in Fenton, *Great Law and the Longhouse*, 86n3; as well as in Kanetohare, "Ohontsiawakon."

13. Jake Swamp, former Wolf Clan subchief of the Mohawk Nation Council of Chiefs, founded the Tree of Peace Society, which has traveled around North America and other parts of the world planting thousands of white pine trees and conducting presentations to share the message of the Great Law of Peace.

14. Kanetohare, "Ohontsiawakon."

15. I have seen both terms used to express this third concept. Kanikon-ri:io is used in King, "Value of Water"; and Kanetohare, "Ohontsiawakon." Kariwiio is used in ATFE RAC, "Akwesasne Good Mind Research Protocol." In an informal survey among Mohawk friends, I found mixed opinions on which is the more appropriate term to fill this spot.

16. The present-day longhouse religion is based on the teachings of Handsome Lake, known as the Kariwiio. At Akwesasne, the Haudenosaunee Confederacy–affiliated longhouse follows these teachings.

17. Alfred, "Peace, Power, Righteousness"; ATFE RAC, "Akwesasne Good Mind Research Protocol."

18. King, "Value of Water."

Introduction

1. In 2000, Alcoa purchased Reynolds Metals, which became Alcoa East, and the existing Alcoa plant in Massena became Alcoa West. During the time I conducted these interviews, the community still referred to the eastern plant as Reynolds, and so that is the name I maintain for that factory.

2. The community is commonly referred to in written work as over-lapping or being based in Ontario and Quebec in the region north of the U.S.–Canadian border, and within New York State's Saint Lawrence and Franklin Counties south of the border. Community members have pointed out to me that they were there long before these entities formed themselves around Akwesasne, and so to say that their community falls within these other political boundaries normalizes the unfair claims these other entities have on Akwesasne's land and political independence. Instead, I describe them as sharing boundaries.

3. The population in this community is notoriously difficult to enu-merate. Residents have been suspicious of and resistant to national censuses, and some are enrolled with both federally recognized tribal governments. George Fulford states that "an estimated 12,918 people live in Akwesasne, 10,219 residents on the Canadian side and 2,699 on the American side." His figures are based on U.S. Census Bureau data from 2000 for the American portion and data from the Mohawk Council of Akwesasne Office of Vital Statistics from 2005 for the Canadian portion. Fulford, "Ahkwesahsne Mo-hawk Board of Education," 29. According to the Mohawk Council of Akwe-sasne website (http://www.akwesasne.ca), as of April 1, 2016, approximately 12,315 people were registered/affiliated with the MCA, but this does not necessarily mean that all of these members live in Akwesasne.

4. U.S. Government Accountability Office, *Superfund.*

5. Katsi's story is pieced together from the following sources: several

conversations I had with her in 2007, a formal interview I conducted with her in 2008, and our ongoing conversations since then; a folder of papers she lent me containing grant applications, articles she had written, and letters to her from personnel at the State University of New York (SUNY) at Albany; the Katsi Cook Papers (1976–2005), MS 528, in the Sophia Smith Collection at Smith College in Northampton, Massachusetts; the transcript of an interview conducted with Katsi in 2005 by Joyce Follet of Smith College; and Katsi's published articles and book chapters. Citations specify the sources of direct quotes taken from Follet's 2005 interview and Katsi's published works; other pieces of information presented here were gained from our 2008 interview as well as from various conversations, meetings, and e-mails from 2007 through 2016. In selecting names and terminology for this book, I have chosen those that were most familiar to the community members with whom I was interacting. Therefore, Katsi and other community members are generally referred to by first name, in contrast to the scientists interviewed, who are generally referred to by last name (as they are known through their publications and throughout the community). My decision to use primarily first names for community members was also influenced by the fact that the Cook family name has been a common one in Akwesasne since Colonel Louis Cook helped to establish the community in its current form in the eighteenth century. Thus, to distinguish Katsi from her relatives, first names are useful.

6. WARN, formed initially in South Dakota in the 1970s, was affiliated with the American Indian Movement but provided a female complement to that largely male-dominated group. WARN supported improved educational opportunities, health care, and reproductive rights for American Indian women and pushed to combat violence against women, to end stereotyping and exploitation of American Indians, to uphold treaties over Indian lands, and to fight against contamination of American Indian lands and environments.

7. She describes the experience of giving birth to her second son in Cook, "Coming of Anontaks."

8. In this book, I use *Tribe* and *Tribal,* capitalized, to refer to the official federally recognized SRMT government, as distinct from the tribe as a group or tribal governments in general.

9. Katsi Cook, "Akwesasne Community Health Project," grant application submitted to the John H. Whitney Foundation, New York, by the Women's Dance Health Program, 1981, 6. Katsi provided me with a copy of this application from her personal files.

10. Ten Fingers, "Rejecting, Revitalizing, and Reclaiming"; Quigley, "Review of Improved Ethical Practices."

11. See Mohai et al.,, "Environmental Justice"; Bullard, *Dumping in Dixie.*

12. Mohai et al., "Environmental Justice," 407.

13. Robert D. Bullard, quoted in Mohai et al., "Environmental Justice," 407.

14. Bryant, "Introduction," 5.

15. U.S. Environmental Protection Agency, "Environmental Justice."

16. U.S. Environmental Protection Agency, "Tribal Superfund Program."

17. LaDuke, *All Our Relations.*

18. Ranco et al., "Environmental Justice."

19. Holifield, "Environmental Justice."

20. Cook, "Critical Contexts."

21. Wildcat, *Red Alert!*

22. Weaver, *Defending Mother Earth,* 3.

23. Wolfe, *Settler Colonialism.*

24. Morgensen, "Biopolitics of Settler Colonialism," 52.

25. Whyte, "Indigenous Experience."

26. Voyles, *Wastelanding,* 23.

27. Ibid., 24.

28. Ranco, "Trust Responsibility," 360.

29. Schlosberg, *Defining Environmental Justice.*

30. Faber and McCarthy, "Neoliberalism, Globalization"; Pellow, *Resisting Global Toxics.*

31. LaDuke, *Winona LaDuke Chronicles,* 142.

32. Hoover et al., "Indigenous Peoples of North America."

33. Harris and Harper, "Native American Exposure Scenario," 789. See also Harris and Harper, "Using Eco-cultural Dependency Webs"; Harris and Harper, "Method for Tribal Environmental Justice Analysis."

34. Whyte, "Justice Forward."

35. Gottlieb and Fisher, "Community Food Security."

36. Whyte, "Indigenous Food Systems," 144.

37. Ibid., 145.

38. See Adamson, "Medicine Food."

39. Whyte, "Indigenous Food Systems," 144.

40. Pellow and Brulle, "Power, Justice, and the Environment."

41. Pellow and Brulle, "Future of Environmental Justice Movements"; Sze, *Noxious New York.*

42. Robbins, *Political Ecology.*

43. Middleton, "Political Ecology of Healing," 2.

44. Carroll, *Roots of Our Renewal.*

45. Carney, "Biopolitics of 'Food Insecurity,'" 2.

46. Baer, "Toward a Political Ecology of Health"; King, "Political Ecologies of Health"; Hayes-Conroy and Hayes-Conroy, "Veggies and Visceralities"; Carney, "Biopolitics of 'Food Insecurity.'"

47. Carney, "Biopolitics of 'Food Insecurity.'"

48. Smith, *Decolonizing Methodologies*; Wilson, *Research Is Ceremony*.

49. TallBear, *Native American DNA*, 20.

50. Wilson, *Research Is Ceremony*, 7.

51. Ibid., 40.

52. I have mixed Indigenous ancestry (Mohawk and Mi'kmaq) but am not enrolled in a community, so I am grateful to the Bear Clan, and especially Bear Clan mother Wakerakatsiteh, for giving me a place to sit with them in the longhouse; to Jean and Henry Laffin, who took me in as their daughter; to Ionawaiienhawi, who became my niece and her parents my dearest friends; and to the dozens of others who took me in, made me their friend and family, and put me to work.

53. See, for example, ATFE RAC, "Superfund Clean-up at Akwesasne"; Tarbell and Arquette, "Akwesasne"; Arquette et al., "Holistic Risk-Based Environmental Decision Making"; Arquette et al., "Restoring Our Relationships."

54. Unless otherwise noted, all quotations of community members and scientists come from my interviews with them.

55. Ottinger, *Refining Expertise*.

56. Nader, "Up the Anthropologist."

57. The term *ecosocial history* comes from Edelstein, *Contaminated Communities*.

58. The term *mitigation politics* comes from Little, *Toxic Town*.

59. Bourdieu, *Language and Symbolic Power*.

60. Fischler, "Food Habits, Social Change"; Fischler, "Food, Self and Identity."

61. Lock, "Cultivating the Body"; Hamdy, *Our Bodies Belong to God*.

62. Scheper-Hughes and Lock, "The Mindful Body."

63. Ibid., 12.

64. Ibid., 7.

65. Douglas, *Purity and Danger*, 122.

66. Salmón, "Kincentric Ecology."

67. ATFE RAC, "Superfund Clean-up at Akwesasne," 283.

68. Harris and Harper, "Environmental Justice in Indian Country," 4.

69. Scheper-Hughes and Lock, "The Mindful Body."

70. Simpson, *Mohawk Interruptus*; Dennison, *Colonial Entanglement*.

71. Alfred, *Peace, Power, Righteousness*; Coulthard, *Red Skin, White Masks*.

1. Driving Tour through the Political and Environmental History of Akwesasne

1. The General Motors Central Foundry was placed on the National Priorities List as a Superfund site in 1984, and the Alcoa plant in 2013. Reynolds Metals is not on the list, but remedial actions under EPA enforcement have occurred there.

2. These charges were adjourned by a town justice when the town's attorney was not on hand to argue the case. Odato, "Indian Cigarette Chaos."

3. The department was disbanded in 1980 after an extended two-year political confrontation between the Tribal Council and the Mohawk Nation. In 1989 the SRMT began creating a new Tribal police force, for which the Tribe received funding from the Bureau of Indian Affairs in 1990. See Bonaparte, "Too Many Chiefs," chaps. 18, 23.

4. The Tribal Court has the following divisions: Traffic Court; Civil Court, for all noncriminal cases; Family Court, which includes the Child Support Enforcement Unit; and Healing-to-Wellness/Drug Court.

5. "Historic Tribal Police Certifications"; New York Law, Indian, Art. 8, Sec. 114, Saint Regis Mohawk Tribal Police.

6. Akwesasne Mohawk Police Service, "History of Akwesasne Mohawk Police Service."

7. New York State, Department of Taxation and Finance, "View/Report"; Public Health and Tobacco Policy Center, "Collecting Cigarette Taxes."

8. "Akwesasne Cigarette Plant Legalizes Operations."

9. Kesmodel, "Tribes Rolling Out Cigarettes."

10. Odato, "Indian Cigarette Chaos."

11. See the Akwesasne Mohawk Casino Resort website, http://mohawk casino.com.

12. Johansen, *Life and Death.*

13. Sack, "Cuomo Urges Internal Police."

14. George-Kanentiio, *Iroquois Culture,* 193.

15. Saint Regis Mohawk Tribe, "How Gaming Benefits Our Community." Proceeds from the Akwesasne Mohawk Casino only benefit programs under the SRMT on the southern half of the community. The Mohawk Council of Akwesasne, the governing body of the northern half of the community, receives a share of the Casino Rama revenue that are distributed to all of the First Nations in Ontario. Funds distributed to the First Nations are intended to fund initiatives under five general areas: community development, health, education, economic development, and cultural development. See Mohawk Council of Akwesasne, "Akwesasne Community Fund."

16. Dupuis, "St. Regis Casino Operators Indicted."

17. Toensing, "Mohawk Elected Government."

18. Fenton and Tooker, "Mohawk," 477; Frisch, "Revitalization, Nativism, and Tribalism," 72.

19. George-Kanentiio, *Iroquois on Fire*, 19.

20. Fenton and Tooker, "Mohawk," 477; King, "New York State Breaks Off."

21. Starna and Campisi, "When Two Are One."

22. "Mohawk Council of Akwesasne Files Baxter and Barnhart Islands Claim."

23. Hauptman, *Iroquois Struggle for Survival*, 146.

24. King, "New York State Breaks Off."

25. Ibid.

26. Graham, "Issue of Mohawk Land Claim."

27. Cayuga Indian Nation of New York v. Pataki, 413 F.3d 266, 273 (2d Cir. 2005), *cert. denied*, 547 U.S. 1128 (2006); City of Sherrill v. Oneida Indian Nation of New York, 544 U.S. 197 (2005).

28. Raymo, "Land-Reclamation Arrest"; Kader, "Bear Clan Representative Arrested"; Kader, "Land Theft Charges."

29. Sommerstein, "Mohawk Chiefs."

30. Office of the Minister of Aboriginal Affairs and Northern Development, Canada, "Canada and the Mohawks of Akwesasne."

31. King, "Land Claims Update."

32. "Overview of Akwesasne's North Shore Claim."

33. The radio station's call letters, CKON, are a play on the Mohawk word for "hello," spelled she:kon or sekon and pronounced "say-go." The Native American Music Awards are known as the Nammy Awards.

34. George-Kanentiio, "Mohawk Nation Council."

35. Bonaparte, "History of the St. Regis Catholic Church."

36. Frey, "Mohawks."

37. Fenton and Tooker, "Mohawk."

38. Fadden, *History of the St. Regis Akwesasne Mohawks*.

39. Hough, *History of St. Lawrence*; Bonaparte, "History of Akwesasne."

40. Hough, *History of St. Lawrence*, 110.

41. Frisch, "Revitalization, Nativism, and Tribalism," 61.

42. According to Akwesasne scholar Salli Benedict: "Our oral history says that the loud roar of the rapids that once existed near Akwesasne, at what is now known as Long Sault, could be heard for great distances, far in advance of our approach to the area. It is said that the sound of the rapids under freezing ice sounded like the drumming sound that emanates from the chest of a partridge in its spring courtship rituals." Benedict, "Made in Akwesasne," 422n1.

43. While some archaeologists contend that this region had previously been settled by an Indigenous people other than the Mohawk (called the "Saint Lawrence Iroquoians"), Akwesasro:non scholars argue that "Akwesasne includes the land and waters where the Mohawk people have raised their families, fished, hunted, and buried their dead for thousands of years." Tarbell and Arquette, "Akwesasne," 94. For discussion of the possibility of earlier Indigenous settlers, see Trigger and Pendergast, "Saint Lawrence Iroquoians." Scholars' claims of later settlement by the Mohawk are viewed as efforts to dispossess the Mohawk people of proper title to the land. In this way, Akwesasne Mohawks are being alienated from their land through historical writing as well as through the land claims process. Doug George-Kanentiio cites oral tradition around a large Mohawk village on the peninsula that juts into the confluence of the Saint Lawrence and Saint Regis Rivers, where the Catholic church now stands. He writes that by the end of the sixteenth century, the Mohawks had retreated from Akwesasne because of various European-borne plagues and the onset of war with Algonkians and their allies, which compelled them to draw back to the Mohawk Valley area in central New York State. After several generations, Mohawks returned to the area, after first settling at Kahnawà:ke. George-Kanentiio, *Iroquois on Fire*. Darren Bonaparte concludes that the Saint Lawrence Iroquoians "spring from the same ancestral source as the Five Nations." These Saint Lawrence Iroquoians of Hochelaga, "although scattered and absorbed by the Five Nations and other surrounding tribes, would one day return to that region where their adoptive nations established settlements there in the seventeenth century." Bonaparte, "Too Many Chiefs," chap. 1.

44. Bonaparte, *Lily among Thorns*. A note on spelling: In writing about institutions like the Saint Kateri Tekakwitha Hall, I have utilized their spelling, which omits accents and punctuation. In writing about Káteri Tekahkwí:tha the person, I have adopted the spelling that includes Mohawk language accent and punctuation, as utilized by Bonaparte and others.

45. Ibid.

46. Eng, "Boy's Survival."

47. Sara Ciborski cites community estimates that 75 percent of residents are Catholic, 20 percent are longhouse, 5 percent are Protestant, and 1 percent are "Jehovas." Ciborski, "Culture and Power," 78. In a random sample of 353 Akwesasne Mohawk adults, Azara Santiago-Rivera et al. found that "religious affiliations were predominantly Catholic, Protestant, and traditional Longhouse religions, with 50%, 6% and 28% membership respectively. About 16% did not wish to respond or did not have affiliation." Santiago-Rivera et al., "Exposure to an Environmental Toxin," 34.

48. Barreiro, "Complexity of Ecstasy."

49. For more information, see Bonaparte, "History of Akwesasne."

50. The position had previously been held by the Mohawks of the Six Nations reserve.

51. George-Kanentiio, *Iroquois on Fire*, 25.

52. Starna, "Repeal of Article 8." The end of every press release issued by the SRMT includes the statement "The Saint Regis Mohawk Tribal Council is the duly elected and federally recognized government of the Saint Regis Mohawk People."

53. Bonaparte, "Too Many Chiefs."

54. Berman, "Violation of the Human Rights of the Mohawk People."

55. Ibid.

56. Bonaparte, "Too Many Chiefs"; Johansen and Mann, *Encyclopedia of the Haudenosaunee*; George-Kanentiio, "*Akwesasne Notes*."

57. Stone, "Legal Mobilization," 385.

58. Hauptman, *Iroquois Struggle for Survival*; Hauptman, *Formulating American Indian Policy*; Hauptman, *Seven Generations*; Wunder, *Indian Bill of Rights*.

59. Hauptman, *Iroquois Struggle for Survival*, 38.

60. Alaska was added to the list after it gained statehood in 1959.

61. Bonaparte, "Too Many Chiefs"; Starna, "Repeal of Article 8"; Fenton and Tooker, "Mohawk."

62. Parker, "Code of Handsome Lake"; Wallace, *Religion*.

63. Bonaparte, "Kaniatarowanenneh"; Thorp et al., "St Lawrence River Basin"; "St Lawrence River."

64. Hauptman, *Iroquois Struggle for Survival*, 134–35; Hauptman, *Formulating American Indian Policy*, 20.

65. Hauptman, *Seven Generations*, 175. Moses, the chairman of the New York State Power Authority at the time, was responsible for $27 billion in public works projects over his career, many of which displaced poor communities and communities of color. See Hauptman, *Iroquois Struggle for Survival*; Choodaro, *Power Broker*.

66. Hauptman, *Seven Generations*, 177.

67. Ibid., 133.

68. Ibid., 135.

69. Parham, *St. Lawrence Seaway*, xxv.

70. Cox et al., "Drowning Voices."

71. Arquette et al., "Restoring Our Relationships," 338–39.

72. Cook, "Mother's Milk Project."

73. Hauptman, *Iroquois Struggle for Survival*, 123.

74. Mitchell, *Teiontsikwaeks*; Bonaparte, "History of Akwesasne."

75. See the Mohawk International Lacrosse website, http://www.moh awklacrosse.net.

76. Vennum, *American Indian Lacrosse*; Herne, "Our Native Game."

77. Canadian Press, "Fire Adds to Lacrosse Stick Shortage."

78. Frisch, "Factionalism, Pan-Indianism, Tribalism," 80.

79. This information comes from the recollections of William D. Fraser, Draft #4 Environmental History of Akwesasne (Env. 1–Env. 9), compiled by Salli M. K. Benedict, principal investigator, Mohawk Council of Akwesasne Land Claim Office, October 9, 1996.

80. Martin, "Life along the Line."

81. George-Kanentiio, *Iroquois on Fire*.

82. Hill, "Akwesasne Busiest Spot."

83. Martin, "Smuggled Aliens."

84. Hawley, "Agents Fight Drug War."

85. Freedman, "Lawlessness on the Borderline."

86. Hawley, "Agents Fight Drug War."

87. Phaneuf, "Indian Reserve Boundaries and Rights."

88. Hauptman, *Iroquois Struggle for Survival*.

89. Nickels, "Native American Free Passage Rights."

90. Barnouw, *Documentary*; Ginsburg, "The After-Life of Documentary."

91. Ginsburg, "The After-Life of Documentary," 67.

92. See the June 1970 issue of *Akwesasne Notes*, which contains excerpts of articles from local newspapers that covered the island takeovers.

93. George-Kanentiio, "*Akwesasne Notes*."

94. Ibid.

95. Johansen, *Encyclopedia of the American Indian Movement*, entries "Akwesasne Mohawk Counselor Organization," 7–8; "*Akwesasne Notes*," 8–12; "White Roots of Peace," 286–87.

96. George-Kanentiio, "*Akwesasne Notes*," 122.

97. Johansen, *Encyclopedia of the American Indian Movement*.

98. George-Kanentiio, "*Akwesasne Notes*"; Blansett, "Journey to Freedom."

99. Johansen, *Encyclopedia of the American Indian Movement*.

100. George-Kanentiio, *Iroquois on Fire*.

101. White, *Free to Be Mohawk*.

102. Matthiessen, *Indian Country*; Lemelin, "Social Movements"; Bonaparte, "Too Many Chiefs."

103. George-Kanentiio, *Iroquois on Fire*. As noted above, the SRMT reconstituted the Tribal police force in 1989.

104. Bonaparte, "Saiowisakeron."

105. Barrera, "Ontario bridge reopens after tense native-police standoff."

106. Sommerstein, "Border Agent Standoff"; "Mohawk Council of Akwesasne Daily Briefing."

107. Hazelton, "Temporary Border Fix."

108. Smith, "Idle No More Border Peaceful Blockade"; Moe, "Idle No More."

109. Smith, "Idle No More Border Peaceful Blockade."

110. Toensing, "Two Officials Bash Mohawk Idle No More Protest."

111. Altman et al., "Pollution Comes Home"; Couch and Kroll-Smith, *Communities at Risk*; Edelstein *Contaminated Communities*.

112. Altman et al., "Pollution Comes Home," 420.

113. Whyte, "Indigenous Experience," 159.

2. Environmental Contamination, Health Studies, and Mitigation Politics

1. In 1919, the Toronto Manufacturing Company was acquired by Howard Smith Paper Mills, which merged with Dominion Tar & Chemical in 1961; the company was rebranded as Domtar in 1965. The plant closed in 2006. "Domtar," The Info List, accessed February 28, 2017, http://www.theinfolist.com. Although this plant contributed to pollution in the river through the release of mercury and other wastes, relatively few studies have been conducted connecting the plant to human health effects, so it will not be discussed as extensively as others in this chapter.

2. Hauptman, *Iroquois Struggle for Survival*.

3. Hoover, "Dying Turtle," 18.

4. Hauptman, *Iroquois Struggle for Survival*, 143.

5. Krook and Maylin, "Industrial Fluoride Pollution."

6. Ibid.

7. McIntyre, "Pollution Clouds Indian Way of Life."

8. "Future of Mohawks at Akwesasne."

9. Hauptman, *Formulating American Indian Policy*, 63.

10. Hoover, "Dying Turtle."

11. "Future of Mohawks at Akwesasne"; Hoover, "Dying Turtle."

12. McIntyre, "Pollution Clouds Indian Way of Life."

13. Krook and Maylin, "Industrial Fluoride Pollution," 14.

14. Ibid., 61.

15. Ibid.

16. Ibid.

17. Ibid., 62.

18. Saint Regis Mohawk Tribe, *St. Regis Mohawk Tribe Data Report*, 3.

19. Emery, "Mt. Sinai Study."

20. Goldstein, "PCBs Dump Poses 'Danger to Health.'"

21. McIntyre, "Pollution Clouds Indian Way of Life."

22. Emery, "Mt. Sinai Study."

23. Ransom and Lickers, "Akwesasne Environment."

24. Forti et al., *Health Risk Assessment.*

25. Hauptman, *Formulating American Indian Policy.*

26. The Mount Sinai report concluded that fish consumption per week should be further reduced for men from 2 pounds to 0.2 pound, for women from 1.6 pounds to 0.16 pound, for pregnant women or those planning pregnancy from 0.16 pound to no fish at all, and for children from 0.07 pound to no fish at all. See Hauptman, *Formulating American Indian Policy,* 64.

27. The list of contaminated fish to be avoided included carp, catfish, and suckers.

28. Everyone was advised to avoid carp, channel catfish, walleye, pike, red horse suckers, white suckers, and brown bullhead. They were also advised to eat no more than one-half pound per week of yellow perch, pumpkinseed, rock bass, whitefish, and bowfin.

29. Cook, interview by Follet, 81.

30. Quoted in Cook and Nelson, "Mohawk Women Resist," 6.

31. Cook and Nelson, "Mohawk Women Resist."

32. Andrews, "Ruin on the Reservation."

33. Spears, *Baptized in PCBs.*

34. Carpenter et al., "University–Community Partnership."

35. "Public Meeting General Motors Corporation Central Foundry Division Superfund Site," Massena, N.Y., April 25, 1990, 9, transcript provided by the EPA Office of Public Affairs. The 1248 in Aroclor 1248's name indicates the weight of the chlorine in the mixture.

36. Skinner, *Chemical Contaminants in Wildlife.*

37. Grinde and Johansen, *Ecocide of Native America,* 181.

38. "Superfund Proposed Plan General Motors Corporation Central Foundry Division," Hogansburg, N.Y., June 26, 1991, 12, transcript provided by the EPA Office of Public Affairs.

39. Ibid., 29.

40. Goldstein, "PCBs Dump Poses 'Danger to Health'"; "GM/PCBs Chronology"; Hart, "State Is Skeptical of Pollutant Claim."

41. GM's distribution of bottled water is noted in Negoita and Swamp, *Human Health and Disease Patterns.*

42. Of the $507,000 fine, GM paid only $395,000. "GM Agrees to Pay $395,000."

43. See the ATFE website, https://sites.google.com/site/atfeonline.

44. ATFE RAC, "Akwesasne Good Mind Research Protocol," 95.

45. Swamp, "St. Regis Mohawk Division," 16.

46. Haraway, "Situated Knowledges."

47. Bush et al., "Polychlorinated Biphenyl Congeners."

48. Cook, interview by Follet, 84.

49. Brian Bush to Dr. Eadon, regarding "Meeting Concerning Mo-hawks' Milk," April 18, 1984.

50. Skoog, "Stone Finds GM Contaminating Animals."

51. Foy, "Animals at Massena GM Dump."

52. Andrews, "Ruin on the Reservation."

53. Ward Stone, quoted in Tomsho, "Dumping Grounds." When I asked one young mother, Randi, if Stone's remark affected how people in Akwe-sasne saw their homeland, she replied: "I think when you are told that where you live is so dirty that animals can't survive there and your kids are going to be diseased and damaged no matter what you do, it kind of brings the whole community's self-esteem down a whole lot, and whether you feel that way or not I think it does anyway. . . . For a while, you know, you could introduce yourself as being from Akwesasne and 'Oh, that is where a giant Superfund site is.' Yeah, that is us."

54. Foy, "Animals at Massena GM Dump."

55. "Ward Stone, Once Clipped, Now Bound, Gagged."

56. Ibid.

57. While the residents of Akwesasne were happy with Stone's per-formance, other people, including his coworkers, were not, as described in a 2012 report by New York State Inspector General Ellen Biben. The re-port details the accusations against Stone, including that he failed to follow agency processes and that he behaved abusively toward coworkers. Biben, *Report of Investigation into Allegations of Misconduct.*

58. Martin, "$100 Million Clean Up."

59. Jim Ransom, quoted in Andrews, "Ruin on the Reservation."

60. Cook, interview by Follet, 87.

61. "Barefoot epidemiology" is a concept borrowed from China's "bare-foot doctors"—community-level health workers who brought basic care to China's countryside in the mid-twentieth century. Hipgrave, "Communi-cable Disease Control." According to a "workers' manual" published by the International Labour Organization, barefoot research is often qualitative, and qualitative research is not the standard approach for conducting health studies, which tend to be based on laboratory experiments and clinical find-ings. See Keith et al., *Barefoot Research.*

62. Cook, interview by Follet, 84–85.

63. Brian Bush to Katsi Cook, May 22, 1985.

64. Brian Bush to Katsi Cook, November 24, 1986.

65. For information on the specific species Akwesasro:non were in-structed to cut back on and avoid, see Tarbell and Arquette, "Akwesasne."

66. H.R. 2005 Superfund Amendments and Reauthorization Act of 1986, https://www.congress.gov/bill/99th-congress/house-bill/2005. See also Du Bey and Grijalva, "Closing the Circle."

67. Forti et al., *Health Risk Assessment*; Emery, "Study Only Partly GM Funded."

68. This chapter does not go as in depth into the Reynolds PCB contamination, but in addition to the fluoride contamination detailed earlier in the chapter, Reynolds was also discharging PCBs into the river through permitted outfalls. The contamination at the Reynolds Metals site (now known as Alcoa Massena East Plant) is being addressed under an EPA-issued Unilateral Administrative Order that requires the potentially responsible party (Alcoa) to investigate and clean up the site. Under the EPA Record of Decision (ROD), dredging the Saint Lawrence River adjacent to the Reynolds facility was required and has been completed. Just a little farther upriver Alcoa (now known as Alcoa West), was also leaching PCBs into the Grasse River (now the Grasse River Superfund Site), which feeds into the Saint Lawrence River.

69. Swamp, "St. Regis Mohawk Division," 16.

70. Sloan and Jock, *Chemical Contaminants in the Fish*; Skinner, *Chemical Contaminants in Wildlife*; Fitzgerald et al., "Chemical Contaminants in the Milk."

71. Sloan and Jock, *Chemical Contaminants in the Fish*; Kinney et al., "Human Exposure to PCBs."

72. Kinney et al., "Human Exposure to PCBs"; Skinner, *Chemical Contaminants in Wildlife*; Forti et al., *Health Risk Assessment*, 8.

73. Women who ate fish had a geometric mean milk total PCB concentration of 0.640 ppm, whereas the controls had a concentration of 0.385 ppm and the Mohawk women who did not report eating local fish had a concentration of 0.368 ppm. Fitzgerald et al., "Chemical Contaminants in the Milk."

74. In the 1979–80 dietary survey conducted by the Mount Sinai researchers, 90 percent of Mohawks reported consuming locally caught fish, and the average Mohawk obtained 89 percent of his or her total fish intake locally. Cited in Forti et al., *Health Risk Assessment*. The dietary information collected in the breast milk study indicated that 79 percent of the women ate locally caught fish more than one year before pregnancy, 58 percent ate these fish one year or less before pregnancy, and 45 percent ate locally caught fish during pregnancy. Fitzgerald et al., "Chemical Contaminants in the Milk."

75. Tarbell and Arquette, "Akwesasne," 101.

76. National Environmental Justice Advisory Council, *Fish Consumption*; O'Neill, "Variable Justice"; O'Neill, "Risk Avoidance"; O'Neill, "Mercury, Risk, and Justice"; Harper and Harris, "Possible Approach"; Hoover, "Cultural and Health Implications."

77. ATFE RAC, "Superfund Clean-up at Akwesasne"; Arquette et al.,

"Holistic Risk-Based Environmental Decision Making"; Tarbell and Arquette, "Akwesasne"; Schell et al., "Organochlorines, Lead and Mercury."

78. Harris and Harper, "Native American Exposure Scenario," 793.

79. The Superfund Basic Research Program, developed in 1987 and renamed the Superfund Research Program in 2009, funds a network of grants for university projects that are designed to seek solutions to the complex health and environmental issues associated with hazardous waste sites. Universities develop multidisciplinary projects around particular hazardous sites (usually but not always Superfund sites), studying aspects such as health risks, toxicity, exposure predictions, and potential treatments for the hazardous waste. For more information, see the NIEHS website, http://www.niehs.nih.gov.

80. Tarbell and Arquette, "Akwesasne," 107.

81. The adjusted geometric mean breast milk total PCB concentration of Mohawk mothers who gave birth from 1986 through 1989 was 0.602 ppm, compared with 0.375 ppm for the controls during the same period. Fitzgerald et al., "Chemical Contaminants in the Milk."

82. Fitzgerald et al., "Fish Consumption and Breast Milk PCB."

83. Fitzgerald et al., "Fish PCB Concentrations"; Fitzgerald et al., "Fish Consumption and Breast Milk PCB"; Hwang et al., "Fingerprinting PCB Patterns."

84. Hwang et al., "Fingerprinting PCB Patterns."

85. Cook, interview by Follet, 85.

86. Fitzgerald et al., *Exposure to PCBs from Hazardous Waste.*

87. Fitzgerald et al., "Fish Consumption and Other Environmental Exposures."

88. Fitzgerald et al., "Environmental and Occupational Exposures."

89. Ibid.

90. Centers for Disease Control and Prevention, *Third National Report on Human Exposure,* 4.

91. A geometric mean of 1.5 ppm was found for North Carolina mothers, as opposed to a geometric mean of 0.404 ppm for the Mohawk mothers. Cited in Fitzgerald et al., "Chemical Contaminants in the Milk." On Atlanta, see Fitzgerald et al., "PCB Exposure and In Vivo CYP1A2 Activity." Regarding the two Ontario communities, Fitzgerald et al. reference the results of a 1992 study that reported a mean PCB concentration among women of reproductive age who did not consume Great Lakes fish that was slightly higher than that of the Mohawk women. Fitzgerald et al., "Fish Consumption and Other Environmental Exposures." Higher serum PCB levels have been found among other Native populations that consume more local fish, such as Ojibwa people in a Wisconsin study who were consuming twice as many fish meals per year as Fitzgerald's team was documenting. Fitzgerald

et al., "Fish Consumption and Other Environmental Exposures." Research on Lake Michigan charter boat captains is cited in Fitzgerald et al., "Local Fish Consumption." The Inuit of Hudson Bay, Quebec, have been especially noted as an example of a population with much higher levels of PCBs than have been found in other populations. See DeWailly et al., "High Levels of PCBs."

92. Katsi Cook, conversation with author, January 22, 2010, Washington, D.C.

93. Fitzgerald et al., "Fish Consumption and Breast Milk," 170.

94. Altman et al., "Pollution Comes Home," 425.

95. Twenty-one interviewees responded yes, and fifteen responded no.

96. The SBRP studies also included projects that were limited to laboratory science, but here I focus only on those that dealt directly with Mohawk community members.

97. Congeners having six or more chlorines are classified as higher chlorinated, according to DeCaprio et al., "Polychlorinated Biphenyl (PCB) Exposure."

98. Dioxin, or 2,3,7,8-tetrachlorodibenzo-p-dioxin (TCDD), is considered the most highly toxic environmental contaminant ever made. It is given a toxic equivalency value of 1, and all other contaminants are scored relative to it.

99. Bruner-Tran and Osteen, "Dioxin-like PCBs."

100. Carpenter, "Polychlorinated Biphenyls (PCBs)."

101. Lawrence Schell, community presentation, December 11, 2014.

102. Schell et al., "Organochlorines, Lead and Mercury."

103. DeCaprio et al., "Polychlorinated Biphenyl (PCB) Exposure."

104. Ibid.

105. Ravenscroft et al., "Dietary Patterns." Akwesasne Mohawk children are average height as compared to other U.S. children, but at every age males who participated in the studies were in the ninetieth percentile for weight, and females were in the eighty-fifth percentile. Of the Akwesasne youth in this sample, 26 percent were at risk of being overweight and 33 percent were already overweight. Gallo et al., "Height, Weight, and Body Mass Index." Both male and female Akwesasne youth at all ages had significantly larger suprailiac skinfolds than average among U.S. children, with means exceeding the eightieth percentile and the seventy-fifth percentile, respectively. Gallo et al. "Selected Anthropometric Measurements," 530.

106. Rosenthal, *Thyroid Source Book*.

107. Schell and Gallo, "Relationships of Putative Endocrine Disruptors."

108. Schell et al., "Relationship of Thyroid Hormone Levels."

109. Schell et al., "Persistent Organic Pollutants."

110. Ibid., 91.

111. Negoita et al., "Chronic Diseases Surveillance."

112. Denham et al., "Relationship of Lead," e132.

113. Ibid.

114. Goncharov et al., "Lower Serum Testosterone."

115. Schell et al., "Relationships of Polychlorinated Biphenyls."

116. David Carpenter, community presentation, December 11, 2014.

117. Gallo et al., "Endocrine Disrupting Chemicals."

118. These measures included subtests for comprehension/knowledge, long-term memory retrieval, and delayed recall. Newman et al., "PCBs and Cognitive Functioning."

119. Newman et al., "Analysis of PCB Congeners."

120. Newman et al., "PCBs and ADHD."

121. Newman reiterated this observation during a community presentation on December 11, 2014.

122. Haase et al., "Evidence of an Age-Related Threshold Effect."

123. Newman et al., "PCBs and Cognitive Functioning," 442; Haase et al., "Evidence of an Age-Related Threshold Effect," 83; Carpenter, community presentation.

124. Carpenter, community presentation.

125. Goncharov et al., "Lower Serum Testosterone."

126. Codru et al., "Diabetes in Relation to Serum Levels."

127. Aminov et al., "Diabetes Prevalence."

128. Carpenter, community presentation.

129. Little, *Toxic Town*, 21.

130. For details on the development of these policies, see Grijalva, *Closing the Circle*.

131. See Du Bey and Grijalva, "Closing the Circle."

132. Ibid.

133. U.S. Environmental Protection Agency, "Applicable or Relevant and Appropriate Requirements (ARARs)," https://www.epa.gov/superfund.

134. Saint Regis Mohawk Tribal Council, Resolution No. 89-19, "A Resolution of the Saint Regis Mohawk Tribal Council Adopting Ambient Standards for PCBs on the Saint Regis Mohawk Reservation," 1989, cited in Lewis and DelVecchio, *Data Report*. As a side note, all of the land contaminated by GM is Mohawk territory and considered within the land claims territory. However, for legal purposes, the Tribe's standards for PCB cleanup could be applied only to land technically within the current boundaries of the reservation.

135. Jim Ransom, e-mail communication with author, June 9, 2015.

136. George Pavlou, associate director for New York programs for the EPA (although he introduced himself as "captain of the EPA"), stated at a

public meeting held April 25, 1990, regarding the GM Central Foundry Division Superfund site in Massena: "Please bear in mind that EPA Regulations recognize that the Tribe is a sovereign state and require that we apply their standards for any cleanups that we undertake on Akwesasne lands. The law is very specific in requiring EPA to apply the more stringent requirements be it State or Federal for Superfund cleanups." "Public Meeting General Motors Corporation," 6.

137. ATFE RAC, "Superfund Clean-up at Akwesasne," 272.

138. "Public Meeting General Motors Corporation," 38, 84.

139. Ibid., 84.

140. "Superfund Proposed Plan," 68.

141. Ibid., 111.

142. ATFE RAC, "Superfund Clean-up at Akwesasne."

143. Ibid.

144. Bruun, "EPA, GM Plans Blasted by Tribe."

145. U.S. Environmental Protection Agency, "Third Five-Year Review Report"; U.S. Environmental Protection Agency, "EPA Superfund Program."

146. Berman, "New GM Shirks Responsibility."

147. Hayden, "RACER Trust Concentrates"; Sommerstein, "Massena GM Redevelopers."

148. U.S. Environmental Protection Agency, "Second Five-Year Review Report," ES1.

149. Associated Press, "New York Mohawk."

150. Ibid.

151. "Kanietekeron (Larry Thompson) Arraigned."

152. Dupuis, "Akwesasne Man Pleads Guilty."

153. Jasanoff, "Civilization and Madness," 223.

154. Ibid.

155. Carroll, *Roots of Our Renewal*.

156. Swamp, "St. Regis Mohawk Division," 16.

3. "We're Not Going to Be Guinea Pigs"

1. See, for example, Latour, *Science in Action*; Gusterson, "Nuclear Weapons Testing."

2. Ingold, "Introduction"; Nader, "Up the Anthropologist."

3. Nadasdy, "Politics of TEK," 11; Ingold, "Introduction." Examples of such an anthropology include Duster, "Prism of Heritability"; Rapp, *Testing Women*.

4. Knorr-Cetina, *Manufacture of Knowledge*; Latour and Woolgar, *Laboratory Life*; Ottinger, *Refining Expertise*.

5. See, for example, TallBear, *Native American DNA*; Cajete, *Native Science*; Kimmerer, *Braiding Sweetgrass*; Whyte, "Indigenous Food Systems"; Whyte et al., "Weaving Indigenous Science."

6. TallBear, *Native American DNA*, 11.

7. Nowotony et al., *Re-thinking Science*.

8. Edwards et al., "Introduction."

9. Ottinger, *Refining Expertise*.

10. Wylie et al., "Institutions for Civic Technoscience"; Shepard et al., "Advancing Environmental Justice"; Ottinger and Cohen, *Technoscience and Environmental Justice*.

11. Among the thirty-two community members who had been involved in the health studies, five had served as fieldworkers to collect the data, and six had consulted with the SUNY researchers as members of ATFE. Two of those consultants were also among the four people who had children enrolled in a study. Five women participated in the adolescent well-being study with their children, since that study also tested the mothers. One man was part of the caffeine breath test study, and four other men gave blood for the men's study. Four women were involved in the breast milk study (two of whom would later become fieldworkers, and so have been counted above as well), and four women gave blood for a study. One woman remembered being part of the cognitive study, and another woman insisted that someone from the Superfund project came by and did a survey with her, asking a lot of questions about fish consumption, but did not take any samples from her. Everyone I spoke with in the community was aware that the health studies had been done, and many others not counted here had family members who were participants.

12. See, for example, Quigley, "Review of Improved Ethical Practices"; Ten Fingers, "Rejecting, Revitalizing, and Reclaiming."

13. Trumbull et al., "Thinking Scientifically"; McCormick, "After the Cap."

14. Corburn, *Street Science*; Brown, "Popular Epidemiology."

15. Corburn, *Street Science*.

16. Brown, "Popular Epidemiology," 269.

17. Ramirez-Andreotta et al., "Environmental Research Translation."

18. Minkler and Wallerstein, *Community-Based Participatory Research for Health*, 7.

19. Wing, "Whose Epidemiology, Whose Health?," 250. See also Cornwall and Jewkes, "What Is Participatory Research?"

20. Chavis et al., "Returning Basic Research to the Community."

21. Schell et al., "Advancing Biocultural Models," 512.

22. Hatch et al., "Community Research."

23. Israel et al., "Review of Community-Based Research."

24. Bishop, "Addressing Issues of Self-Determination"; Vega, "Theoretical and Pragmatic Implications"; Israel et al., "Review of Community-Based Research."

25. Brown et al., "Measuring the Success of Community Science"; Altman et al., "Pollution Comes Home"; Morello-Frosch et al., "Toxic Ignorance and Right-to-Know."

26. De Koning and Martin, "Participatory Research in Health."

27. Brody et al., "'Is It Safe?'"

28. Shepard et al., "Advancing Environmental Justice"; Minkler and Wallerstein, *Community-Based Participatory Research for Health*; Ramirez-Andreotta et al., "Environmental Research Translation."

29. Epstein, *Inclusion*; Moreno-John et al., "Ethnic Minority Older Adults"; Lex and Norris, "Health Status of American Indian."

30. Cochran et al., "Indigenous Ways of Knowing," 22.

31. Schnarch, "Ownership, Control, Access, and Possession."

32. Moreno-John et al., "Ethnic Minority Older Adults."

33. Morton et al., "Creating Research Capacity," 2160; Burhansstipanov et al., "Lessons Learned from Community-Based Participatory Research."

34. Castellano, "Ethics of Aboriginal Research," 98.

35. Bourdieu, *Language and Symbolic Power*.

36. Tarbell and Arquette, "Akwesasne," 93.

37. Tsosie, "Indigenous Peoples and Epistemic Injustice," 1136.

38. Arquette et al., "Holistic Risk-Based Environmental Decision Making," 261.

39. Nadasdy, *Hunters and Bureaucrats*.

40. White et al., "Communicating Results," 488.

41. Nadasdy, *Hunters and Bureaucrats*, 5.

42. Potvin et al., "Implementing Participatory Intervention," 296. See also Smith-Morris, "Autonomous Individuals or Self-Determined Communities?"; Cummins et al., "Community-Based Participatory Research."

43. See, for example, Garwick and Auger, "Participatory Action Research"; Strickland, "Challenges in Community-Based Participatory Research"; Chrisman et al., "Community Partnership Research"; Dignan et al., "Evaluation Lessons Learned"; Fisher and Ball, "Tribal Participatory Research."

44. Cochran et al., "Indigenous Ways of Knowing," 22.

45. In a survey, Noe et al. found that a number of factors would lead Native people to be more likely to take part in a study, including (1) if the study was to be conducted by a tribal organization and the community would be involved in study development, (2) if a Native person was to have a leading role in the study, (3) if the study would address serious health problems of concern to the community, (4) if the study would bring money

to the community, and (5) if the study would provide new treatments or services, or use the information gathered to answer new questions. Noe et al., "Influence of Community-Based Participatory Research." Many Mohawk fieldworkers felt that Akwesasne residents took part in the SBRP studies because familiar faces were collecting the data and because the studies were addressing an issue of concern for the community. See also Chrisman et al., "Community Partnership Research"; Fisher and Ball, "Tribal Participatory Research."

46. Morton et al., "Creating Research Capacity."

47. Burhansstipanov et al., "Lessons Learned from Community-Based Participatory Research"; LaVeaux and Christopher, "Contextualizing CBPR"; Fisher and Ball, "Tribal Participatory Research"; Schell and Tarbell, "Partnership Study of PCBs."

48. The eight key principles are as follows: CBPR (1) recognizes community as a unit of identity, (2) builds on strengths and resources of the community, (3) facilitates collaborative partnerships in all phases of the research, (4) integrates knowledge and action for mutual benefit of all partners, (5) promotes a colearning and empowering process that attends to social inequalities, (6) involves a cyclical and iterative process, (7) addresses health from both positive and ecological perspectives, and (8) disseminates findings and knowledge gained to all partners. Described initially in Israel et al., "Review of Community-Based Research," the principles are reviewed in LaVeaux and Christopher, "Contextualizing CBPR."

49. LaVeaux and Christopher, "Contextualizing CBPR."

50. Smith, "Interorganizational Collaboration"; Chrisman et al., "Community Partnership Research."

51. Strickland, "Challenges in Community-Based Participatory Research"; Burhansstipanov et al., "Lessons Learned from Community-Based Participatory Research"; Garwick and Auger, "Participatory Action Research"; Fisher and Ball, "Tribal Participatory Research"; Dignan et al., "Comparison of Two Native American Navigator Formats"; Burhansstipanov et al., "Lessons Learned While Developing"; Dickson, "Aboriginal Grandmothers' Experience"; Chrisman et al., "Community Partnership Research"; Castelden et al., "'I Spent the First Year Drinking Tea.'"

52. Fisher and Ball, "Tribal Participatory Research."

53. Ibid.; Gallo et al., "Selected Anthropometric Measurements."

54. Quigley, "Review of Improved Ethical Practices"; Foster and Sharp, "Race, Ethnicity, and Genomics."

55. U.S. Department of Health, Education, and Welfare, *The Belmont Report.*

56. Brugge and Missaghian, "Protecting the Navajo People."

57. Oetzel et al. define community-engaged research as including tribal

participatory research, community-based participatory research, and participatory action research. All phases of community-engaged research involve collaborative partnership and shared leadership between community members and academic researchers. Oetzel et al., "Enhancing Stewardship of Community-Engaged Research."

58. In seeking approval for the dissertation research that led to this book, I submitted a document to ATFE containing all of the information required by the Good Mind Research Protocol, as described in note 60 below. After consulting with Akwesasne community members about a series of appropriate research topics, I met with ATFE members to discuss the best way to meet the stipulations. I mailed my submission to ATFE on April 3, 2007, and I received an e-mail on June 13, 2007, granting approval. During the spring of 2008, I further met with individual ATFE members to ensure that my interview questions were appropriate. Additionally, the final drafts of the dissertation and the manuscript for this book were submitted to ATFE for approval.

59. ATFE RAC, "Akwesasne Good Mind Research Protocol."

60. The Good Mind Research Protocol requires that the synopsis address the following twelve points: (1) statement of problem/research question; (2) intent of the research and the benefits the project will have to the community; (3) methods for collecting data; (4) methods for protecting confidentiality; (5) methods for disposition of the data; (6) any potential legal, financial, social, physical, or psychological risks; (7) funding/budget; (8) arrangements for all principal investigators, researchers, graduate students, and any others involved in data collection to undergo cultural sensitivity training, which is provided at the researchers' expense; (9) equity, or how study participants and the community at large will be given fair and appropriate return, including copies of research findings, authorship or acknowledgments, royalties, fair monetary compensation, copyrights, and patents; (10) empowerment, or mechanisms for informed consent as well as how individuals and community members will be empowered by the research process through employment, training, or outreach efforts; (11) intellectual property rights and review of product or research results, which must include community authorship (community access to the results of the project and use of the research data must be included, and researchers must inform the RAC before submitting or presenting papers on the study results to journals, publishing houses, or conferences); and (12) data ownership/ archive—ATFE reserves the right to require the deposit of raw materials or data, working papers, or study products in a tribally designated repository, with specific safeguards to preserve confidentiality.

61. Not all researchers have been fortunate enough to receive approval from the ATFE RAC. In his 2002 PhD dissertation, Stephen Garson

of George Mason University describes how he wanted to use in-person interviews with both Akwesasne and Massena community members about the local Superfund site as primary source material to answers questions about the elements of concern that constitute a community's construction of risk. He prepared a research synopsis and submitted it to ATFE. Much to his dismay, "ATFE rejected my proposal on the grounds that it did not see how the research would benefit tribal members. . . . ATFE also noted the amount of research that had been performed on the Akwesasne community—some of it much needed human and environmental health research, but some of it unwanted and unsolicited political research." Garson, "Talking Toxics," 157. In lieu of in-person interviews, Garson turned to the transcripts from public meetings that the EPA held to receive public comments on three separate cleanup proposals.

62. Cook, interview by Follet, 87.

63. Schell et al., "Advancing Biocultural Models."

64. The citation count comes from Web of Science, accessed May 30, 2014, http://login.webofknowledge.com.

65. Ten interviewees responded this way.

66. Thirty-seven out of fifty interviewees who were asked about rates of fish consumption mentioned decreasing their frequency of eating fish because of the advisories.

67. Burhansstipanov et al., "Lessons Learned from Community-Based Participatory Research."

68. Castellano, "Ethics of Aboriginal Research."

69. Arquette et al., "Holistic Risk-Based Environmental Decision Making," 261.

70. Jernigan et al., "Beyond Health Equity"; Andrews et al., "Training Partnership Dyads."

71. Goodman et al., "Identifying and Defining the Dimensions," 259. See also Ramirez-Andreotta et al. "Environmental Research Translation," 656; Freudenberg, "Community Capacity," 473.

72. Corburn, *Street Science.*

73. Chavis et al., "Returning Basic Research to the Community."

74. Schell et al., "Advancing Biocultural Models," 522.

75. As Santiago-Rivera et al. noted about ATFE in 1998: "Members of this group hold formal academic degrees (i.e., AA, BS, BA, MS, PhD degrees), and have expertise in a variety of areas including wildlife biology, ecotoxicology, aquaculture, civil and environmental engineering, biology, and in traditional medicine, environmental and cultural knowledge. Through formal training, life experiences, and leadership roles, they are well respected in their community." Santiago-Rivera et al., "Building a Community-Based Research Partnership," 165. Since this list was compiled

almost two decades ago, the areas of expertise have grown, and more ATFE members have obtained academic degrees.

76. See also Jernigan et al., "Beyond Health Equity."

77. Schell and Tarbell, "Partnership Study of PCBs," 838.

78. Schell et al., "Advancing Biocultural Models," 513.

79. Carpenter et al., "Polychlorinated Biphenyls"; Carpenter and Miller, "Environmental Contamination"; Miller et al., "Community-Based Participatory Research."

80. For a description of the conference and its outcomes, see Hoover et al., "Indigenous Peoples of North America."

81. See Minkler and Wallerstein, *Community-Based Participatory Research for Health*; Israel et al., "Review of Community-Based Research"; Fisher and Ball, "Tribal Participatory Research."

82. Schell et al., "Advancing Biocultural Models," 521.

83. In a March 2008 interview, Carpenter told me: "We lost our funding in 2000 and one of the major reasons we lost our funding, we'd gotten to the point where the next obvious avenue to take was to look at genetic susceptibility. And [we] knew very well the reservations in many Native communities about anything that involved genetic testing, so we talked about it very, very early on. And I think partly because of the trust we had generated over a period of time, we got a fairly strong 'maybe' kind of answer. But then at the last moment, we got an 'absolutely not.' And it was just too late to revamp the project." Similarly, also in a March 2008 interview, Schell noted: "This is the age of genomics and they are—the reviewers and the agency people at NIH—are very keen on having genetic testing done. They want to know whether some genes are better at metabolizing these things or some people who are exposed to PCBs don't have thyroid hormone effects and so on. You smile, you just [know] how contentious or even abhorrent the notion of genetic testing is. When I explain this to people who weren't familiar with the issue at all, and once I explain it, it makes a lot of sense to them. But it doesn't serve you well when you're applying for grants. We've had grants turned down because we didn't have genetic testing involved, and we know that that's just not going to fly with the tribe. So we don't argue until we're blue in the face. We've been told it's not going to work out. We don't even bring it up. I always bring it up but I always expect, and I'm not disappointed, to learn the position hasn't changed on that. So I don't know whether we'll be able to do or anyone will ever be able to do any work at . . . Akwesasne that could possibly involve differences in physiology within the community because there'll be some demand for [a] genetic basis to that. We'll see."

84. LaDuke, *Recovering the Sacred*; TallBear, *Native American DNA*.

85. TallBear, *Native American DNA*.

86. Quigley, "Review of Improved Ethical Practices"; Quigley, "Applying Bioethical Principles"; Foster and Agzarian, "Reporting Results of Biomonitoring Studies."

87. Morello-Frosch et al., "Toxic Ignorance and Right-to-Know."

88. Brown et al., "Institutional Review Board Challenges."

89. Morello-Frosch et al., "Toxic Ignorance and Right-to-Know."

90. Brody et al., "'Is It Safe?,'" 1548.

91. Quandt et al., "Reporting Pesticide Assessment Results," 643.

92. Altman et al., "Pollution Comes Home"; Brown et al., "Measuring the Success of Community Science"; Curtis and Wilding, *Is It In Us?*; Morello-Frosch et al., "Toxic Ignorance and Right-to-Know."

93. Schell et al., "Advancing Biocultural Models," 516.

94. On the exposure experience, see Altman et al., "Pollution Comes Home"; Adams et al., "Disentangling the Exposure Experience."

95. Henry Lickers, community meeting, December 11, 2014.

96. Little, "Negotiating Community Engagement," 100. See also White et al., "Communicating Results."

97. White et al., "Communicating Results," 487.

98. Two of the women who said that they were happy with the report-back they received later worked on subsequent health studies. It is possible that as they became part of the process and gained a greater understanding through that experience, they also gained a better appreciation of what went into reporting results back to the community and of the limitations of the data. With this greater understanding of the process and its limitations, they could be happy with what they had previously received.

99. A previously conducted study on reducing childhood obesity at Akwesasne concluded that an intervention involving obesity prevention plus parenting support would have greater success in reducing the prevalence of obesity in high-risk Native American children than an intervention involving parent support only. The major finding of this study was that a home-visiting program, in which the intervention was delivered one-on-one in homes by an Indigenous peer educator focused on changing lifestyle behaviors and improving parenting skills, showed promise for obesity prevention in high-risk Native American children. Harvey-Berino and Rourke, "Obesity Prevention." In a previous study of diabetes in Akwesasne, Hood et al. distributed the information gathered through surveys by attending meetings of and presenting to seventeen community organizations and two public forums, writing letters to participants, and writing articles for local newspapers. In this way, they were able to reach hundreds of community members, present their results, and get feedback. Hood et al., "Native American Community Initiative." Presenting results in these ways is clearly more work for the researchers and their staff, but Hood et al. found that by fully

utilizing preexisting networks they achieved better results. Future health studies could follow a similar model.

100. Ottinger and Cohen, *Technoscience and Environmental Justice*, 4.

101. Ibid., 9.

102. *OED* Online, s.v. "citizen," accessed February 21, 2017, http://www.oed.com.

103. Bruyneel, *Third Space of Sovereignty*.

4. Contamination, Convenience, and a Changing Food Culture

1. Tsionkwanati:io is Mohawk for "We have a nice place again."

2. Caplan, "Approaches to the Study of Food."

3. Quoted in ibid., 3.

4. Fischler, "Food, Self and Identity," 275.

5. Dombrowski, "Subsistence Livelihood."

6. Million, *Therapeutic Nations*, 171.

7. Whyte, "Recognition Dimensions of Environmental Justice."

8. Fitzgerald et al., "Fish PCB Concentrations"; Hwang et al., "Exposure to PCBs"; Fitzgerald et al., "Local Fish Consumption"; Fitzgerald et al., "Fish Consumption and Other Environmental Exposures."

9. Of the fifty community members I interviewed about their fish consumption, thirty-seven said they had cut down or stopped eating fish entirely, eight said they still ate fish, and five said they stopped eating fish during the height of the advisories but had since gone back to it, now that they are older and less worried about their health.

10. For information on PCB impacts on fish, see National Oceanic and Atmospheric Administration, "Assessing Fish Health." See also Barron et al., "Association between PCBs, Liver Lesions." A study published by Environment Canada showed a higher level of parasitism among yellow perch from Lake Saint-François, a regulated aquatic environment with water-level fluctuations of approximately fifteen centimeters, than among those from Lake Saint-Pierre, where water levels vary significantly, with fluctuations of approximately two meters. See Environment Canada, "Effects of Water Level and Flow Fluctuations." Since Akwesasne is directly west of Lake Saint-François, it is quite possible that Mohawk fishermen were catching fish tainted by this parasite.

11. For a review of studies on the immunotoxic impact of PCBs on fish, see Duffy et al., "PCB-Induced Hepatic CYP1A Induction."

12. Hart, "High PCB Level."

13. ATFE RAC, "Superfund Clean-up at Akwesasne," 283.

14. Parker, "Code of Handsome Lake," 14.

15. Quintana, "Agricultural Survey."

16. Ibid.

17. Ostendorf and Terry, "Toward a Democratic Community."

18. The U.S. Department of Agriculture defines a farm as any place from which one thousand dollars or more of agricultural products are produced and sold in a year. The USDA designates places with agricultural activity that do not qualify as farms as "agricultural places." U.S. Department of Agriculture, *2012 Census of Agriculture*. For purposes of this chapter, I will simply use the term *gardens* to refer to most of these "agricultural places."

19. Onkwehonwe means "original people" in Mohawk.

20. Tsí Yotsihstokwáthe Dakota Brant, "*Onhehste'ón:we*: 'The Original Corn,'" posting on Indigenous Food Sovereignty Network's Facebook page, March 1, 2009, http://www.facebook.com. Dakota's mother is Terrylynn Brant, who founded the Mohawk Seedkeepers organization and has hosted a number of events and conferences on the topic.

21. Harper, *Changing Works*, 24.

22. Many Native American farmers and ranchers have suffered difficulties in procuring loans and subsidies, even where they should have been eligible. In 1999, this led to the *Keepseagle v. Vilsack* class action lawsuit against the USDA. Although this case, which was settled in 2010, did not directly affect most farmers at Akwesasne, it demonstrates that Indian farmers nationwide have had to struggle to maintain and fund their operations.

23. Quintana, "Agricultural Survey," 32.

24. White, "Sustaining Diversity," 100. White, who is originally from Akwesasne, is a renowned seed saver and expert on Haudenosaunee heritage seed varieties. She is currently the director of the Sierra Seed Cooperative and chair of the board of directors of Seed Savers Exchange.

25. George-Kanentiio, "*Akwesasne Notes*," 124.

26. Saint Regis Mohawk Tribe, *St. Regis Mohawk Tribe Data Report*, 3.

27. Twenty-one respondents blamed community concerns about contaminated soil for the fact that there were now fewer gardens in Akwesasne than in the past.

28. Fitzgerald et al., "Polychlorinated Biphenyl."

29. Hwang et al., "Assessing Environmental Exposure."

30. Ibid.

31. The lowest level that can be detected is 0.2 ppb per congener.

32. Fitzgerald et al., "Fish Consumption and Other Environmental Exposures." The highest levels there were 29 ppb and 119.7 ppb in corn and 26.5 ppb and 149.5 ppb in tobacco.

33. Chiarenzelli et al., "Defining the Sources"; Fitzgerald et al., "Fish Consumption and Other Environmental Exposures," 167.

34. Saint Regis Mohawk Tribe, *St. Regis Mohawk Tribe Data Report*, 24.

35. Shapin, *Social History of Truth*, xxv.

36. Ibid., xxvi.

37. Mackie and Queller, "Impact of Group Membership."

38. Fourteen interviewees said they get their information about the environment from the SRMT Environment Division. Four interviewees said they look to ATFE for information about the environment, four said the MCA Department of Environment, four mentioned the newspaper or news, four rely on family members or friends, and seven said they rely on themselves to seek out information, through the Internet, reading different sources, or through direct observation.

39. Carroll, *Roots of Our Renewal*; Alfred, *Peace, Power, Righteousness*.

40. As part of the environmental health research carried out in Akwesasne, SUNY scientists conducted food frequency interviews with youth and found that nutrient-dilute but energy-dense foods (e.g., fries, soda, cookies) characterized up to a quarter of the diets of most the young people. Ravenscroft et al., "Dietary Patterns." People tend to acquire these foods at local convenience stores, fry shacks, and the grocery stores and Walmart Supercenter located in Massena, the town to the west.

41. Caplan, "Approaches to the Study of Food," 19.

42. Belasco, *Food*.

43. Cook, interview by Follet, 83.

44. When I was recruited to take part in a three-day fast with a group of other women, some of my Akwesasro:non friends expressed concern that I did not have the necessary "stores" that most Mohawk women did, and might not make it through the experience. Fortunately, I did survive, and the end of the fast was celebrated with a lavish feast of traditional foods.

45. Mintz, "Meals without Grace"; Mintz, *Sweetness and Power*; Caplan, "Approaches to the Study of Food."

46. Fischler, "Food Habits, Social Change."

47. Ibid.

48. Fischler, "Food, Self, and Identity," 290.

49. Ibid., 289.

50. Crowther, *Eating Culture*, 279.

51. Mohawk, "From the First to the Last Bite," 174.

52. Milburn, "Indigenous Nutrition," 423.

53. Katsi Cook, quoted in Brant, "*Onhehste'ón:we*."

54. White, "Sustaining Diversity, " 18.

55. Tarbell and Arquette, "Akwesasne."

56. Schell et al., "What's NOT to Eat."

57. Arquette et al., "Holistic Risk-Based Environmental Decision Making."

58. See Bushkin-Bedient and Carpenter, "Benefits versus Risks." Turyk

et al. argue that most of our knowledge about the nutritional benefits of fish consumption is based on marine fish, which generally have higher concentrations of omega-3 fatty acids than freshwater fish. They point to studies that have found no association between local fish intake and serum omega-3 fatty acids in Great Lakes fishermen. Since omega-3 fatty acids are one of the most highly cited health-promoting compounds in fish, Turyk et al. conclude that we do not have enough data to quantitatively analyze the costs and benefits of the consumption of fish from the Great Lakes and the Saint Lawrence River. Turyk et al., "Risks and Benefits."

59. See Schell et al., "Organochlorines, Lead and Mercury"; Schell et al., "What's NOT to Eat"; Gallo et al., "Levels of Persistent Organic Pollutant."

60. Cook, "Critical Contexts."

61. Whyte, "Justice Forward."

62. Ibid., 518.

63. Dombrowski, "Subsistence Livelihood," 217.

64. Ibid., 212.

65. Edelstein, *Contaminated Communities,* 11.

66. Hayes-Conroy and Hayes-Conroy, "Veggies and Visceralities," 87.

5. PCBs and Thrifty Genes

1. Harris and Harper, "Using Eco-cultural Dependency Webs."

2. Baer et al., *Medical Anthropology and the World System,* 5.

3. McMullin, *Healthy Ancestor,* 141.

4. Hull et al., "Increased Dietary Fat."

5. Centers for Disease Control and Prevention, *National Diabetes Fact Sheet, 2011.*

6. Burkitt, "Emergence of a Concept."

7. Milburn, "Indigenous Nutrition."

8. Judkins, "Diabetes and Perception of Diabetes"; Wiedman, "Diabetes Mellitus and Oklahoma Native Americans"; Wiedman, "Type II Diabetes Mellitus"; Wiedman, "Striving for Healthy Lifestyles."

9. Wiedman, "Diabetes Mellitus and Oklahoma Native Americans"; Wiedman, "Native American Embodiment."

10. Wiedman, "Native American Embodiment."

11. U.S. Department of Health and Human Services, *Healthy People 2010 Midcourse Review,* sec. 5.

12. Centers for Disease Control and Prevention, *National Diabetes Fact Sheet, 2011.*

13. Sharp, "Environmental Toxins."

14. Martinez and Strauss, "Diabetes in St. Regis Mohawk Indians."

15. Negoita et al., "Chronic Diseases Surveillance."

16. Gallo et al., "Height, Weight, and Body Mass Index"; Schell and Gallo, "Overweight and Obesity."

17. Schell, community presentation, December 11, 2014.

18. Hamdy, "When the State and Your Kidneys Fail."

19. Scheper-Hughes, *Death without Weeping*; Scheper-Hughes, "Diabetes and Genocide"; Farmer, "On Suffering and Structural Violence."

20. Nguyen and Peschard, "Anthropology, Inequality, and Disease," 459.

21. Scheper-Hughes, "Diabetes and Genocide," xviii.

22. Ferreira and Lang, "Introduction," 25.

23. Hagey, "Phenomenon, the Explanations and the Responses"; Hagey, "Native Diabetes Program."

24. Scheper-Hughes, "Diabetes and Genocide," xviii–xix.

25. Phil Brown describes the dominant epidemiological paradigm as the generally accepted perspective on a disease, "the status quo of science and government policy and public understanding." According to Brown, "The DEP is a set of beliefs and practices about a disease and its causation embedded within science, government, and public life. It includes established institutions entrusted with the diagnosis, treatment, and care of disease sufferers, as well as journals, media, universities, medical philanthropies, and government officials. . . . The DEP is both a model and a process. It is a model in that it helps us understand the complexity of disease discovery. It is a process in that it delineates a variety of locations of action." The DEP "emphasizes individual behavioral factors rather than environmental and social factors as keys to disease prevention." Brown, *Toxic Exposures*, 18, 20.

26. Centers for Disease Control and Prevention, *National Diabetes Fact Sheet, 2011*.

27. Neel, "Diabetes Mellitus."

28. Neel, "'Thrifty Genotype' in 1998."

29. Sahota, "Genetic Histories."

30. Ibid.

31. TallBear, *Native American DNA*.

32. On genetics and obesity, see Bouchard, "Biological Predisposition to Obesity." On the thrifty gene, see, for example, Ayub et al., "Revisiting the Thrifty Gene Hypothesis."

33. Ferreira and Lang, "Introduction," 13.

34. Scheper-Hughes, "Diabetes and Genocide," xx.

35. Kozak, "Surrendering to Diabetes."

36. Chaufan, "Sugar Blues"; Chaufan, "What Does Justice Have to Do with It?"

37. Bailey et al., "Qsource Quality Initiative."

38. On the concept of the individual fallacy, see Chaufan, "Sugar Blues."

On the ecological fallacy, see Brown, "Environment and Health"; Freedman, "Ecological Inference."

39. Chaufan, "Sugar Blues"; Chaufan, "What Does Justice Have to Do with It?" While Chaufan considers "environment" in the sociological sense as encompassing the principles of distribution of social resources such as institutional arrangements, power arrangements, and formal and informal normative structures, many residents of Akwesasne define "environment" in the more conventional sense, implicating environmental contamination of fish and gardens in the root causes of diabetes in the community.

40. Codru et al., "Diabetes in Relation to Serum Levels."

41. Ibid., 1444.

42. Carpenter, community presentation, December 11, 2014; Aminov et al. "Diabetes Prevalence."

43. Saint Regis Mohawk Tribe, "Diabetes Center for Excellence."

44. Macaulay et al., "Community Empowerment," 409.

45. Coates, *Between the World and Me*, 29.

46. Wiedman, "Native American Embodiment."

47. Nineteen interviewees expressed this opinion.

48. Tarbell and Arquette, "Akwesasne," 102.

49. See, for example, Schell et al., "Organochlorines, Lead and Mercury," 960–61; Schell et al., "Thyroid Function," 97.

50. Schell et al., "Thyroid Function."

51. Schell et al., "Organochlorines, Lead and Mercury," 961.

52. Hood et al., "Native American Community Initiative."

53. Wiedman, "Native American Embodiment," 606.

54. Bev went on to become the director of the clinic, and then an elected SRMT chief.

55. During his 1967–70 fieldwork among the Akwesasne Mohawk, Jack Frisch noted that there were many political and religious divisions (or "factions," as he called them) within the community. However, he also found that "when the Mohawks are politically threatened by the dominant non-Indian society, their response to this threat is manifested as tribalism and their extratribal political behavior tends to bring the community together and a sense of Mohawk ethnic identity is shared by all." Frisch, "Factionalism, Pan-Indianism, Tribalism," 81. Frisch defines tribalism as "the process whereby a society, such as the Mohawks, with a common territory, common traditions, and common values and interests, goes about establishing its self-identity. The need for establishing this self-identity arises out of specific socio-political conditions." Ibid., 79. Frisch sees tribalism as "a healing bridge between factions." The divisions in the community are as strong today as when Frisch observed them in the late 1960s, and threats from the outside have come to include factors of diet, health, and the environment.

56. Smith-Morris, "Reducing Diabetes in Indian Country."

57. Halpern, *Obesity and American Indians/Alaska Natives.*

58. Macaulay et al., "Kahnawake Schools Diabetes Prevention Project"; Macaulay et al., "Community Empowerment."

59. In addition to the elected Saint Regis Mohawk Tribe and Mohawk Council of Akwesasne and the traditional Mohawk Nation Council of Chiefs, during the summer of 2008 there was a group called the Community Spokespeople. The members of this group were looking to replace the SRMT with what they saw as a more effective, more traditional form of government.

60. Krieger, "Embodying Inequality," 296, quoted in Walters et al., "Bodies Don't Just Tell Stories," 180.

61. McMullin, *Healthy Ancestor,* 159.

62. Arquette et al., "Holistic Risk-Based Environmental Decision Making," 262.

Conclusion

1. See, for example, Arquette et al., "Holistic Risk-Based Environmental Decision Making"; Giles et al. "Integrating Conventional Science."

2. Brenda was also kind enough to serve as the "community editor" for this book.

3. O'Neill, *Five Bodies,* 36.

4. Cook, "Critical Contexts."

5. ATFE RAC, "Superfund Clean-up at Akwesasne," 268. See also Tarbell and Arquette, "Akwesasne," 95.

6. Tarbell and Arquette, "A Native American Community's Resistance," 102.

7. Whyte, "Justice Forward."

8. See especially the works in this volume's bibliography by Stuart G. Harris and Barbara L. Harper, Catherine A. O'Neill, and Kyle Powys Whyte on this issue.

9. Arquette et al., "Holistic Risk-Based Environmental Decision Making," 261. See also Hoover et al., "Social Science Collaboration."

10. Bruyneel, *Third Space of Sovereignty,* xvii.

11. Simpson, *Mohawk Interruptus,* 128.

12. Phaneuf, "Indian Reserve Boundaries and Rights."

13. "Public Meeting General Motors Corporation," 11.

14. Ibid., 7.

15. Boswell-Penc, *Tainted Milk,* 12.

16. Ibid., 169.

17. Sze, "Boundaries and Border Wars," 791.

18. Cook, interview by Follet, 85.

19. Sze, "Boundaries and Border Wars," 808, citing Haraway, *Simians, Cyborgs, and Women*.

20. Ottinger and Cohen, *Technoscience and Environmental Justice*.

21. See, for example, Mihesuah, *Recovering Our Ancestors' Gardens*.

22. I have been working remotely with Kanenhi:io since 2007, and I participated more intensively when I lived in Akwesasne in 2008. My role in 2008 included taking care of the community garden and taking notes at meetings. Since moving away, I have mostly been involved through networking and assisting with grant applications.

23. Much of my summary of the three arms of the NRDA restoration project is based on U.S. Fish and Wildlife Service, "Natural Resource Damages Settlement"; Lafrance, "Natural Resource Damages," 8–9; and Tarbell, "Akwesasne Cultural Restoration Program."

24. See the EPA's Superfund web page, http://www.epa.gov/superfund.

25. Alfred, *Cultural Impact Study*; Alfred, "Akwesasne Cultural Restoration Program."

26. Alfred, "Akwesasne Cultural Restoration Program."

27. Tom Cook to Saint Regis Mohawk Tribe, August 19, 2015.

28. Ohseraséia:hawi, "St Regis Mohawk Tribe Community Meeting."

29. Tuck, "Suspending Damage," 413–14.

30. Ibid., 416, 422.

31. Gerald Vizenor, quoted in ibid., 422.

32. Alfred, *Wasáse*, 34.

33. Whyte, "Indigenous Food Systems."

34. Corntassle, "Re-envisioning Resurgence," 88.

Bibliography

Adams, Crystal, Phil Brown, Rachel Morello-Frosch, Julia Green Brody, Ruthann Rudel, Ami Zota, Sarah Dunagan, Jessica Tovar, and Sharyle Patton. "Disentangling the Exposure Experience: The Roles of Community Context and Report-Back of Environmental Exposure Data." *Journal of Health and Social Behavior* 52, no. 2 (2011): 180–96.

Adamson, Joni. "Medicine Food: Critical Environmental Justice Studies, Native North American Literature, and the Movement for Food Sovereignty." *Environmental Justice* 4, no. 4 (2011): 213–19.

"Akwesasne Cigarette Plant Legalizes Operations." CBC News Ottawa, April 14, 2010. http://www.cbc.ca/news.

Akwesasne Mohawk Police Service. "History of Akwesasne Mohawk Police Service." http://www.akwesasnepolice.ca.

Akwesasne Task Force on the Environment Research Advisory Committee. "Akwesasne Good Mind Research Protocol." *Akwesasne Notes* 28, no. 1 (1996): 94–99.

———. "Superfund Clean-up at Akwesasne: A Case Study in Environmental Justice." *International Journal of Contemporary Sociology* 34, no. 2 (1997): 267–90.

Alfred, Taiaiake. "The Akwesasne Cultural Restoration Program: A Mohawk Approach to Land-Based Education." *Decolonization: Indigeneity, Education & Society* 3, no. 3 (2014): 134–44.

———. *Cultural Impact Study: Assessment and Overview of the Effects of Environmental Contamination on the Mohawks of Akwesasne.* Report for the Environment Division, Saint Regis Mohawk Tribe, September 27, 2006. http://www.srmtenv.org/web_docs.

———. *Peace, Power, Righteousness: An Indigenous Manifesto.* Oxford: Oxford University Press, 1999.

———. *Wasáse: Indigenous Pathways of Action and Freedom.* Peterborough, Ont.: Broadview Press, 2005.

Altman, Rebecca Gasior, Rachel Morello-Frosch, Julia Green Brody, Ruthann Rudel, Phil Brown, and Mara Averick. "Pollution Comes Home and Gets Personal: Women's Experience of Household Chemical Exposure." *Journal of Health and Social Behavior* 49, no. 4 (2008): 417–35.

Aminov, Zafar, Richard Haase, Robert Rej, Maria J. Schymura, Azara L. Santiago-Rivera, Gayle Morse, Anthony DeCaprio, David O. Carpenter, and Akwesasne Task Force on the Environment. "Diabetes Prevalence in Relation to Serum Concentrations of Polychlorinated Biphenyl (PCB) Congener Groups and Three Chlorinated Pesticides in a Native American Population." *Environmental Health Perspectives* 124, no. 9 (2016): 1376–83.

Andrews, Jeannette O., Melissa J. Cox, Susan D. Newman, Gwen Gillenwater, Gloria Warner, Joyce A. Winkler, Brandi White, Sharon Wolf, Renata Leite, Marvella E. Ford, and Sabra Slaughter. "Training Partnership Dyads for Community-Based Participatory Research Strategies and Lessons Learned from the Community Engaged Scholars Program." *Health Promotion Practice* 14, no. 4 (2013): 524–33.

Andrews, Roberts. "Ruin on the Reservation." *Post Standard* (Syracuse, N.Y.), 1989, A4–A6.

Arquette, Mary, Maxine Cole, Katsi Cook, Brenda LaFrance, Margaret Peters, James Ransom, Elvera Sargent, Vivian Smoke, and Arlene Stairs. "Holistic Risk-Based Environmental Decision Making: A Native Perspective." *Environmental Health Perspectives* 110, no. S2 (2002): 259–64.

Arquette, Mary, Maxine Cole, and Akwesasne Task Force on the Environment. "Restoring Our Relationships for the Future." In *In the Way of Development: Indigenous Peoples, Life Projects and Globalization,* edited by Mario Blaser, Harvey A. Feit, and Glenn McRae, 332–50. London: Zed Books, 2004.

Associated Press. "New York Mohawk: Move Toxic General Motors Dump from Tribal Lands." *Post Standard* (Syracuse, N.Y.), March 26, 2012. http://www.syracuse.com/news.

Ayub, Qasim, Loukas Moutsianas, Yuan Chen, Kalliope Panoutsopoulou, Vincenza Colonna, Luca Pagani, Inga Prokopenko, Graham R. S. Ritchie, Chris Tyler-Smith, Mark I. McCarthy, Eleftheria Zeggini, and Yali Xue. "Revisiting the Thrifty Gene Hypothesis via 65 Loci Associated with Susceptibility to Type 2 Diabetes." *American Journal of Human Genetics* 94, no. 2 (2014): 176–85.

Baer, Hans A. "Toward a Political Ecology of Health in Medical Anthropology." *Medical Anthropology Quarterly* 10, no. 4 (1996): 451–54.

Baer, Hans A., Merrill Singer, and Ida Susser. *Medical Anthropology and the World System.* 2nd ed. Westport, Conn.: Praeger, 2003.

Bailey, James E., Deborah V. Gibson, Manoj Jain, Stephanie A. Connelly, Kathryn M. Ryder, and Samuel Dagogo-Jack. "Qsource Quality Initiative: Reversing the Diabetes Epidemic in Tennessee." *Tennessee Medicine* 96, no. 12 (2003): 559–63.

Barnouw, Erik. *Documentary: A History of the Non-fiction Film.* New York: Oxford University Press, 1993.

Barreiro, Randi Rourke. "Complexity of Ecstasy: The Life and Sainthood of St. Kateri Tekakwitha." *National Museum of the American Indian* 14, no. 1 (2013): 33–37.

Barrera, Jorge. "Ontario Bridge Reopens after Tense Native–Police Standoff." *Ottawa Citizen,* June 12 2009. http://www.caledoniawakeupcall.com.

Barron, Mace G., Michael Anderson, Doug Beltman, Tracy Podrabsky, William Walsh, Dave Cacela, and Josh Lipton. "Association between PCBs, Liver Lesions, and Biomarker Responses in Adult Walleye (*Stizostedium vitreum vitreum*) Collected from Green Bay, Wisconsin." *Journal of Great Lakes Research* 3 (2000): 156–70.

Benedict, Salli M. Kawennotakie. "Made in Akwesasne." In *Archaeology of the Iroquois,* edited by Jordan E. Kerber, 422–41. Syracuse, N.Y.: Syracuse University Press, 2007.

Belasco, Warren. *Food: The Key Concepts.* Oxford: Berg, 2008.

Berman, Brad. "New GM Shirks Responsibility for Old Toxic Dumps and Mercury Disposal." *Hybrid Cars,* August 27, 2009. http://www.hybridcars.com.

Berman, Howard. "Violation of the Human Rights of the Mohawk People by the United States of America." In *Rethinking Indian Law,* edited by National Lawyers Guild Committee on North American Struggles, 155–61. New Haven, Conn.: Advocate Press, 1982.

Biben, Ellen. *Report of Investigation into Allegations of Misconduct by State Wildlife Pathologist Ward Stone.* Albany: State of New York, Office of the Inspector General, February 2012. https://www.ig.ny.gov.

Bishop, Russell. "Addressing Issues of Self-Determination and Legitimation in Kaupapa Maori Research." In *Research Perspectives in Maori Education,* edited by Bev Webber, 143–60. Wellington: New Zealand Council for Educational Research, 1996.

Blansett, Kent. "A Journey to Freedom: The Life of Richard Oakes, 1942–1972." PhD diss., University of New Mexico, 2011. https://repository.unm.edu.

Bonaparte, Darren. "The History of Akwesasne from Pre-contact to Modern Times." Wampum Chronicles. Accessed February 16, 2017. http://www.wampumchronicles.com.

———. "The History of the St. Regis Catholic Church and the Early Pastors." Wampum Chronicles. Accessed February 16, 2017. http://www.wampumchronicles.com.

———. "Kaniatarowanenneh, River of the Iroquois: The Aboriginal History of the St. Lawrence River." Wampum Chronicles. Accessed February 16, 2017. http://www.wampumchronicles.com.

———. *A Lily among Thorns: The Mohawk Repatriation of Káteri Tekahkwí:tha.* New York: BookSurge, 2009.

———. "Saiowisakeron: The Jake Ice Story." Wampum Chronicles. Accessed February 16, 2017. http://www.wampumchronicles.com.

———. "Too Many Chiefs, Not Enough Indians: The History of the Three Chief System and the Constitution of the St. Regis Mohawk Tribe." Submitted to the Saint Regis Mohawk Tribal Council. Wampum Chronicles, August 26, 2007. http://www.wampumchronicles.com.

Boswell-Penc, Maia. *Tainted Milk: Breastmilk, Feminisms, and the Politics of Environmental Degradation.* Albany: State University of New York Press, 2006.

Bouchard, Claude. "The Biological Predisposition to Obesity: Beyond the Thrifty Genotype Scenario." *International Journal of Obesity* 31, no. 9 (2007): 1337–39.

Bourdieu, Pierre. *Language and Symbolic Power.* Cambridge, Mass.: Harvard University Press, 1991.

Brody, Julia Green, Rachel Morello-Frosch, Phil Brown, Ruthann Rudel, Rebecca Gasior Altman, Margaret Frye, Cheryl. A. Osimo, Carla Pérez, and Liesel M. Seryak. "'Is It Safe?': New Ethics for Reporting Personal Exposures to Environmental Chemicals." *American Journal of Public Health* 97, no. 9 (2007): 1547–54.

Brody, Julia Green, Rachel Morello-Frosch, Ami Zota, Phil Brown, Carla Pérez, and Ruthann Rudel. "Linking Exposure Assessment Science with Policy Objectives for Environmental Justice and Breast Cancer Advocacy: The Northern California Household Exposure Study." *American Journal of Public Health* 99, no. S3 (2009): S600–S609.

Brown, Phil. "Environment and Health." In *Handbook of Medical Sociology,* edited by Chloe E. Bird, Peter Conrad, and Allen M. Fremont, 143–59. Upper Saddle River, N.J.: Prentice Hall, 2000.

———. "Popular Epidemiology and Toxic Waste Contamination: Lay and Professional Ways of Knowing." *Journal of Health and Social Behavior* 33, no. 3 (1992): 267–81.

———. *Toxic Exposures: Contested Illnesses and the Environmental Health Movement*. New York: Columbia University Press, 2007.

Brown, Phil, Julia Green Brody, Rachel Morello-Frosch, Jessica Tovar, Ami R. Zota, and Ruthann Rudel. "Measuring the Success of Community Science: The Northern California Household Exposure Study." *Environmental Health Perspectives* 120, no. 3 (2012): 326–31.

Brown, Phil, Rachel Morello-Frosch, Julia Green Brody, Rebecca Gasior Altman, Ruthann Rudel, Laura Senier, Carla Pérez, and Ruth Simpson. "Institutional Review Board Challenges Related to Community-Based Participatory Research on Human Exposure to Environmental Toxins: A Case Study." *Environmental Health* 9, no. 1 (2010): 39.

Brugge, Doug, and Mariam Missaghian. "Protecting the Navajo People through Tribal Regulation of Research." *Science and Engineering Ethics* 12, no. 3 (2006): 491–507.

Bruner-Tran, K. L., and K. G. Osteen. "Dioxin-like PCBs and Endometriosis." *Systems Biology in Reproductive Medicine* 56, no. 2 (2010): 132–46.

Bruun, Matthew. "EPA, GM Plans Blasted by Tribe." *Daily Courier-Observer* (Massena/Potsdam, N.Y.), June 14, 1995.

Bruyneel, Kevin. *The Third Space of Sovereignty: The Postcolonial Politics of U.S.–Indigenous Relations*. Minneapolis: University of Minnesota Press, 2007.

Bryant, Bunyan. "Introduction." In *Environmental Justice: Issues, Policies, and Solutions*, edited by Bunyan Bryant, 1–7. Washington, D.C.: Island Press, 1995.

Bullard, Robert D. *Dumping in Dixie: Race, Class, and Environmental Quality*. 3rd ed. Boulder, Colo.: Westview Press, 2000.

Burhansstipanov Linda, Suzanne Christopher, and Ann Schumacher. "Lessons Learned from Community-Based Participatory Research in Indian Country." *Cancer Control* 12, no. S2 (2005): 70–76.

Burhansstipanov, Linda, Linda U. Krebs, Alice Bradley, Eduard Gamito, Kyle Osborn, Mark B. Dignan, and Judith S. Kaur. "Lessons Learned While Developing 'Clinical Trials Education for Native Americans' Curriculum." *Cancer Control* 10, no. 5 (2003): 29–36.

Burkitt, Denis Parsons. "The Emergence of a Concept." In *Western Diseases: Their Dietary Prevention and Reversibility*, edited by Norman J. Temple and Denis Parsons Burkitt, 1–13. Totowa, N.J.: Humana Press, 1994.

Bush, B., J. Snow, S. Connor, and R. Koblintz. "Polychlorinated Biphenyl Congeners (PCBs) *p,p´*-DDE and Hexachlorobenzene in Human Milk in Three Areas of Upstate New York." *Archives of Environmental Contamination and Toxicology* 14 (1985): 443–50.

Bushkin-Bedient, Sheila, and David O. Carpenter. "Benefits versus Risks

Associated with Consumption of Fish and Other Seafood." *Review of Environmental Health* 25 (2010): 161–91.

Cajete, Gregory. *Native Science: Natural Laws of Interdependence.* Santa Fe, N.M.: Clear Light, 2000.

Canadian Press. "Fire Adds to Lacrosse Stick Shortage." *Montreal Gazette,* June 6, 1968. https://news.google.com/newspapers.

Caplan, Pat. "Approaches to the Study of Food, Health and Identity." In *Food, Health and Identity,* edited by Pat Caplan, 1–31. London: Routledge, 1997.

Carney, Megan A. "The Biopolitics of 'Food Insecurity': Towards a Critical Political Ecology of the Body in Studies of Women's Transnational Migration." *Journal of Political Ecology* 21 (2014): 1–18.

Carpenter, David O. "Polychlorinated Biphenyls (PCBs): Routes of Exposure and Effects on Human Health." *Reviews on Environmental Health* 21, no. 1 (2006): 1–23.

Carpenter David O., Anthony P. DeCaprio, David O'Hehir, Farooq Akhtar, Glenn Johnson, Ronald J. Scrudato, Lucy Apatiki, Jane Kava, Jesse Gologergen, Pamela K. Miller, and Lorraine Eckstein. "Polychlorinated Biphenyls in Serum of the Siberian Yupik People from St. Lawrence Island, Alaska." *International Journal of Circumpolar Health* 64, no. 4 (2005): 322–35.

Carpenter, David O., and Pamela K. Miller. "Environmental Contamination of the Yupik People of St. Lawrence Island, Alaska." *Journal of Indigenous Research* 1, no. 1 (2011). http://digitalcommons.usu.edu/kicjir/vol1/iss1/1.

Carpenter, David O, Alice Tarbell, Edward Fitzgerald, Michael J. Kadlec, David O'Hehir, and Brian Bush. "University–Community Partnership for the Study of Environmental Contamination at Akwesasne." In *Biomarkers of Environmentally Associated Disease: Technologies, Concepts, and Perspectives,* edited by Samuel H. Wilson and William A. Suk, 507–23. Boca Raton, Fla.: Lewis, 2002.

Carroll, Clint. *Roots of Our Renewal: Ethnobotany and Cherokee Environmental Governance.* Minneapolis: University of Minnesota Press, 2015.

Castelden, Heather, Vanessa Sloan Morgan, and Christopher Lamb. "'I Spent the First Year Drinking Tea': Exploring Canadian University Researchers' Perspectives on Community-Based Participatory Research Involving Indigenous Peoples." *Canadian Geographer/Géographe canadien* 56, no. 2 (2012): 160–79.

Castellano, Marlene Brant. "Ethics of Aboriginal Research." *Journal of Aboriginal Health* 1, no. 1 (2004): 98–114.

Centers for Disease Control and Prevention. *National Diabetes Fact Sheet,*

2011. Atlanta, Ga.: U.S. Department of Health and Human Services. https://www.cdc.gov.

———. *Third National Report on Human Exposure to Environmental Chemicals.* NCEH Pub. No. 05-0570. Atlanta, Ga.: National Center for Environmental Health, July 2005. https://www.cdc.gov.

Chaufan, Claudia. "Sugar Blues: A Social Anatomy of the Diabetes Epidemic in the United States." In *Unhealthy Health Policy: A Critical Anthropological Examination,* edited by Arachu Castro and Merrill Singer, 257–74. Walnut Creek, Calif.: AltaMira Press, 2004.

———. "What Does Justice Have to Do with It? A Bioethical and Sociological Perspective on the Diabetes Epidemic." In *Bioethical Issues, Sociological Perspectives,* edited by Barbara Katz Rothman, Elizabeth Mitchell Armstrong, and Rebecca Tiger, 269–300. Oxford: Elsevier, 2008.

Chavis, David M., Paul E. Stucky, and Abraham Wandersman. "Returning Basic Research to the Community: A Relationship between Scientist and Citizen." *American Psychologist* 38 (1983): 424–34.

Checker, Melissa. *Polluted Promises: Environmental Racism and the Search for Justice in a Southern Town.* New York: New York University Press, 2005.

Chiarenzelli, Jeff, Brian Bush, Ann Casey, Ed Barnard, Bob Smith, Patrick O'Keefe, Eileen Gilligan, and Glenn Johnson. "Defining the Sources of Airborne Polychlorinated Biphenyls: Evidence for the Influence of Microbially Dechlorinated Congeners from River Sediment?" *Canadian Journal of Fisheries and Aquatic Sciences* 57, no. S1 (2000): 86–94.

Choodaro, Robert A. *The Power Broker: Robert Moses and the Fall of New York.* New York: Alfred A. Knopf, 1974.

Chrisman, Noel J., C. June Strickland, Kolynn Powell, Marian Dick Squeochs, and Martha Yallup. "Community Partnership Research with the Yakama Indian Nation." *Human Organization* 58 (1999): 134–41.

Ciborski, Sara. "Culture and Power: The Emergence and Politics of Akwesasne Mohawk Traditionalism." PhD diss., State University of New York, 1990.

Coates, Ta-Nehisi. *Between the World and Me.* New York: Columbia University Press, 2015.

Cochran, Patricia A. L., Catherine A. Marshall, Carmen Garcia-Downing, Elizabeth Kendall, Doris Cook, Laurie McCubbin, and Reva Mariah S. Gover. "Indigenous Ways of Knowing: Implications for Participatory Research and Community." *American Journal of Public Health* 98, no. 1 (2008): 22–27.

Codru, Neculai, Maria Schymura, Serban Negoita, Akwesasne Task Force on the Environment, Robert Rej, and David Carpenter. "Diabetes in Relation to Serum Levels of Polychlorinated Biphenyls and Chlorinated

Pesticides in Adult Native Americans." *Environmental Health Perspectives* 115, no. 10 (2007): 1442–47.

Cook, Katsi. "The Coming of Anontaks." In *Reinventing the Enemy's Language: Contemporary Native Women's Writings of North America*, edited by Joy Harjo and Gloria Bird, 45–51. New York: W. W. Norton, 1997.

———. "Critical Contexts: Research to Support Community Environmental Reproductive Health." Keynote speech delivered at the Social Science Environmental Health Research Institute conference, Northeastern University, Boston, May 21, 2015.

———. "Mother's Milk Project." *First Environment* 1, no. 1 (1992): 8–9.

———. Interview by Joyce Follet. Transcript of video recording, October 26–27, 2005. Voices of Feminism Oral History Project, Sophia Smith Collection, Smith College, Northampton, Mass. http://www.smith.edu.

Cook, Katsi, and Lin Nelson. "Mohawk Women Resist Industrial Pollution." *Indian Time,* January 9, 1986, 6.

Corburn, Jason. *Street Science: Community Knowledge and Environmental Health Justice.* Cambridge: MIT Press, 2005.

Corntassle, Jeff. "Re-envisioning Resurgence: Indigenous Pathways to Decolonization and Sustainable Self-Determination." *Decolonization: Indigeneity, Education & Society* 1, no 1 (2012): 86–101.

Cornwall, Andrea, and Rachel Jewkes. "What Is Participatory Research?" *Social Science & Medicine* 41, no. 12 (1995): 1667–76.

Couch, Stephen Robert, and J. Stephen Kroll-Smith, eds. *Communities at Risk: Collective Responses to Technological Hazards.* New York: Peter Lang, 1991.

Coulthard, Glen Sean. *Red Skin, White Masks: Rejecting the Colonial Politics of Recognition.* Minneapolis: University of Minnesota Press, 2014.

Cox, Heather M., Brendan G. DeMelle, Glenn R. Harris, Christopher P. Lee, and Laura K. Montondo. "Drowning Voices and Drowning Shoreline: A Riverside View of the Social and Ecological Impacts of the St. Lawrence Seaway and Power Project." *Rural History* 10, no. 2 (1999): 235–57.

Crowther, Gillian. *Eating Culture: An Anthropological Guide to Food.* Toronto: University of Toronto Press, 2013.

Cummins, Crescentia, John Doyle, Larry Kindness, Myra J. Lefthand, Urban J. Bear Don't Walk, Ada L. Bends, Susan C. Broadaway, Anne K. Camper, Roberta Fitch, Tim E. Ford, Steve Hamner, Athalia R. Morrison, Crystal L. Richards, Sara L. Young, and Margaret J. Eggers. "Community-Based Participatory Research in Indian Country: Improving Health through Water Quality Research and Awareness." *Family & Community Health* 33, no. 3 (2010): 166–74.

Curtis, Kathleen, and Bobbi Chase Wilding. *Is It in Us? Chemical Contamination in Our Bodies: Toxic Trespass, Regulatory Failure and Opportunities for Action.* Bolinas, Calif.: Body Burden Work Group and Commonweal Biomonitoring Resource Center, 2007.

DeCaprio, Anthony P., Glen W. Johnson, Alice M. Tarbell, David O. Carpenter, Jeffrey R. Chiarenzelli, Gail S. Morse, Azara L. Santiago-Rivera, Maria J. Schymura, and Akwesasne Task Force on the Environment. "Polychlorinated Biphenyl (PCB) Exposure Assessment by Multivariate Statistical Analysis of Serum Congener Profiles in an Adult Native American Population." *Environmental Research* 98, no. 3 (2005): 284–302.

de Koning, Korrie, and Marion Martin. "Participatory Research in Health: Setting the Context." In *Participatory Research in Health: Issues and Experiences,* edited by Korrie de Koning and Marion Martin, 1–18. London: Zed Books, 1996.

Denham, Melinda, Lawrence M. Schell, Glenn Deane, Mia V. Gallo, Julia Ravenscroft, Anthony P. DeCaprio, and Akwesasne Task Force on the Environment. "Relationship of Lead, Mercury, Mirex, Dichlorodphenyl-dichloroethylene, Hexachlorobenzene and Polychlorinated Biphenyls to Timing of Menarche among Akwesasne Mohawk Girls." *Pediatrics* 115 (2005): e127–34.

Dennison, Jean. *Colonial Entanglement: Constituting a Twenty-First-Century Osage Nation.* Chapel Hill: University of North Carolina Press, 2012.

Dewailly, Eric, Albert Nantel, Jean-Philippe Weber, and François Meyer. "High Levels of PCBs in Breast Milk of Inuit Women from Arctic Quebec." *Bulletin of Environmental Contamination and Toxicology* 43 (1989): 641–46.

Dickson, Geraldine. "Aboriginal Grandmothers' Experience with Health Promotion and Participatory Action Research." *Qualitative Health Research* 10, no. 2 (2000): 188–213.

Dignan, Mark B., Linda Burhansstipanov, Judy Hariton, Lisa D. Harjo, Terri Rattler, Rose Lee, and Mondi Mason. "A Comparison of Two Native American Navigator Formats: Face-to-Face and Telephone." *Cancer Control* 12, no. S2 (2005): 28–33.

Dignan, Mark B., Kate Jones, Linda Burhansstipanov, and Arthur M. Michalek. "Evaluation Lessons Learned from Implementing CBPR in Native American Communities." *Journal of Cancer Education* 29 (2014): 412–13.

Dombrowski, Kirk. "Subsistence Livelihood, Native Identity and Internal Differentiation in Southeast Alaska." *Anthropologica* 49, no. 2 (2007): 211–29.

Douglas, Mary. *Purity and Danger: An Analysis of Concepts of Pollution and Taboo.* 1966. Reprint, London: Routledge, 1996.

Du Bey, Richard, and James Grijalva. "Closing the Circle: Tribal Implementation of the Superfund Program in the Reservation Environment." *Journal of Natural Resources and Environmental Law* 9 (1993–94): 279–96.

Duffy, J. E., Y. Li, and J. T. Zelikoff. "PCB-Induced Hepatic CYP1A Induction Is Associated with Innate Immune Dysfunction in Feral Teleost Fish." *Bulletin of Environmental Contamination and Toxicology* 74 (2005): 107–13.

Dupuis, Roger. "Akwesasne Man Pleads Guilty to Criminal Mischief at GM Site: 'I Have No Regrets.'" *Watertown Daily Times,* December 12, 2012. http://www.watertowndailytimes.com.

———. "St. Regis Casino Operators Indicted on Illegal-Gambling Charges." *Watertown Daily Times,* December 19, 2012. http://www.watertowndaily times.com.

Duster, Troy. "The Prism of Heritability and the Sociology of Knowledge." In *Naked Science: Anthropological Inquiry into Boundaries, Power, and Knowledge,* edited by Laura Nader, 119–30. New York: Routledge, 1996.

Edelstein, Michael R. *Contaminated Communities: The Social and Psychological Impacts of Residential Toxic Exposure.* 2nd ed. Boulder, Colo.: Westview Press, 2004.

Edwards, Jeanette, Penny Harvey, and Peter Wade. "Introduction: Epistemologies in Practice." In *Anthropology and Science: Epistemologies in Practice,* edited by Jeanette Edwards, Penny Harvey, and Peter Wade, 1–18. Oxford: Berg, 2007.

Emery, Ellen. "Mt. Sinai Study Took Six Years." *Massena (N.Y.) Observer,* December 3, 1985.

———. "Study Only Partly GM Funded." *Massena (N.Y.) Observer,* July 2, 1987.

Eng, James. "Boy's Survival from Flesh-Eating Bacteria Deemed a Miracle by His Family—and the Pope." MSNBC News, December 20, 2011. http://www.nbcnews.com/news/us-news.

Environment Canada. "Effects of Water Level and Flow Fluctuations in the St. Lawrence River on Fish Health." January 1, 2001, updated July 18, 2006. http://www.qc.ec.gc.ca.

Epstein, Steven. *Inclusion: The Politics of Difference in Medical Research.* Chicago: University of Chicago Press, 2007.

Faber, Daniel R., and Deborah McCarthy. "Neo-liberalism, Globalization and the Struggle for Ecological Democracy: Linking Sustainability and Environmental Justice." In *Just Sustainabilities: Development in an Unequal World,* edited by Julian Agyeman, Robert D. Bullard, and Bob Evans, 38–63. Cambridge: MIT Press, 2005.

Fadden, Ray. *History of the St. Regis Akwesasne Mohawks.* New York: Malone, 1947.

Farmer, Paul. "On Suffering and Structural Violence: A View from Below."

In *Social Suffering,* edited by Arthur Kleinman, Veena Das, and Margaret Lock, 261–84. Berkeley: University of California Press, 1997.

Fenton, William N. *The Great Law and the Longhouse: A Political History of the Iroquois Confederacy.* Norman: University of Oklahoma Press, 1998.

———. "Leadership in the Northeastern Woodlands of North America." *American Indian Quarterly* 10, no. 1 (1986): 21–43.

Fenton, William N., and Elisabeth Tooker. "Mohawk." In *Handbook of North American Indians: Northeast,* vol. 15, edited by Bruce G. Trigger, 466–80. Washington, D.C.: Smithsonian Institution, 1978.

Ferreira, Mariana Leal, and Gretchen Chesley Lang. "Introduction: Deconstructing Diabetes." In *Indigenous Peoples and Diabetes: Community Empowerment and Wellness,* edited by Mariana Leal Ferreira and Gretchen Chesley Lang, 3–32. Durham, N.C.: Carolina Academic Press, 2006.

Fingers, Keely Ten. "Rejecting, Revitalizing, and Reclaiming: First Nations Work to Set the Direction of Research and Policy Development." *Canadian Journal of Public Health/Revue Canadienne de Santé Publique* 96 (2005): S60–63.

Fischler, Claude. "Food Habits, Social Change, and the Nature/Culture Dilemma." *Social Science Information* 19 (1980): 937–53.

———. "Food, Self and Identity." *Social Science Information* 27, no. 2 (1988): 275–93.

Fisher, Philip A., and Thomas J. Ball. "Tribal Participatory Research: Mechanisms of a Collaborative Model." *American Journal of Community Psychology* 32 (2003): 207–16.

Fitzgerald, Edward F., Kelley A. Brix, Debra A. Deres, Syni-An Hwang, Brian Bush, George Lambert, and Alice Tarbell. "Polychlorinated Biphenyl (PCB) and Dichlorodiphenyl Dichloroethylene (DDE) Exposure among Native American Men from Contaminated Great Lakes Fish and Wildlife." *Toxicology and Industrial Health* 12, nos. 3/4 (1996): 361–68.

Fitzgerald, Edward F., Debra A. Deres, Syni-An Hwang, Brian Bush; Baozhu Yang, Alice Tarbell, and Agnes Jacobs. "Local Fish Consumption and Serum PCB Concentrations among Mohawk Men at Akwesasne." *Environmental Research* 80, no. 2 (1999): S97–103.

Fitzgerald, Edward F., Syni-An Hwang, and Kelley A. Brix. *Exposure to PCBs from Hazardous Waste among Mohawk Women and Infants at Akwesasne.* Report for the Agency for Toxic Substances and Disease Registry, PB95-159935 ATSDR. Atlanta, 1995.

Fitzgerald, Edward F., Syni-An Hwang, Kelley A. Brix, Brian Bush, Judith Quinn, and Katsi Cook. "Chemical Contaminants in the Milk of Mohawk Women from Akwesasne." In *Report for the Health Risk Assessment of the General Motors Central Foundry Division Superfund Waste.* Albany: New York State Department of Health, 1992.

Fitzgerald, Edward F., Syni-An Hwang, Kelley A. Brix, Katsi Cook, and Priscilla Worswick. "Fish PCB Concentrations and Consumption Patterns among Mohawk Women at Akwesasne." *Journal of Exposure Analysis and Environmental Epidemiology* 5 (1995): 1–19.

Fitzgerald, Edward F., Syni-An Hwang, Brian Bush, Katsi Cook, and Priscilla Worswick. "Fish Consumption and Breast Milk PCB Concentrations among Mohawk Women at Akwesasne." *American Journal of Epidemiology* 148, no. 2 (1998): 164–72.

Fitzgerald, Edward F., Syni-An Hwang, Debra A. Deres, Brian Bush, Katsi Cook, and Priscilla Worswick. "The Association between Local Fish Consumption and DDE, Mirex, and HCB Concentrations in the Breast Milk of Mohawk Women at Akwesasne." *Journal of Exposure Analysis and Environmental Epidemiology* 11 (2001): 381–88.

Fitzgerald, Edward F., Syni-An Hwang, Marta Gomez, Brian Bush, Bao-zhu Yang, and Alice Tarbell. "Environmental and Occupational Exposures and Serum PCB Concentrations and Patterns among Mohawk Men at Akwesasne." *Journal of Exposure Science and Environmental Epidemiology* 17 (2007): 269–78.

Fitzgerald, Edward F., Syni-An Hwang, George Lambert, Marta Gomez, and Alice Tarbell. "PCB Exposure and In Vivo CYP1A2 Activity among Native Americans." *Environmental Health Perspectives* 113, no. 3 (2005): 272–77.

Fitzgerald, Edward F., Syni-An Hwang, Karyn Langguth, Michael Cayo, Bao-zhu Yang, Brian Bush, Priscilla Worswick, and Trudy Lauzon. "Fish Consumption and Other Environmental Exposures and Their Associations with Serum PCB Concentrations among Mohawk Women at Akwesasne." *Environmental Research* 94 (2004): 160–70.

Forti, Anthony, Kenneth G. Bogdan, and Edward Horn. *Health Risk Assessment for the Akwesasne Mohawk Population from Exposure to Chemical Contaminants in Fish and Wildlife.* Albany: New York State Department of Health, Bureau of Toxic Substance Assessment, 1995.

Foster, Morris W., and Richard R. Sharp. "Race, Ethnicity, and Genomics: Social Classifications as Proxies of Biological Heterogeneity." *Genome Research* 12, no. 6 (2002): 844–50.

Foster, Warren G., and John Agzarian. "Reporting Results of Biomonitoring Studies." *Analytical and Bioanalytical Chemistry* 387, no. 1 (2007): 137–40.

Foy, Paul. "Animals at Massena GM Dump Laden with PCBs." *Watertown Daily Times,* August 24, 1985.

Freedman, Dan. "Lawlessness on the Borderline." *Times Union* (Albany, N.Y.), January 23, 2011. http://www.timesunion.com.

Freedman, David A. "Ecological Inference and the Ecological Fallacy." In

International Encyclopedia of the Social and Behavioral Sciences, edited by Neil J. Smelser and Paul B. Baltes, 4027–30. Amsterdam: Elsevier, 1999.

Freudenberg, Nicholas. "Community Capacity for Environmental Health Promotion: Determinants and Implications for Practice." *Health Education & Behavior* 31, no. 4 (2004): 472–90.

Frey, S. L. "The Mohawks." *Transactions of the Oneida Historical Society* 8 (1898): 1–41.

Frisch, Jack A. "Factionalism, Pan-Indianism, Tribalism, and the Contemporary Political Behaviour of the St. Regis Mohawk." *Man in the North-East* 2 (1971): 75–81.

———. "Revitalization, Nativism, and Tribalism among the St. Regis Mohawk." PhD diss., Indiana State University, 1971.

Fulford, George, with Jackie Moore Daigle, Blair Stevenson, Chuck Tolley, and Tracey Wade. "Ahkwesahsne Mohawk Board of Education." In *Sharing Our Success: More Case Studies in Aboriginal Schooling,* 29–58. Kelowna, B.C.: Society for the Advancement of Excellence in Education, 2007.

"Future of Mohawks at Akwesasne." *Akwesasne Notes* 13, no. 1 (1981): 26.

Gallo, Mia V., Julia Ravenscroft, David O. Carpenter, C. Frye, Akwesasne Task Force on the Environment, Beverly Cook, and Lawrence M. Schell. "Endocrine Disrupting Chemicals and Ovulation: Is There a Relationship?" *Environmental Research* 17, no. 151 (2016): 410–18.

Gallo, Mia V., Julia Ravenscroft, Melinda Denham, Lawrence M. Schell, Anthony P. DeCaprio, and Akwesasne Task Force on the Environment. "Environmental Contaminants and Growth of Mohawk Adolescents at Akwesasne." In *Human Growth from Conception to Maturity,* edited by Giulio Gilli, Lodovico Benso, and Lawrence M. Schell, 279–87. London: Smith-Gordon, 2002.

Gallo, Mia V., Lawrence M. Schell, and Akwesasne Task Force on the Environment. "Height, Weight, and Body Mass Index among Akwesasne Mohawk Youth." *American Journal of Human Biology* 17, no. 3 (2005): 269–79.

———. "Selected Anthropometric Measurements of Akwesasne Mohawk Youth: Skinfolds, Circumferences, and Breadths." *American Journal of Human Biology* 19, no. 4 (2007): 525–536.

Gallo, Mia V., Lawrence M. Schell, Anthony P. DeCaprio, and Agnes Jacobs. "Levels of Persistent Organic Pollutant and Their Predictors among Young Adults." *Chemosphere* 83 (2011): 1374–82.

Garson, Stephen C. "Talking Toxics: Narrative Constructions of Environmental Risk in Conflict." PhD diss., Institute for Conflict Analysis and Resolution, George Mason University, 2002.

Garwick, Ann W., and Sally Auger. "Participatory Action Research: The Indian Family Stories Project." *Nursing Outlook* 51 (2003): 261–66.

George-Kanentiio, Doug. "*Akwesasne Notes*: How the Mohawk Nation Created a Newspaper and Shaped Contemporary Native America." In *Insider Histories of the Vietnam Era Underground Press, Part 1*, edited by Ken Wachsberger, 109–37. East Lansing: Michigan State University Press, 2011.

———. *Iroquois Culture and Commentary*. Santa Fe, N.M.: Clear Light, 2000.

———. *Iroquois on Fire: A Voice from the Mohawk Nation*. Lincoln: University of Nebraska Press, 2006.

———. "Mohawk Nation Council Has Authority over CKON." *Indian Time*, November 29, 2012. http://www.indiantime.net.

Giles, Brian G., C. Scott Findlay, George Haas, Brenda LaFrance, Wesley Laughing, and Sakakohe Pembleton. "Integrating Conventional Science and Aboriginal Perspectives on Diabetes Using Fuzzy Cognitive Maps." *Social Science & Medicine* 64, no. 3 (2007): 562–76.

Ginsburg, Faye. "The After-Life of Documentary: The Impact of *You Are on Indian Land*." *Wide Angle* 21, no. 2 (1999): 60–67.

"GM Agrees to Pay $395,000 in Penalties for PCB Violations." *Wall Street Journal*, eastern ed., August 23, 1985, 1.

"GM/PCBs Chronology." *Watertown Daily Times*, October 5, 1983, 16.

Goldstein, Mark. "PCBs Dump Poses 'Danger to Health.'" *Watertown Daily Times*, October 5, 1983.

Goncharov, Alexey, Richard F. Haase, Azara L. Santiago-Rivera, Gayle Morse, Akwesasne Task Force on the Environment, Robert J. McCaffrey, Robert Rej, and David O. Carpenter. "High Serum PCBs Are Associated with Elevation of Serum Lipids and Cardiovascular Disease in a Native American Population." *Environmental Research* 106, no. 2 (2008): 226–39.

Goncharov, Alexey, Robert Rej, Serban Negoita, Maria Schymura, Azara L. Santiago-Rivera, Gayle Morse, Akwesasne Task Force on the Environment, and David O. Carpenter. "Lower Serum Testosterone Associated with Elevated Polychlorinated Biphenyl Concentrations in Native American Men." *Environmental Health Perspectives* 117, no. 9 (2009): 1454–60.

Goodman, Robert M., Marjorie A. Speers, Kenneth McLeroy, Stephen Fawcett, Michelle Kegler, Edith Parker, Steven Rathgeb Smith, Terrie D. Sterling, and Nina Allerstein. "Identifying and Defining the Dimensions of Community Capacity to Provide a Basis for Measurement." *Health Education & Behavior* 25, no. 3 (1998): 258–78.

Gottlieb, Robert, and Andy Fisher. "Community Food Security and Environmental Justice: Converging Paths Towards Social Justice and Sustainable Communities." *Race, Poverty & the Environment* 7, no. 2 (2000): 18–20.

Graham, Elizabeth. "Issue of Mohawk Land Claim Lawsuit Resurrected." *Watertown Daily Times*, May 23, 2009. http://www.watertowndailytimes .com.

Gray (Kanatiiosh), Barbara, and Pat Lauderdale. "The Web of Justice: Restorative Justice Has Presented Only Part of the Story." *Wicazo Sa Review* 21, no. 1 (2006): 29–41.

Grijalva, James M. *Closing the Circle: Environmental Justice in Indian Country.* Durham, N.C.: Carolina Academic Press, 2008.

Grinde, Donald, and Bruce Johansen. *Ecocide of Native America.* Santa Fe, N.M.: Clear Light, 1995.

Gusterson, Hugh. "Nuclear Weapons Testing: Scientific Experiment as Political Ritual." In *Naked Science: Anthropological Inquiry into Boundaries, Power, and Knowledge,* edited by Laura Nader, 131–47. New York: Routledge, 1996.

Haase, Richard F., Robert J. McCaffrey, Azara L. Santiago-Rivera, Gayle S. Morse, and Alice Tarbell. "Evidence of an Age-Related Threshold Effect of Polychlorinated Biphenyls (PCBs) on Neuropsychological Functioning in a Native American Population." *Environmental Research* 109, no. 1 (2009): 73–85.

Hagey, Rebecca. "The Native Diabetes Program: Rhetorical Process and Praxis." *Medical Anthropology* 12, no. 1 (1989): 7–33.

———. "The Phenomenon, the Explanations and the Responses: Metaphors Surrounding Diabetes in Urban Canadian Indians." *Social Science & Medicine* 18, no. 3 (1984): 265–72.

Halpern, Peggy. *Obesity and American Indians/Alaska Natives.* Report prepared for the U.S. Department of Health and Human Services, Washington, D.C., April 2007. https://aspe.hhs.gov.

Hamdy, Sherine F. *Our Bodies Belong to God: Organ Transplants, Islam, and the Struggle for Human Dignity in Egypt.* Berkeley: University of California Press, 2012.

———. "When the State and Your Kidneys Fail: Political Etiologies in an Egyptian Dialysis Ward." *American Ethnologist* 35, no. 4 (2008): 553–69.

Haraway, Donna. *Simians, Cyborgs, and Women: The Reinvention of Nature.* New York: Routledge, 1991.

———. "Situated Knowledges: The Science Question in Feminism and the Privilege of Partial Perspective." *Feminist Studies* 14, no. 3 (1988): 575–99.

Harper, Barbara L., and Stuart G. Harris. "A Possible Approach for Setting a Mercury Risk-Based Action Level Based on Tribal Fish Ingestion Rates." *Environmental Research* 107, no. 1 (2008): 60–68.

———. "Tribal Environmental Justice: Vulnerability, Trusteeship, and Equity under NEPA." *Environmental Justice* 4, no. 4 (2011): 193–97.

Harper, Douglas. *Changing Works: Visions of a Lost Agriculture.* Chicago: University of Chicago Press, 2001.

Harris, Stuart G., and Barbara L. Harper. "Environmental Justice in Indian Country: Using Equity Assessments to Evaluate Impacts to Trust Resources, Watersheds and Eco-cultural Landscapes." Paper presented at the conference "Environmental Justice: Strengthening the Bridge between Tribal Governments and Indigenous Communities, Economic Development and Sustainable Communities," Hilton Head, S.C., June 11, 1999.

———. "A Method for Tribal Environmental Justice Analysis." *Environmental Justice* 4, no. 4 (2011): 231–37.

———. "A Native American Exposure Scenario." *Risk Analysis* 17, no. 6 (1997): 789–95.

———. "Using Eco-cultural Dependency Webs in Risk Assessment and Characterization of Risks to Tribal Health and Cultures." Special issue, *Environmental Science and Pollution Research* 2 (2000): 91–100.

Hart, Bill. "High PCB Level in Fish Prompts Warning at St Regis." *Post Standard* (Syracuse, N.Y.), July 24, 1986, B1.

———. "State Is Skeptical of Pollutant Claim from Reservation." *Post Standard* (Syracuse, N.Y.), February 19, 1982.

Harvey-Berino, Jean, Virginia Hood, Janine Rourke, Terrie Terrance, Anne Dorwaldt, and Roger Secker-Walker. "Food Preferences Predict Eating Behavior of Very Young Mohawk Children." *Journal of the American Dietetic Association* 97, no. 7 (1997): 750–53.

Harvey-Berino, Jean, and Janine Rourke. "Obesity Prevention in Preschool Native American Children: A Pilot Study Using Home Visits." *Obesity Research* 11, no. 5 (2003): 603–11.

Hatch, J., N. Moss, A. Saran, L. Presley-Cantrell, and C. Mallory. "Community Research: Partnership in Black Communities." *American Journal of Preventive Medicine* 9, no. S6 (1993): 27–31.

Haudenosaunee Environmental Task Force. *Words That Come before All Else: Environmental Philosophies of the Haudenosaunee.* Akwesasne: North American Traveling College, 1999.

Hauptman, Laurence M. *Formulating American Indian Policy in New York State, 1970–1986.* Albany: State University of New York Press, 1988.

———. *The Iroquois Struggle for Survival: World War II to Red Power.* Syracuse, N.Y.: Syracuse University Press, 1986.

———. *Seven Generations of Iroquois Leadership.* Syracuse, N.Y.: Syracuse University Press, 2008.

Hawley, Chris. "Agents Fight Drug War on Ice at Northern Border." Huffington Post, February 14, 2011. http://www.huffingtonpost.com.

Hayden, Bryan. "RACER Trust Concentrates on Massena GM Plant." *Watertown Daily Times,* May 26, 2011. http://www.watertowndailytimes.com.

Hayes-Conroy, Jessica, and Allison Hayes-Conroy. "Veggies and Visceralities: A Political Ecology of Food and Feeling." *Emotion, Space and Society* 6 (2013): 81–90.

Hazelton, Cheryl. "Temporary Border Fix Proposed by CBSA." *Cornwall Standard-Freeholder,* January 14, 2013. http://www.standard-freeholder .com.

Herne, Shawn. "Our Native Game." Babe Ruth Birthplace and Museum, May 13, 2011. http://baberuthmuseum.org/our-native-game.

Hill, Michael. "Akwesasne Busiest Spot for Cigarette Smuggling." *Press-Republican* (Plattsburgh, N.Y.), November 24, 2007. http://pressrepubl ican.com.

Hipgrave, David. "Communicable Disease Control in China: From Mao to Now." *Journal of Global Health* 1, no. 2 (2011): 224–38.

"Historic Tribal Police Certifications Announced by State Police and Akwesasne." New York State Police News, May 30, 2007. https://www .nyspnews.com.

Holifield, Ryan. "Environmental Justice as Recognition and Participation in Risk Assessment: Negotiating and Translating Health Risk at a Superfund Site in Indian Country." *Annals of the Association of American Geographers* 102, no. 3 (2012): 591–613.

Hood, Virginia L., Benson Kelly, Charlene Martinez, Shevonne Shuman, and Roger Secker-Walker. "A Native American Community Initiative to Prevent Diabetes." *Ethnicity & Health* 2, no. 4 (1997): 277–85.

Hoover, Elizabeth. "Cultural and Health Implications of Fish Advisories in a Native American Community." *Ecological Processes* 2, no. 4 (2013). doi:10.1186/2192-1709-2-4.

Hoover, Elizabeth, Katsi Cook, Ron Plain, Kathy Sanchez, Vi Waghiyi, Pamela Miller, Renee Dufault, Caitlin Sislin, and David O. Carpenter. "Indigenous Peoples of North America: Environmental Exposures and Reproductive Justice." *Environmental Health Perspectives* 120, no. 12 (2012): 1645–49.

Hoover, Elizabeth, Mia Renauld, Michael R. Edelstein, and Phil Brown. "Social Science Collaboration with Environmental Health." *Environmental Health Perspectives* 123, no. 11 (2015): 1100–1106.

Hoover, Mary. "The Dying Turtle: Mohawk Lands under Siege." *Akwesasne Notes* 18, no. 5 (1986): 18.

Hough, Franklin B. *History of St. Lawrence and Franklin Counties, from the Earliest Period to the Present Time.* Albany, N.Y.: Little, 1853.

Hull, R. L., S. Andrikopoulos, C. B. Verchere, J. Vidal, F. Wang, M. Cnop,

R. L. Prigeon, and S. E. Kahn. "Increased Dietary Fat Promotes Islet Amyloid Formation and Beta-Cell Secretory Dysfunction in a Transgenic
Mouse Model of Islet Amyloid." *Diabetes* 52, no. 2 (2003): 372–79.

Hwang, Syni-An, Edward F. Fitzgerald, Brian Bush, and Katsi Cook. "Exposure to PCBs from Hazardous Waste among Mohawk Women and
Infants at Akwesasne." *Technology Journal of the Franklin Institute* 333A
(1996): 17–23.

Hwang, Syni-An, Edward F. Fitzgerald, Mike Cayo, Bao-zhu Yang, Alice
Tarbell, and Agnes Jacobs. "Assessing Environmental Exposure to PCBs
among Mohawks at Akwesasne through the Use of Geostatistical Methods." *Environmental Research* 80, no. 2 (1999): S189–S199.

Hwang, Syni-An, L. Gensburg, Edward F. Fitzgerald, P. Herzfeld, and Brian
Bush. "Fingerprinting Sources of Contamination: Statistical Techniques
for Identifying Point Sources of PCBs." *Journal of Occupational Medicine
and Toxicology* 4 (1993): 365–82.

Hwang, Syni-An, Bao-zhu Yang, Edward F. Fitzgerald, Brian Bush, and Katsi
Cook. "Fingerprinting PCB Patterns among Mohawk Women." *Journal
of Exposure Analysis and Environmental Epidemiology* 11 (2001): 184–92.

Ingold, Tim. "Introduction: Anthropology after Darwin." *Social Anthropology*
12, no. 2 (2004): 177–79.

Israel, Barbara A., Amy J. Schulz, Edith A. Parker, and Adam B. Becker. "Review of Community-Based Research: Assessing Partnership Approaches
to Improve Public Health." *Annual Review of Public Health* 19 (1998):
173–202.

Jasanoff, Sheila. "Civilization and Madness: The Great BSE Scare of 1996."
Public Understanding of Science 6, no. 3 (1997): 221–32.

Jernigan, Valarie Blue Bird, Michael Peercy, Dannielle Branam, Bobby
Saunkeah, David Wharton, Marilyn Winkleby, John Lowe, Alicia L. Sal-
vatore, Daniel Dickerson, Annie Belcourt, Elizabeth D'Amico, Christi
A. Patten, Myra Parker, Bonnie Duran, Raymond Harris, and Dedra
Buchwald. "Beyond Health Equity: Achieving Wellness within Ameri-
can Indian and Alaska Native Communities." *American Journal of Public
Health* 105, no. S3 (2015): S376–S379.

Johansen, Bruce E. *Encyclopedia of the American Indian Movement.* Santa
Barbara, Calif.: Greenwood, 2013.

———. *Life and Death in Mohawk Country.* Golden, Colo.: North American
Press, 1993.

Johansen, Bruce E., and Barbara A. Mann, eds. *Encyclopedia of the Haudenosaunee (Iroquois Confederacy).* Westport, Conn.: Greenwood Press, 2000.

Judkins, Russell A. "Diabetes and Perception of Diabetes among Seneca
Indians." *New York State Journal of Medicine* 78, no. 8 (1978): 1320–23.

Kader, Charles. "Bear Clan Representative Arrested for 'Stealing' What

He Considers His Homeland." *Indian Country Today*, January 16, 2012. http://indiancountrytodaymedianetwork.com.

———. "Land Theft Charges and National Debt." *Indian Country Today*, September 20, 2012. http://indiancountrytodaymedianetwork.com.

Kanetohare. "Ohontsiawakon." Ronathahonni Cultural Center video, April 15, 2010. http://vimeo.com.

"Kanietekeron (Larry Thompson) Arraigned in St. Lawrence County." *Indian Time*, March 1, 2012. http://www.indiantime.net.

Keith, Margaret, James J. Brophy, Peter Kirby, and Ellen Rosskam. *Barefoot Research: A Workers' Manual for Organising on Work Security*. Geneva: International Labour Organization, 2002. http://www.ilo.org.

Kesmodel, David. "Tribes Rolling Out Cigarettes." *Wall Street Journal*, August 17, 2011. http://www.wsj.com.

Kimmerer, Robin Wall. *Braiding Sweetgrass: Indigenous Wisdom, Scientific Knowledge, and the Teachings of Plants*. Minneapolis: Milkweed Editions, 2015.

———. "Weaving Traditional Ecological Knowledge into Biological Education: A Call to Action." *Bio Science* 52, no. 5 (2002): 432–38.

King, Brian. "Political Ecologies of Health." *Progress in Human Geography* 34, no. 1 (2010): 38–55.

King, Joyce Tekahnawiiaks. "New York State Breaks Off Negotiations." Press release from the Kahniakehaka (Mohawk) Nation Council of Chiefs (traditional government), the Saint Regis Mohawk Tribe (United States), and the Mohawk Council of Akwesasne (Canada), October 3, 1996.

———. "The Value of Water and the Meaning of Water Law for the Native Americans Known as the Haudenosaunee." *Cornell Journal of Law and Public Policy* 16, no. 3 (2007): 449–72.

King, Larry. "Land Claims Update." *Onkwe'ta:ke: For the People* (newsletter of the Mohawk Council of Akwesasne), June 2012, 6–8. http://www.akwesasne.ca/pdf/Onkwetake/OnkwetakeJune2012.pdf.

Kinney, Andrea, Edward F. Fitzgerald, Syni-An Hwang, Brian Bush, Alice Tarbell, and Mohawk Nation at Akwesasne. "Human Exposure to PCBs: Modeling and Assessment of Environmental Concentrations of the Akwesasne Reservation." *Drug and Chemical Toxicology* 20, no. 4 (1997): 313–28.

Knorr-Cetina, Karin D. *The Manufacture of Knowledge: An Essay on the Constructivist and Contextual Nature of Science*. Oxford: Pergamon Press, 1981.

Kozak, David. "Surrendering to Diabetes: An Embodied Response to Perceptions of Diabetes and Death in the Gila River Indian Community." *Omega: Journal of Death and Dying* 35, no. 4 (1997): 347–59.

Krieger, Nancy. "Embodying Inequality: A Review of Concepts, Measures, and Methods for Studying Health Consequences of Discrimination." *International Journal of Health Services* 29, no. 2 (1999): 295–352.

Krook, Lennart, and George A. Maylin. "Industrial Fluoride Pollution: Chronic Fluoride Poisoning in Cornwall Island Cattle." *Cornell Veterinarian* 69, no. S8 (1979).

LaDuke, Winona. *All Our Relations: Native Struggles for Land and Life.* Cambridge, Mass.: South End Press, 1999.

——. *Recovering the Sacred: The Power of Naming and Claiming.* Cambridge, Mass.: South End Press, 2005.

——. *The Winona LaDuke Chronicles.* Ponsford, Minn.: Spotted Horse Press, 2016.

Lafrance, Amberdawn. "Natural Resource Damages." *Kawenni:ios* (newsletter of the Saint Regis Mohawk Tribe), October 2013, 8–9. http://www.srmt-nsn.gov/_uploads/site_files/Oct13.pdf.

Latour, Bruno. *Science in Action.* Cambridge, Mass.: Harvard University Press, 1987.

Latour, Bruno, and Steve Woolgar. *Laboratory Life: The Construction of Scientific Facts.* Princeton, N.J.: Princeton University Press, 1986.

LaVeaux, Deborah, and Suzanne Christopher. "Contextualizing CBPR: Key Principles of CBPR Meet the Indigenous Research Context." *Pímatísíwín* 7, no. 1 (2009): 1–25.

Lemelin, Raynald Harvey. "Social Movements and the Great Law of Peace in Akwesasne." Master's thesis, University of Ottawa, 1996.

Lewis, Christopher, and Rachel DelVecchio. *Data Report: PCBs in Garden Soils of Akwesasne.* Report prepared for the Environment Division, Saint Regis Mohawk Tribe, April 17, 2007. http://www.srmtenv.org/web_docs.

Lex, Barbara W., and Janice Racine Norris. "Health Status of American Indian and Alaska Native Women." In *Women and Health Research: Ethical and Legal Issues of Including Women in Clinical Studies*, vol. 2, edited by Anna C. Mastroianni, Ruth Faden, and Daniel. Federman, 192–215. Washington, D.C.: National Academies Press, 1999.

Little, Peter C. "Negotiating Community Engagement and Science in the Federal Environmental Public Health Sector." *Medical Anthropology Quarterly* 23, no. 2 (2009): 94–118.

——. *Toxic Town: IBM, Pollution, and Industrial Risks.* New York: New York University Press, 2014.

Lock, Margaret. "Cultivating the Body: Anthropology and Epistemologies of Bodily Practice and Knowledge." *Annual Review of Anthropology* 22 (1993): 133–55.

Macaulay, Ann C., Gilles Paradis, Louise Potvin, Edward J. Cross, Chantal Saad-Haddad, Alex M. McComber, Serge Desrosiers, Rhonda Kirby, Louis T. Montour, Donna L. Lamping, Nicole Leduc, and Michèle Rivard. "The Kahnawake Schools Diabetes Prevention Project: Intervention, Evaluation, and Baseline Results of a Diabetes Primary Prevention Program with a Native Community in Canada." *Preventive Medicine* 26 (1997): 779–90.

Macaulay, Ann C., Margaret Cargo, Sherri Bisset, Treena Delormier, Lucie Levesque, Louise Potvin, and Alex M. McComber. "Community Empowerment for the Primary Prevention of Type 2 Diabetes: Kanien'kehá:ka (Mohawk) Ways for the Kahnawake Schools Diabetes Prevention Project." In *Indigenous Peoples and Diabetes: Community Empowerment and Wellness*, edited by Mariana Leal Ferreira and Gretchen Chesley Lang, 407–34. Durham, N.C.: Carolina Academic Press, 2006.

Mackie, Diane M., and Sarah Queller. "The Impact of Group Membership on Persuasion: Revisiting 'Who Says What to Whom with What Effect?'" In *Attitudes, Behavior, and Social Context: The Role of Norms and Group Membership*, edited by Deborah J. Terry and Michael A. Hogg, 135–55. Mahwah, N.J.: Lawrence Erlbaum, 2000.

Mann, Barbara A., and Jerry L. Fields. "A Sign in the Sky: Dating the League of the Haudenosaunee." *American Indian Culture and Research Journal* 21, no. 2 (1997): 105–63.

Martin, Douglas. "Smuggled Aliens Now Cross Mohawk Land." *New York Times*, October 14, 1996. http://www.nytimes.com.

Martin, Kallen M. "Life along the Line: Landscape Contestation and Place among the Mohawks of Akwesasne." Paper presented at the conference "First Nations, First Thoughts," University of Edinburgh, May 5–6, 2005.

Martin, Ryne R. "$100 Million Clean Up; DEC's Stone Says Clean Up Will Be Investment for Industries." *Daily Courier* (Massena, N.Y.), October 7, 1989, 2.

Martinez, Charlene B., and Karen Strauss. "Diabetes in St. Regis Mohawk Indians." *Diabetes Care* 16, no. 1 (1993): 260–62.

Matthiessen, Peter. *Indian Country*. New York: Viking Press, 1984.

McCormick, Sabrina. "After the Cap: Risk Assessment, Citizen Science, and Disaster Recovery." *Ecology and Society* 17, no. 4 (2012). doi:10.5751/ES-05263-170431.

McIntyre, Mark. "Pollution Clouds Indian Way of Life." *Newsday* (Long Island, N.Y.), October 13, 1985.

McMullin, Juliet. *The Healthy Ancestor: Embodied Inequality and the Revitalization of Native Hawaiian Health*. Walnut Creek, Calif.: Left Coast Press, 2010.

McNaughton, Laticia Gail. "Tetewatskà:hons ne Sewatokwà:tshera: Revitalizing Haudenosaunee Food Traditions through Mohawk Language." Paper presented at the annual meeting of the Native American and Indigenous Studies Association, Washington, D.C., June 2015.

Middleton, Beth Rose. "A Political Ecology of Healing." *Journal of Political Ecology* 17 (2010): 1–28.

———. *Trust in the Land: New Directions in Tribal Conservation.* Tucson: University of Arizona Press, 2011.

Mihesuah, Devon Abbott. *Recovering Our Ancestors' Gardens.* Lincoln: University of Nebraska Press, 2005.

Milburn, Michael P. "Indigenous Nutrition: Using Traditional Food Knowledge to Solve Contemporary Health Problems." *American Indian Quarterly* 28, nos. 3/4 (2004): 411–34.

Miller, Pamela K., Viola Waghiyi, Gretchen Welfinger-Smith, Samuel Carter Byrne, Jane Kava, Jesse Gologergen, Lorraine Eckstein, Ronald Scrudato, Jeff Chiarenzelli, David O. Carpenter, and Samarys Seguinot-Medina. "Community-Based Participatory Research Projects and Policy Engagement to Protect Environmental Health on St. Lawrence Island, Alaska." *International Journal of Circumpolar Health* 72, no. 1 (2013). doi:10.3402/ijch.v72i0.21656.

Million, Dian. *Therapeutic Nations: Healing in an Age of Indigenous Human Rights.* Tucson: University of Arizona Press, 2013.

Minkler, Meredith, and Nina Wallerstein, eds. *Community-Based Participatory Research for Health: From Process to Outcome.* 2nd ed. San Francisco: Jossey-Bass, 2008.

Mintz, Sydney. "Meals without Grace." *Boston Review,* December 1984.

———. *Sweetness and Power: The Place of Sugar in Modern History.* New York: Viking Press, 1985.

Mitchell, Michael Kanentakeron. *Teiontsikwaeks: Lacrosse, the Creator's Game.* Akwesasne, Ont.: Ronathahon:ni Cultural Center, 2010.

Moe, Kristin. "Idle No More: Indigenous Uprising Sweeps North America." *Yes Magazine,* January 9, 2013. http://www.yesmagazine.org.

Mohai, Paul, David Pellow, and J. Timmons Roberts. "Environmental Justice." *Annual Review of Environment and Resources* 34 (2009): 405–30.

Mohawk, John. "From the First to the Last Bite: Learning from the Food Knowledge of Our Ancestors." In *Original Instructions: Indigenous Teachings for a Sustainable Future,* edited by Melissa K. Nelson, 170–79. Rochester, Vt.: Bear, 2008.

Mohawk Council of Akwesasne. "Akwesasne Community Fund: Guidelines and Application Form." December 2013. http://www.akwesasne.ca/sites/default/files/pdf/communityfund/community_fund_info_guidelines.pdf.

"Mohawk Council of Akwesasne Daily Briefing." June 3, 2009. http://www.akwesasne.ca/node/200.

"Mohawk Council of Akwesasne Files Baxter and Barnhart Islands Claim." *Onkwe'ta:ke: For the People* (newsletter of the Mohawk Council of Akwesasne), June 2012, 4–5, http://www.akwesasne.ca/pdf/Onkwetake/OnkwetakeJune2012.pdf.

Morello-Frosch, Rachel, Julia Green Brody, Phil Brown, Rebecca Gasior Altman, Ruthann A. Rudel, and Carla Pérez. "Toxic Ignorance and Right-to-Know in Biomonitoring Results Communication: A Survey of Scientists and Study Participants." *Environmental Health* 8, no. 6 (2009). doi:10.1186/1476-069X-8-6.

Moreno-John, Gina, Anthony Gachie, Candace M. Fleming, Anna Nápoles-Springer, Elizabeth Mutran, Spero M. Manson, and Eliseo J. Perez-Stable. "Ethnic Minority Older Adults Participating in Clinical Research: Developing Trust." *Journal of Aging and Health* 16, no. S5 (2004): 93S–123S.

Morgensen, Scott Lauria. "The Biopolitics of Settler Colonialism: Right Here, Right Now." *Settler Colonial Studies* 1, no. 1 (2011): 52–76.

Morton, Deborah J., Joely Proudfit, Daniel Calac, Martina Portillo, Geneva Lofton-Fitzsimmons, Theda Molina, Raymond Flores, Barbara Lawson-Risso, and Romelle Majel-McCauley. "Creating Research Capacity through a Tribally Based Institutional Review Board." *American Journal of Public Health* 103, no. 12 (2013): 2160–64.

Nadasdy, Paul. *Hunters and Bureaucrats: Power, Knowledge, and Aboriginal–State Relations in the Southwest Yukon.* Vancouver: University of British Columbia Press, 2003.

———. "The Politics of TEK: Power and the 'Integration' of Knowledge." *Arctic Anthropology* 36, nos. 1/2 (1999): 1–18.

Nader, Laura. "Up the Anthropologist—Perspectives Gained from Studying Up." In *Reinventing Anthropology,* edited by Dell Hymes, 284–311. New York: Pantheon, 1969.

National Environmental Justice Advisory Council. *Fish Consumption and Environmental Justice.* Washington, D.C.: U.S. Environmental Protection Agency, 2002. https://www.epa.gov.

National Oceanic and Atmospheric Administration. "Assessing Fish Health." Status report on the Hudson River Natural Resource Damage Assessment, Fall 2001. https://casedocuments.darrp.noaa.gov.

Neel, James V. "Diabetes Mellitus: A 'Thrifty' Genotype Rendered Detrimental by 'Progress'?" *American Journal of Human Genetics* 14, no. 4 (1962): 353–62.

———. "The 'Thrifty Genotype' in 1998." *Nutrition Reviews* 57, no. 5 (1999): 2–9.

Negoita, Serban, and Levi Swamp. *Human Health and Disease Patterns at Akwesasne.* Akwesasne: Akwesasne Task Force on the Environment, 1997.

Negoita, Serban, Levi Swamp, Benson Kelley, and David O. Carpenter. "Chronic Diseases Surveillance of St. Regis Mohawk Health Service Patients." *Journal of Public Health Management and Practice* 7, no. 1 (2001): 84–91.

Newman, Joan, Amy Aucompaugh, Lawrence M. Schell, Melinda Denham, Anthony P. DeCaprio, Mia V. Gallo, Julia Ravenscroft, Chin-Cheng Kao, MaryEllen Rougas Hanover, Dawn David, Agnes Jacobs, Alice Tarbell, Priscilla Worswick, and Akwesasne Task Force on the Environment. "PCBs and Cognitive Functioning of Mohawk Adolescents." *Neurotoxicology and Teratology* 28 (2006): 429–45.

Newman, Joan, Bita Behforooz, Amy G. Khuzwayo, Mia V. Gallo, Lawrence M. Schell, and Akwesasne Task Force on the Environment. "PCBs and ADHD in Mohawk Adolescents." *Neurotoxicology and Teratology* 42 (2014): 25–34.

Newman, Joan, Mia V. Gallo, Lawrence M. Schell, Anthony P. DeCaprio, Melinda Denham, Glenn D. Deane, and Akwesasne Task Force on the Environment. "Analysis of PCB Congeners Related to Cognitive Functioning in Adolescents." *Neurotoxicology* 30, no. 4 (2009): 686–96.

New York State, Department of Taxation and Finance. "View/Report Indian Tax-Exempt Cigarette Sales." June 30, 2011. https://www.tax.ny.gov.

Nguyen, Vinh-Kim, and Karine Peschard. "Anthropology, Inequality, and Disease: A Review." *Annual Review of Anthropology* 32 (2003): 447–74.

Nickels, Brian. "Native American Free Passage Rights under the 1794 Jay Treaty: Survival under United States Statutory Law and Canadian Common Law." *Boston College International and Comparative Law Review* 24, no. 2 (2001): 313–39.

Noe Tim D., Spero M. Manson, Calvin Croy, Helen McGough, Jeffrey A. Henderson, and Dedra S. Buchwald. "The Influence of Community-Based Participatory Research Principles on the Likelihood of Participation in Health Research in American Indian Communities." *Ethnicity and Disease* 17, no. S1 (2007): S6–S14.

Nowotony, Helga, Peter Scott, and Michael Gibbons. *Re-thinking Science: Knowledge and the Public in an Age of Uncertainty.* Oxford: Polity Press, 2001.

Odato, James M. "Indian Cigarette Chaos." *Times Union* (Albany, N.Y.), April 30, 2012. http://www.timesunion.com.

Oetzel, John G., Malia Villegas, Heather Zenone, Emily R. White Hat, Nina Wallerstein, and Bonnie Duran. "Enhancing Stewardship of Community-Engaged Research through Governance." *American Journal of Public Health* 105, no. 6 (2015): 1161–67.

Office of the Minister of Aboriginal Affairs and Northern Development, Canada. "Canada and the Mohawks of Akwesasne Finalize Kawehnoke-Easterbrook Settlement Agreement." Press release, October 17, 2012. http://www.marketwired.com.

Ohseraséia:hawi. "St Regis Mohawk Tribe Community Meeting." Akwesasne TV, June 14, 2016. http://www.akwesasnetv.com.

O'Neill, Catherine A. "Mercury, Risk, and Justice." *Environmental Law Reporter* 34 (2004): 11070–115.

———. "Risk Avoidance, Cultural Discrimination, and Environmental Justice for Indigenous Peoples." *Ecology Law Quarterly* 30 (2003): 1–57.

———. "Variable Justice: Environmental Standards, Contaminated Fish, and 'Acceptable' Risk to Native Peoples." *Stanford Environmental Law Review* 19 (2000): 3–118.

O'Neill, John. *Five Bodies: Re-figuring Relationships.* London: Sage, 2004.

Ostendorf, David, and Dixon Terry. "Toward a Democratic Community of Communities: Creating a New Future with Agriculture in Rural America." In *Environmental Justice: Issues, Policies, and Solutions,* edited by Bunyan Bryant, 149–71. Washington, D.C.: Island Press, 1995.

Ottinger, Gwen. *Refining Expertise: How Responsible Engineers Subvert Environmental Justice Challenges.* New York: New York University Press, 2013.

Ottinger, Gwen, and Benjamin R. Cohen, eds. *Technoscience and Environmental Justice: Expert Cultures in a Grassroots Movement.* Cambridge: MIT Press, 2011.

"Overview of Akwesasne's North Shore Claim." *Onkwe'ta:ke: For the People* (newsletter of the Mohawk Council of Akwesasne), September 2012, 13. http://www.akwesasne.ca/pdf/Onkwetake/OnkwetakeSeptember2012 .pdf.

Parham, Claire Puccia. *The St. Lawrence Seaway and Power Project: An Oral History of the Greatest Construction Show on Earth.* Syracuse, N.Y.: Syracuse University Press, 2009.

Parker, Arthur Caswell. "The Code of Handsome Lake, the Seneca Prophet." In *Parker on the Iroquois,* edited by William Nelson Fenton. Syracuse, N.Y.: Syracuse University Press, 1968.

———. *The Constitution of the Five Nations; or, The Iroquois Book of the Great Law.* Albany: University of the State of New York, 1916.

Pellow, David Naguib. *Resisting Global Toxics: Transnational Movements for Environmental Justice.* Cambridge: MIT Press, 2007.

Pellow, David Naguib, and Robert J. Brulle. "Power, Justice, and the Environment: Toward Critical Environmental Justice Studies." In *Power, Justice, and the Environment: A Critical Appraisal of the Environmental Justice Movement,* edited by David Naguib Pellow and Robert J. Brulle, 1–22. Cambridge: MIT Press, 2005.

———. "The Future of Environmental Justice Movements." In *Power, Justice, and the Environment: A Critical Appraisal of the Environmental Justice*

Movement, edited by David Naguib Pellow and Robert J. Brulle, 293–300. Cambridge: MIT Press, 2005.

Phaneuf, Richard. "Indian Reserve Boundaries and Rights: Enforcement on the St. Lawrence River." *Canadian Water Resources Journal* 4, no. 3 (1979): 30–34.

Philibert, Aline, Claire Vanier, Nadia Abdelouahab, Hing Man Chan, and Donna Mergler. "Fish Intake and Serum Fatty Acid Profiles from Freshwater Fish." *American Journal of Clinical Nutrition* 84, no. 6 (2006): 1299–1307.

Potvin, Louise, Margaret Cargo, Alex M. McComber, Treena Delormier, and Ann C. Macaulay. "Implementing Participatory Intervention and Research in Communities: Lessons from the Kahnawake Schools Diabetes Prevention Project in Canada." *Social Science & Medicine* 56, no. 6 (2003): 1295–1305.

Public Health and Tobacco Policy Center. "Collecting Cigarette Taxes from Native American Retailers." October 4, 2013. http://tobaccopolicycen ter.org.

Quandt, Sara A., Alicia M. Doran, Pamela Rao, Jane A. Hoppin, Beverly M. Snively, and Thomas A. Arcury. "Reporting Pesticide Assessment Results to Farmworker Families: Development, Implementation, and Evaluation of a Risk Communication Strategy." *Environmental Health Perspectives* 112, no. 5 (2004): 636–42.

Quigley, Dianne. "Applying Bioethical Principles to Place-Based Communities and Cultural Group Protections: The Case of Biomonitoring Results Communication." *Journal of Law, Medicine & Ethics* 40, no. 2 (2012): 348–58.

———. "A Review of Improved Ethical Practices in Environmental and Public Health Research: Case Examples from Native Communities." *Health Education & Behavior* 33, no. 2 (2006): 130–47.

Quintana, Jorge. "Agricultural Survey of New York State Iroquois Reservations 1990." *Northeast Indian Quarterly* 8, no. 1 (1991): 32–36.

Ramirez-Andreotta, Monica D., Mark L. Brusseau, Janick F. Artiola, Raina M. Maier, and A. Jay Gandolfi. "Environmental Research Translation: Enhancing Interactions with Communities at Contaminated Sites." *Science of the Total Environment* 497–98 (November 1, 2014): 651–64.

Ranco, Darren J. "The Trust Responsibility and Limited Sovereignty: What Can Environmental Justice Groups Learn from Indian Nations?" *Society & Natural Resources* 21, no. 4 (2008): 354–62.

Ranco, Darren J., Catherine A. O'Neill, Jamie Donatuto, and Barbara L. Harper. "Environmental Justice, American Indians, and the Cultural Dilemma: Developing Environmental Management for Tribal Health and Well-Being." *Environmental Justice* 4, no. 4 (2011): 221–30.

Ransom, James, and Henry Lickers. "Akwesasne Environment: Appraisals of Toxic Contamination at the St. Regis Mohawk Reservation." *Northeast Indian Quarterly* 5, no. 3 (1988): 22–26.

Rapp, Rayna. *Testing Women, Testing the Fetus: The Social Impact of Amniocentisis in America.* New York: Routledge, 1999.

Ravenscroft, Julia, Lawrence M. Schell, and Akwesasne Task Force on the Environment. "Dietary Patterns of Akwesasne Mohawk Adolescents." *Annals of Human Biology* 41, no. 5 (2014): 403–14.

Ravenscroft, Julia, Lawrence M. Schell, and Tewentahawih'tha' Cole. "Applying the Community Partnership Approach to Human Biology Research." *American Journal of Human Biology* 27, no. 1 (2015): 6–15.

Raymo, Denise A. "Land-Reclamation Arrest." *Press-Republican* (Plattsburgh, N.Y.), December 9, 2011. http://pressrepublican.com.

Robbins, Paul. *Political Ecology.* Malden, Mass.: Blackwell, 2004.

Rosenthal, M. Sara. *The Thyroid Source Book.* 5th ed. New York: McGraw-Hill, 2008.

Sack, Kevin. "Cuomo Urges Internal Police for Mohawks." *New York Times,* May 9, 1990. http://www.nytimes.com.

Sahota, Puneet Chawla. "Genetic Histories: Native Americans' Accounts of Being at Risk for Diabetes." *Social Studies of Science* 42, no. 6 (2012): 821–42.

"St Lawrence River." In *The Crystal Reference Encyclopedia.* West Chiltington, England: Crystal Semantics, 2005.

Saint Regis Mohawk Tribe. "Diabetes Center for Excellence." *Kawenni:ios* (newsletter of the Saint Regis Mohawk Tribe), February 2008, 14–15.

———. "How Gaming Benefits Our Community." 2009–10. http://www .srmt-nsn.gov.

———. *St. Regis Mohawk Tribe Data Report: Fluoride.* Akwesasne: Environment Division, Saint Regis Mohawk Tribe, 2008. http://www.srmtenv .org/web_docs.

Salmón, Enrique. *Eating the Landscape: American Indian Stories of Food, Identity, and Resilience.* Tucson: University of Arizona Press, 2012.

———. "Kincentric Ecology: Indigenous Perceptions of the Human–Nature Relationship." *Ecological Applications* 10, no. 5 (2000): 1327–32.

Santiago-Rivera, Azara L., Gayle Skawenio Morse, Richard F. Haase, Robert J. McCaffrey, and Alice Tarbell. "Exposure to an Environmental Toxin, Quality of Life and Psychological Distress." *Journal of Environmental Psychology* 27, no. 1 (2007): 33–43.

Santiago-Rivera, Azara L., Gayle Skawenio Morse, Anne Hunt, and Henry Lickers. "Building a Community-Based Research Partnership: Lessons from the Mohawk Nation of Akwesasne." *Journal of Community Psychology* 26, no. 2 (1998) 163–74.

Schell, Lawrence M., and Mia V. Gallo. "Overweight and Obesity among North American Indian Infants, Children, and Youth." *American Journal of Human Biology* 24, no. 3 (2012): 302–13.

———. "Relationships of Putative Endocrine Disruptors to Human Sexual Maturation and Thyroid Activity in Youth." *Physiology and Behavior* 99 (2010): 246–53.

Schell, Lawrence M., Mia V. Gallo, and Katsi Cook. "What's NOT to Eat— Food Adulteration in the Context of Human Biology." *American Journal of Human Biology* 24, no. 2 (2012): 139–48.

Schell, Lawrence M., Mia V. Gallo, Glenn D. Deane, Kyrie R. Nelder, Anthony P. DeCaprio, Agnes Jacobs, and Akwesasne Task Force on the Environment. "Relationships of Polychlorinated Biphenyls and Dichlorodiphenyldichloroethylene (p,p'-DDE) with Testosterone Levels in Adolescent Males." *Environmental Health Perspectives* 122, no. 3 (2014): 304–9.

Schell, Lawrence M., Mia V. Gallo, Anthony P. DeCaprio, Lech A. Hubicki, Melinda Denham, Julia Ravenscroft, and Akwesasne Task Force on the Environment. "Thyroid Function in Relation to Burden of PCBs, p,p'-DDE, HCB, Mirex and Lead among Akwesasne Mohawk Youth: A Preliminary Study." *Environmental Toxicology and Pharmacology* 18 (2004): 91–99.

Schell, Lawrence M., Mia V. Gallo, Melinda Denham, Julia Ravenscroft, Anthony P. DeCaprio, and David O. Carpenter. "Relationship of Thyroid Hormone Levels to Levels of Polychlorinated Biphenyls, Lead, p,p'-DDE, and Other Toxicants in Akwesasne Mohawk Youth." *Environmental Health Perspectives* 116, no. 6 (2008): 806–13.

Schell, Lawrence M., Mia V. Gallo, Julia Ravenscroft, Anthony P. DeCaprio. "Persistent Organic Pollutants and Anti-thyroid Peroxidase Levels in Akwesasne Mohawk Young Adults." *Environmental Research* 109, no. 1 (2009): 86–92.

Schell, Lawrence M., Lech A. Hubicki, Anthony P. DeCaprio, Mia V. Gallo, Julia Ravenscroft, Alice Tarbell, Agnes Jacobs, Dawn David, Priscilla Worswick, and Akwesasne Task Force on the Environment. "Organochlorines, Lead and Mercury in Akwesasne Mohawk Youth." *Environmental Health Perspectives* 11, no. 7 (2003): 954–61.

Schell, Lawrence M., Julia Ravenscroft, Mia Gallo, and Melinda Denham. "Advancing Biocultural Models by Working with Communities: A Partnership Approach." *American Journal of Human Biology* 19, no. 4 (2007): 511–24.

Schell, Lawrence M., and Alice M. Tarbell. "A Partnership Study of PCBs and the Health of Mohawk Youth: Lessons from Our Past and Guidelines for Our Future." *Environmental Health Perspectives* 106, no. S3 (1998): 833–40.

Scheper-Hughes, Nancy. *Death without Weeping: The Violence of Everyday Life in Brazil.* Berkeley: University of California Press, 1993.

———. "Diabetes and Genocide—beyond the Thrifty Gene." In *Indigenous Peoples and Diabetes: Community Empowerment and Wellness,* edited by Mariana Leal Ferreira and Gretchen Chesley Lang, xvii–xxi. Durham, N.C.: Carolina Academic Press, 2006.

Scheper-Hughes, Nancy, and Margaret M. Lock. "The Mindful Body: A Prolegomenon to Future Work in Medical Anthropology." *Medical Anthropology Quarterly* 1, no. 1 (1987): 6–41.

Schlosberg, David. *Defining Environmental Justice.* New York: Oxford University Press, 2004.

Schnarch, Brian. "Ownership, Control, Access, and Possession (OCAP) or Self-Determination Applied to Research: A Critical Analysis of Contemporary First Nations Research and Some Options for First Nations Communities." *Journal of Aboriginal Health* 1, no. 1 (2004): 80–95.

Shapin, Steven. *A Social History of Truth: Civility and Science in Seventeenth-Century England.* Chicago: University of Chicago Press, 1994.

Sharp, Donald. "Environmental Toxins, a Potential Risk Factor for Diabetes among Canadian Aboriginals." *International Journal of Circumpolar Health* 68 (2009): 316–26.

Shepard, Peggy M., Mary E. Northridge, Swati Prakash, and Gabriel Stover. "Advancing Environmental Justice through Community-Based Participatory Research." *Environmental Health Perspectives* 110, no. S2 (2002): 139–40.

Simpson, Audra. *Mohawk Interruptus: Political Life across the Borders of Settler States.* Durham, N.C.: Duke University Press, 2014.

Skinner, Lawrence C. *Chemical Contaminants in Wildlife from the Mohawk Nation at Akwesasne and the Vicinity of the General Motors Corporation/ Central Foundry Division, Massena, NY Plant.* Albany: New York State Department of Environmental Conservation, 1992.

Skoog, Joanne. "Stone Finds GM Contaminating Animals." *Massena (N.Y.) Observer,* August 1, 1985.

Sloan, R., and K. Jock. *Chemical Contaminants in the Fish from the Mohawk Nation at Akwesasne and the Vicinity of the General Motors Corporation/ Central Foundry Division, Massena NY Plant.* Albany: New York State Department of Environmental Conservation, 1990.

Smith, Debra M. "Interorganizational Collaboration: A Cautionary Note for Tribal Health Nurses." *Public Health Nursing* 15 (1998): 131–35.

Smith, Don. "Idle No More Border Peaceful Blockade in Akwesasne." *Cornwall Free News,* January 6, 2013. http://cornwallfreenews.com.

Smith, Linda Tuhiwai. *Decolonizing Methodologies: Research and Indigenous Peoples.* London: Zed Books, 2002.

Smith-Morris, Carolyn. "Autonomous Individuals or Self-Determined Communities? The Changing Ethics of Research among Native Americans." *Human Organization* 66 (2007): 327–35.

———. "Reducing Diabetes in Indian Country: Lessons from the Three Domains Influencing Pima Diabetes." *Human Organization* 63 (2004): 34–46.

Snow, Dean. *The Iroquois.* Oxford: Blackwell, 1994.

Sommerstein, David. "Border Agent Standoff Lingers on Cornwall Island." North Country Public Radio, August 12, 2010. http://www.northcountry publicradio.org.

———. "Massena GM Redevelopers 'Confident' of Sale." North Country Public Radio, November 30, 2012. http://www.northcountrypublicradio.org.

———. "Mohawk Chiefs: 'The Most Important Thing Is Our Land.'" North Country Public Radio, June 6, 2014. http://www.northcountrypublicra dio.org.

Spears, Ellen Griffith. *Baptized in PCBs: Race, Pollution, and Justice in an All-American Town.* Chapel Hill: University of North Carolina Press, 2014.

Starna, William A. "The Repeal of Article 8: Law, Government, and Cultural Politics at Akwesasne." *American Indian Law Review* 18, no. 2 (1993): 297–311.

Starna, William A., and Jack Campisi. "When Two Are One: The Mohawk Indian Community at St. Regis (Akwesasne)." *European Review of Native American Studies* 14, no. 2 (2000): 39–45.

Stone, Thomas. "Legal Mobilization and Legal Penetration: The Department of Indian Affairs and the Canadian Party at St. Regis, 1876–1918." *Ethnohistory* 22, no. 4 (1975): 375–408.

Strickland, C. June. "Challenges in Community-Based Participatory Research Implementation: Experiences in Cancer Prevention with Pacific Northwest American Indian Tribes." *Cancer Control* 13, no. 3 (2006): 230–36.

Swamp, Lawrence C. "St. Regis Mohawk Tribe Environment Division." *Akwesasne Notes* 29, no. 2 (1997): 16.

Sze, Julie. "Boundaries and Border Wars: DES, Technology, and Environmental Justice." *American Quarterly* 58, no. 3 (2006): 791–814.

———. *Noxious New York: The Racial Politics of Urban Health and Environmental Justice.* Cambridge: MIT Press, 2006.

TallBear, Kim. *Native American DNA: Tribal Belonging and the False Promise of Genetic Science.* Minneapolis: University of Minnesota Press, 2013.

Tarbell, Alice, and Mary Arquette. "Akwesasne: A Native American Community's Resistance to Cultural and Environmental Damage." In *Reclaiming the Environmental Debate: The Politics of Health in a Toxic Culture,* edited by Richard Hofrichter, 93–112. Cambridge: MIT Press, 2000.

Tarbell, Barbara. "Akwesasne Cultural Restoration Program." Talk presented at the Akwesasne Mohawk Casino, April 30, 2015.

Ten Fingers, Keely. "Rejecting, Revitalizing, and Reclaiming: First Nations Work to Set the Direction of Research and Policy Development." *Canadian Journal of Public Health* 96, no. S1 (2005): S60–S63.

Thorp, James H., Gary A. Lamberti, and Andrew F. Casper. "St Lawrence River Basin." In *Field Guide to Rivers of North America.* Oxford: Elsevier Science & Technology, 2009.

Toensing, Gale Courey. "Mohawk Elected Government and Traditional Longhouse Council in Casino Rift." *Indian Country Today,* February 3, 2012. http://indiancountrytodaymedianetwork.com.

———. "Two Officials Bash Mohawk Idle No More Protest; One Apologizes." *Indian Country Today,* January 14, 2013. http://indiancountrytodaymedianetwork.com.

Tomsho, Robert. "Dumping Grounds: Indian Tribes Contend with Some of Worst of America's Pollution." *Wall Street Journal,* eastern ed., November 29, 1990, A1.

Tooker, Elisabeth. "The League of the Iroquois: Its History, Politics, and Ritual." In *Handbook of North American Indians, Northeast,* vol. 15, edited by Bruce G. Trigger, 418–41. Washington, D.C.: Smithsonian Institution, 1978.

Trigger, Bruce G., and James F. Pendergast. "Saint Lawrence Iroquoians." In *Handbook of North American Indians, Northeast,* vol. 15, edited by Bruce G. Trigger. Washington, D.C.: Smithsonian Institution, 1978.

Trumbull, Deborah J., Rick Bonney, Derek Bascom, and Anna Cabral. "Thinking Scientifically during Participation in a Citizen-Science Project." *Science Education* 84, no. 2 (2000): 265–75.

Tsosie, Rebecca. "Indigenous Peoples and Epistemic Injustice: Science, Ethics, and Human Rights." *Washington Law Review* 87 (2012): 1133–1201.

Tuck, Eve. "Suspending Damage: A Letter to Communities." *Harvard Educational Review* 79, no. 3 (2009): 409–27.

Turyk, Mary E., Satyendra P. Bhavsar, William Bowerman, Eric Boysen, Milton Clark, Miriam Diamond, Donna Mergler, Peter Pantazopoulos, Susan Schantz, and David O. Carpenter. "Risks and Benefits of Consumption of Great Lakes Fish." *Environmental Health Perspectives* 120 (2012): 11–18.

U.S. Department of Agriculture. *2012 Census of Agriculture: Farm Typology,* vol. 2, subject series, pt. 10. Washington, D.C.: U.S. Department of Agriculture, January 2015. https://www.agcensus.usda.gov.

U.S. Department of Health and Human Services. *Healthy People 2010 Mid-*

course Review. Washington, D.C.: DHHS, April 12, 2010. http://www
.healthypeople.gov.

U.S. Department of Health, Education, and Welfare. *The Belmont Report: Ethical Principles and Guidelines for the Protection of Human Subjects of Research*. Washington, D.C.: U.S. Government Printing Office, April 18, 1979. http://www.hhs.gov.

U.S. Environmental Protection Agency. "Environmental Justice." Accessed February 22, 2017. http://www.epa.gov.

———. "EPA Superfund Program: General Motors (Central Foundry Division), Massena, NY." Accessed March 1, 2016. https://www.epa.gov.

———. "Second Five-Year Review Report: General Motors (Central Foundry Division) Superfund Site, St. Lawrence County, Town of Massena, New York." July 2010. https://quicksilver.epa.gov/work/02/108531.pdf.

———. "Third Five-Year Review Report: General Motors (Central Foundry Division) Superfund Site, St. Lawrence County, Town of Massena, New York." September 2015. https://semspub.epa.gov/src/collection/02/SC 32295.

———. "Tribal Superfund Program Needs Clear Direction and Actions to Improve Effectiveness." Evaluation Report No. 2004-P-00035. September 30, 2004. https://www.epa.gov.

U.S. Fish and Wildlife Service. "Natural Resource Damages Settlement: For the St. Lawrence Environment." April 17, 2013. http://www.fws.gov.

U.S. Government Accountability Office. *Superfund: Trends in Federal Funding and Cleanup of EPA's Nonfederal National Priorities List Sites*. GAO-15-812. Washington, D.C.: U.S. GAO, September 2015. http://www.gao.gov.

Vega, William A. "Theoretical and Pragmatic Implications of Cultural Diversity for Community Research." *American Journal of Community Psychology* 20, no. 3 (1992): 375–91.

Vennum, Thomas, Jr. *American Indian Lacrosse: Little Brother of War*. Baltimore: Johns Hopkins University Press, 2007.

Voyles, Traci Brynne. *Wastelanding: Legacies of Uranium Mining in Navajo Country*. Minneapolis: University of Minnesota Press, 2015.

Wallace, Anthony F. C. *Religion: An Anthropological View*. New York: Random House, 1966.

Walters, Karina L., Selina A. Mohammed, Teresa Evans-Campbell, Ramona E. Beltran, David H. Chae, and Bonnie Duran. "Bodies Don't Just Tell Stories, They Tell Histories." *Du Bois Review: Social Science Research on Race* 8, no. 1 (2011): 179–89.

"Ward Stone, Once Clipped, Now Bound, Gagged." *Post Standard* (Syracuse, N.Y.), May 23, 1989.

Weaver, Jace. *Defending Mother Earth: Native American Perspectives on Environmental Justice*. Maryknoll, N.Y.: Orbis Books, 1996.

White, Kevin J. "Rousing a Curiosity in Hewitt's Iroquois Cosmologies." *Wicazo Sa Review* 28, no. 2 (2013): 87–111.

White, Louellyn. *Free to Be Mohawk: Indigenous Education at the Akwesasne Freedom School*. Norman: University of Oklahoma Press, 2015.

White, Mary C., Sherri Berger-Frank, Dave Campagna, Steven G. Inserra, Dan Middleton, M. Deborah Millette, Curtis W. Noonan, Lucy A. Peipins, Dhelia M. Williamson, and Health Investigations Communications Work Group. "Communicating Results to Community Residents: Lessons from Recent ATSDR Health Investigations." *Journal of Exposure Analysis and Environmental Epidemiology* 14, no. 7 (2004): 484–91.

White, Rowen M. "Sustaining Diversity for Culture's Sake: Haudenosaunee Native Seed Conservation." Master's thesis, Hampshire College, 2002.

Whyte, Kyle Powys. "Indigenous Experience, Environmental Justice and Settler Colonialism." In *Nature and Experience: Phenomenology and the Environment*, edited by Bryan E. Bannon, 157–74. Lanham, Md.: Rowman & Littlefield, 2016.

———. "Indigenous Food Systems, Environmental Justice, and Settler–Industrial States." In *Global Food, Global Justice: Essays on Eating under Globalization*, edited by Mary C. Rawlinson and Caleb Ward, 143–66. Newcastle upon Tyne: Cambridge Scholars, 2015.

———. "Justice Forward: Tribes, Climate Adaptation and Responsibility." *Climatic Change* 120, no. 3 (2013): 517–30.

———. "The Recognition Dimensions of Environmental Justice in Indian Country." *Environmental Justice* 4, no. 4 (2011): 199–205.

Whyte, Kyle Powys, Joseph P. Brewer II, and Jay T. Johnson. "Weaving Indigenous Science, Protocols and Sustainability Science." *Sustainability Science* 11, no. 1 (2016): 25–32.

Wiedman, Dennis. "Diabetes Mellitus and Oklahoma Native Americans: A Case Study of Culture Change in Oklahoma Cherokee." PhD diss., University of Oklahoma, 1979.

———. "Native American Embodiment of the Chronicities of Modernity: Reservation Food, Diabetes, and the Metabolic Syndrome among the Kiowa, Comanche, and Apache." *Medical Anthropology Quarterly* 26, no. 4 (2012): 595–612.

———. "Striving for Healthy Lifestyles: Contributions of Anthropologists to the Challenges of Diabetes in Indigenous Communities." In *Indigenous Peoples and Diabetes: Community Empowerment and Wellness*, edited by Mariana Leal Ferreira and Gretchen Chesley Lang, 511–34. Durham, N.C.: Carolina Academic Press, 2006.

———. "Type II Diabetes Mellitus, Technological Development and the Oklahoma Cherokee." In *Encounters with Biomedicine: Case Studies in*

Medical Anthropology, edited by Hans A. Baer, 43–71. New York: Gordon and Breach, 1987.

Wildcat, Daniel R. *Red Alert!* Golden, Colo.: Fulcrum, 2009.

Wilson, Shawn. *Research Is Ceremony: Indigenous Research Methods.* Winnipeg: Fernwood, 2008.

Wing, Steve. "Whose Epidemiology, Whose Health?" *International Journal of Health Services* 28, no. 2 (1998): 241–52.

Wolfe, Patrick. *Settler Colonialism and the Transformation of Anthropology.* London: Cassell, 1999.

Wunder, John R. *The Indian Bill of Rights.* New York: Garland, 1996.

Wylie, Sara Ann, Kirk Jalbert, Shannon Dosemagen, and Matt Ratto. "Institutions for Civic Technoscience: How Critical Making Is Transforming Environmental Research." *Information Society* 30, no. 2 (2014): 116–26.

Index

Elizabeth Hoover is Manning Assistant Professor of American Studies and Ethnic Studies at Brown University.